THE SOUND OF CHARLIE CHAPLIN

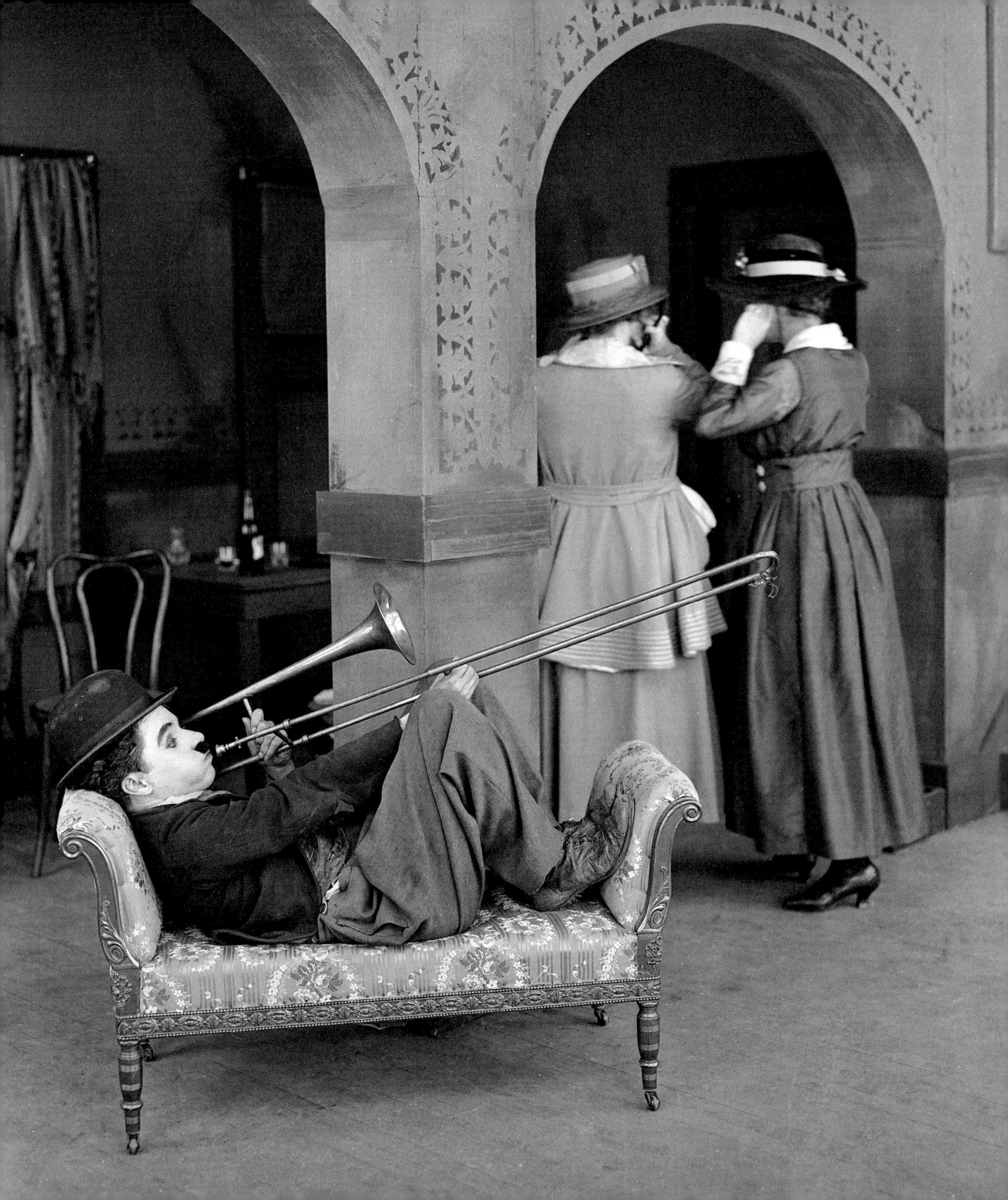

THE SOUND OF
CHARLIE CHAPLIN

Exhibition catalogue
Kate Guyonvarch and Mathilde Thibault-Starzyk

Curator
Sam Stourdzé

Éditions
de La Martinière

PHILHARMONIE
DE PARIS
MUSÉE DE LA MUSIQUE

THE SOUND OF CHARLIE CHAPLIN

October 11, 2019 – January 26, 2020

Catalogue

Editors
Kate Guyonvarch
Mathilde Thibault-Starzyk

Cité de la Musique – Philharmonie de Paris

Editorial coordinators
Julie Bénet
Marianne Lagueunière

Picture researcher
Raphaëlle Sabouraud

Éditions de La Martinière

Graphic design
ABM Studio, David Longuein

Translation from French
Chrisoula Petridis

Copy editor
Bernard Wooding

Editorial coordinator
Isabelle Dartois
assisted by **Louise Green**

Production
Nathalie Voyer

The Cité de la Musique – Philharmonie de Paris thank the following partners, museums, and collectors—as well as those who wished to remain anonymous —whose help and support made this exhibition possible.

Archives de Montreux: Nicole Meystre
British Film Institute: Espen Bale, Claire Smith
Chaplin's World: Béatrice de Reyniès, Annick Barbezat-Perrin
Cinémathèque Française: Jacques Ayroles, Frédéric Bonnaud, Sandra Laupa, Françoise Lemerige, Laurent Mannoni, Laure Parchomenko, Isabelle Regelsperger, Cécile Touret, Gilles Veyrat
Cinémathèque Suisse: Frédéric Maire, Thomas Bissegger, Sophie Pujol, Nadia Roche
Cineteca di Bologna: Gian Luca Farinelli, Cecilia Cenciarelli
Conservatoire National des Arts et Métiers: Catherine Cuenca, Karine Alexandrian, Marie-Sophie Corcy, Mélanie Drappier
Deutsches Filminstitut & Filmmuseum: Isabelle Louise Bastian
Fondation Jérôme Seydoux-Pathé: Dominique Erenfrid, Stéphanie Salmon, Manon Billaut, Julie Chartier
Lobster Films: Serge Bromberg, Éric Lange, Anne Simon
Musée de l'Élysée: Tatyana Franck, Nora Mathys, Carole Sandrin
Musée National d'Art Moderne: Bernard Blistène, Isabelle Daire, Olga Makhroff, Rania Moussa, Laurine Leblanc
RMN-Grand Palais: Raphaëlle Cartier, Fatima Louli
ADAGP: Michel Donval, Chantale Bermude, Anita Pognon

Our deepest gratitude to those whose cooperation helped bring this project to fruition, particularly:
The Chaplin family
Philippe Baudoin, N. T. Binh, Patrick Bouteloup, Timothy Brock, Ian Burley, Juliette Collomb, Karoline Consigny, Florence Darbre, Régis Fromaget, Audrey Guillemet, Bernard Hermann, Ken Heyman, Sylvie Kohler, Jane Koszuta, Léo Kouper, Jim Lochner, Arnold Lozano, Lucy Lyall-Grant, Marie-Laure Metge-Escuriol, Paula Mutel, Adam Stoltman, Jeffrey Vance

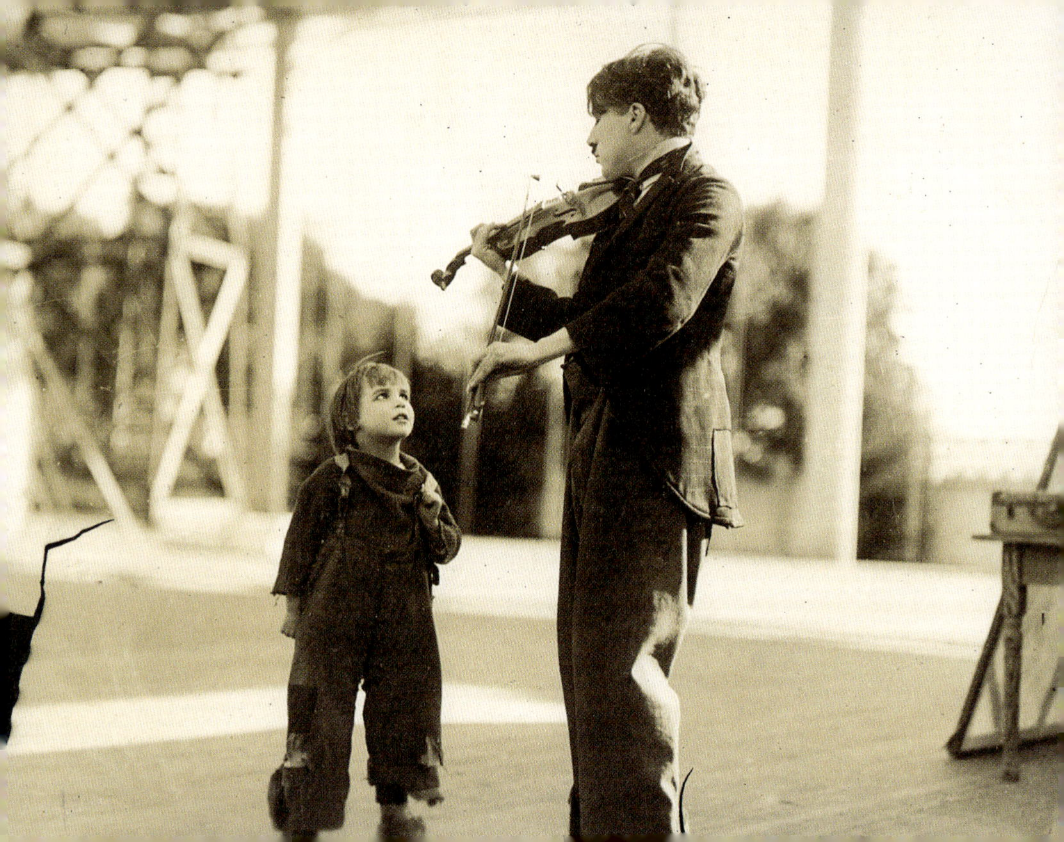

Foreword

Language for the eye as well as the ear

Sam Stourdzé,
exhibition curator
Marie-Pauline Martin,
director, Musée de la Musique
Laurent Bayle,
managing director, Philharmonie de Paris

It is no paradox to welcome the master of silent cinema to the Musée de la Musique-Philharmonie de Paris, but a fascinating way to rediscover his work through its musical dimension and, more generally, through Charlie Chaplin's close relationship to dance, rhythm, speech and sound, all rigorously "orchestrated" in each of his films.

A self-taught musician, Chaplin left the world of music hall at the age of twenty-five for that of the cinema. With the invention of the Tramp character, he confirmed the superiority of pantomime: his dancing, almost musical figure, whose movements were reflected in the rhythm of the film editing, touched the hearts of people worldwide and became a poetical and comic representation of the art of cinema.

So much so that in 1927, when world cinema switched from silent film to talkies, Chaplin resisted dialogue and instead highlighted the musical eloquence of his work. From then onwards he composed the scores for all his films and developed comic sound, in which sound effects and music mirrored each other.

Bringing Chaplin's cinema together with numerous works, machines, scores, and manuscripts, the exhibition renders the entire "eloquence" of this genius, whose influence extended from avant-garde artists to popular culture. Examining everything in his work that makes "noise" and "talks" to the eye as much as to the ear, it demonstrates the extent to which the quest for sound and musical expression was a catalyst for his entire imagination. This exhibition, part of the Musée de la Musique's recent quest to showcase *musique concrète*, opens up the (often limited) field of music to embrace elements such as noise, gesture, and rhythm. Chaplin's silent heritage stands as one of the most emblematic, visionary, and politically committed "sound corpuses" of the twentieth century.

This new approach to the work of Chaplin the musician would not have been possible without the generous collaboration of his family, remarkably and discerningly represented by Kate Guyonvarch. Finally, our sincere thanks go to Béatrice de Reyniès, director of Chaplin's World in Corsier-sur-Vevey, where an adapted version of our exhibition will be presented in 2020.

Left

Chaplin and Jackie Coogan on the set of *The Kid*, c. 1919–20.

Next page

Chaplin playing violin during filming of *The Vagabond*, 1916.

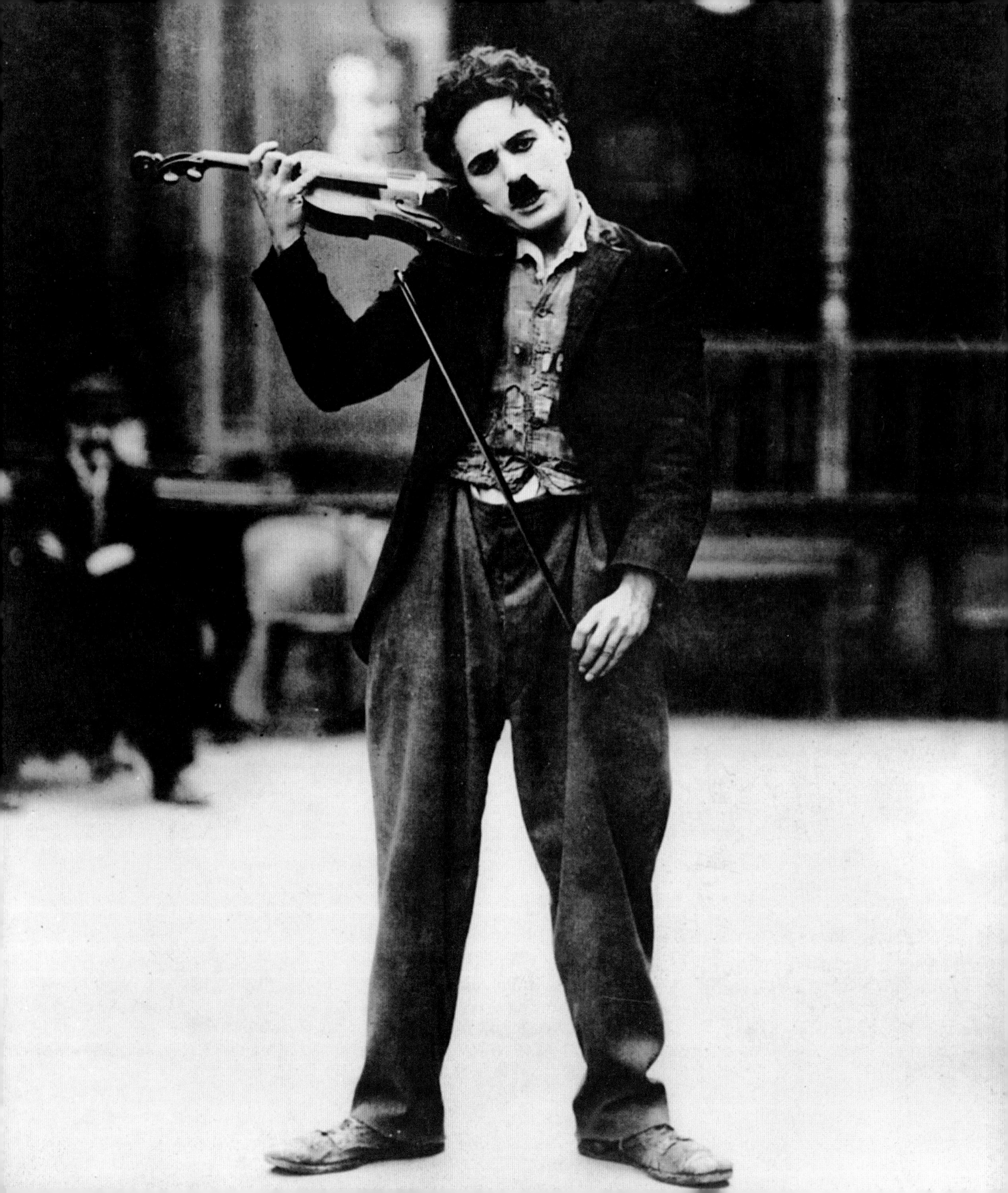

There is so much of the English music hall in my father's film music. Whether it comments on the human condition, whether it conveys hope, longing, or sadness, whether it satirizes or simply hints at the innuendo, the music is always beautifully constructed and paced. It is the audible melodic counterpoint to the silent verbosity of the balletic pantomime.

CHRISTOPHER CHAPLIN

Contents

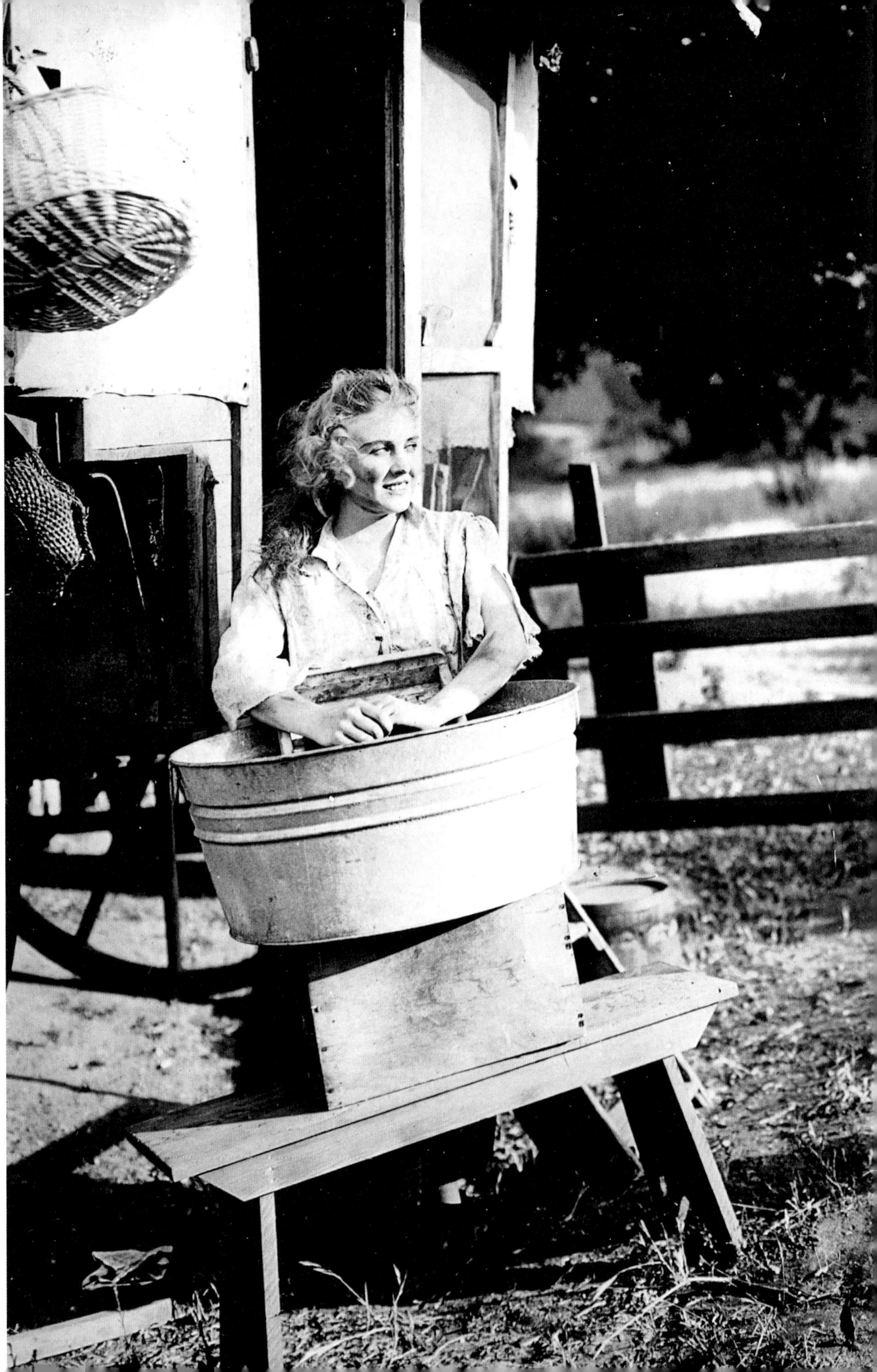

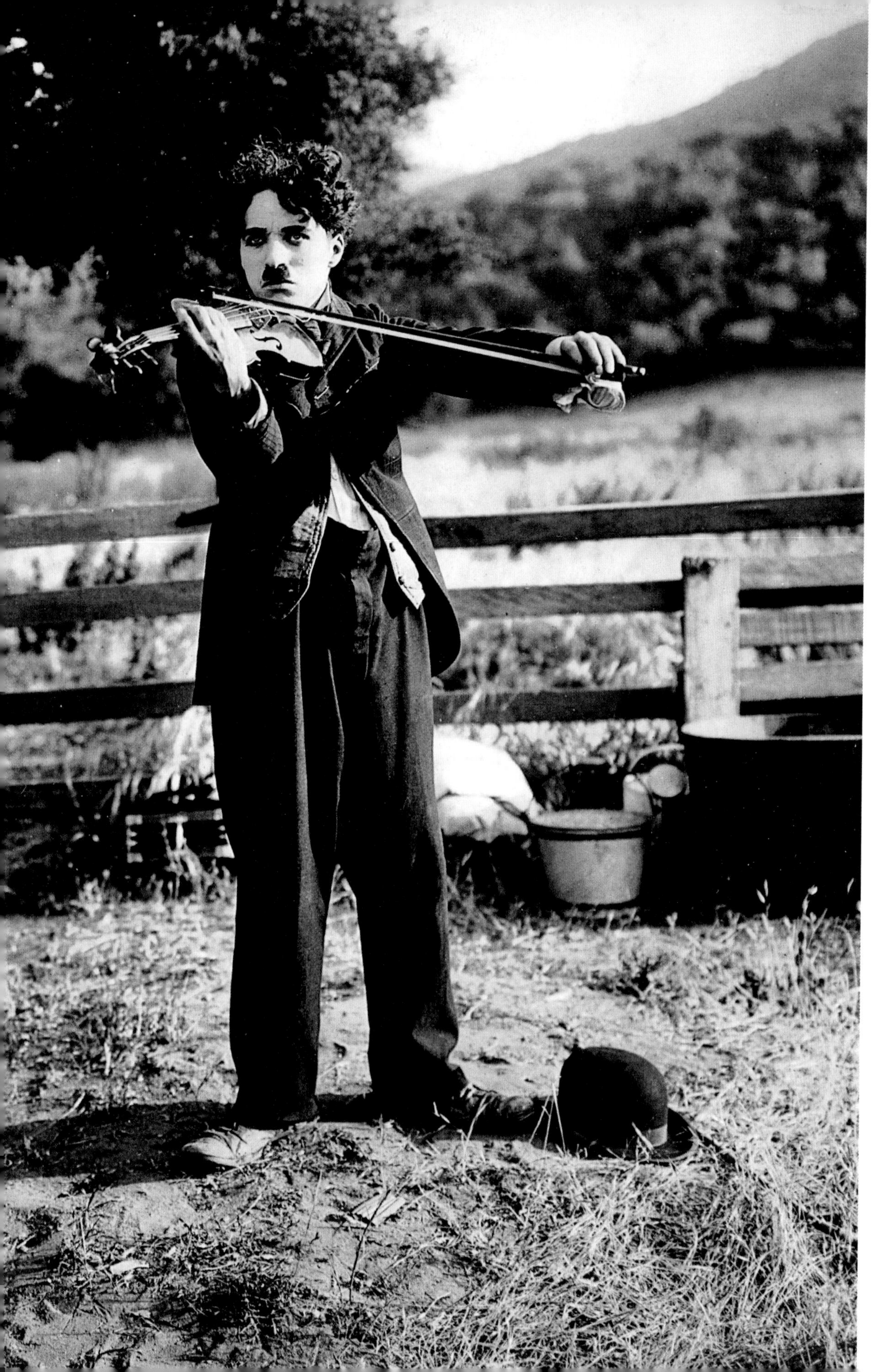

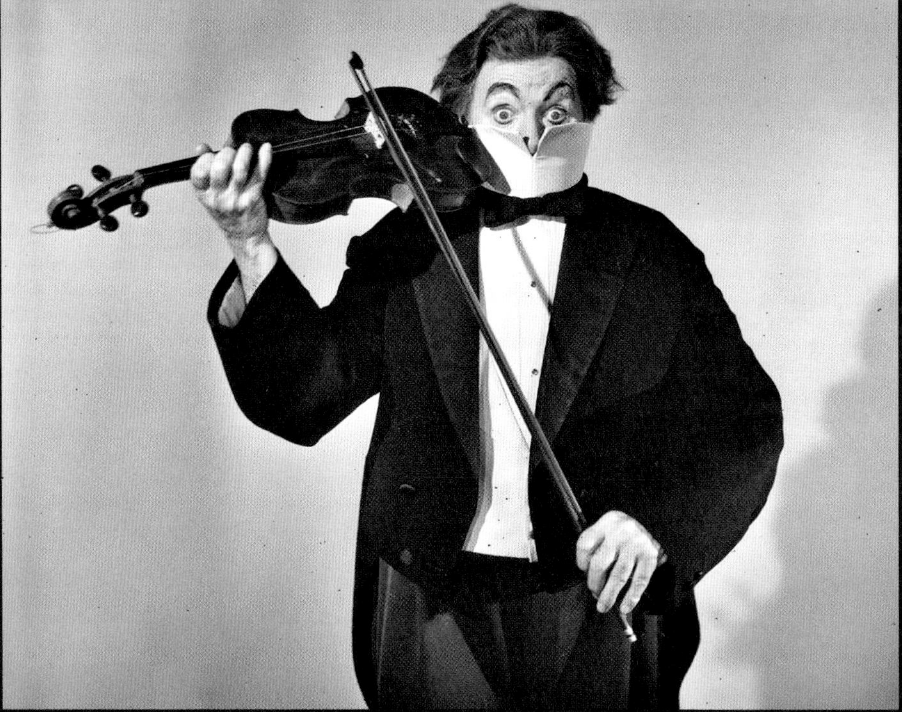

FROM MUSIC HALL TO CINEMA

Born in a poor neighborhood of London on April 16, 1889, Charles Spencer Chaplin, known as Charlie Chaplin, made use of his artistic talents from an early age. His parents, Charles Chaplin and Hannah Hill (stage name Lily Harley) were music hall singers and Charlie himself began to tread the boards from around the age of five. He learned the art of pantomime in sketches in which music and mime figured prominently. He also quickly discovered the cinema, born at the same time as he.

Early films, only a few minutes long, were usually screened as part of music hall programming or as fairground attractions, and like the acts whose content and themes they regularly copied, were always accompanied by a live piano or small orchestra. Music hall, cinema, and music were thus closely related and to audiences often seemed one and the same form of entertainment.

At the age of eighteen, Charlie Chaplin joined the troupe of the British music hall's preeminent impresario, Fred Karno. During a Karno tour of the United States, the young Chaplin was noticed by Mack Sennett, founder of Keystone Studios in Los Angeles, who offered him a contract, and like many music hall performers of the time Chaplin went from stage to screen. Very soon he began directing his own films and used the slapstick techniques that had made his stage success. The short form of gags, the belligerent comedy, the exaggerated mime, the repeated falls, and the frantic running were easily transposed from music hall to cinema.

Throughout his career, Chaplin made multiple tributes to the world of music hall, from *A Night in the Show* (1915) to *Limelight* (1952), for which he seems to have drawn on his memories, with the character of the aging performer Calvero being inspired by his father.

Previous double page

Film still from *The Vagabond*, with Edna Purviance, 1916.

Opposite

Costume trial for the music hall number at the end of *Limelight*, c. 1951–52.

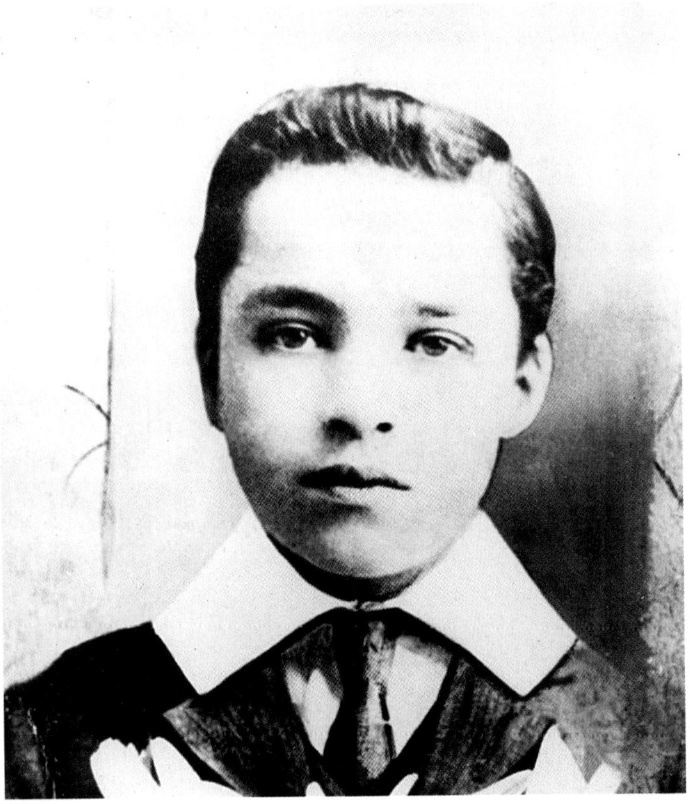

Left

Charles Chaplin at the age of nine or ten, c. 1898–1900.

Opposite

Left

Hannah Hill, Chaplin's mother, c. 1885.
"If it had not been for my mother I doubt if I could have made a success of pantomime. She was one of the greatest pantomime artists I have ever seen." Under the stage name Lily Harley, Hannah met with some success in music hall theaters. But her poor health meant that she could not continue her career; she supported her children by working as a seamstress.

Right

Charles Chaplin Senior, Chaplin's father, c. 1885.
"I was hardly aware of a father, and do not remember him having lived with us. He too was a vaudevillian . . . He had a light baritone voice and was considered a very fine artist. Even in those days he earned the considerable sum of forty pounds a week. The trouble was that he drank too much, which Mother said was the cause of their separation."

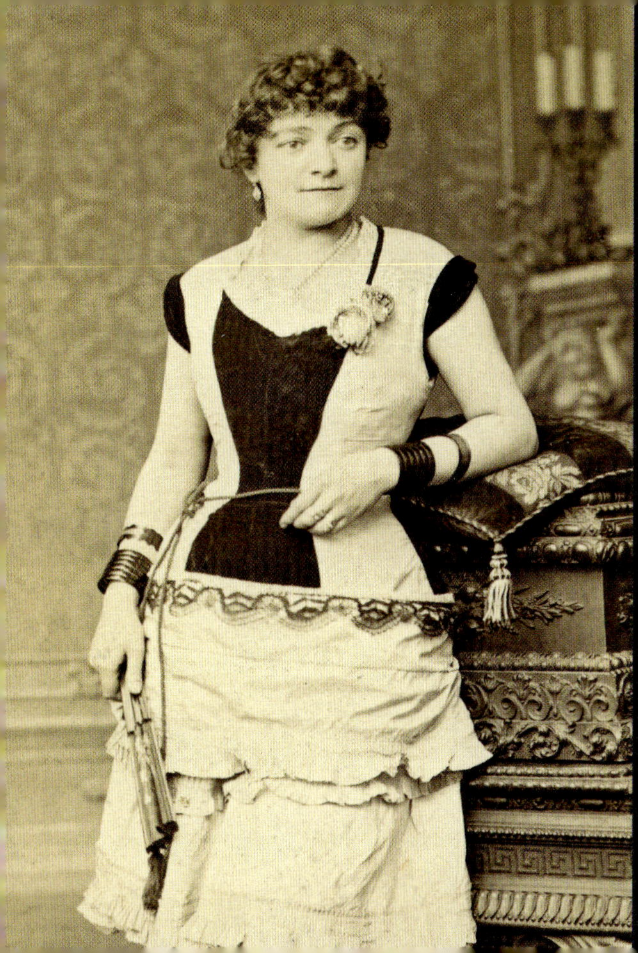
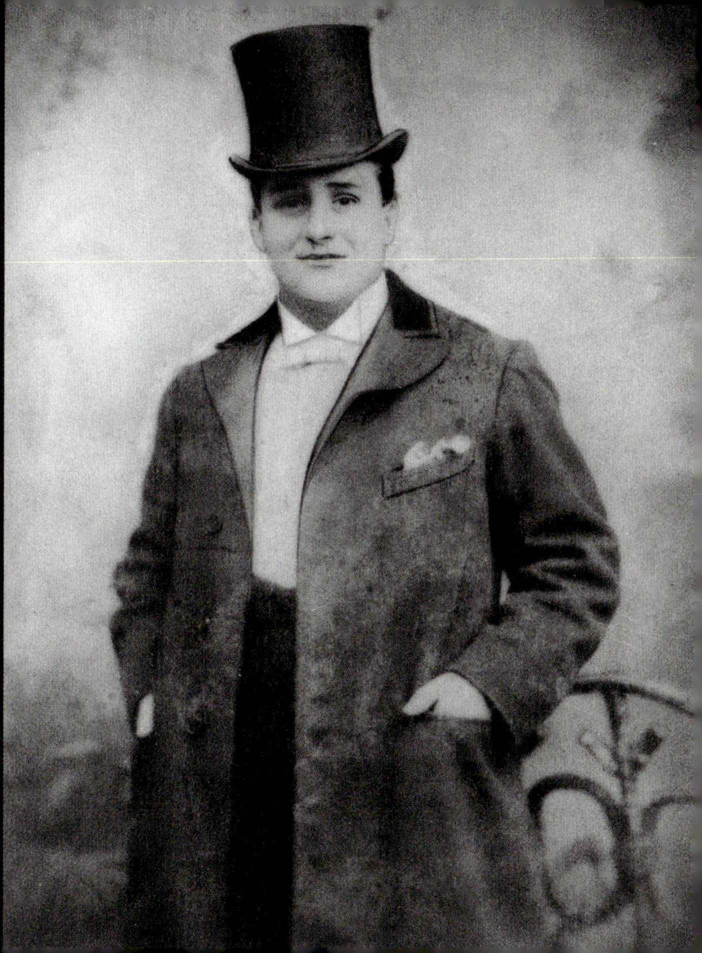

ARGYLE

THEATRE OF VARIETIES.

(Late PRINCE OF WALES), Argyle Street, BIRKENHEAD.

Lessees and Managers ... ... Messrs. CLARKE & RILEY.

THE FOLLOWING MATCHLESS ARRAY OF TALENT WILL APPEAR.] **MONDAY, DEC. 22, 1890** [AND EVERY EVENING DURING THE WEEK.

(CHRISTMAS NIGHT EXCEPTED.)

Most Expensive Engagement and First Appearance of the

4 AUBREYS

In their Great Speciality Act—"20 LAUGHS IN 20 MINUTES."

Return Visit of MISS FLORRIE

VILLER

The Vocal Gem. Descriptive and Ballad Vocalist.

First Appearance of MR. SAM

JESSON

The Celebrated Tyrolean Vocalist and Character Comedian.

Engagement for Six Nights only, of

U N A

The Human Fly.

Important Engagement and First Appearance of MR. CHARLES

CHAPLIN

The Great Metropolitan Vocal Comedian.

First Appearance of

PROF. HOLT

The most Versatile Ventriloquist on the Variety Stage, with his Budget of Comicalities and Funny Companions.

Engagement of MR. HARRY

LEANDER

"Our Musical Fritz."

Engagement of MISS

FRANCES TALBOT

Ballad and Descriptive Vocalist.

Starring Engagement of MR. HARRY

WHALING

Your Old Favourite.

Special Engagement of

POOLE'S MINSTRELS

FIVE IN NUMBER,

TED, TOM, OLIVE, FLORA, LOTTIE.

TED and FLORA will introduce their World-Renowned Champion Acrobatic Dance.

BOXING-DAY, FRIDAY, DECEMBER 26th,

GRAND ILLUMINATED

MORNING PERFORMANCE

IN WHICH THE

ENTIRE COMPANY WILL APPEAR.

Doors Open at 1-30; Commence at 2. Children Half-Price to All Parts.

PRICES OF ADMISSION,

GALLERY.	PIT	SIDE BOXES.	STALLS AND CENTRE BOXES.
3D.	6D.	9D.	1s.

Private Boxes, 2s. Half-price at 9 o'clock to Stalls and Boxes.

Doors open at Seven, to commence at Half-past.

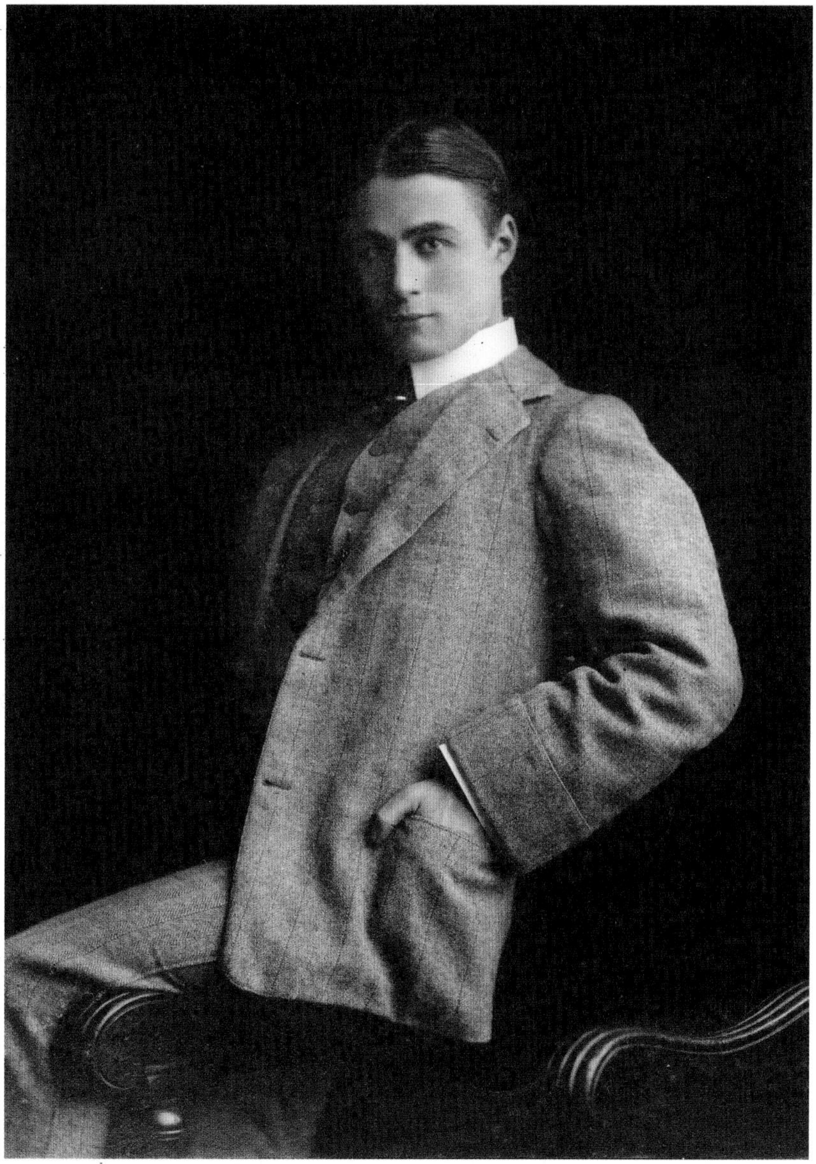

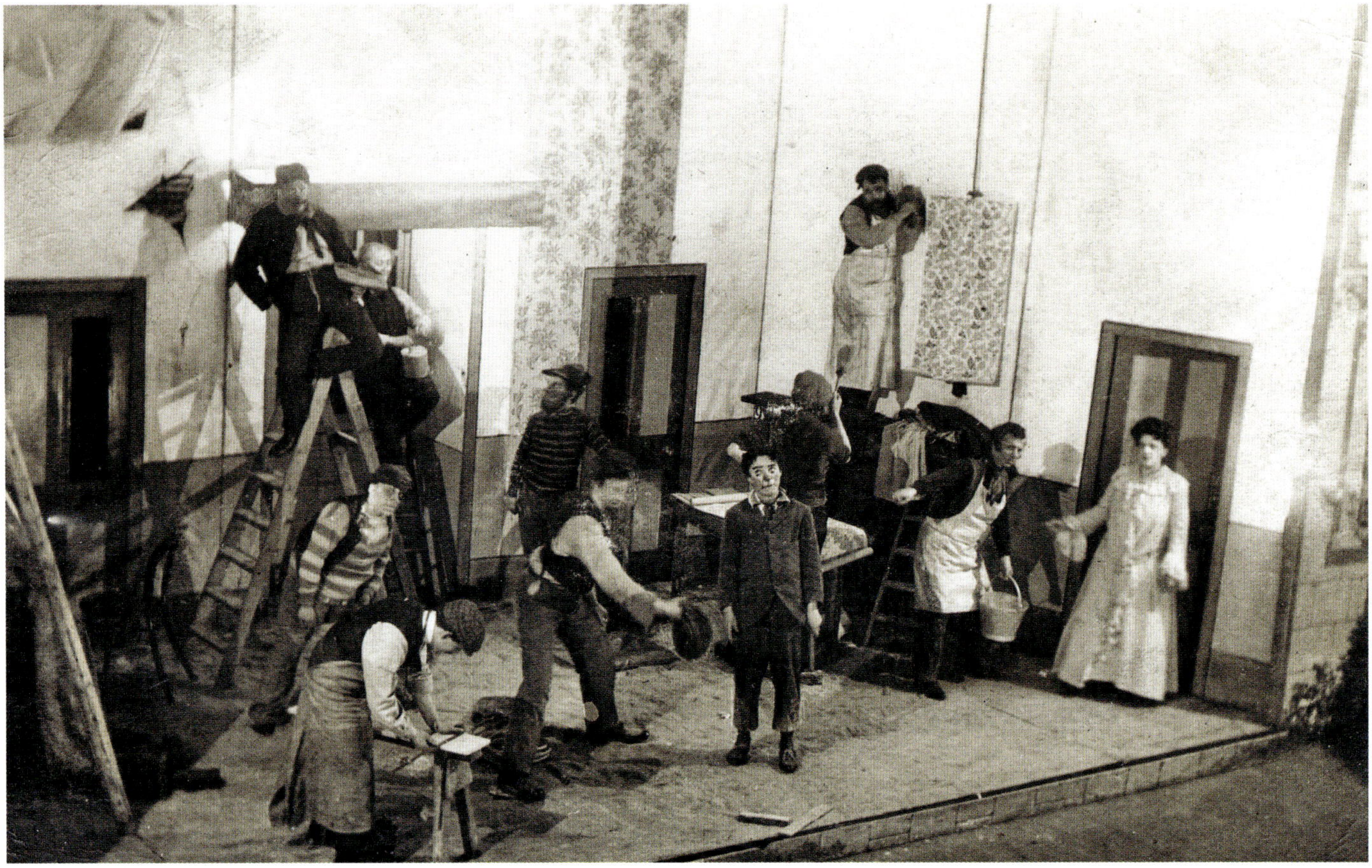

Above

Charlie and Sydney in the play *Repairs*, Wal Pink company, March 1906. Charlie stands in the center, Sydney on the ladder at the back. Charlie played the role of a plumber and Syd that of a carpenter, part of an incompetent team hired to redecorate a house. Charlie left the company after eight weeks to join Casey's Circus and Syd remained until he was recruited by Fred Karno on July 9, 1906.

Opposite

Chaplin third from left, with Fred Karno (seated, center), c. 1910. The Karno company was founded in 1888 and, when Sydney joined it in 1906, the impresario was already heading ten different troupes that toured regularly. Recommended by his brother, Charlie had his first audition in February 1908.

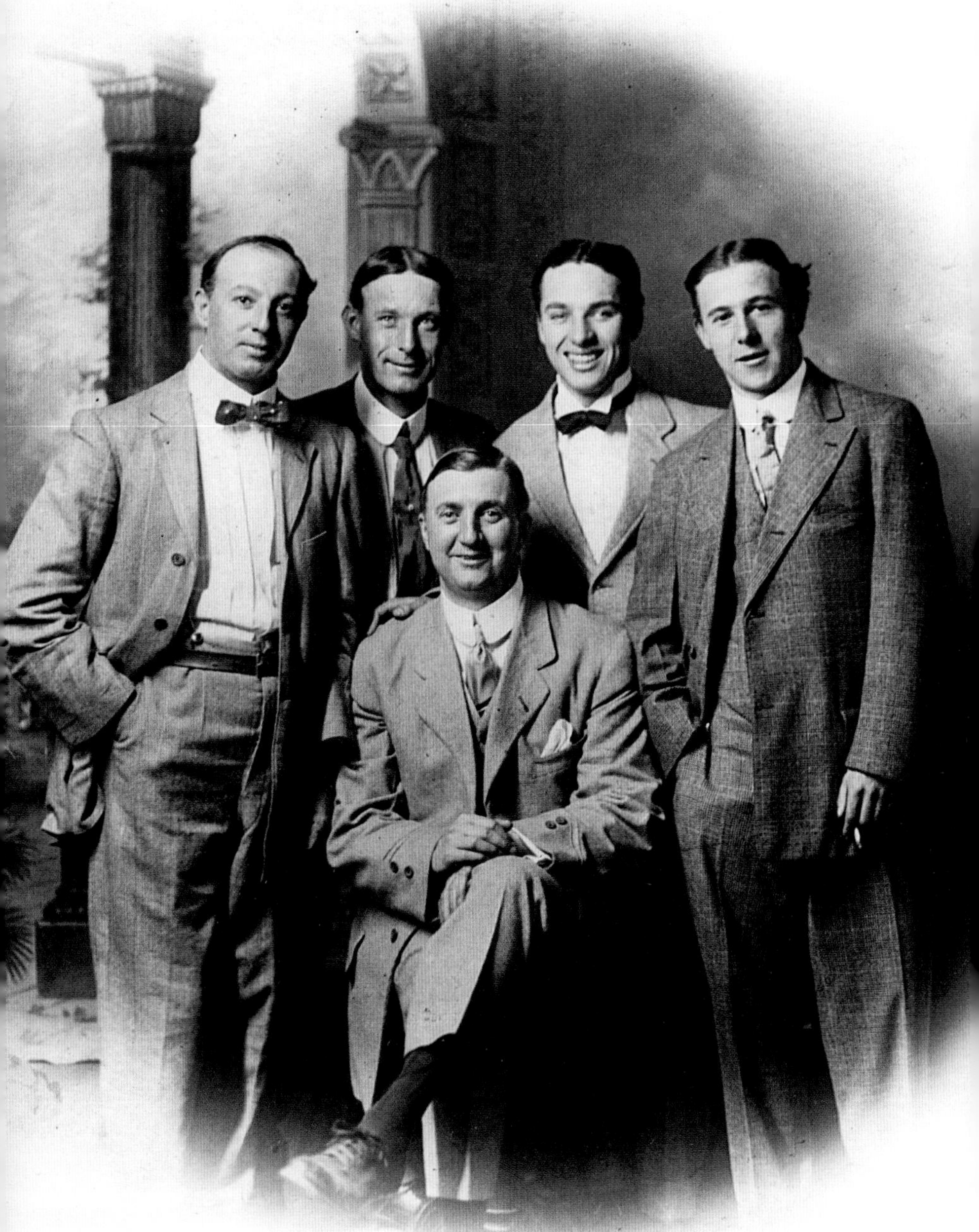

"Tis not in mortals to command success, but we'll do more—deserve it."—ADDISON

SHEFFIELD EMPIRE

PALACE, CHARLES STREET and PINSTONE STREET.

PROPRIETORS . . . . . . MOSS' EMPIRES LIMITED
Managing Director . . . . . . Mr FRANK ALLEN
Acting Manager . . . Mr. L. H. STEWART . . . TELEPHONE No 682.

MONDAY, DEC. 22ND. 1913. TWICE NIGHTLY AT 6-40 & 9-0
(Xmas Day Excepted)

FRED KARNO

Presents his latest laughing creation, entitled

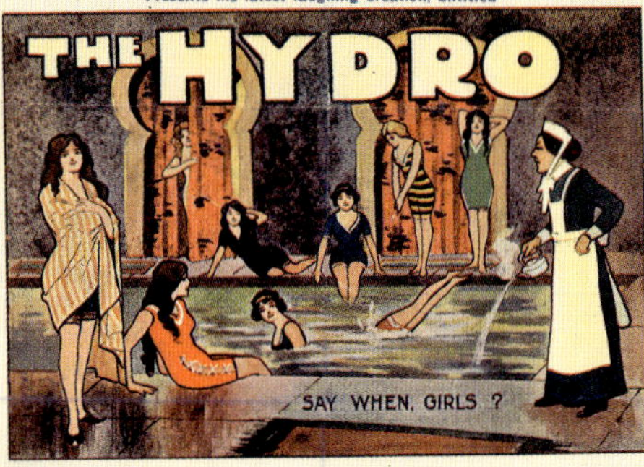

SYD CHAPLIN

As "NICK SHARP." Scene 1 Pump Room at the Hydro, Merryandbad, France
Scene 2 - Interior of bath de luxe at the same Hydro

A REAL SWIMMING BATH WITH A BEVY OF BEAUTIFUL BATHING GIRLS

New Series of Up-to-date Subjects on the AMERICAN BIOSCOPE

LIZZIE **GLENROY**
Scotch Comedienne.

ROSIE **ARCHER**
At the Piano

SCAMP & SCAMP
Comedy Gymnasts

HOLDEN'S MANNIKINS
Presenting a Miniature Vaudeville Programme.

JOCK WHITEFORD
The Smart Scot.

FOUR BOISES
The Human Aeroplanes, in feats of amazing skill and daring.

AUSTIN RUDD
Comedian.

BOXING DAY, Dec. 26th. **MATINEE AT 2·30**
AT WHICH THE FULL COMPANY WILL APPEAR.

GALLERY	BALCONY	PIT	FAMILY CIRCLE	GRAND CIRCLE	Orchestra Stalls	PRIVATE BOXES
2d	4d	6d	9d	1/-	1/6	7/6
Mondays, Saturdays, and Holidays. 3d.			All Nights Bookable in Advance. 3d. extra.	Bookable in Advance. 3d. extra.		(For Four Persons) Extra Seats, 2s.

NOTICE.—The Booking Office for Advance Booking to Boxes, Stalls, Grand Circle and Family Circle will be open Daily from 10 a.m. to 4 p.m.
SEATS NOT GUARANTEED UNLESS PREVIOUSLY BOOKED. NO MONEY RETURNED. The Management reserve the right of refusing Admission. Seats Booked by Telephone not claimed by 7 and 9 respectively will be Sold.

LATE TRAINS FROM SHEFFIELD.

MIDLAND STATION.—10-42 (Wednesdays and Thursdays excepted) all Stations to Barnsley via Chapeltown, except Attercliffe Road. 10-57 all Stations to Chesterfield. 10-58 (Saturdays only) Attercliffe Road and most Intermediate Stations to Mansfield via Cutcliffe and Trenton. 10-55 (Thursdays and Saturdays only) Brightside, Masboro', Parkgate, Kilnhurst, Swinton and Wath. 11-2 (Wednesdays and Thursdays only) all stations to Barnsley via Chapeltown except Attercliffe Road. 11-3 (Saturdays only) all Stations to Eckington. 11-5 (Fridays and Saturdays only) all Stations to Hope except Millhouses and Beauchief. 11-22 all stations to Rotherham (Westgate) except Attercliffe Road. 11-30 (Saturdays only) all Stations to Barnsley via Chapeltown. Excursion fares, Tuesdays and Saturdays, see small bills.

VICTORIA—GREAT CENTRAL STATION—11 o'clock, to Kiveton Park, Worksop and Retford. 11 o'clock, all Stations to Penistone (Saturdays) only. 11-15 for all Stations to Chesterfield. 11-5 (Saturdays only) for all Stations to Barnsley. 11-20 (Thursday and Saturday only) for Rotherham, Mexboro, Conisboro and Doncaster. 12-0 midnight (Saturdays) for Rotherham, Mexboro, Conisboro and Doncaster.

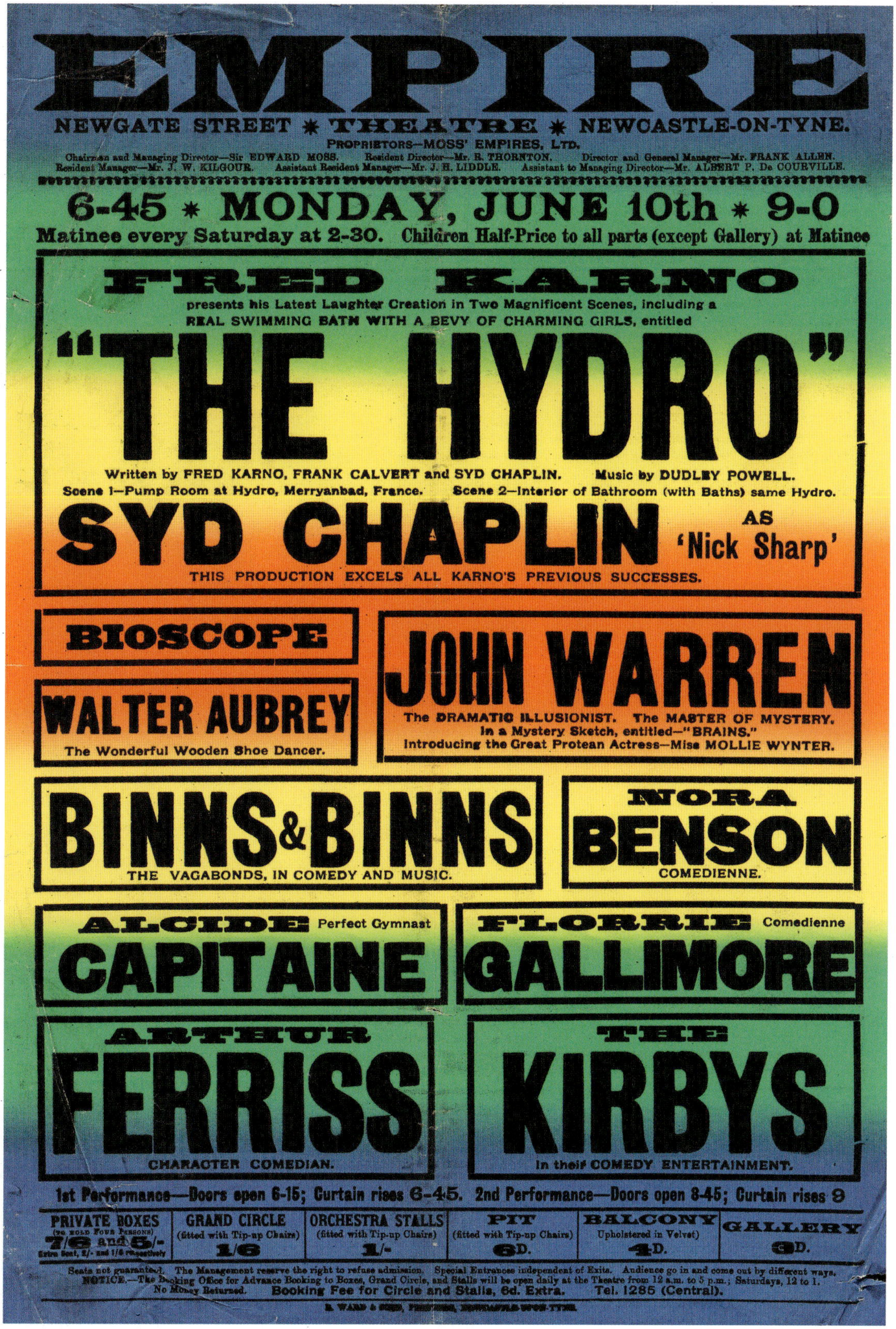
EMPIRE
NEWGATE STREET ✱ THEATRE ✱ NEWCASTLE-ON-TYNE.
PROPRIETORS—MOSS' EMPIRES, LTD.
Chairman and Managing Director—Sir EDWARD MOSS. Resident Director—Mr. R. THORNTON. Director and General Manager—Mr. FRANK ALLEN.
Resident Manager—Mr. J. W. KILGOUR. Assistant Resident Manager—Mr. J. H. LIDDLE. Assistant to Managing Director—Mr. ALBERT P. De COURVILLE.
6-45 ✱ MONDAY, JUNE 10th ✱ 9-0
Matinee every Saturday at 2-30. Children Half-Price to all parts (except Gallery) at Matinee
FRED KARNO
presents his Latest Laughter Creation in Two Magnificent Scenes, including a
REAL SWIMMING BATH WITH A BEVY OF CHARMING GIRLS, entitled
"THE HYDRO"
Written by FRED KARNO, FRANK CALVERT and SYD CHAPLIN. Music by DUDLEY POWELL.
Scene 1—Pump Room at Hydro, Merryanbad, France. Scene 2—Interior of Bathroom (with Baths) same Hydro.
SYD CHAPLIN
AS 'Nick Sharp'
THIS PRODUCTION EXCELS ALL KARNO'S PREVIOUS SUCCESSES.
BIOSCOPE
WALTER AUBREY
The Wonderful Wooden Shoe Dancer.
JOHN WARREN
The DRAMATIC ILLUSIONIST. The MASTER OF MYSTERY.
In a Mystery Sketch, entitled—"BRAINS."
Introducing the Great Protean Actress—Miss MOLLIE WYNTER.
BINNS & BINNS
THE VAGABONDS, IN COMEDY AND MUSIC.
NORA BENSON
COMEDIENNE.
ALCIDE CAPITAINE
Perfect Gymnast
FLORRIE GALLIMORE
Comedienne
ARTHUR FERRISS
CHARACTER COMEDIAN.
THE KIRBYS
In their COMEDY ENTERTAINMENT.
1st Performance—Doors open 6-15; Curtain rises 6-45. 2nd Performance—Doors open 8-45; Curtain rises 9
PRIVATE BOXES (TO HOLD FOUR PERSONS) 7/6 and 5/- Extra Seat, 2/- and 1/6 respectively
GRAND CIRCLE (fitted with Tip-up Chairs) 1/6
ORCHESTRA STALLS (fitted with Tip-up Chairs) 1/-
PIT (fitted with Tip-up Chairs) 6D.
BALCONY Upholstered in Velvet) 4D.
GALLERY 3D.
Seats not guaranteed. The Management reserve the right to refuse admission. Special Entrances independent of Exits. Audience go in and come out by different ways.
NOTICE.—The Booking Office for Advance Booking to Boxes, Grand Circle, and Stalls will be open daily at the Theatre from 12 a.m. to 5 p.m.; Saturdays, 12 to 1.
No Money Returned. Booking Fee for Circle and Stalls, 6d. Extra. Tel. 1285 (Central).

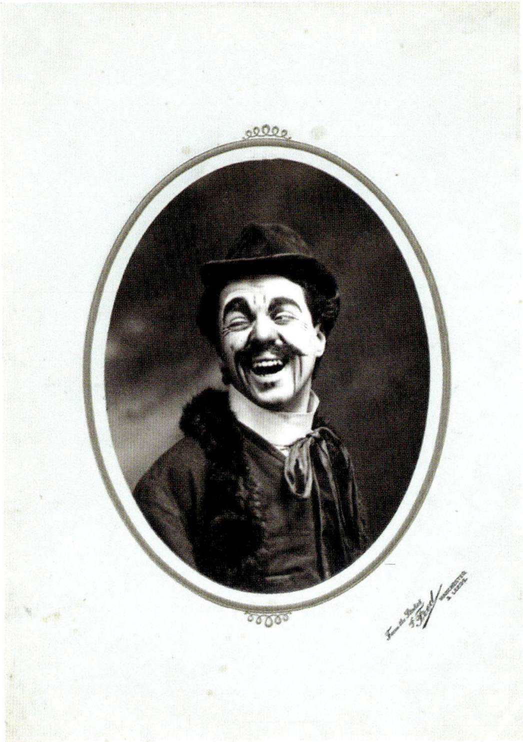

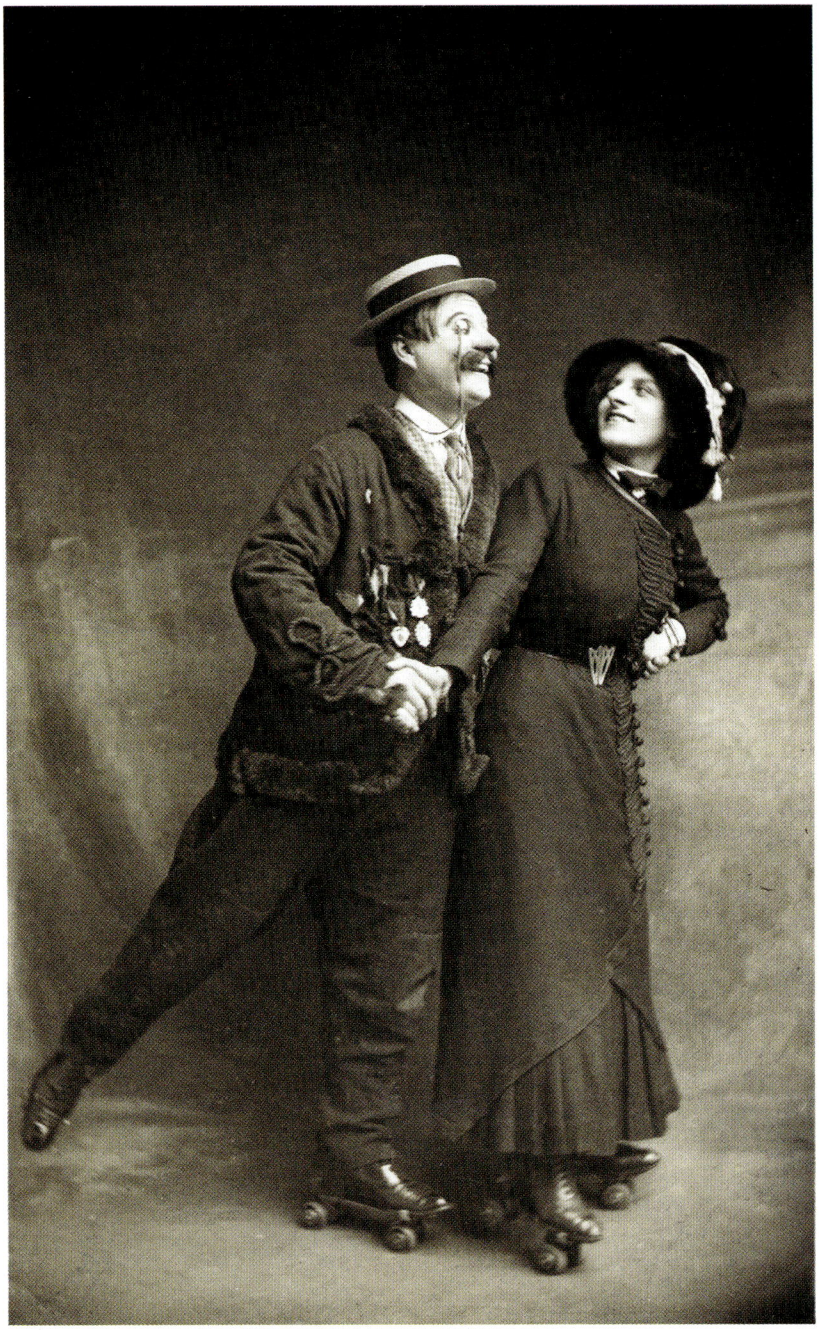

Above left

Chaplin in the role of Archibald Binks in *Skating*, c. 1910. Fred Karno regularly gave the same role to different actors and Chaplin and his brother sometimes played the same characters, as was the case in *Skating*. The story for this sketch was partly written by Sydney Chaplin. Charlie later used it to construct the plot of *The Rink*, a film he shot in 1916.

Above right

Minnie and Sydney Chaplin in *Skating*, c. 1909. Minnie Gilbert was also part of Fred Karno's company. She married Sydney Chaplin before their departure for the United States. She appeared in five films directed by her husband and made a brief appearance in a crowd scene in *A Dog's Life*.

Opposite

Chaplin in costume in the play *Mumming Birds*, November 1911. Whether in *Mumming Birds*, *A Night in a London Club* or *The Wow-Wows*, Chaplin always incarnated a character under the influence of drink, a classic in Karno—and music hall—sketches. Chaplin used the costume and figure of the drunk in his early films.

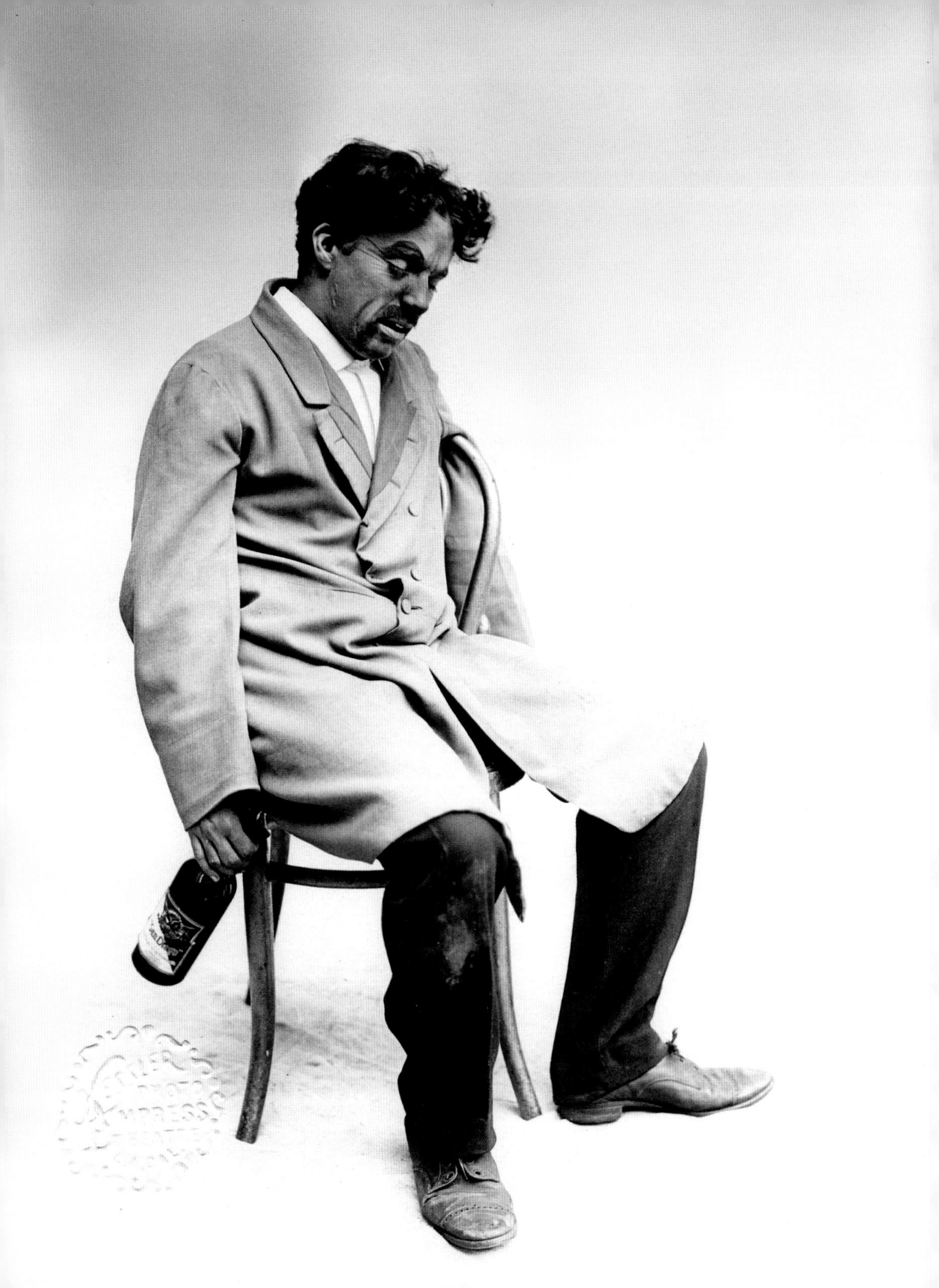

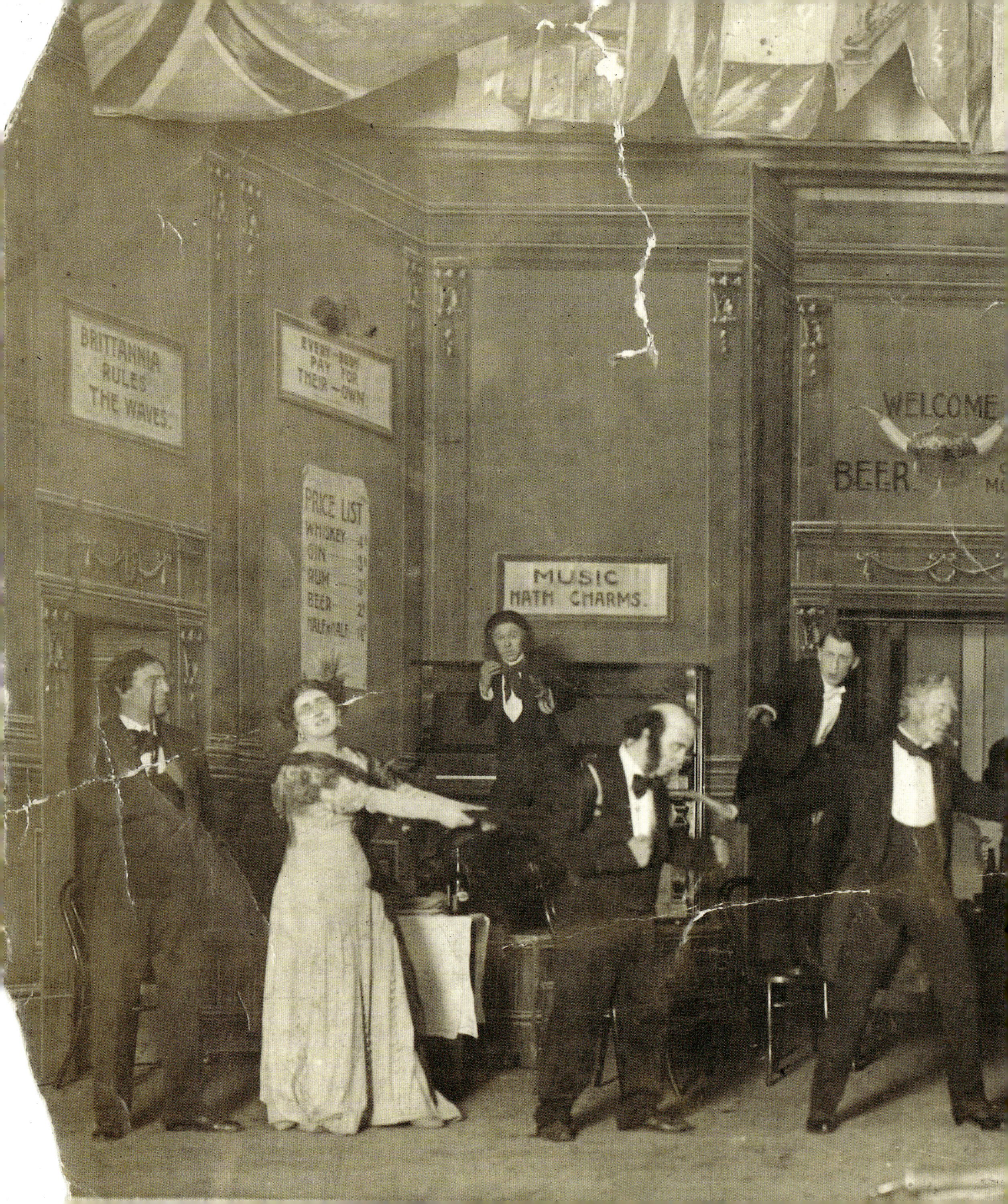
BRITTANNIA RULES THE WAVES.
EVERY BODY PAY FOR THEIR OWN
PRICE LIST
WHISKEY 4d
GIN 3d
RUM 3d
BEER 2d
HALF'N'ALF 1½d
MUSIC HATH CHARMS.
WELCOME
BEER.

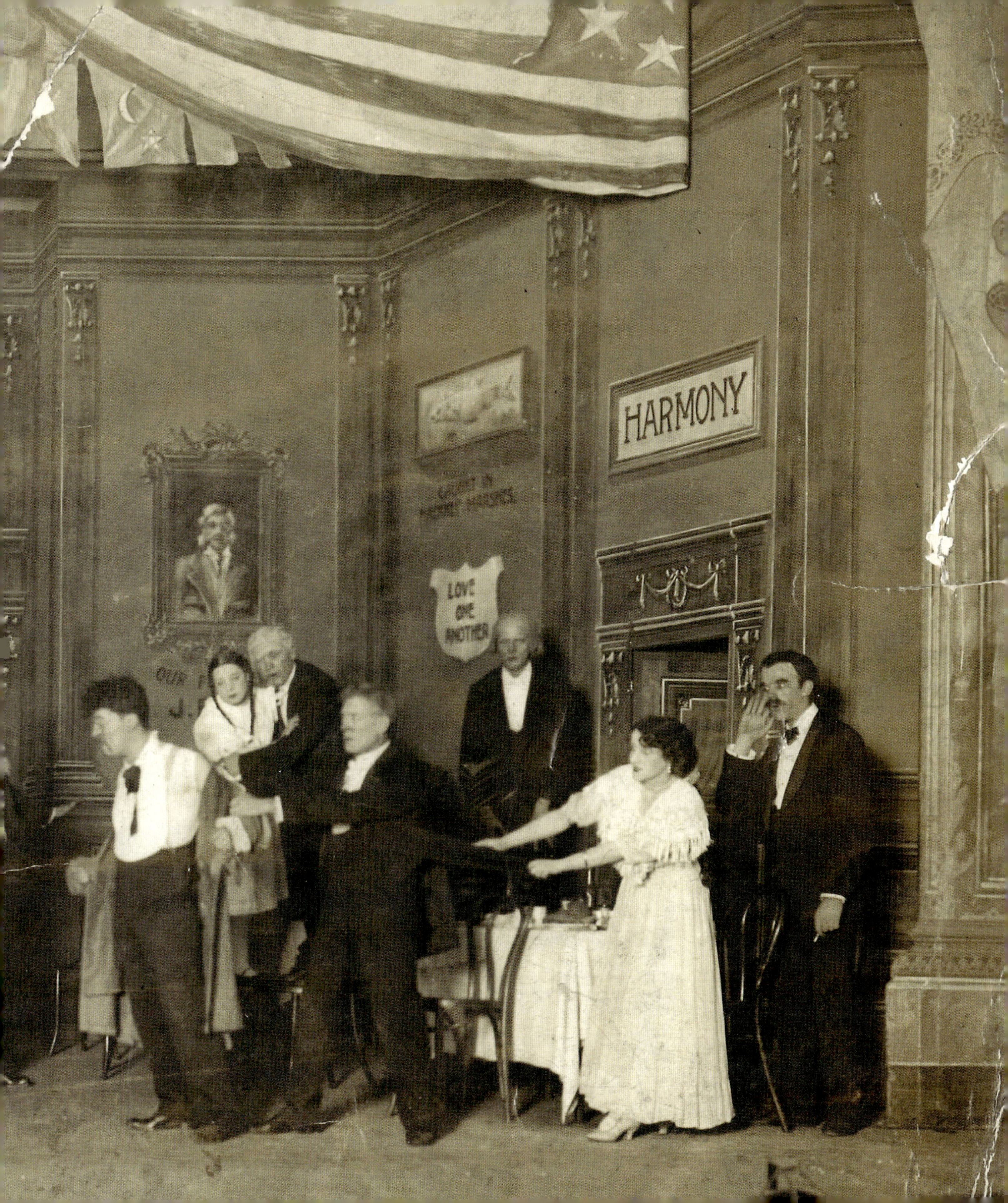
HARMONY
LOVE ONE ANOTHER

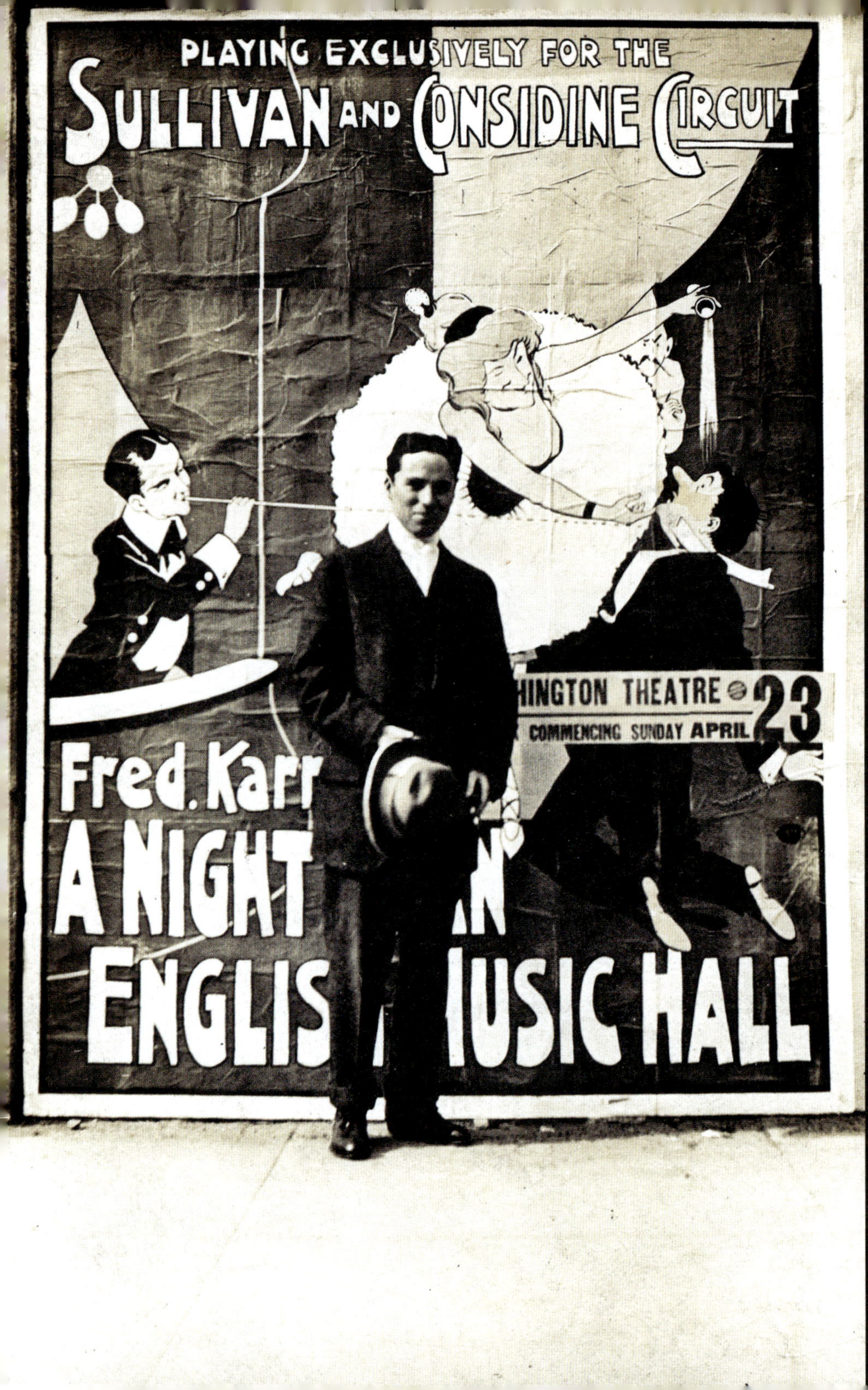

Previous double page

Fred Karno's company on stage in Kansas City, June 23, 1912. Chaplin played a drunk in *A Night in a London Club* during the company's second American tour. This photograph was autographed by Alfred Reeves for a company of acrobats, the Royal Zanettos, who were performing in the same theater.

Left

Chaplin in front of the poster for Fred Karno's *A Night in an English Music Hall*, April 1911. The play toured the theater circuit managed by John W. Considine and Big Tim Sullivan, entrepreneurs from the vaudeville scene who had made their fortune by buying theaters and saloons all over the United States and Canada.

Opposite

Auguste Leymarie, poster design, undated.

Following pages

Keystone Film Company posters for the release of *Dough and Dynamite* at a movie theater entrance, November 1914.

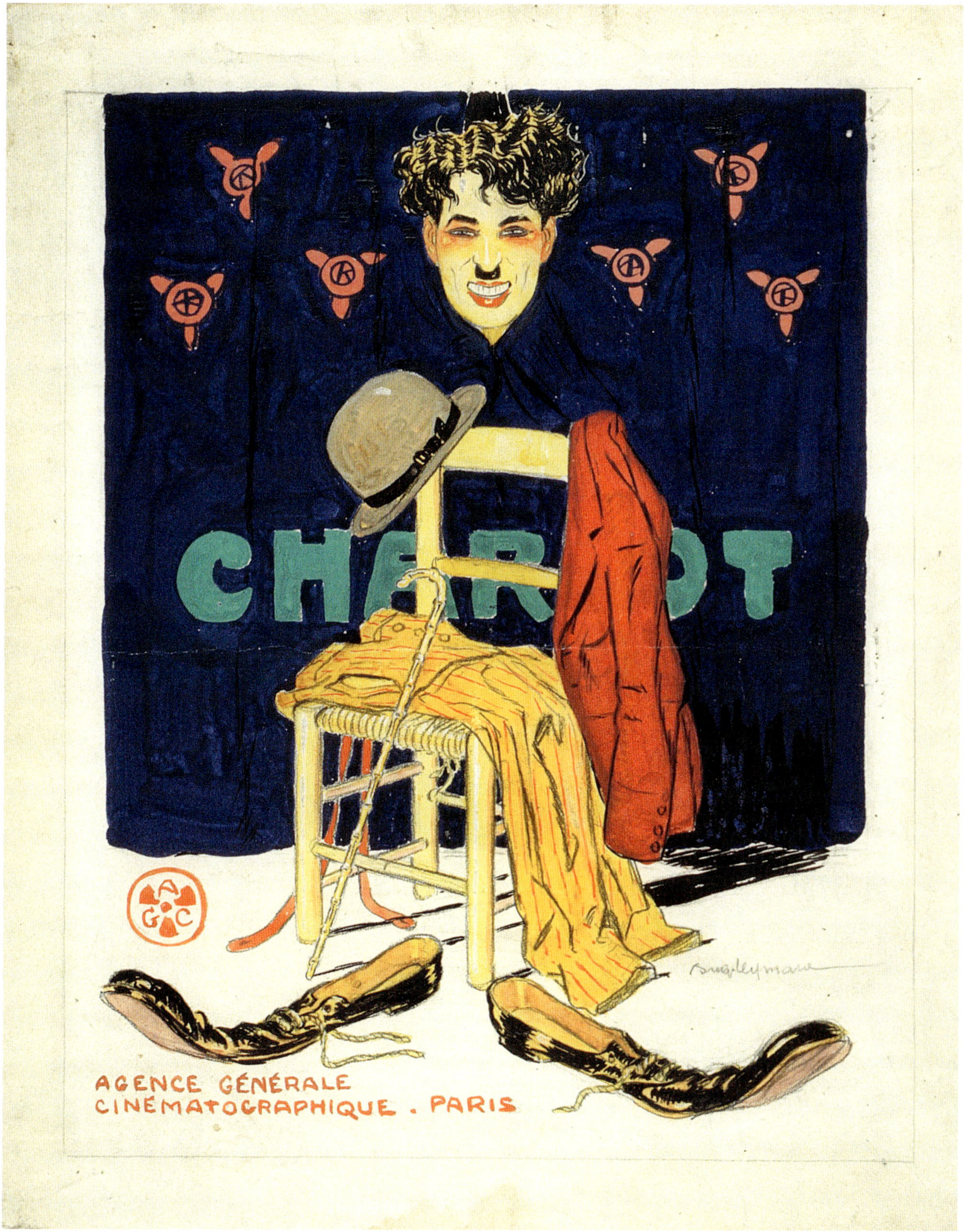
CHARLOT
AGENCE GÉNÉRALE
CINÉMATOGRAPHIQUE . PARIS

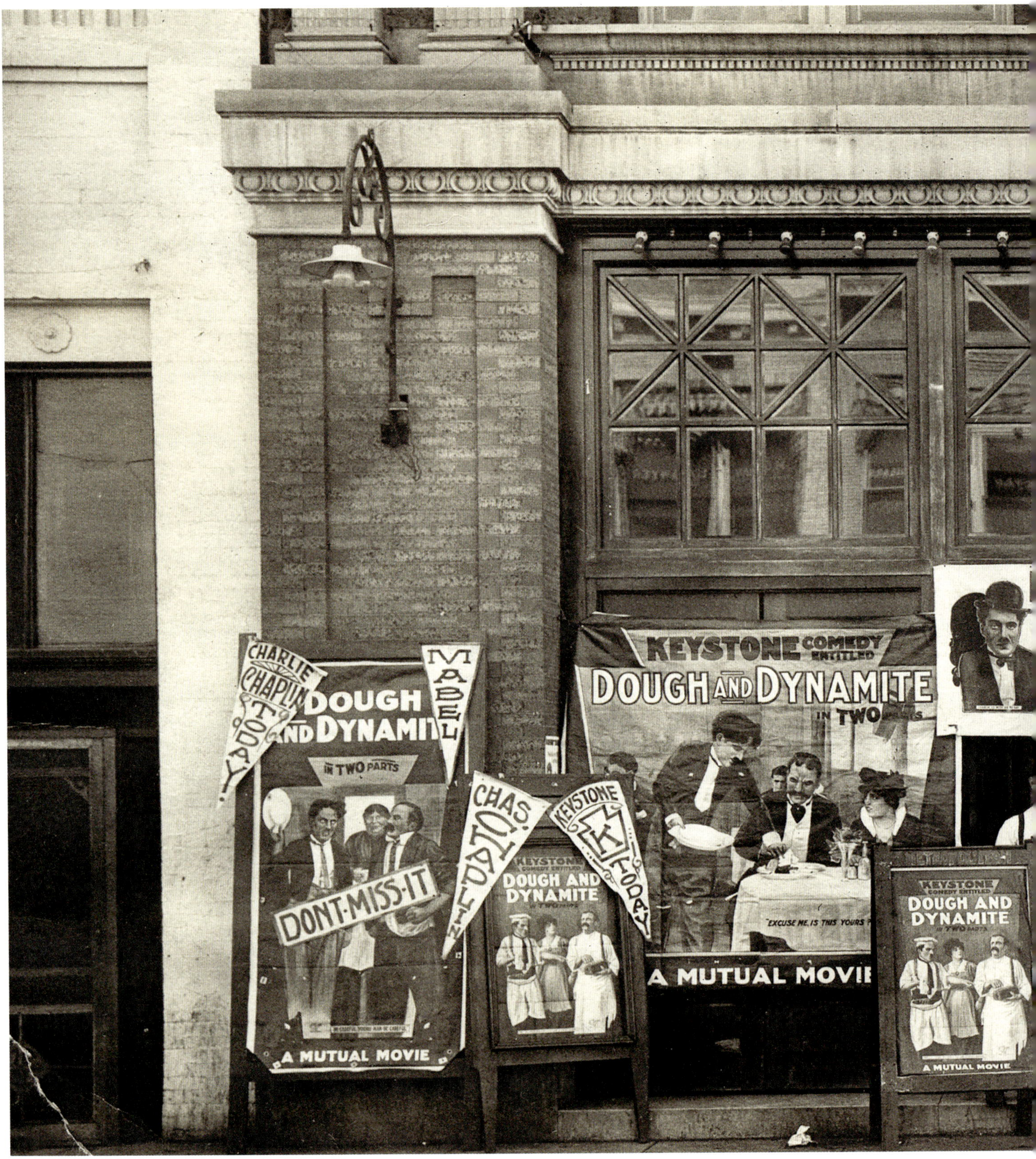
CHARLIE CHAPLIN TODAY
DOUGH AND DYNAMITE
IN TWO PARTS
MABEL
DONT-MISS-IT
A MUTUAL MOVIE
CHAS
KEYSTONE K TODAY
KEYSTONE COMEDY ENTITLED
DOUGH AND DYNAMITE
IN TWO PARTS
KEYSTONE COMEDY ENTITLED
DOUGH AND DYNAMITE
IN TWO
"EXCUSE ME, IS THIS YOURS
A MUTUAL
KEYSTONE COMEDY ENTITLED
DOUGH AND DYNAMITE
IN TWO PARTS
A MUTUAL MOVIE

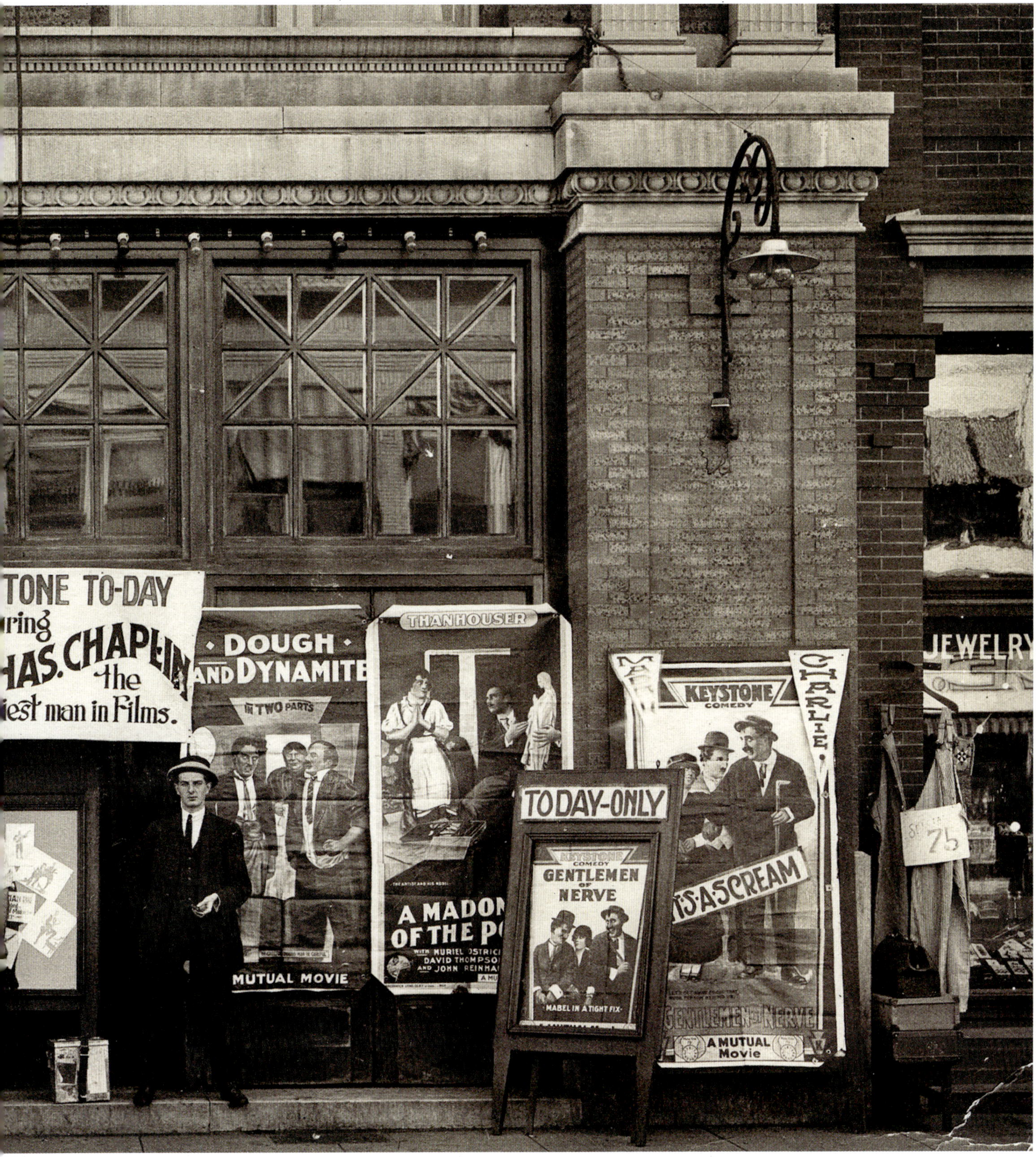

TONE TO-DAY
ring
HAS. CHAPLIN
the
iest man in Films.
DOUGH
AND DYNAMITE
IN TWO PARTS
MUTUAL MOVIE
THANHOUSER
A MADON
OF THE PO
TODAY-ONLY
KEYSTONE COMEDY
GENTLEMEN OF NERVE
MABEL IN A TIGHT FIX
KEYSTONE COMEDY
CHARLIE
IT'S A SCREAM
GENTLEMEN OF NERVE
A MUTUAL Movie
JEWELRY
75

David Robinson

The music hall heritage

Throughout his life Charles Chaplin recalled with joy and awe the moment "when music first entered my soul."[1] He first described it in his 1922 account of his European visit, *My Trip Abroad*. As a young boy, he remembered, wandering late at night in shabby and deserted Kennington Cross, he encountered a duo of wretched musicians performing in the entrance of a public house: "The harmonium player was blind, with scarred sockets where the eyes had been; and a besotted, embittered face played the clarinet."[2] Yet, despite their sad appearance, their music "was played with such feeling that I became conscious for the first time of what melody really was. My first awakening to music . . . It was here that I first discovered music, or where I first learned its rare beauty, a beauty that has gladdened and haunted me from that moment . . . Kennington Cross, where music first entered my soul. Trivial, perhaps, but it was the first time."[3]

Thirty years later, in 1952, he told the same story, in much the same words, to reporters who met him when he disembarked from the *Queen Elizabeth*, which had brought him to Britain for what was to become permanent exile in Europe: "I was seven and now I'm sixty-three, but I'll never forget it." His memory was not quite accurate all the same: he was seven in 1896, and the song in question was not written until 1901. It was not a native tune, but one of the first pieces from the American musical repertoire to reach Britain after the triumph of *The Belle of New York* in 1898. The song, "You Are the Honeysuckle, I Am the Bee," with words by Albert H. Fitz and music by William H. Penn, had been hastily introduced into the third act of a failing New York musical *The Prima Donna* (Herald Square Theatre, April 1901). The rescue effort failed: the show closed after thirty-six performances. The writer Albert Fitz, reverting to his alter ego as Sol Bloom, Chicago music publisher, nevertheless launched a massive assault on the sheet-music market, issuing the song in a large edition with a variety of colorful covers, each with the portrait of a different vaudeville star claimed to have performed the song. His ruse worked: news of the song's ensuing popularity reached Britain where Seymour Hicks incorporated it into the third act of his new Christmas musical show *Bluebell in Fairyland*, whose score had already been completed by Walter Slaughter. Performed by Hicks' wife, Ellaline Terriss, the song became a national hit in Britain, and was rapidly to go on to international popularity.

Right

Street musicians in *Limelight* (Snub Pollard, Julian Ludwig, Loyal Underwood), c. 1951. The trio of musicians Chaplin imagined for *Limelight* is reminiscent of the filmmaker's childhood as described in his autobiography.

1 Charlie Chaplin, *My Trip Abroad* (New York: Harper & Brothers, 1922), 62.
2 Charles Chaplin, *My Autobiography* [1964] (London: Penguin Modern Classics, 2003), 37. Ed. note-In *My Trip Abroad* the instrument is a harmonica and not a harmonium.
3 Charlie Chaplin, *My Trip Abroad*, 62.

It is likely then that Chaplin experienced the impact of the song in the winter of 1901–02, when he was in his twelfth year. What makes the Damascene effect of this particular melody (he only discovered later that it had words) more remarkable is that by this time Chaplin must already have been familiar with a huge repertory of songs of the British music hall, then at the zenith of its appeal, prosperity, and artistry. His parents were both professional singers and lived in Kennington, a London district much inhabited by music hall artists. For a while his father (also Charles Chaplin) was a sufficiently prominent singer for music publishers to portray him on the covers of his songs, some of which were written by, or in collaboration with, outstanding songwriters of the day, including the prolific star team of J.P. Harrington and George Le Brunn. Even though Chaplin senior abandoned his family when young Charles was still a baby, some memory of his repertoire and style must have persisted in the home.

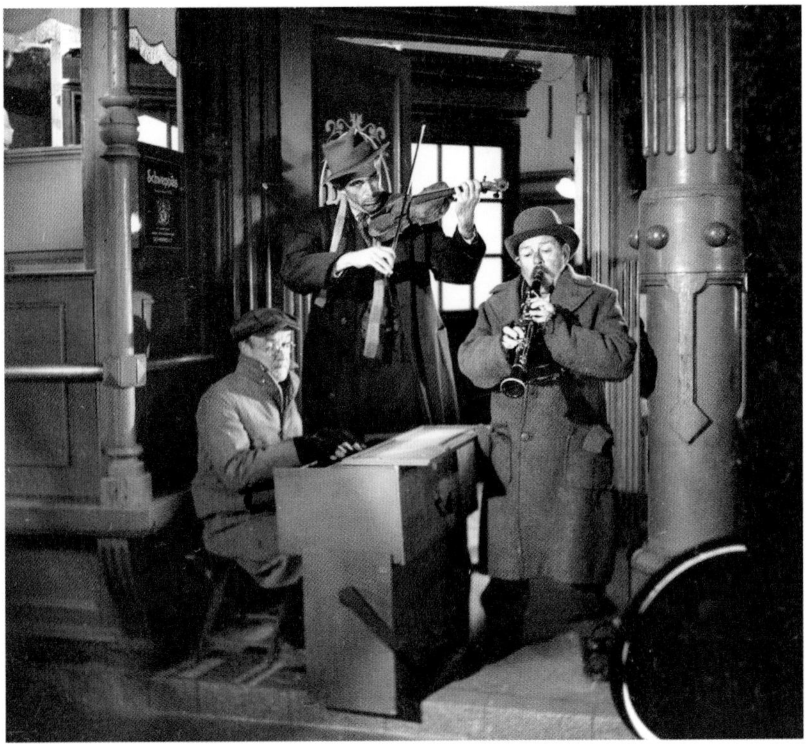

His mother had had a shorter career as a soubrette and dancer, under the name of Lily Harley, and her song repertory was modest, in part composed by herself; but she also seems to have written a couple of songs for her sister, who performed as Kitty Fairdale. For a brief time a bigger star moved in with Mrs. Chaplin and fathered a boy by her. This was Leo Dryden, whose celebrated songs of patriotism, Empire and nobility belied his less gallant private behavior: he soon walked out on the Chaplins and snatched his own son away.

Chaplin's childhood was therefore spent in households in which music hall songs were the stock-in-trade. We know that his mother entertained her young sons, Sydney and Charles, with songs, which Chaplin himself still delighted to recall in his old age. Evidently the boys learned some of these by heart, as we discover from Chaplin's memory of his first stage appearance at the age of around six. His mother had taken him with her to a one-night engagement at an army canteen theater at Aldershot, where the audience was famously unruly and demanding. The ailing Mrs. Chaplin's voice failed her mid-performance, and the quick-thinking manager pushed Charlie, whom he had seen amusing the other artists backstage, onto the stage. The boy obligingly launched into Gus Elen's 1890 success "'E Dunno Where 'E Are," and went on to do a couple of encores, after picking up the coins which the delighted audience had showered upon him. Evidently, then, Mrs. Chaplin not only sang the songs of the day to her boys, but also taught them how to perform them.

Chaplin was soon, however, to be exposed to the whole great lyrical repertory of the music hall at its zenith, when there were close to 200 music hall theaters in the British Isles,

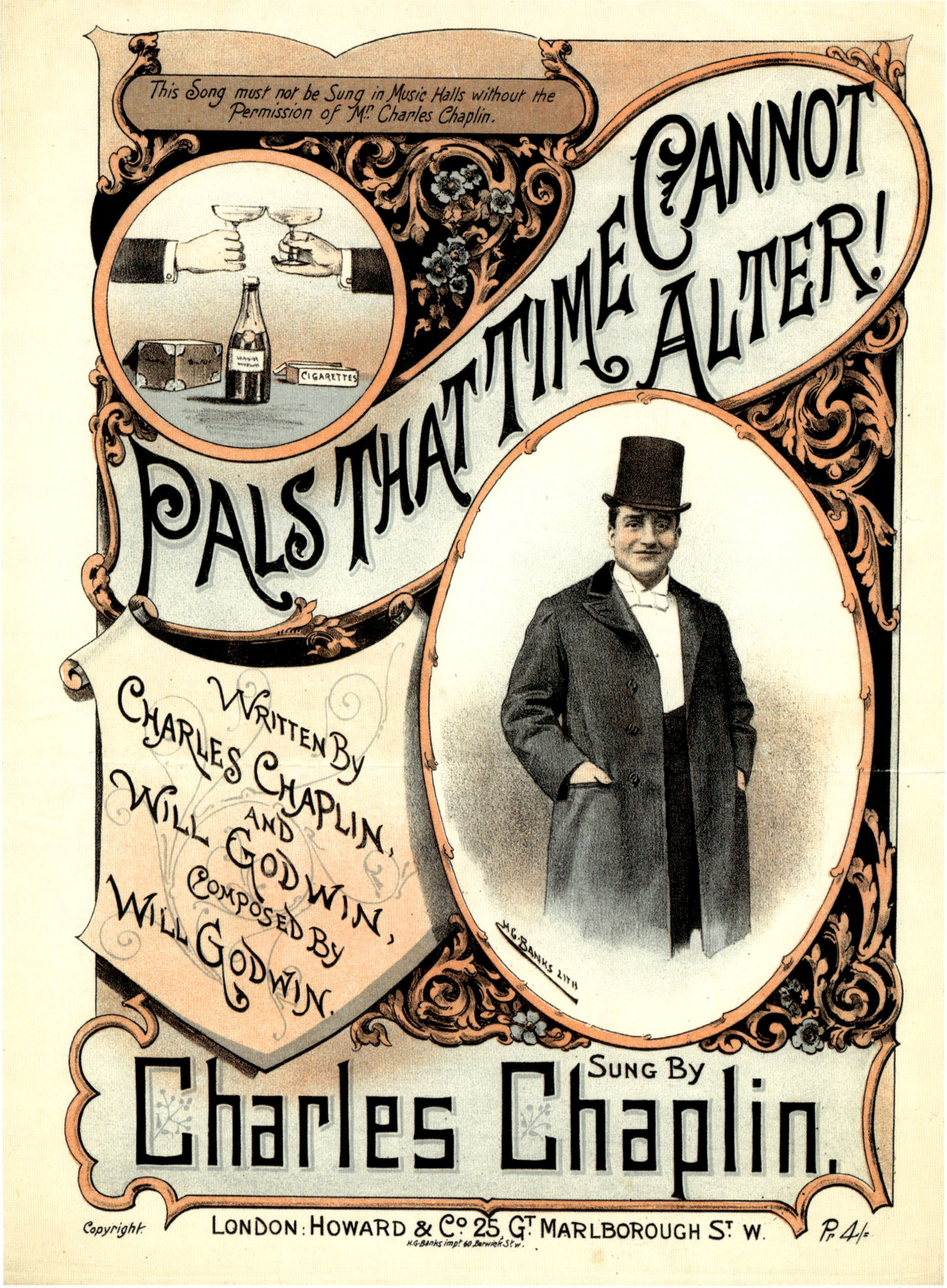
This Song must not be Sung in Music Halls without the Permission of Mr. Charles Chaplin.
PALS THAT TIME CANNOT ALTER!
CIGARETTES
Written By Charles Chaplin, and Will Godwin, Composed By Will Godwin.
H.G. BANKS LITH
Sung By
Charles Chaplin.
Copyright
LONDON: HOWARD & Co. 25 Gt. MARLBOROUGH St. W.
H.G. Banks impt. 60 Berwick St. W.
Pr 4/-

Opposite

Sheet music for "Pals That Time Cannot Alter!" Charles Chaplin Senior, 1900.

Below

The Eight Lancashire Lads, c. 1890.
When he was seven years old, Charlie joined this company of young actor-dancers, traveling from theater to theater all over England.
"I was not particularly enamoured with being just a clog dancer in a troupe of eight lads. Like the rest of them I was ambitious to do a single act, not only because it meant more money but because I instinctively felt it to be more gratifying than just dancing."

each employing between a dozen and twenty acts a night, each act with its own music repertory. He became a professional music hall performer before he was ten, as a member of the Eight Lancashire Lads, a troupe of boy singers and clog-dancers. Finally, after a variety of stage experiences and adventures, in 1908 he was recruited to Fred Karno's Speechless Comedians, who presented comedy sketches that were very much in the style of early one- and two-reel comic films. He remained with Karno for the rest of his stage career, until he entered films in January 1914. Karno was a tough and dictatorial boss, but his companies were incomparable schools of comedy technique. Here, amongst other lessons, Chaplin learned the use of music for comic irony: Karno might for instance accompany a scene of rough knockabout with a dainty romantic gavotte.

A music hall act would be on stage for a maximum of twenty minutes, and it is certain that in the course of the week artists would have the opportunity to watch the other acts on the program. So Chaplin could have seen and heard some of the great music hall singers of the era. In 1901 the Lancashire Lads were for many weeks on the same London bill as Dan Leno, one of the greatest comic artists in British theatre history, then still at the peak of his form. The young Chaplin found himself working on the same stages as the great music hall singing stars of the time—Marie Lloyd, Harry Lauder, George Robey, Marie Kendall, Vesta Tilley, Vesta Victoria, Gus Elen.

The demand for songs was insatiable, and was met by several generations of writers and composers, many of outstanding lyrical talent and invention. In his definitive catalogue of British music hall songs, Michael Kilgarriff lists some 18,000 songs and 600 composers and lyricists.

With a wide range of music skills and inventive gifts, the music hall song writers nevertheless conformed to a consistent

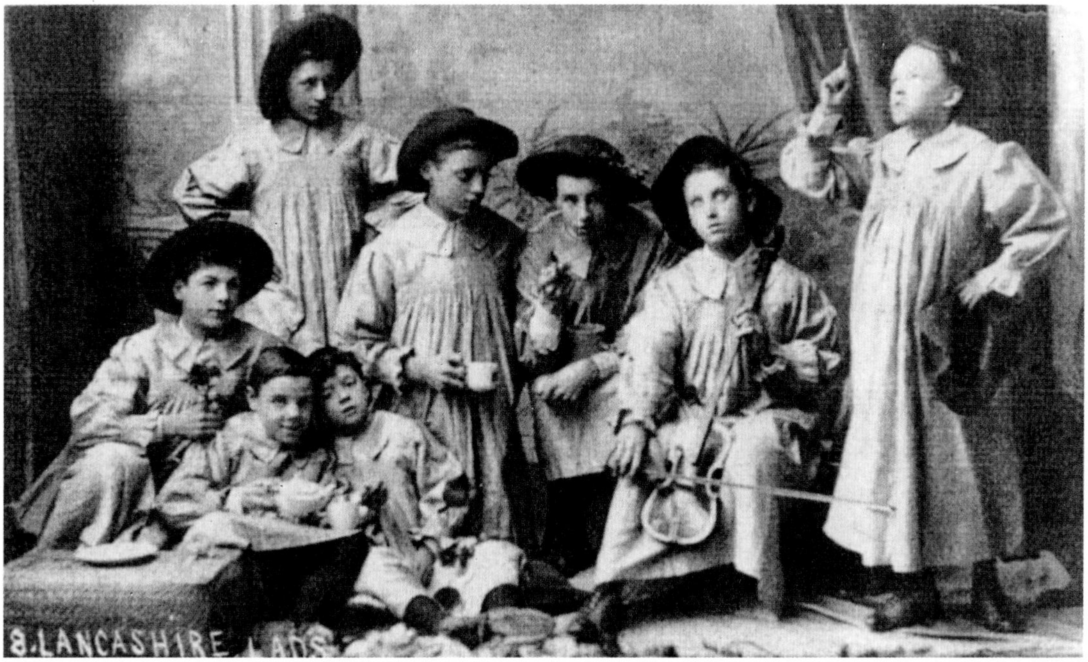

Below

Fred Karno's company, Sacramento, 1911. Chaplin, second from the right, poses beside Alfred Reeves who holds a rifle.

Right

Chaplin, as his character Calvero, and Buster Keaton in *Limelight*, 1952. Chaplin asked Buster Keaton to be his partner for a music hall number marking the climax of the film. It was the first time that the two giants of silent cinema had acted together. The clown duo performance nostalgically evokes the performances of Chaplin's London youth.

format, ultimately derived from native folk song and the minstrel songs popularized in the mid-19th century, and readily handled by the hard-worked orchestras. Each number was introduced with a catchy "till ready" phrase that could be repeated ad lib, as the performer took his time to ready himself and his audience. Then came the verse, often in the style of *recitativo accompagnato*, laying out the story of the song. A song might normally run to between three and six verses, each followed by the chorus, which was the melodic raison d'être of the song, and in which the audience was frequently encouraged to join. The chorus might be unvarying, or have a changing gag-line for each repetition.

Within this constrained format, music hall songs could nevertheless explore a limitless range of themes and moods: romantic ("I'll Be Your Sweetheart"), maudlin ("The Blind Boy"), pathetic ("Are We to Part Like This", "The City Waif"), tragic ("Ring Down the Curtain"), anarchic ("What Funny Things You See When You Haven't Got a Gun"), patriotic ("God Bless Victoria, Albion's Queen"), occupational ("Any Old Iron?"). They might explore family relations ("Her Mother's at the Bottom of It All"), work ("Young Man Who Worked at the Milk Shop"), aging ("My Old Dutch," "I'm One of the Ruins That Cromwell Knocked About a Bit"). A whole genus was dedicated to the joys of alcohol. There was no limit to subject or mood, and in turn the singer would shape his character to suit the song: "true to life" was a constant quest and boast of music hall artists.

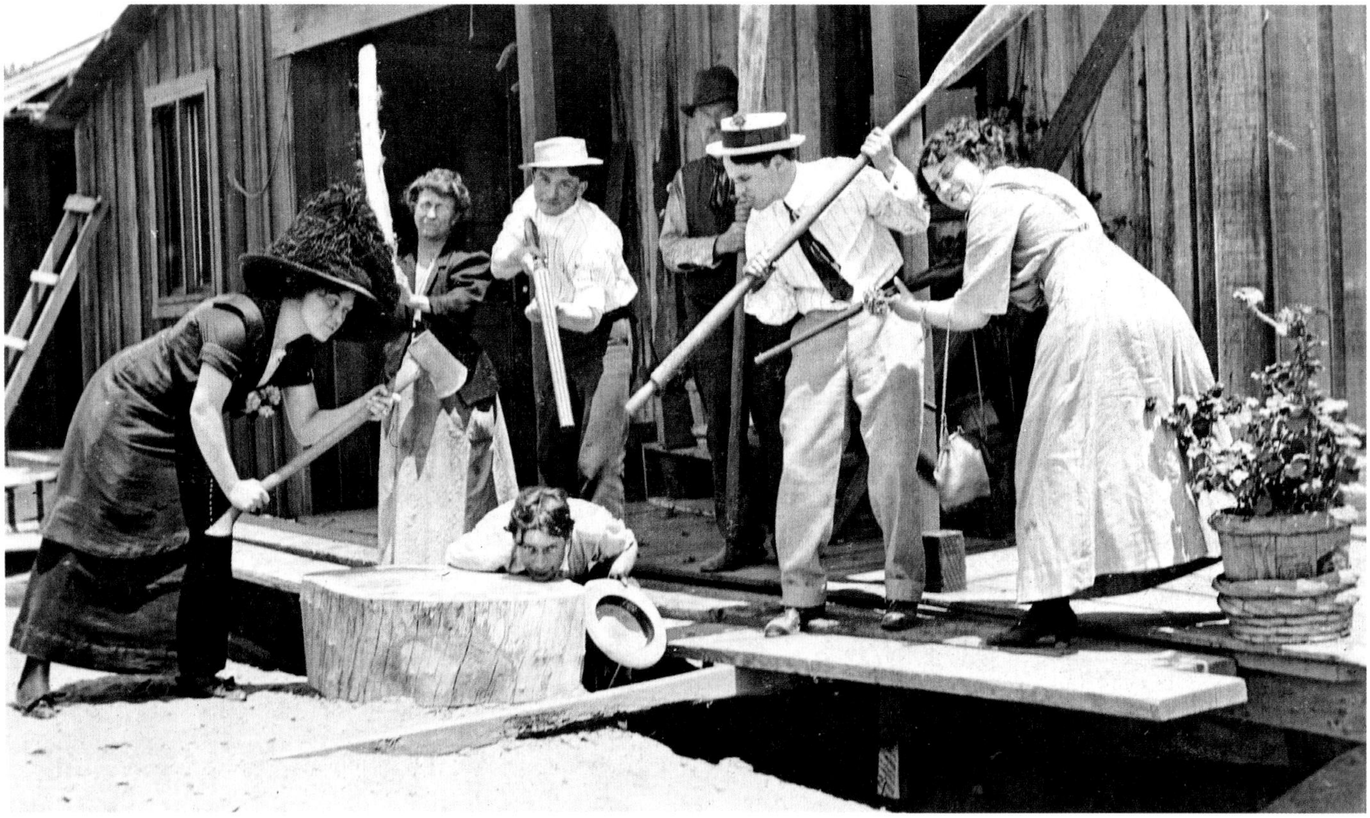

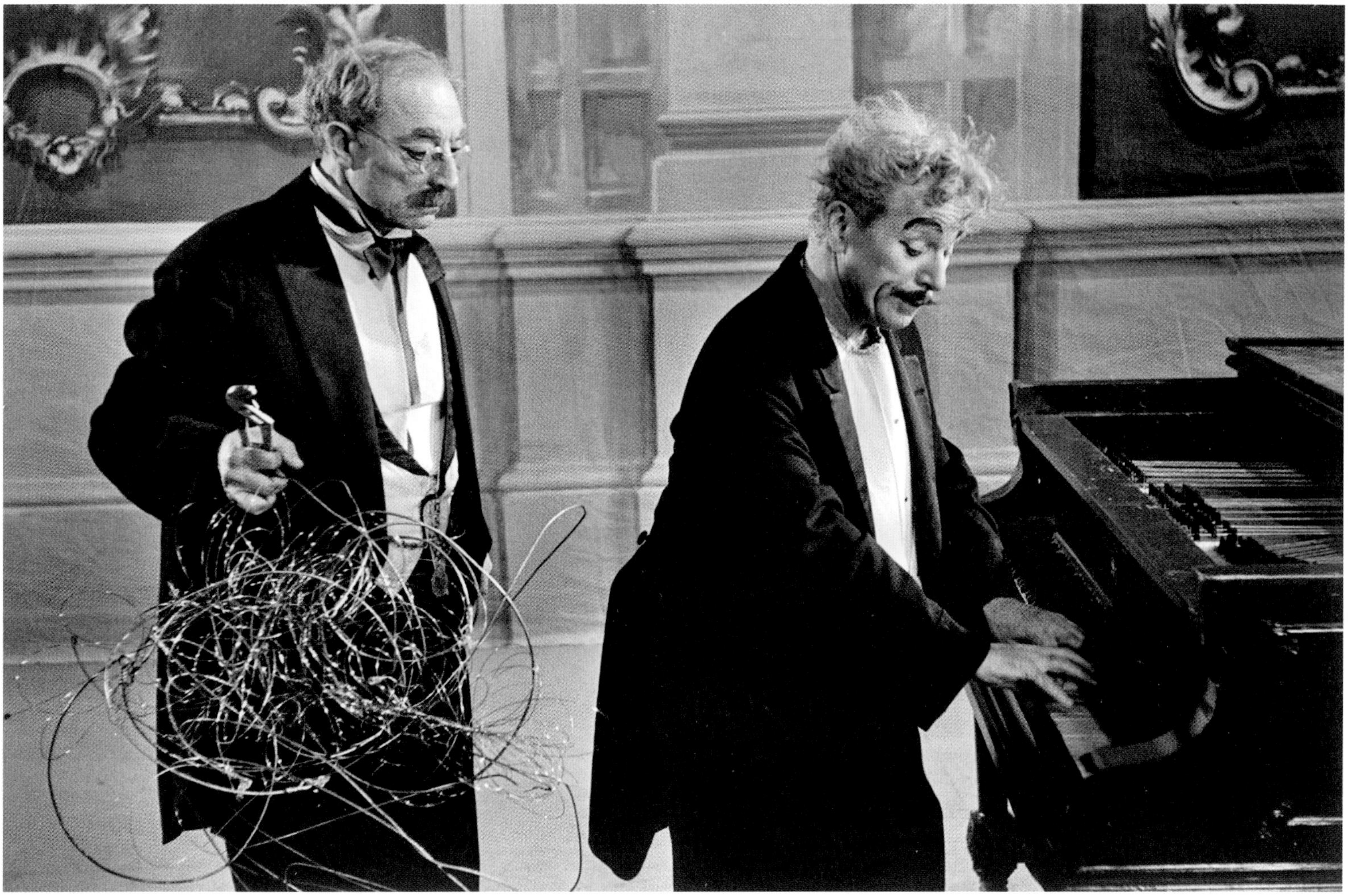

Right

Publicity stills for *Limelight*, 1951. Chaplin plays the role of Calvero, and in the film performs several pastiches of music hall numbers. On the left, he wears the outfit in which he sings "Animal Trainer" and, on the right, that of "Spring Song."

Even though Chaplin declared that it was at the age of twelve that "music entered his soul," from his earliest consciousness and until his entry into films he was inescapably exposed to this vast world of melody. Our question here is to what extent did this experience impact his own work as a composer? The great Hollywood composer David Raksin recalled, "There is a specific kind of genius that traces its ancestry back to the magpie family, and Charlie was one of those. He had accumulated a veritable attic full of memories and scraps of ideas which he converted to his own purposes with great style and individuality."[4] In each of his film scores for *City Lights* and *Modern Times* Chaplin deliberately interpolates and acknowledges themes both from music hall songs and from American vaudeville and jazz. In *Limelight*, he wrote and staged pastiches of music hall numbers for his character of Calvero, the failed comic: "I'm an Animal Trainer," "Oh for the Life of a Sardine," in which he perfectly parodied the vocal manner of George Bastow (1871–1914), and the comic-romantic "Spring Song". But it is hard to know just how much of the vast and rich melodic heritage of the music halls was stored in that attic-mind, to color the overall composition of his film scores and songs. David Raksin, who at twenty-three engaged in a stormy but finally triumphant collaboration with Chaplin as orchestrator of the music of *Modern Times*, remembered, "In the area of music, the influence of the English music hall was very strong, and since I felt that nothing but the best would do for this remarkable film, when I thought his approach was a bit vulgar, I would say, 'I think we can do better than that.' To Charlie this was insubordination, pure and simple—and the culprit had to go."[5] Raksin was, indeed, immediately dismissed, but then, fortunately for *Modern Times* and for posterity, was persuaded to return.

Music had entered the young Chaplin's soul, perhaps—but it also had its place in that attic-mind.

4 David Raksin, "Life with Charlie," *The Quarterly Journal of the Library of Congress*, vol. 40, no. 3, summer 1983.

5 *Ibid.*

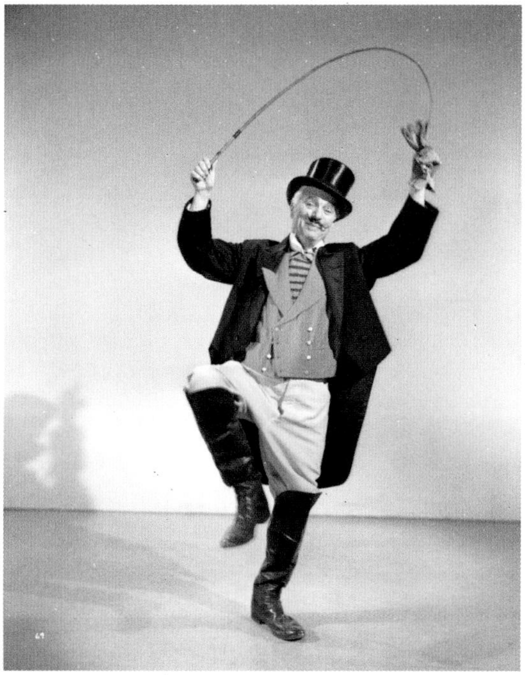

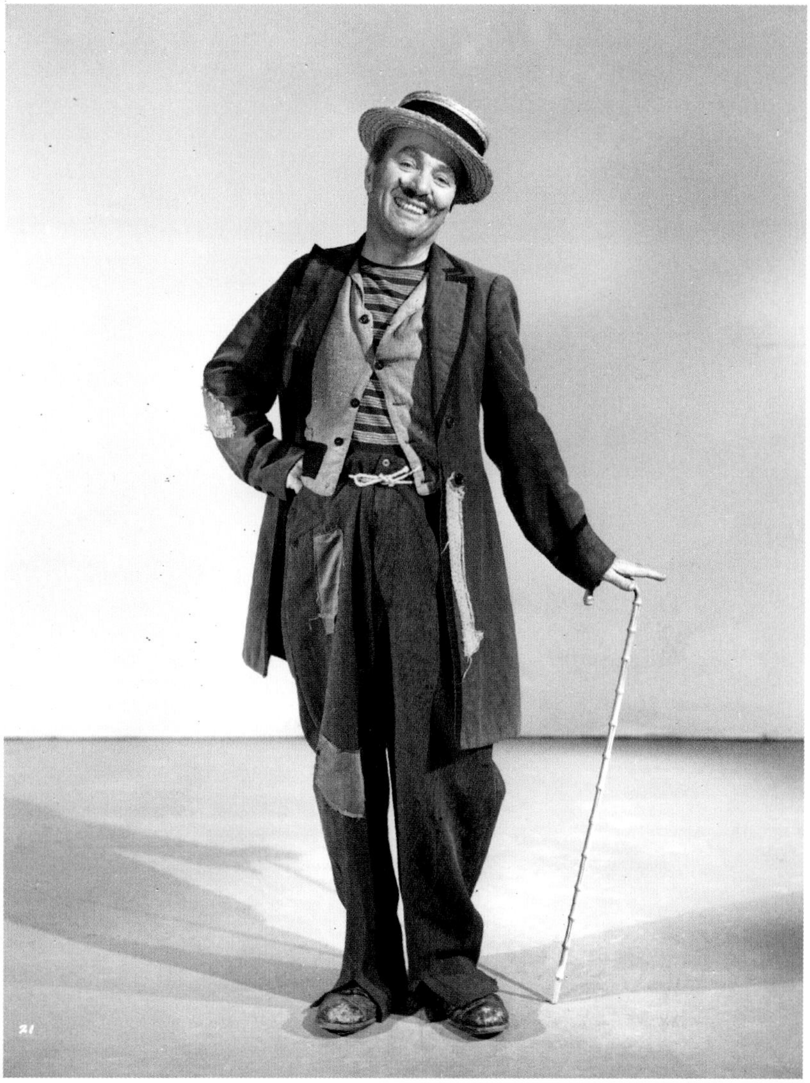

Timothy Brock

Carmen

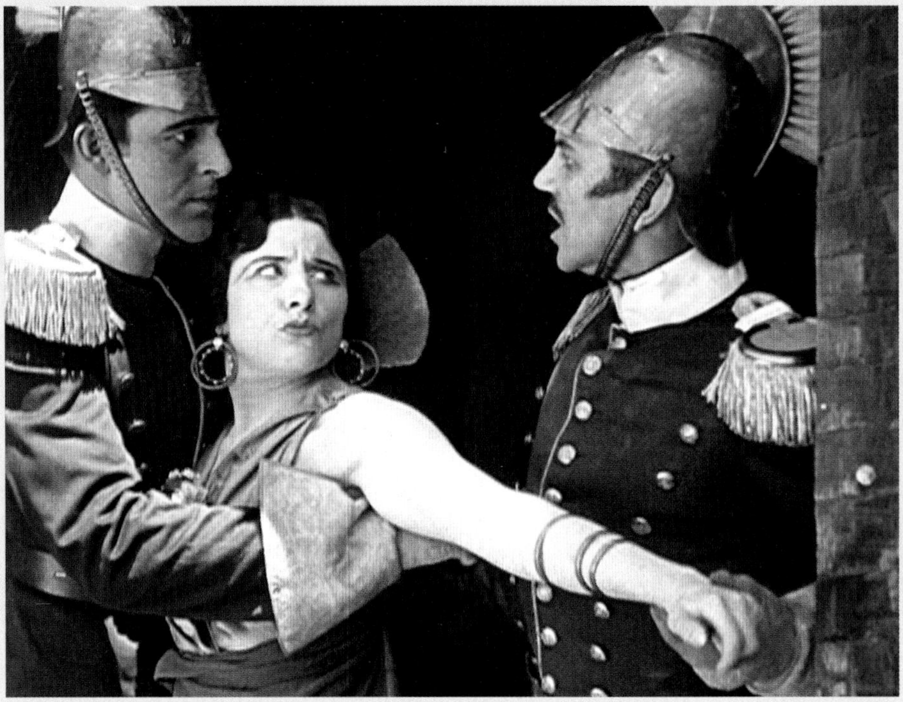

The first true representation of Carmen on film was by the pioneering female director Alice Guy-Blaché in 1906 for Gaumont. By the time Chaplin's *Burlesque on Carmen* made its screen debut in December 1915, no less than twenty-four versions of the Carmen legend had preceded it, and by the end of the following decade nearly forty silent-film portrayals of Carmen had made it to the screen, from a diverse field of directors including Ernst Lubitsch and Raoul Walsh. However, none was more popular or successful than Cecil B. DeMille's *Carmen* from 1915.

Opera synopses were not uncommon fare in the silent period as they had a built-in audience familiar with the storylines. Studios did not rely on the illustrious music to sell the films, having no control over what music was actually played in the local cinemas by the theater-employed musician(s). The first film adaptation of *Tosca*, released in 1909, very much relied on the popularity of the opera to sell cinema tickets, though possibly not one single note of Puccini's score (written only nine years earlier in 1900) was heard accompanying the film.

In the case of *Carmen*, however, there are no practical musical alternatives, and DeMille's vision was to give a much more spectacular and immersive experience, both visually and aurally. Paramount Pictures had allotted a rather lavish budget to their production and in 1915 they were able to procure a three-film contract with the Metropolitan Opera's most coveted singer, American soprano Geraldine Farrar, who had made Bizet's *Carmen*

Above

Geraldine Farrar and Pedro de Cordoba in Cecil B. DeMille's *Carmen*, 1915.

Right

Edna Purviance in the role of Carmen and Chaplin as Darn Hosiery in *A Burlesque on Carmen*, 1915.

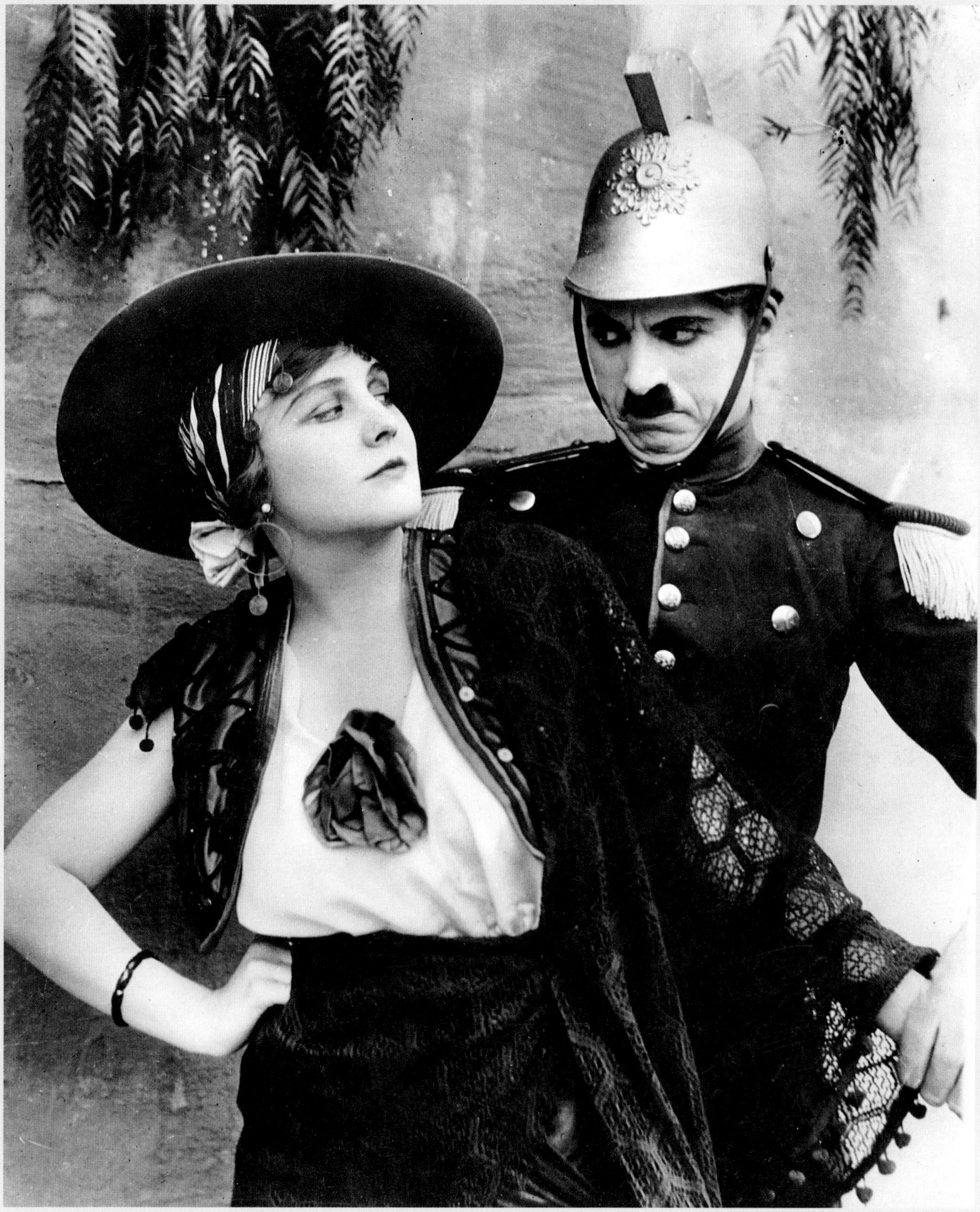

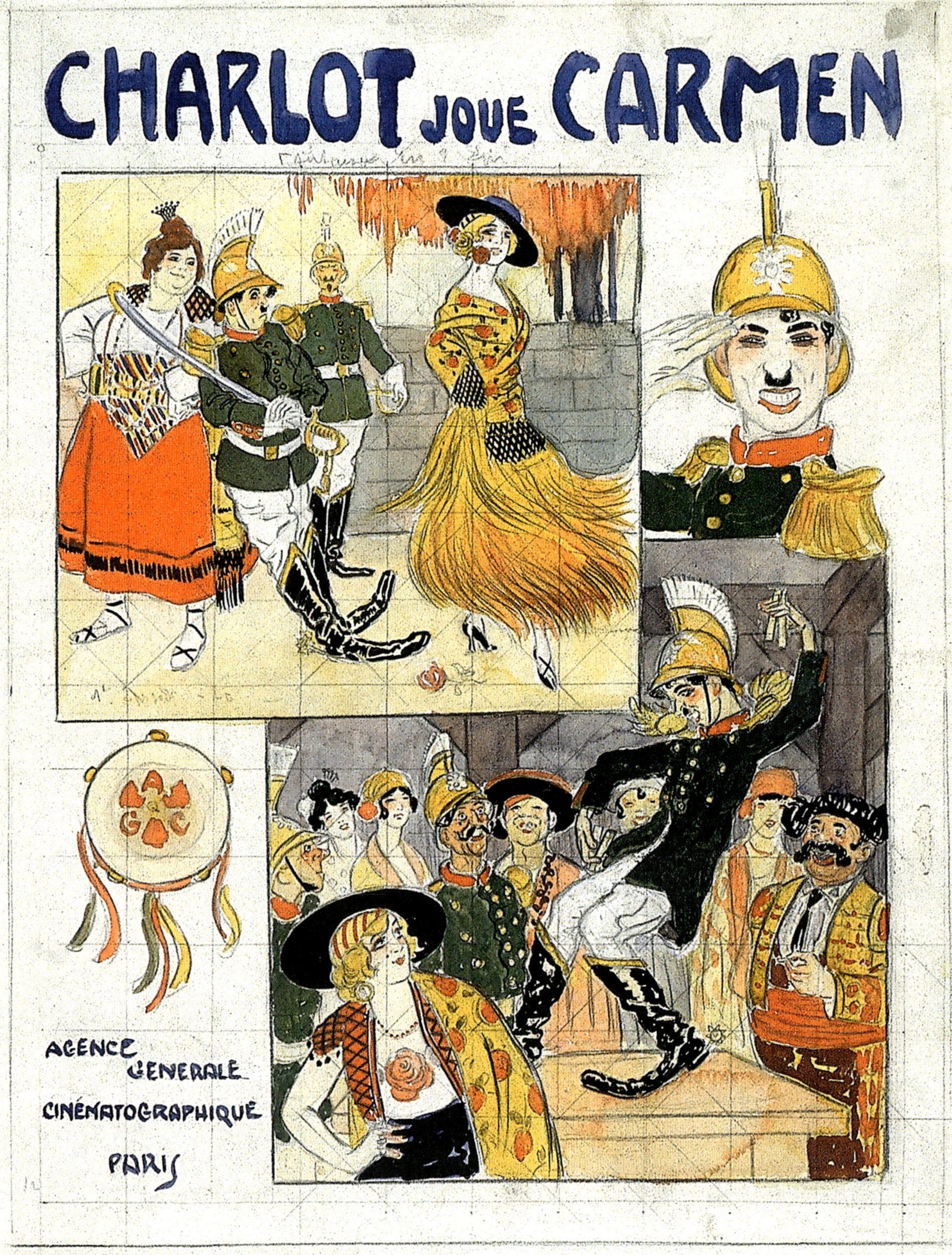
CHARLOT JOUE CARMEN
A G C
AGENCE GENERALE
CINÉMATOGRAPHIQUE
PARIS

her signature role on the stage. Equally extravagant, they commissioned film-music pioneer Hugo Riesenfeld to create an adaptation of Bizet's score to be played at all screenings of the film across the country, by any size of orchestra (one to forty-five musicians). This ensured the public would experience the type of spectacle that DeMille eventually became so famous for with his epics *King of Kings* (1927) and *Cleopatra* (1934). *Carmen* became a rousing success and on screen Farrar together with Wallace Reid as Don José were immense hits with the public.

Enter Chaplin, whose *Burlesque on Carmen* was not so much a parody of Bizet's opera, but a grinning mockery of DeMille's *Carmen*, by this time the most successful version ever produced. He endeavored to duplicate the look and feel of the DeMille production in as many ways as he could: production design, script and intertitle choices, and even some identical filming locations. Casting his ever-present leading lady Edna Purviance in the title role, and himself as army officer Darn Hosiery, Chaplin relied heavily on both the general popularity of the Carmen story and the box-office smash released merely six weeks previously.

We do not have any accounts of what was actually played to accompany the 1915 *Burlesque*, but we do know that the Bizet score was extremely common repertoire for small cinema orchestras and organists. Most cinemas had what was known as a "Photoplay" book, where the musician could reference dozens of short pieces of music that would be apt for accompanying (and improvising to) certain scenes of a film. In addition, they were also required to play before the featured screenings a short set of popular favorites of the day, and highlights from famous operas. All cinema musicians would definitely have had ready access to the Bizet score, especially given the fact that the Riesenfeld score was widely distributed some six weeks earlier.

The question is, did the musicians lampoon the Bizet score to accompany Chaplin's *Burlesque?* Musical parody has been fashionable at least since J. S. Bach's *Cantate Burlesque* (1742), up through Bela Bartok's *Concerto for Orchestra* (1943), where both composers mocked their distinguished musical peers. Chaplin himself was an artist who had used refined and sophisticated music to great comic effect as a stage performer throughout his career in the English musical halls. He never bought into the notion that comedic performances should be accompanied by irreverent music, and said "Elegant music gave my comedies an emotional dimension . . . I wanted no competition, I wanted the music to be a counterpoint of grace and charm." Therefore, I can only hope that if, in fact, Bizet's music was played to accompany *Burlesque on Carmen*, the clever musician played it straight, and let the comedy speak for itself.

Opposite

Auguste Leymarie, poster design for *A Burlesque on Carmen*, c. 1915.

Jürg Stenzl

The musical accompaniment of Chaplin's silent films

A Night in the Show

It has long been established that until the late 1920s silent films were never "silent" when screened. Another certitude is that while Chaplin later became particularly interested in the music for his films, he did not choose music to accompany his first seventy-two shorts. Restored versions of those films are now available on DVD, accompanied by new music whose style is predominantly dependent on that of sound films. The search for music that accompanied silent films at the time also brings to light names of composers and works that are little known by specialists in the history of music of the first third of the 20th century.

Before focusing on a concrete example—Chaplin's film *A Night in the Show* (1915)—we should describe the screening conditions for films at the time.

Movie theaters were widespread in the United States and Europe. But the size of the theaters, their quality, and the audience and its expectations, varied greatly from one place to another. Likewise, depending on the nature of the print screened, the length, quality, and duration of an identical film could also vary considerably. The same was true for the number of intertitles for a film.

The musical accompaniment of screenings was just as varied: certain movie theaters hired a lone pianist who improvised, others featured ensembles of three to twelve musicians, and "film palaces" in larger cities could host orchestras of forty or more musicians.

While several thousands of specifically composed pieces survive, as do an incalculable number of musical extracts in compilation, the actual cue sheets—which give cues and timing, and list the musical choices for individual film titles—are now very rare. For Chaplin films only a dozen or so survive around the world. Analysis of the musical choices within them is nevertheless particularly interesting, especially when documentation for the same film from different countries or cities exists. In addition to the differences generated by cinematographic genres, there are significant local characteristics. For example, resorting to hit songs of the period, particularly their instrumental versions, is common because of the audience "recognition effect."

The son of two music hall artists, Chaplin joined Fred Karno's famous company at the age of eighteen. During a tour of the United States, he was discovered by Mack Sennett, who signed him to the Keystone

Right

Henry Roberty, poster for the French release of *A Night in the Show*, 1915.

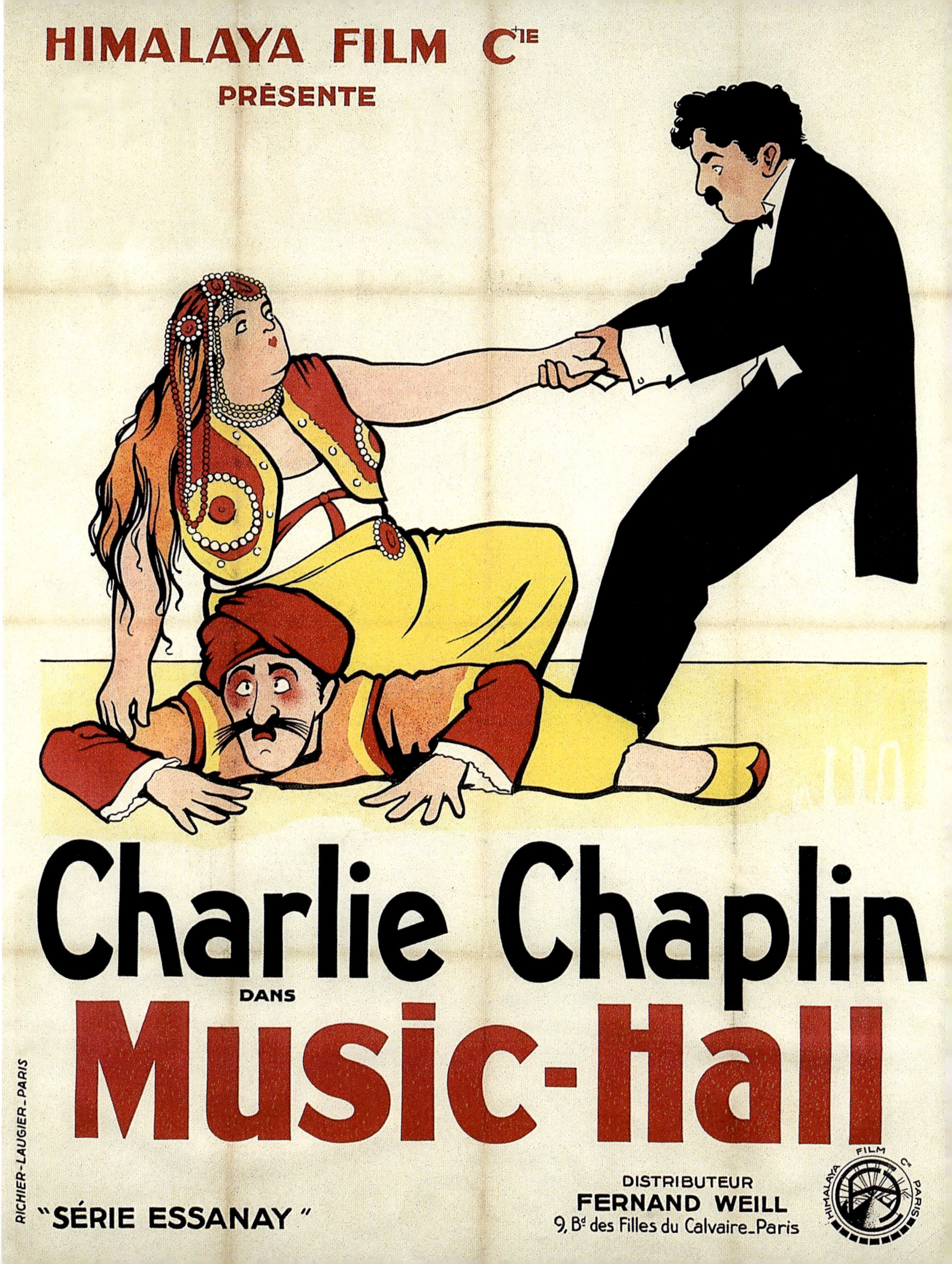
HIMALAYA FILM Cie
PRÉSENTE
Charlie Chaplin
DANS
Music-Hall
RICHIER-LAUGIER-PARIS
"SÉRIE ESSANAY"
DISTRIBUTEUR
FERNAND WEILL
9, Bd des Filles du Calvaire-Paris
HIMALAYA FILM Cie PARIS

Film Company. Chaplin made thirty-five films featuring the Tramp character for Keystone until December 1914. Hired from January 1915 by the Essanay Film Manufacturing Company, Chaplin went on to make fourteen films for them. My example, *A Night in the Show*, is the twelfth of this series. Screened in the United States for the first time on November 20, 1915, its restored version runs twenty-three minutes.

A Night in the Show is one of the rare Chaplin films for which cue sheets still exist. The two surviving cue sheets were both used at the same Parisian movie theater: the Gaumont-Palace. Unfortunately, no cue sheets from other countries have survived, which would have allowed us to observe to what extent the musical accompaniment of the same film could vary from country to country.

Unusually, for this film Chaplin adapted an act that was a hit from his Fred Karno days. Titled "Mumming Birds," it was a play within a play from the music hall world. Chaplin acts two parts with characteristic names—Mr. Pest, sitting in the orchestra, and Mr. Rowdy, in the circle—both attending a music-hall show made up of strange acts.[1] Unusually, Chaplin does not appear as the tramp figure, but as an inebriated, wealthy member of the audience, intervening inopportunely during the acts, and as a belligerent character, obviously less rich but just as drunk.

The plot of the film may be summarized by its nine intertitles:

1 A complete description of the film by Brian J. Robb: https:/chaplinfilmbyfilm.wordpress.com/2015/11/20/a-night-in-the-show-20-november-1915/

	Intertitles	Text	Action
0:20 0:22	1st intertitle	*Get in line and wait your turn.*	Chaplin sits behind the sculpture
0:51 0:53	2nd intertitle	*Mr. Rowdy.*	Gallery of audience member portraits: Chaplin "the drunken bum"
3:03 3:08	3rd intertitle	*My mistake, Sir. Your seat is in the second row.*	Chaplin changes place, a woman behind him—Quarrel
9:51 9:54	4th intertitle	*You're on my hat, Sir.*	Chaplin stands up
10:04 10:07	5th intertitle	*You're on mine, too!*	The two spectators stand up
10:13	6th intertitle	*La Belle Wienerwurst.*	Curtain rises
13:46 13:51	7th intertitle	*Next—Tootsy-Frutti, the snake charmer.*	Curtain rises: a woman in oriental dress
16:44	8th intertitle	*Dot & Dash. They say they are clever. We shall see.*	Man with a dwarf
20:26 20:30	9th intertitle	*Professor Nix, the Fire Eater.*	Curtain
23:06	End		

Paul Fosse was responsible for the musical accompaniment of the 1,600 films screened at the Gaumont-Palace in Place Clichy, Paris, between 1915 and 1928. He headed an orchestra of up to sixty musicians. The musical compositions they played is listed in two large volumes in which we find two "adaptations" of the musical accompaniment for *A Night in the Show*, as the film had been programed twice at the Parisian movie theater, from June 9, 1916, and then five years later, from April 1921.

The first adaptation was most likely written by one of Fosse's assistants, while the second—which was, in the author's words, "much better"—was composed by Fosse himself. This particular situation allows us better to assess the changes made between the two screenings.

For screenings of "ordinary" films, Fosse called on a limited repertoire of pieces. The more "ambitious" films represented a sort of challenge that he rose to by opting for more demanding compositions. Having delegated the job of musical accompaniment to his assistants for some time, the fact that Fosse decided to write the adaptations himself for a considerable number of the thirty or so Chaplin films screened at the Gaumont-Palace was no coincidence.

To begin with, let us examine the first musical accompaniment of *A Night in the Show*. In the list of pieces, the adapters mention the title and author of the musical compositions. Indications of image and sound synchronization are frequent. Most of the time, the first measures of each piece follow the intertitles. This information is completed by the names and dates of birth and/or death of the composers, as well as the printed scores of the works used.

The seven pieces on the first cue sheet were written by only three composers, unknown to us today: Laurent Halet, (the Bibliothèque Nationale de France (BnF) holds no fewer than 409 printed scores of his); Auguste Bosc (560 scores at the BnF); and a certain "Juliano," of whom no trace could be found. Only three out of the seven pieces (nos. 2, 4, and 7 on the list) were also played during screenings of other Chaplin films. The impossibility of finding these particular music pieces is not surprising because many of the works in Fosse's rich musical corpus were written by contemporary composers and were never published or, if they were, printed versions are now hard to find.

Most of the compositions used are either dance tunes or, unsurprisingly, pieces with particularly lively tempos well suited to the requirements of slapstick comedy. The pieces are on average three minutes long and thus comparable to other forms of popular music of the period, even though their structure was often more repetitive than more distinguished examples of this genre. In the present case, only the scores, when we have them, allow us to know with what intertitle such and such a tune corresponded and at what moment it began and ended.

In the corpus of Gaumont-Palace cue sheets, the musical accompaniment of 1915 seems to indicate a certain professional routine. This situation changed greatly five years later when Fosse decided to write an adaptation for this film himself.

Following double page

Paul Fosse, Gaumont-Palace register of musical adaptations (first volume), 1911–28.

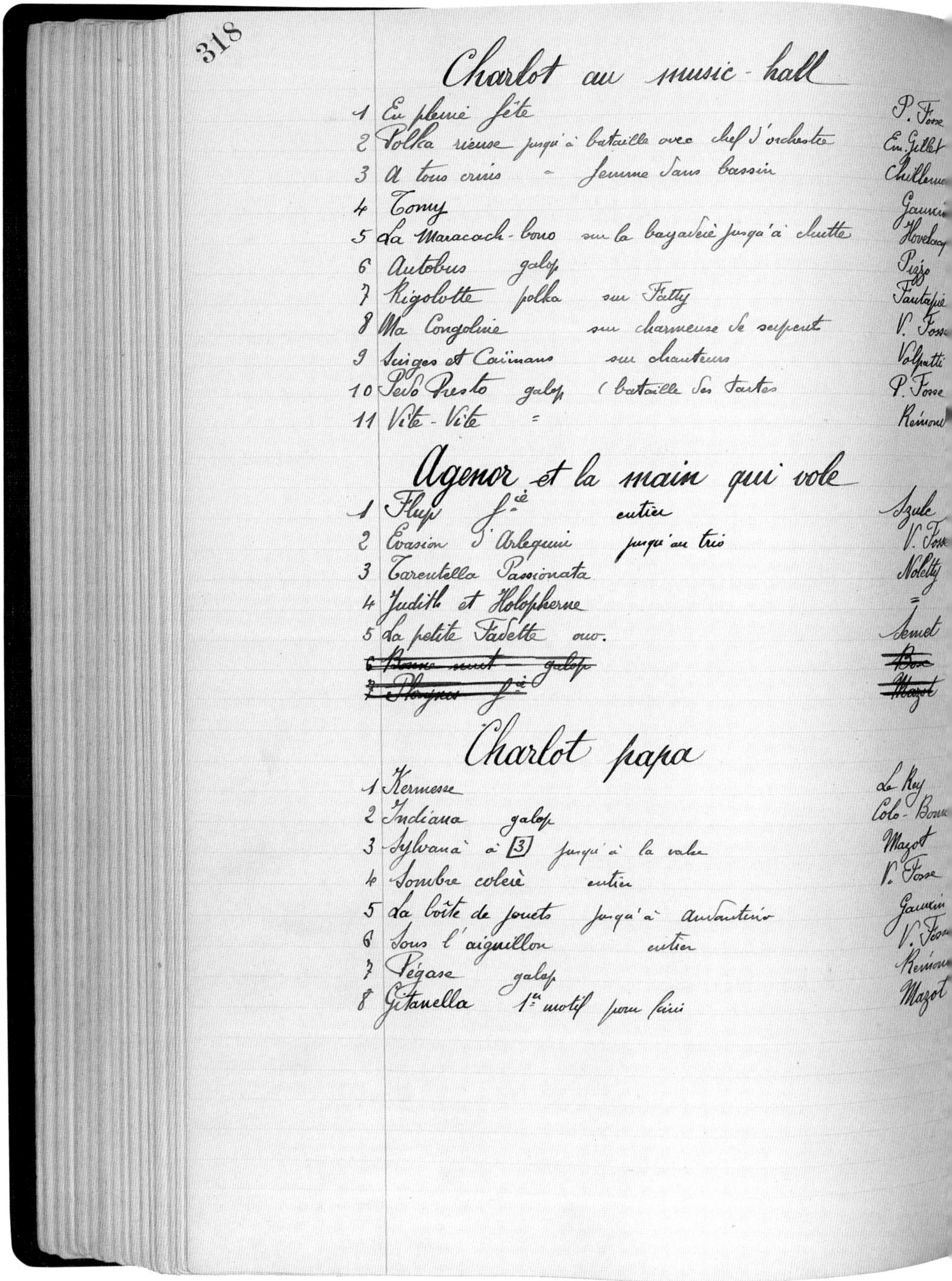
318
Charlot au music-hall
1 En pleine fête — P. Fosse
2 Polka rieuse jusqu'à bataille avec chef d'orchestre — Em. Gillet
3 A tous cris — femme dans bassin
4 Tony — Gauwin
5 La Maracach-boro sur la bayadère jusqu'à chute
6 Autobus galop
7 Rigolotte polka sur Fatty
8 Ma Congoline sur charmeuse de serpent — V. Fosse
9 Singes et Caïmans sur chanteurs — Volpatti
10 Presto Presto galop (bataille des tartes — P. Fosse
11 Vite-Vite =
Agenor et la main qui vole
1 Flup fie entier
2 Evasion d'Arlequin jusqu'au trio — V. Fosse
3 Tarentella Passionata
4 Judith et Holopherne =
5 La petite Fadette ouv. — Semet
6 Bonne nuit galop — Bosc
7 f.ie — Mazot
Charlot papa
1 Kermesse — Le Rey
2 Indiana galop — Colo-Bonnet
3 Sylvana à 3 jusqu'à la valse — Mazot
4 Sombre colère entier — V. Fosse
5 La boîte de jouets jusqu'à andantino — Gauwin
6 Sous l'aiguillon entier — V. Fosse
7 Pégase galop
8 Gitanella 1er motif pour finir — Mazot

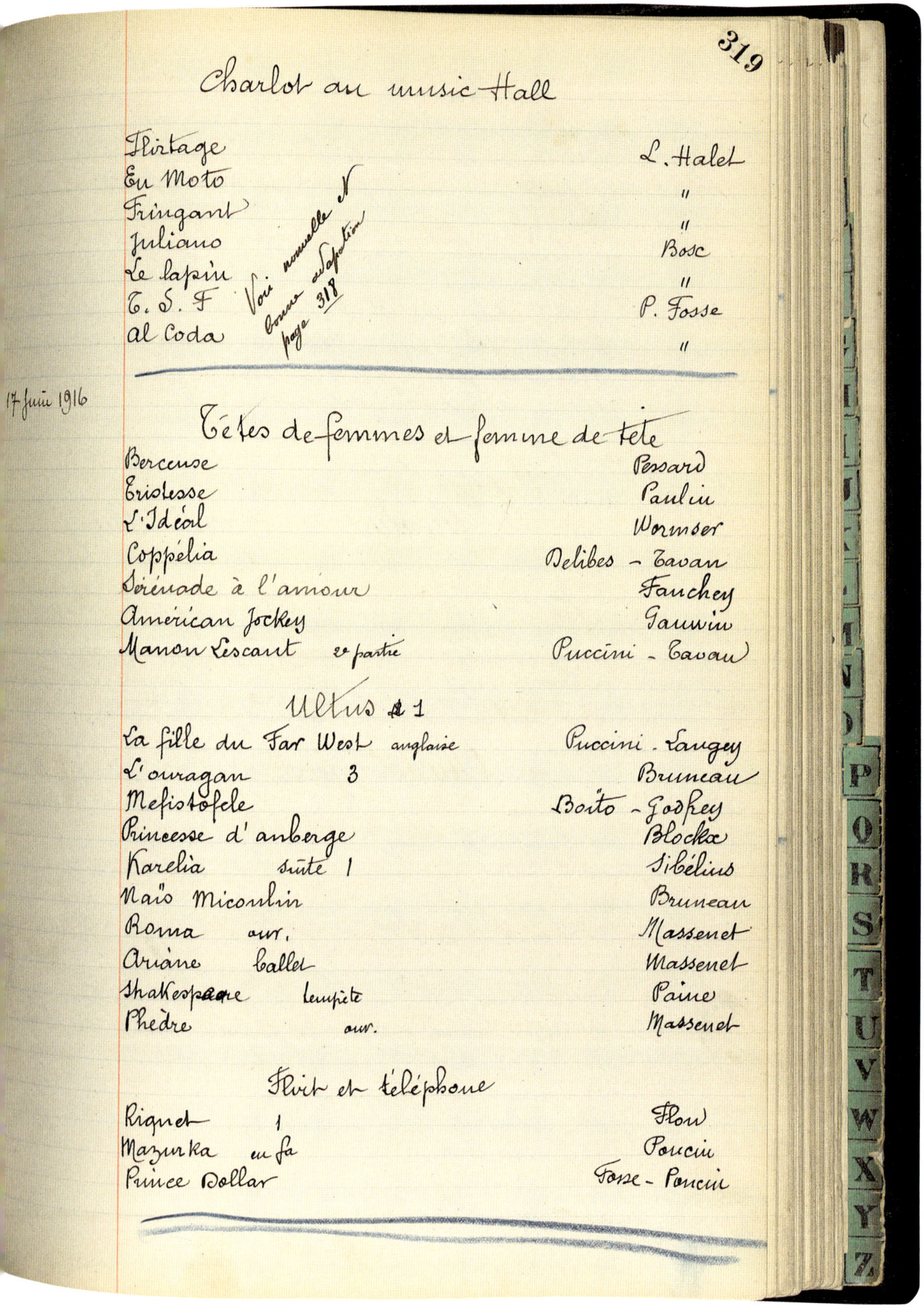

319

Charlot au music Hall

Flirtage		L. Halet
En Moto		"
Fringant		"
Juliano		Bosc
Le lapin		"
T. S. F		P. Fosse
Al Coda		"

Voir nouvelle et bonne adaptation page 318

17 Juin 1916

Têtes de femmes et femme de tête

Berceuse		Pessard
Tristesse		Paulin
L'Idéal		Wormser
Coppélia		Delibes - Tavan
Sérénade à l'amour		Fauchey
American Jockey		Gauwin
Manon Lescaut	2e partie	Puccini - Tavan

Ultus 1

La fille du Far West	anglaise	Puccini - Langey
L'ouragan	3	Bruneau
Mefistofele		Boïto - Godfrey
Princesse d'auberge		Blockx
Karelia	suite 1	Sibélius
Naïs Micoulin		Bruneau
Roma	ouv.	Massenet
Ariane	ballet	Massenet
Shakespeare	tempête	Paine
Phèdre	ouv.	Massenet

Flirt et téléphone

Rigaud	1	Flow
Mazurka	en fa	Poncin
Prince Dollar		Fosse - Poncin

It is not surprising that the new cue sheet is punctuated by fast rhythm dances as well as by two compositions by Fosse. As in the previous adaptation, it is quite easy to understand the synchronization between the image and the sound: numerous indications clearly refer to the intertitles and to easily identifiable events in the film. It is, however, the number of music titles used exclusively to accompany this Chaplin film that is most surprising. Out of them all, only Fosse's composition no. 10 had been used previously for another film. Moreover, the selected composers and works were little known to the public. Although it is a burlesque comedy, *A Night in the Show* and its quasi-exclusive musical repertoire, striking, among other things, because of three pieces written by barely identifiable composers, in fact constitutes an extremely rare example.

After this unique case of musical adaptation, the Gaumont-Palace screened three other Chaplin films: a very early film, *His Trysting Place* (1914), and two later films, *The Pilgrim* (1923) and *The Kid* (1921). The screening of Chaplin films stopped in May 1925, probably because their exclusive contract came to an end.

The differences between the two musical "adaptations"—as Fosse called them—of *A Night in the Show* very clearly demonstrate that the musical accompaniment of silent films up until the late 1920s and the appearance of talkies has a history of its own, rarely found in books dedicated to the history of music.

Opposite

Film still from *A Night in the Show*.

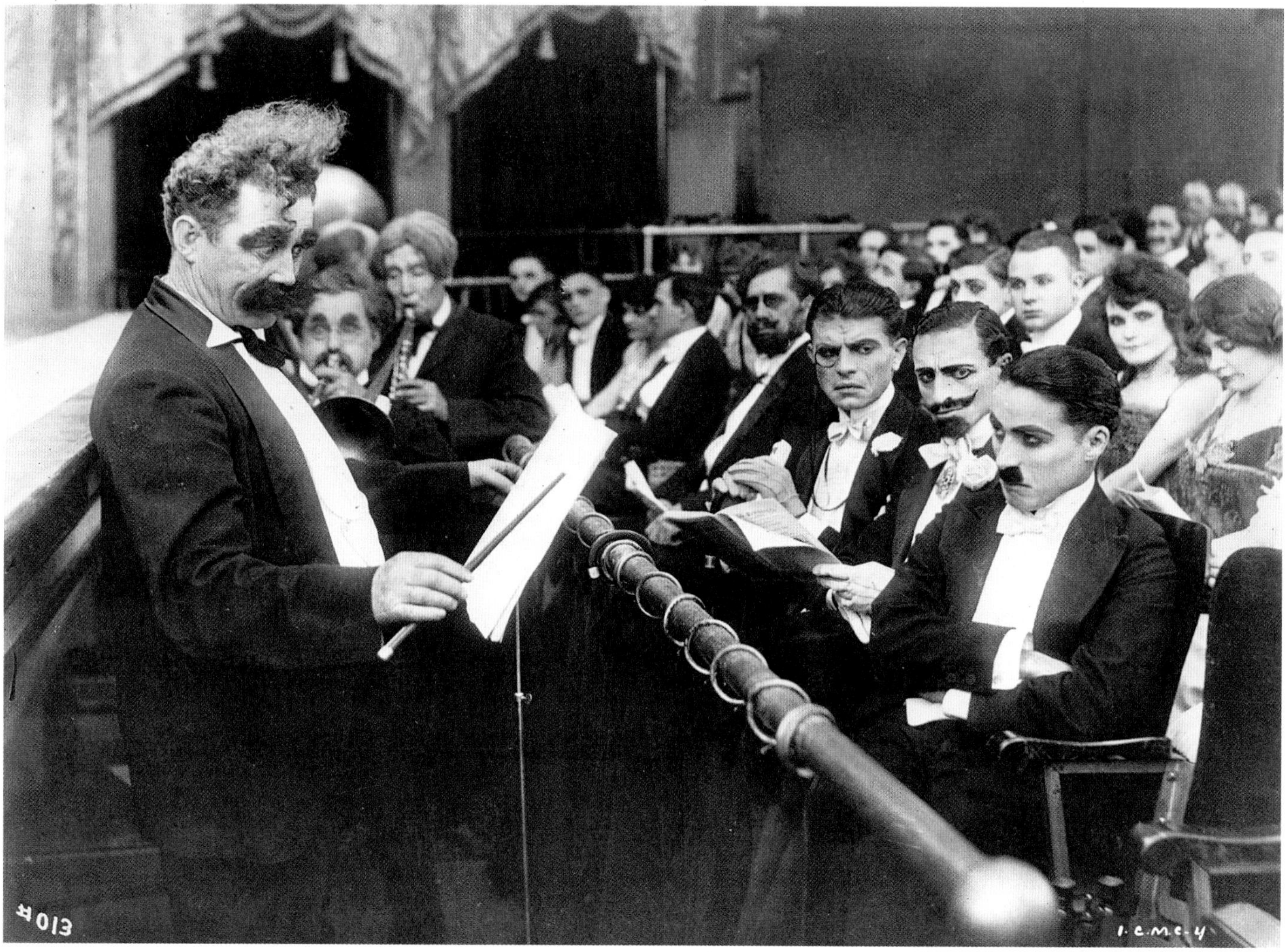

Following double page

Interior view of the Gaumont-Palace movie theater, c. 1912.

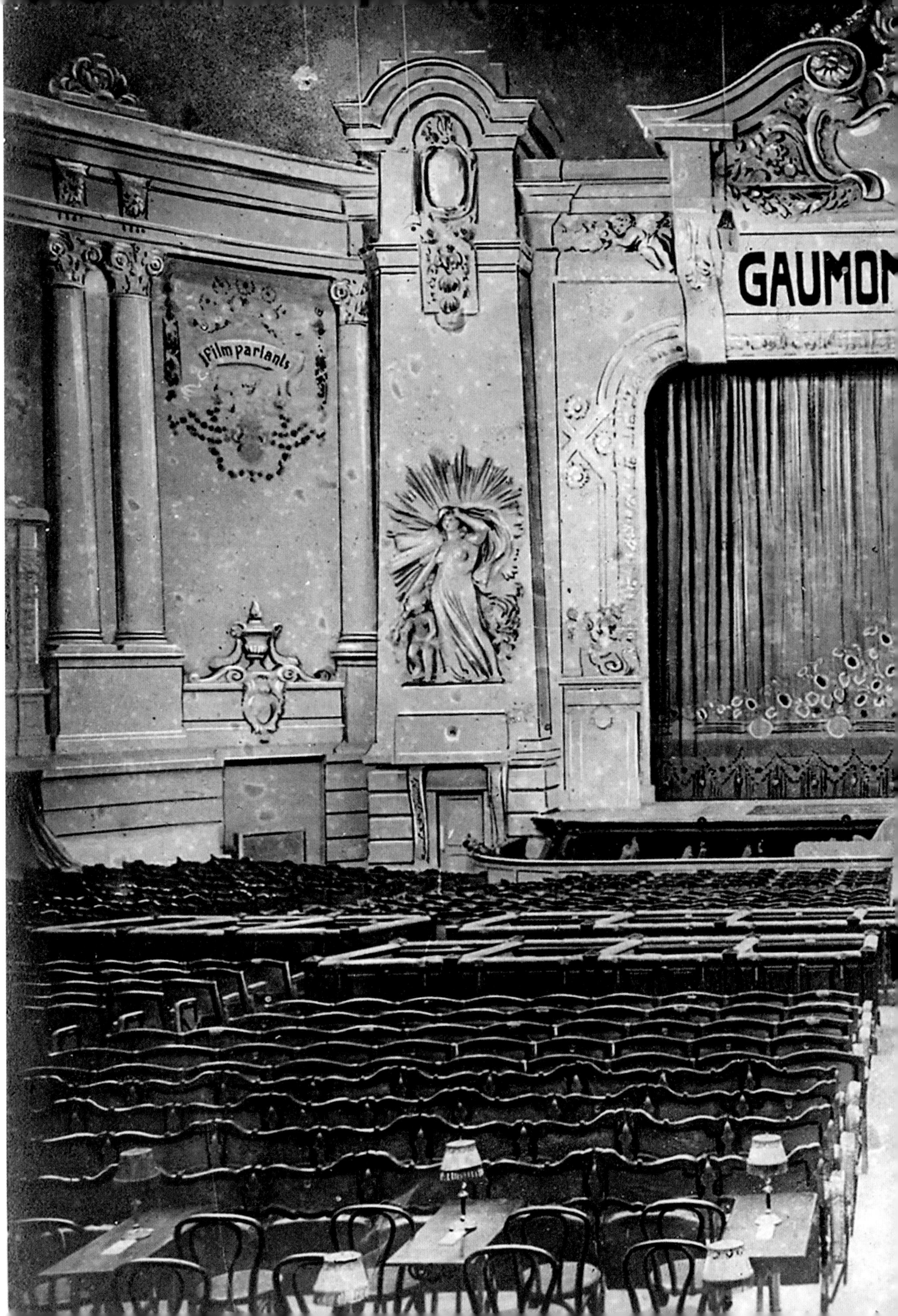
Film parlants
GAUMON

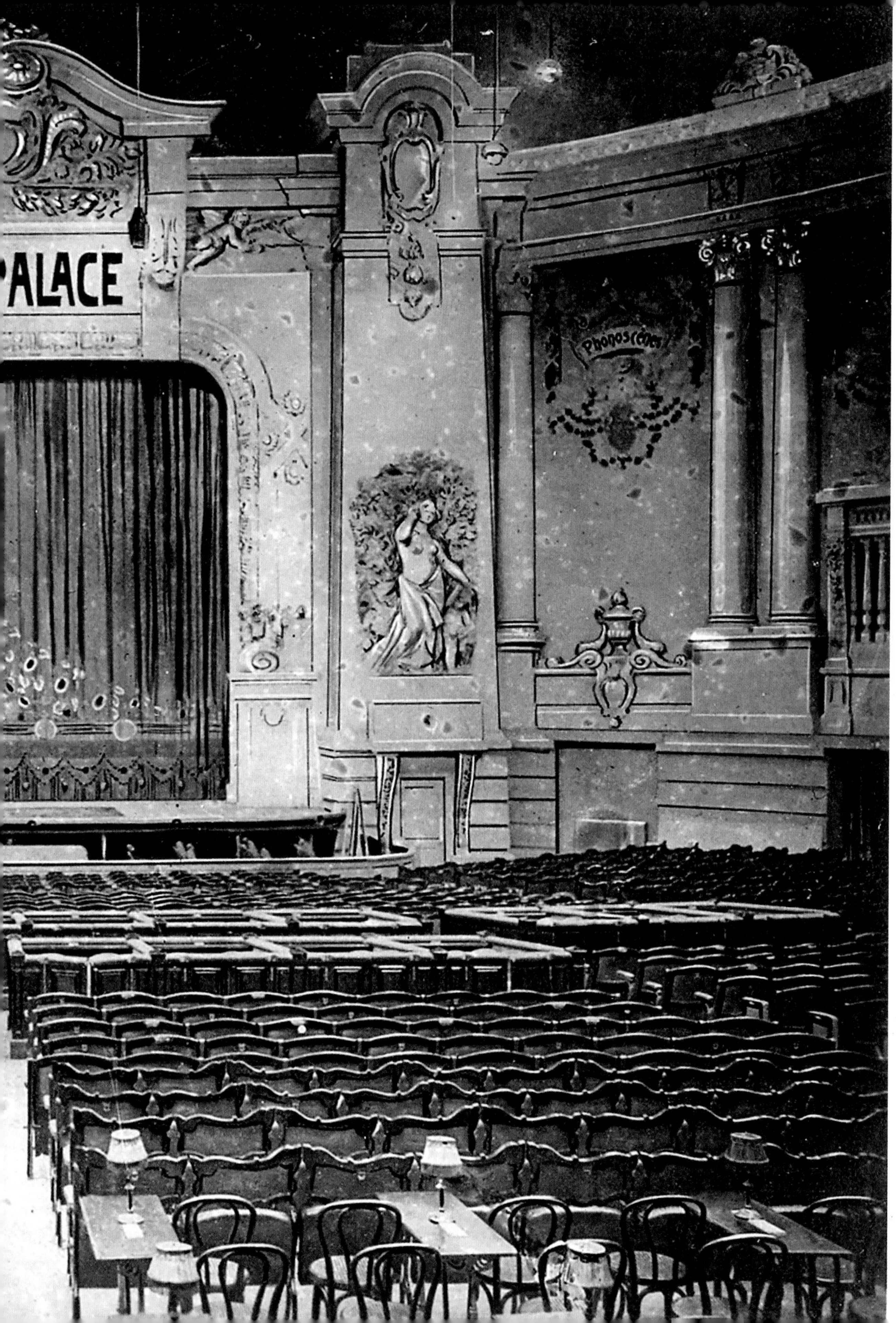
PALACE
Phonoscènes

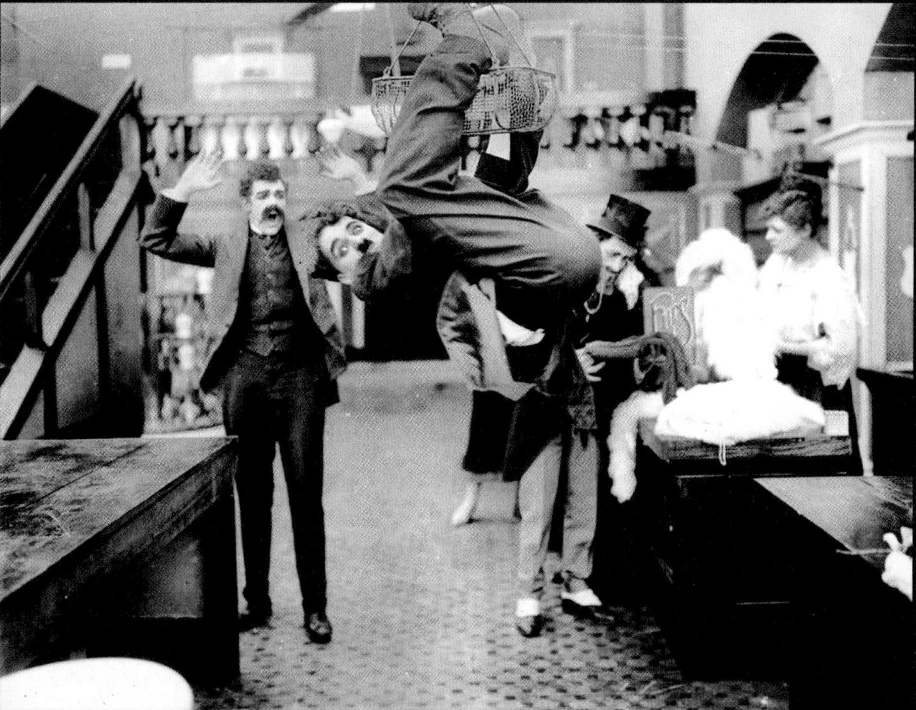

A DANCING BODY: THE INVENTION OF THE TRAMP

The little tramp with his unusual way of walking first appeared in 1914 in *Kid Auto Races at Venice, Cal.* Chaplin invented a character who, four years and sixty films later, was known around the world. His silhouette was instantly recognizable: mustache, hat, cane, baggy pants, over-sized shoes. In his early films the humor was mean, but gradually the cruelty was abandoned in favor of a more poetical tramp. Audiences, accustomed to slap- and kick-based gags, were moved by the illusions and weaknesses of their hero. His language was universal, since the humor was part of this body in motion, choreographed like a dancer; a body constantly in equilibrium, as if moved by opposing forces, in action and reaction with the surrounding world. To this sublime body language, Chaplin added a sense of rhythm, innate to both his character and his film editing. Each film is the result of intricate work in which the tiniest gag was timed to the second.

His universally loved figure very quickly became the embodiment of a popular culture shared by all. While the Tramp was particularly appreciated by the general public, he also influenced avant-garde artists, who hailed him as indissociable from the resolutely modern art in motion that was cinema.

Left

The Floorwalker, 1916.

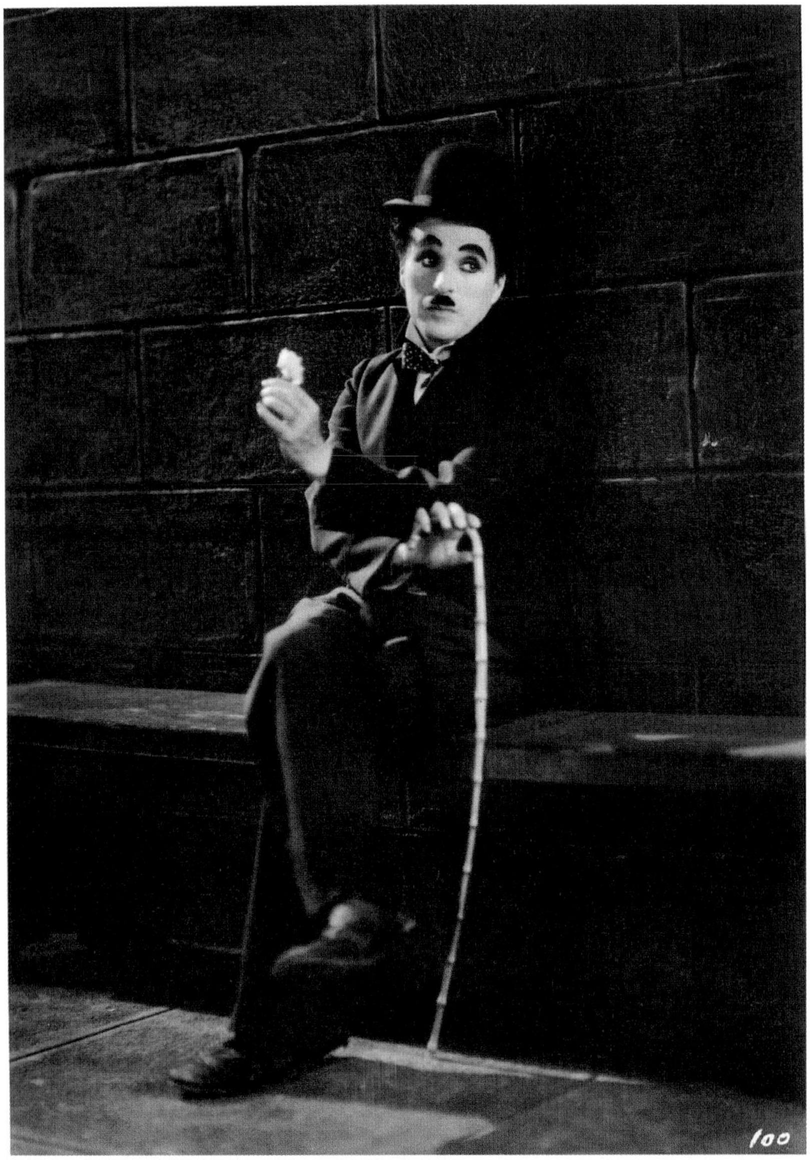

Left

City Lights, 1931.

Opposite

Chaplin as a waiter in *The Rink*, 1916.

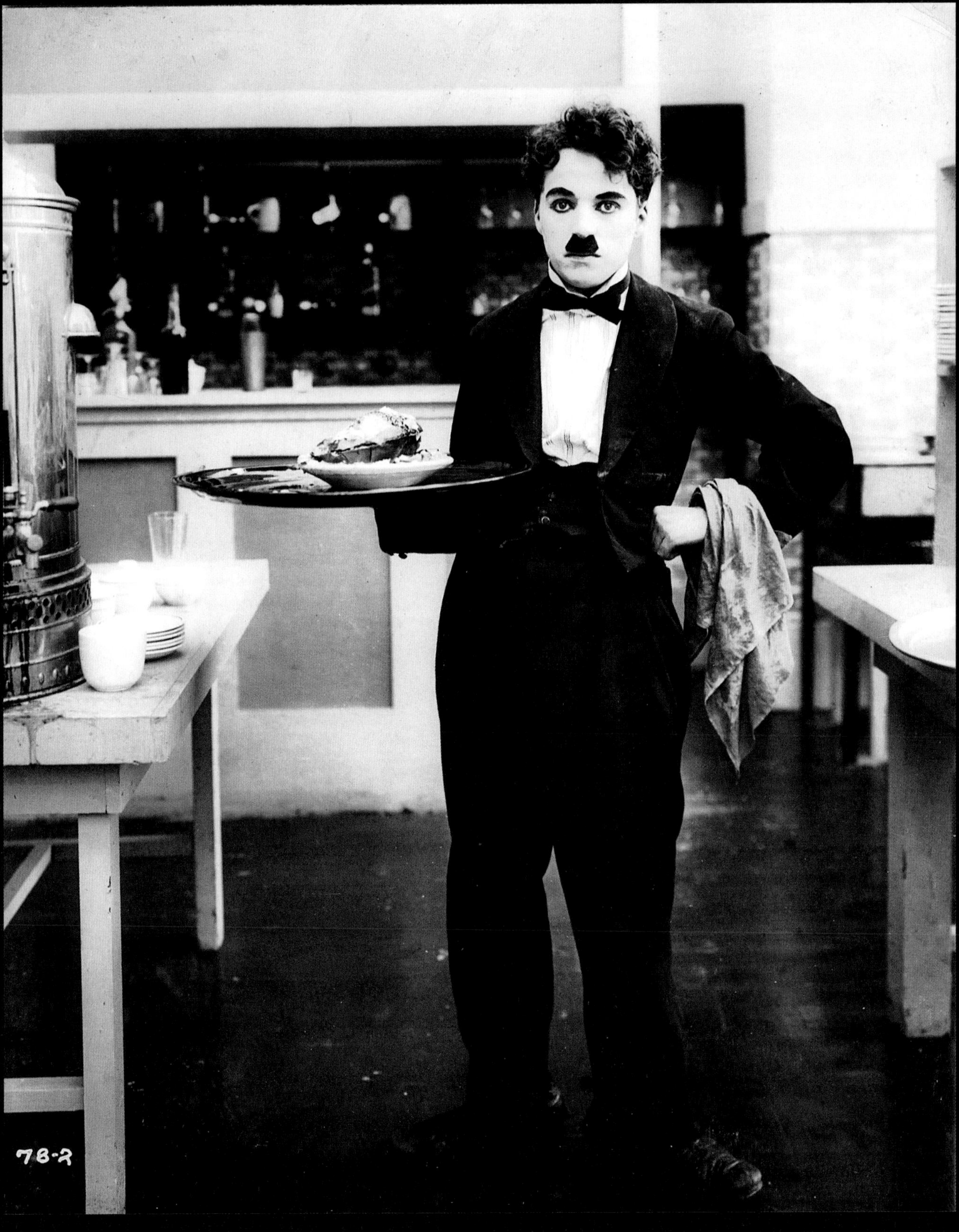
78-2

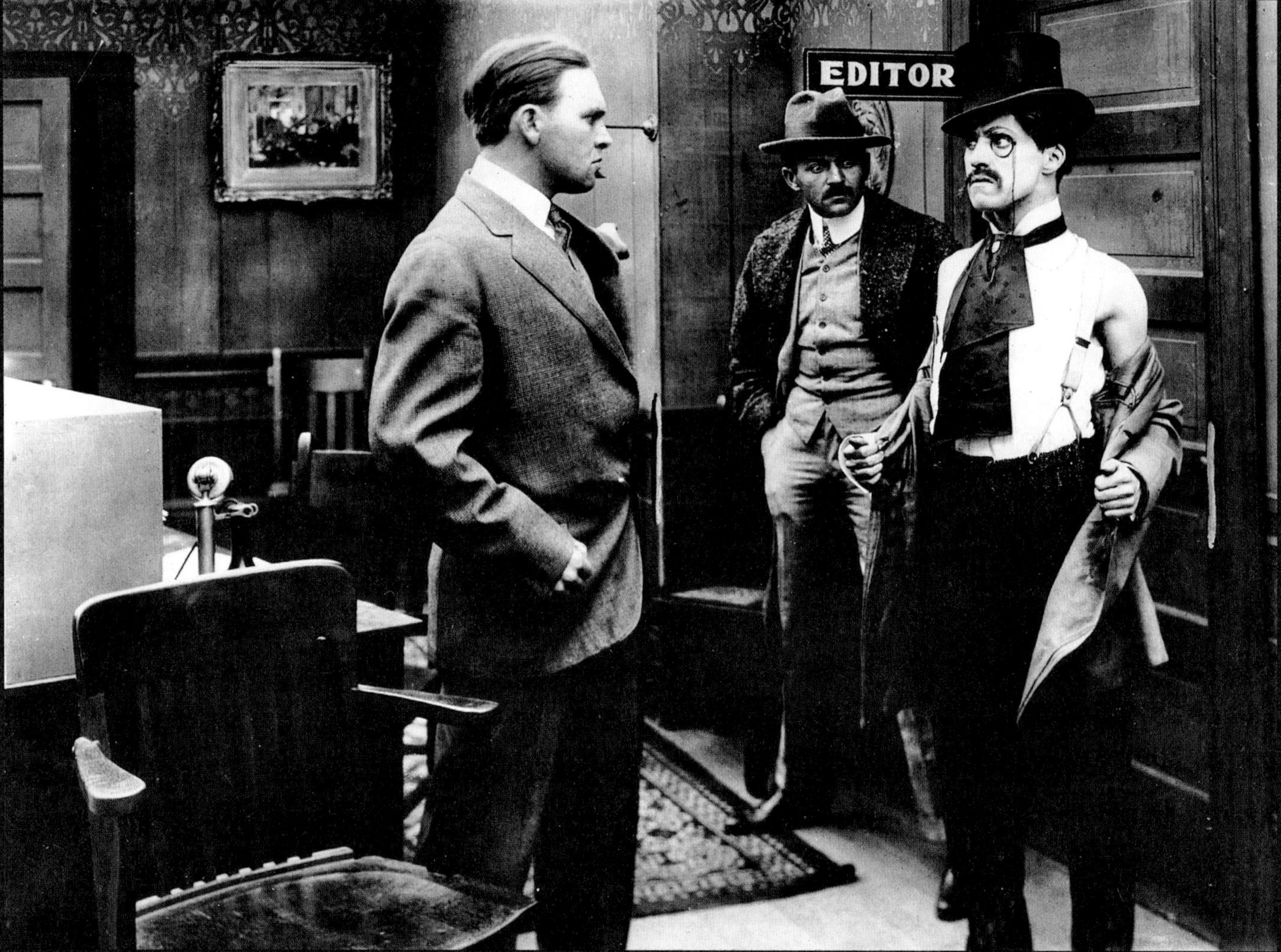
EDITOR

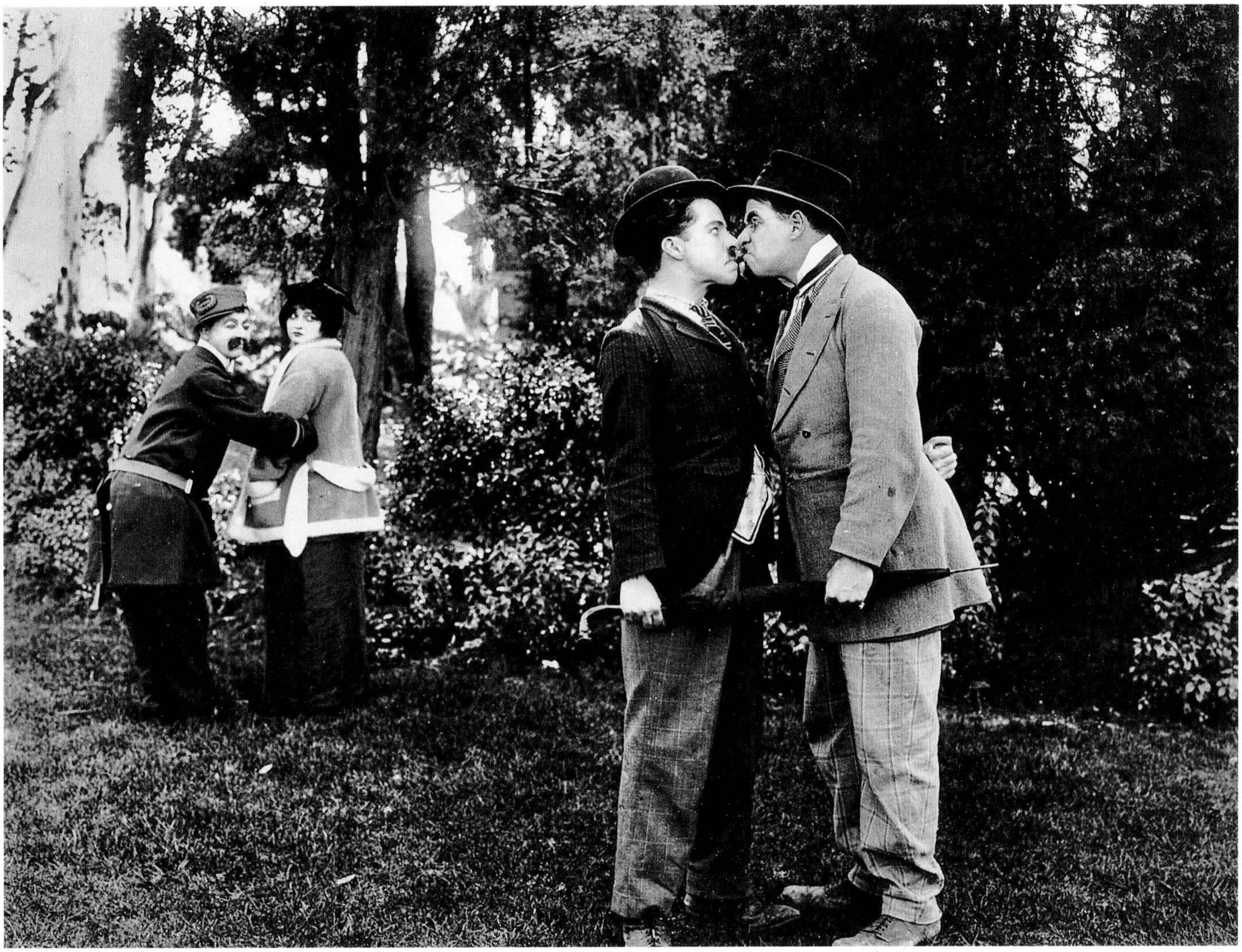

Left

Making a Living, 1914.

Above

Between Showers, 1914.

Below

By the Sea, 1915.

Opposite

The Champion, 1915.

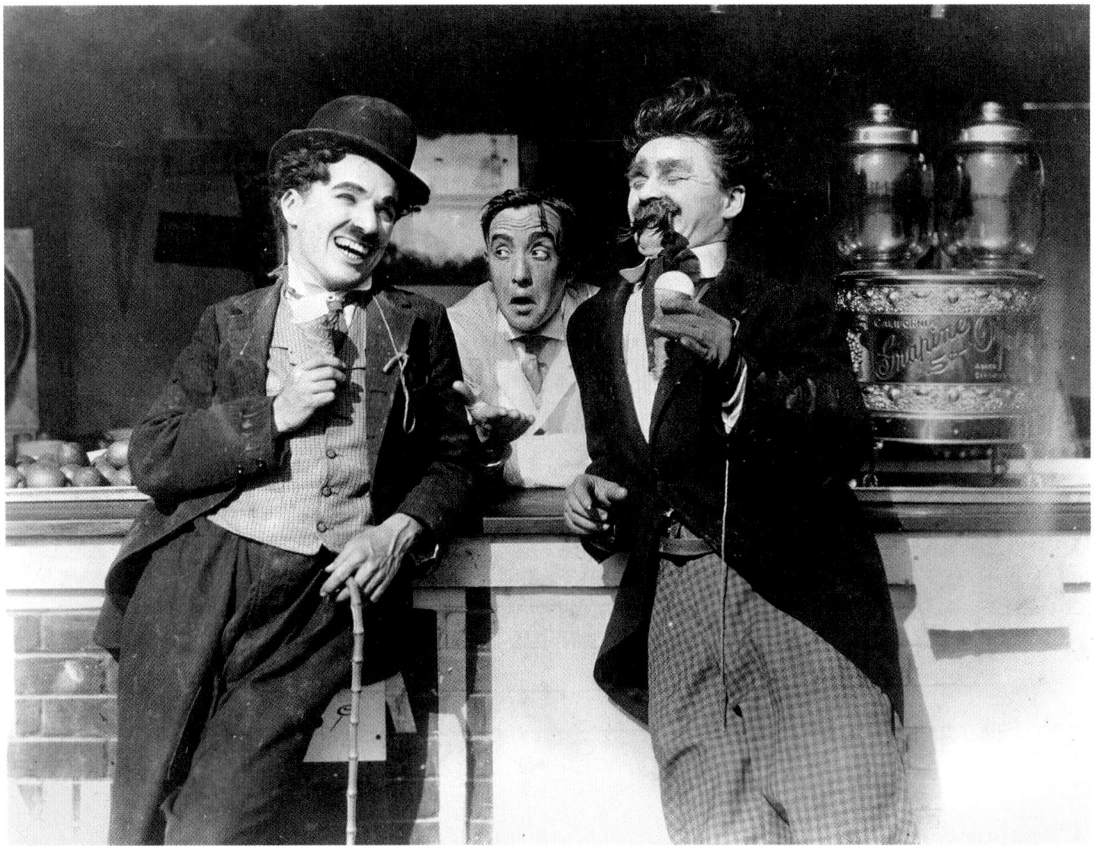

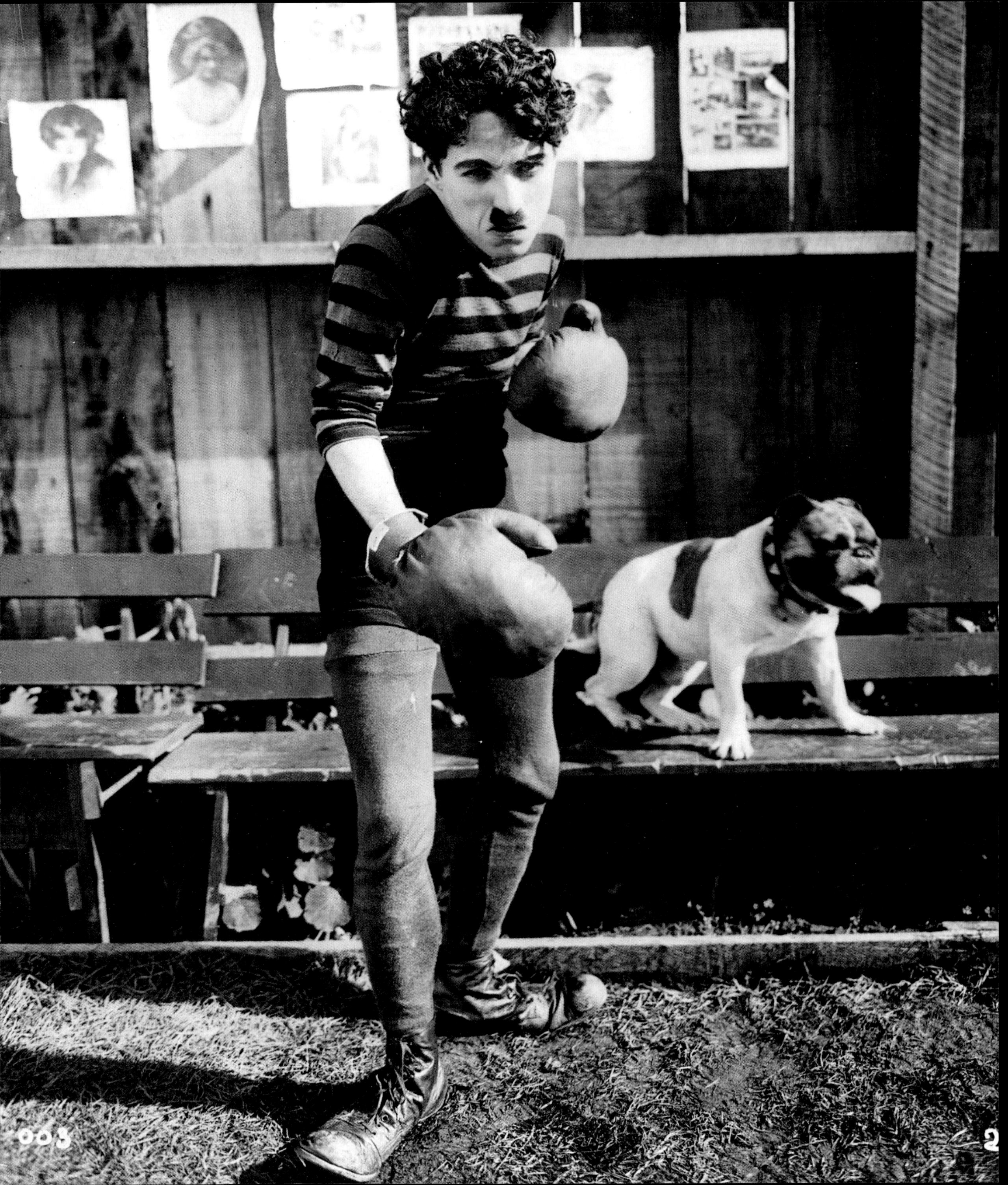

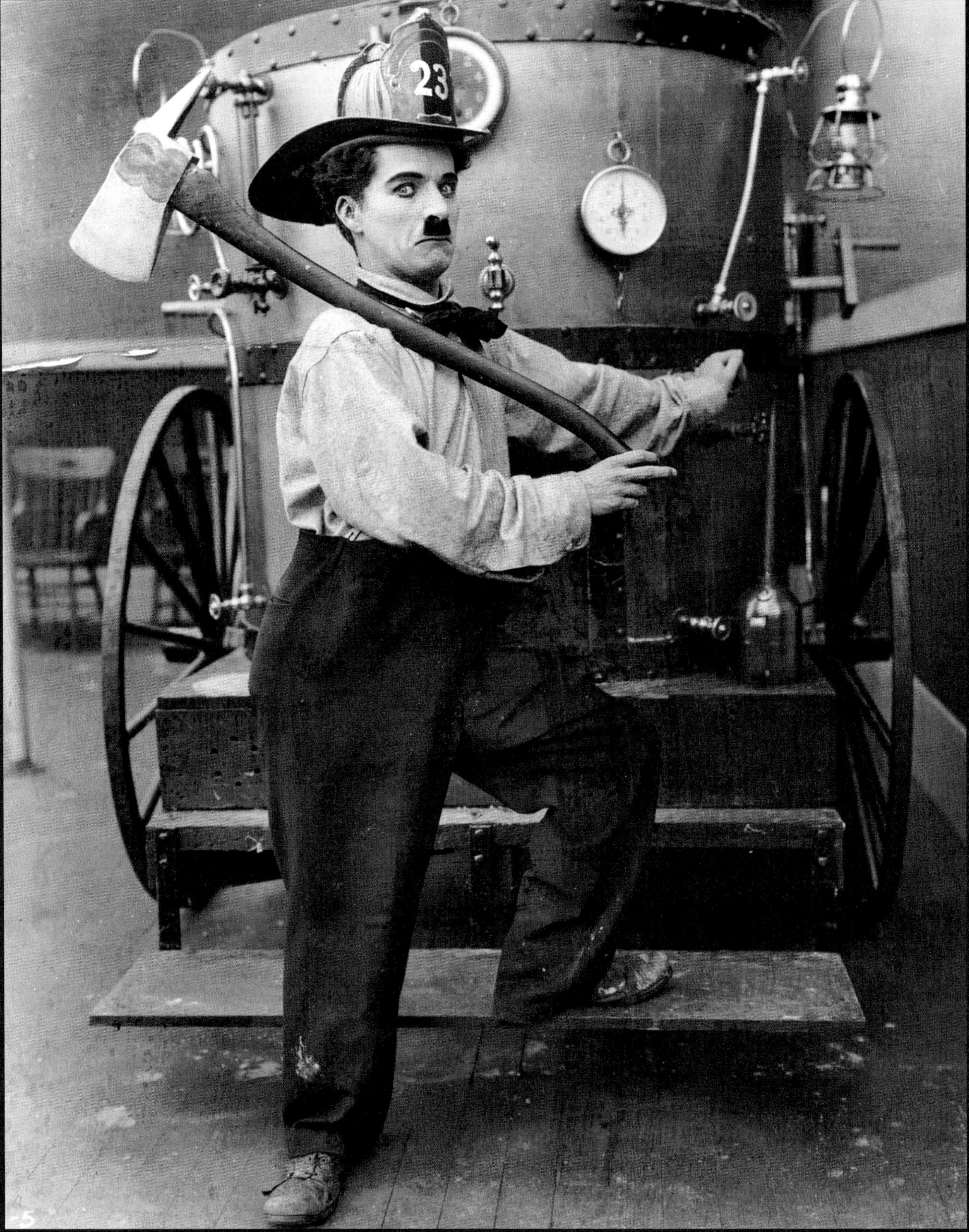
23

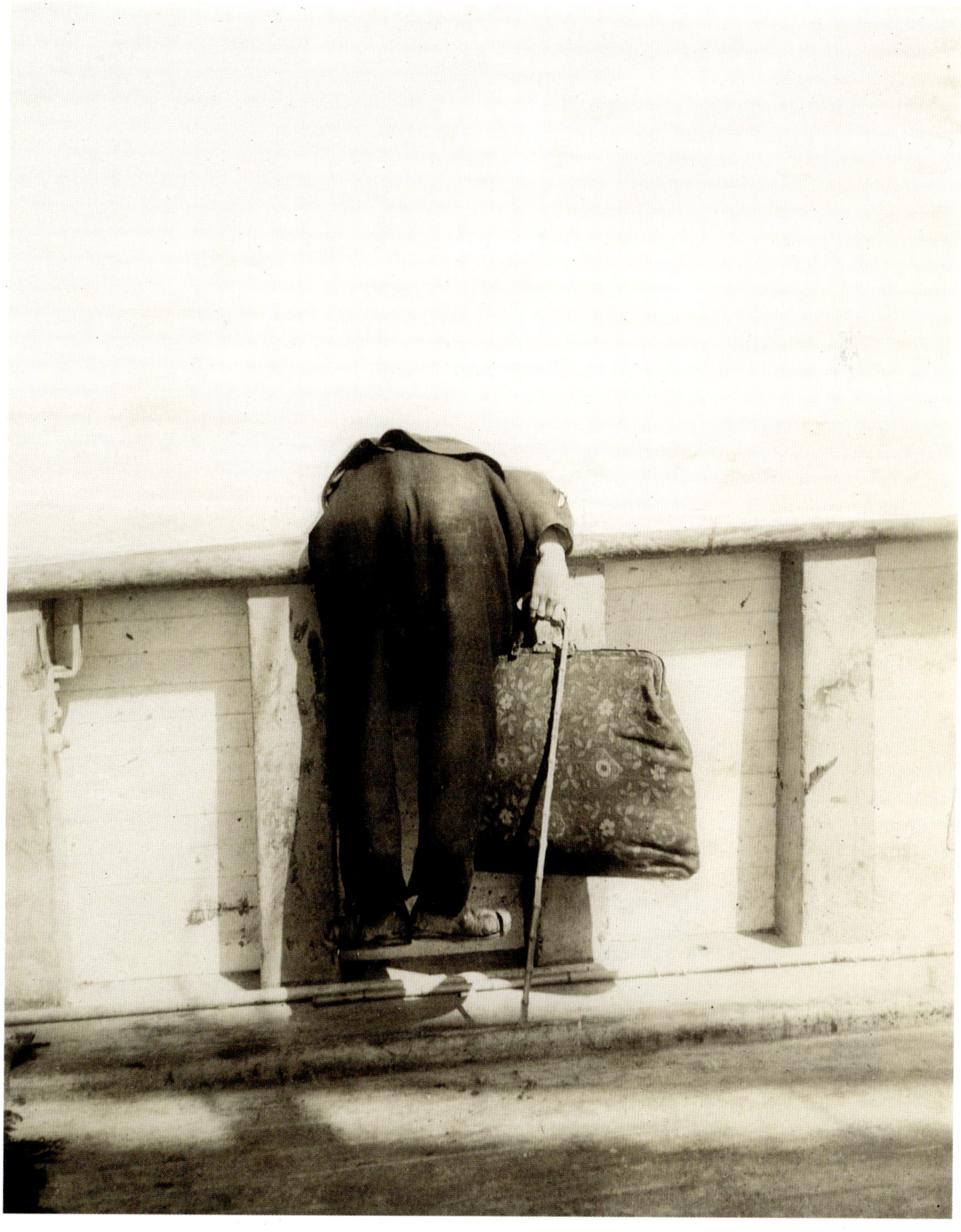

Left

The Fireman, 1916.

Right

The Immigrant, 1917.

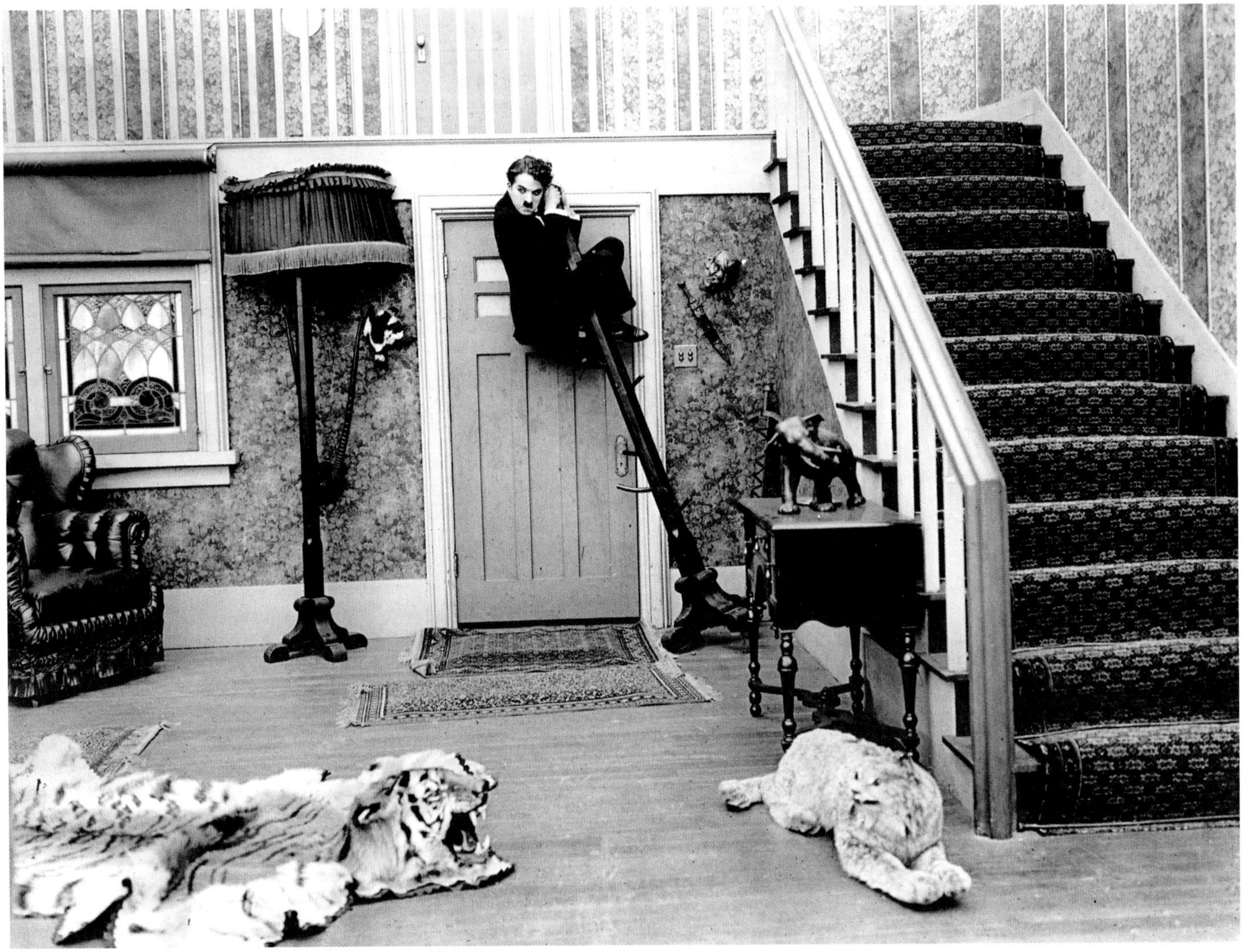

Above

One A.M., 1916.

Opposite

The Pawnshop, 1916.

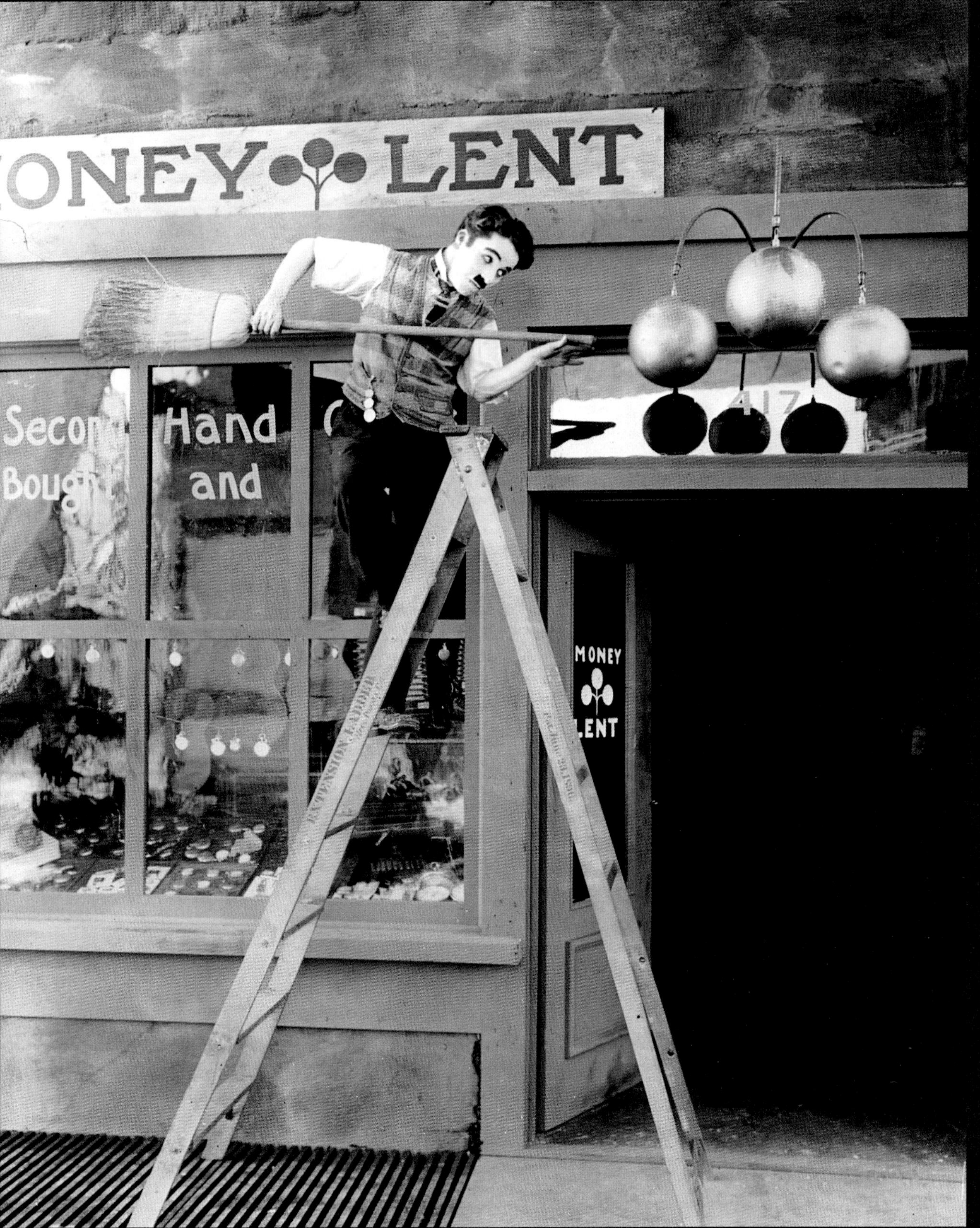
ONEY LENT
Hand
and
417
MONEY
LENT

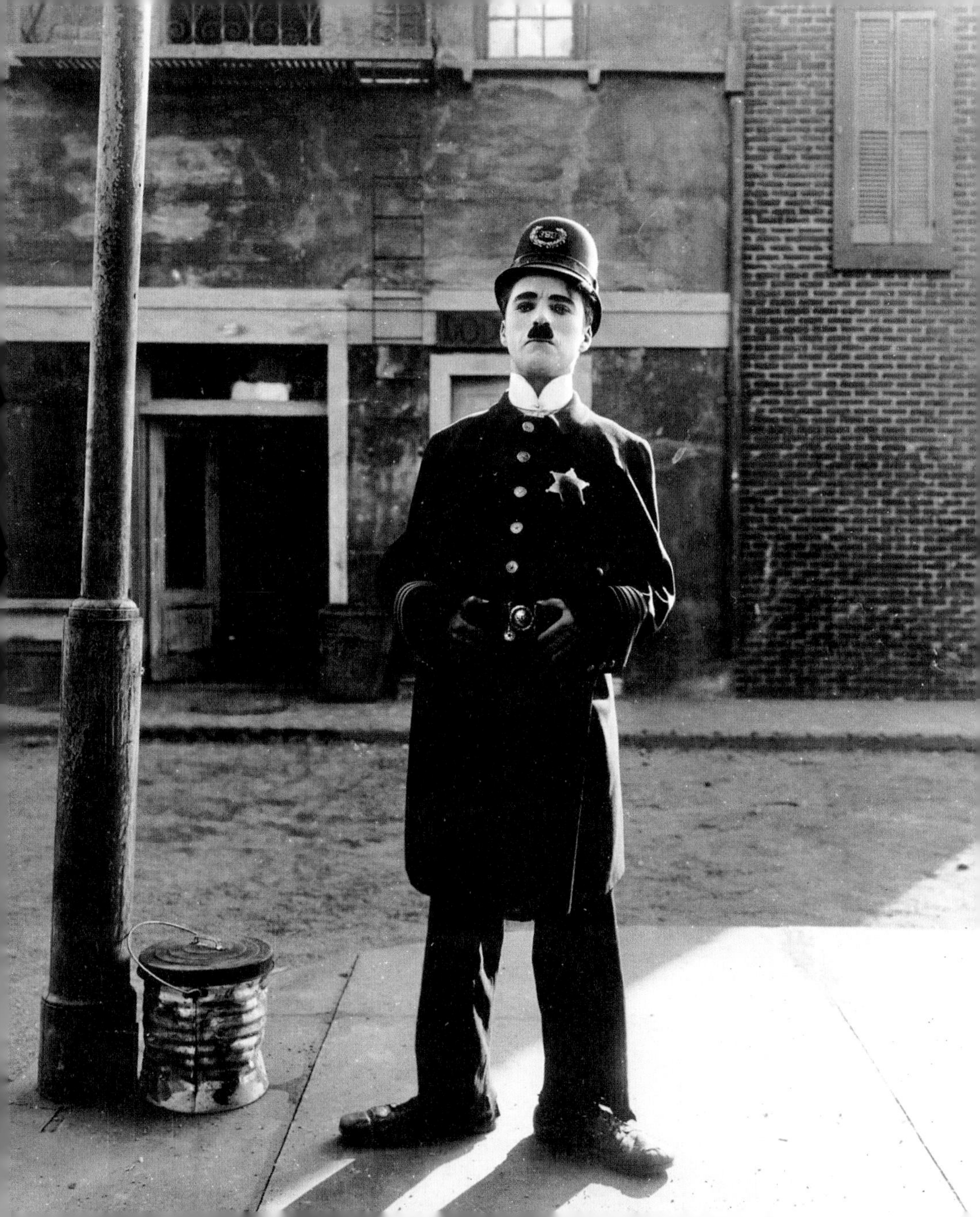

Left

Easy Street, 1917.

Right

The Adventurer, 1917.

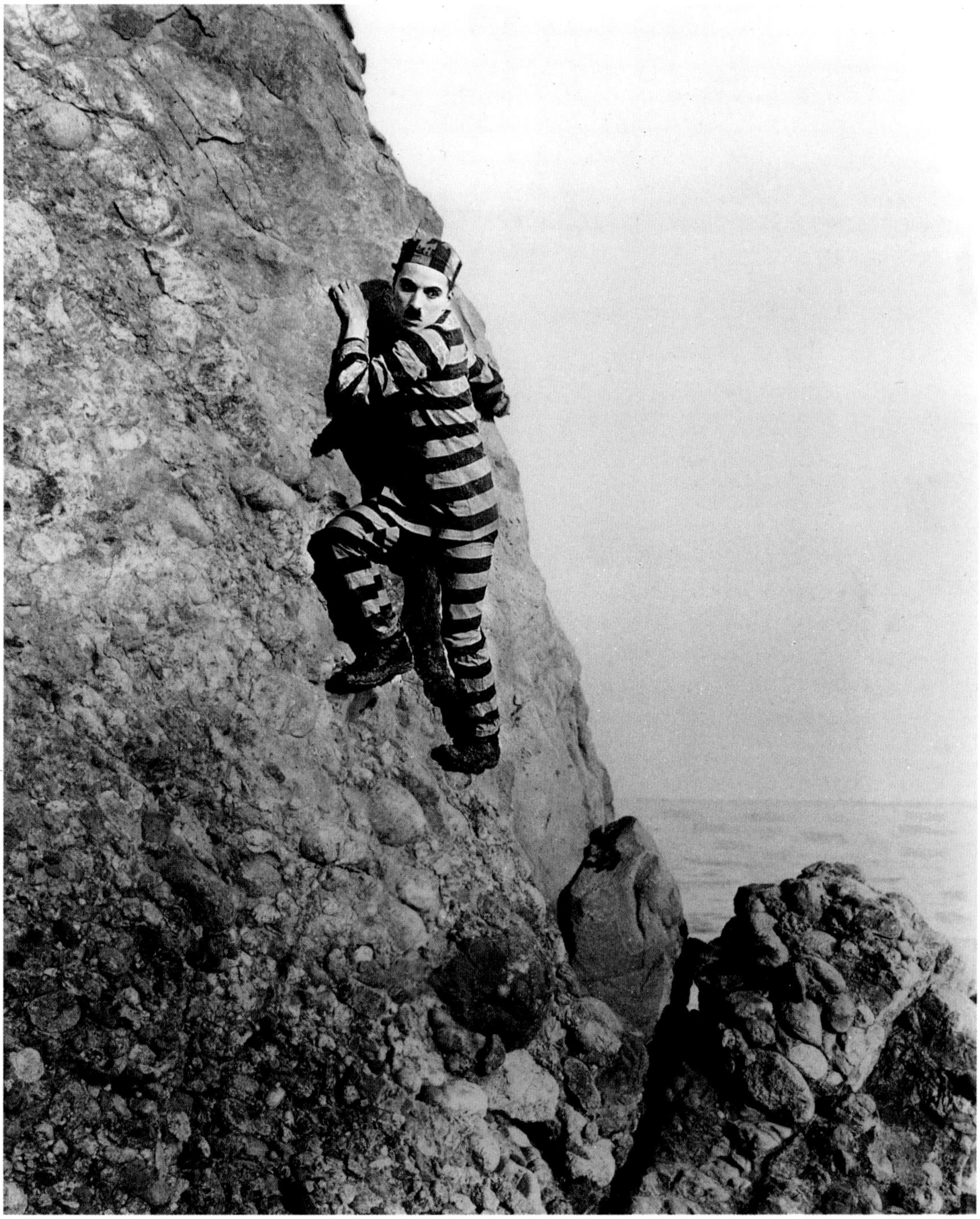

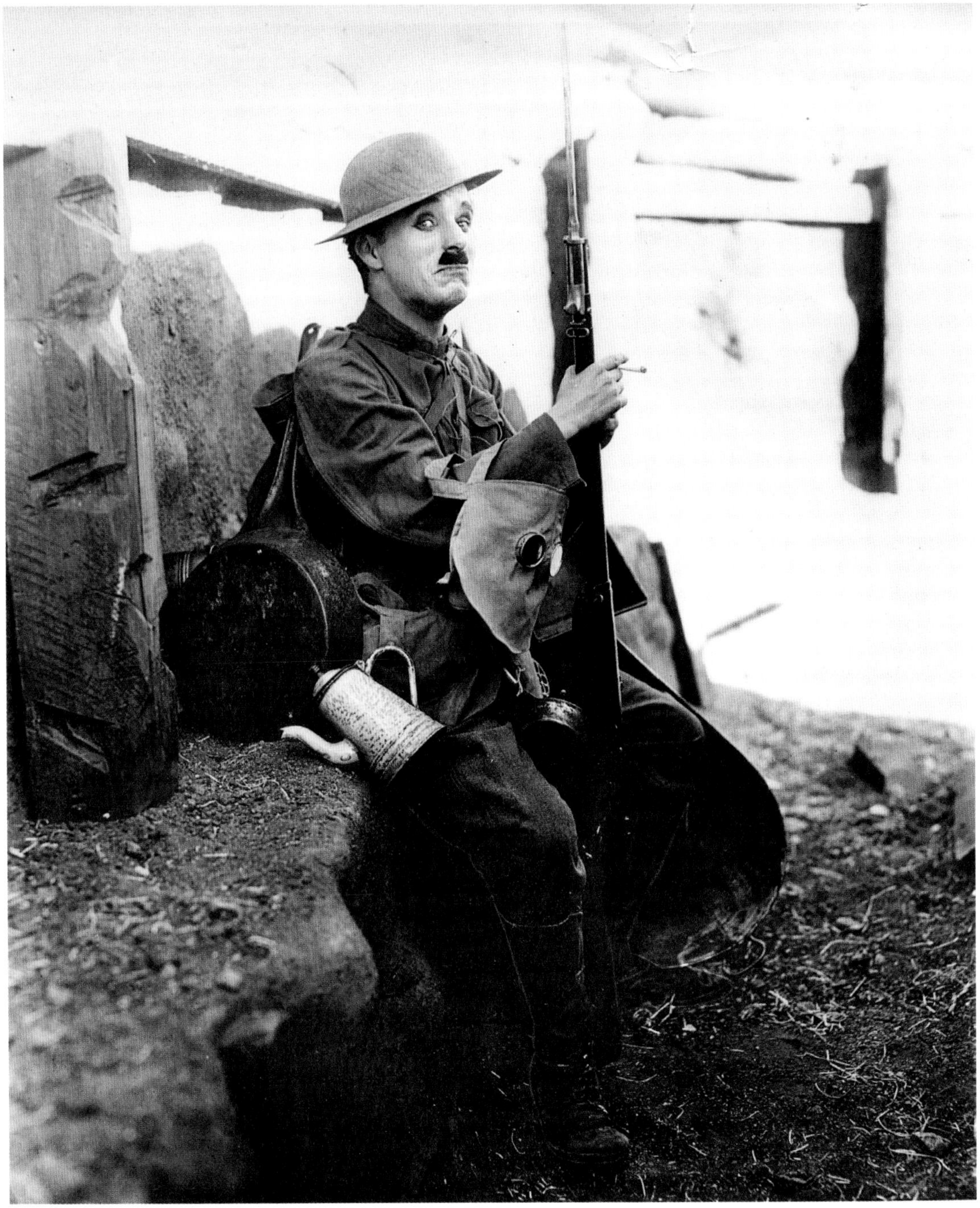

Left

Shoulder Arms, 1918.

Opposite

The Kid, 1921.

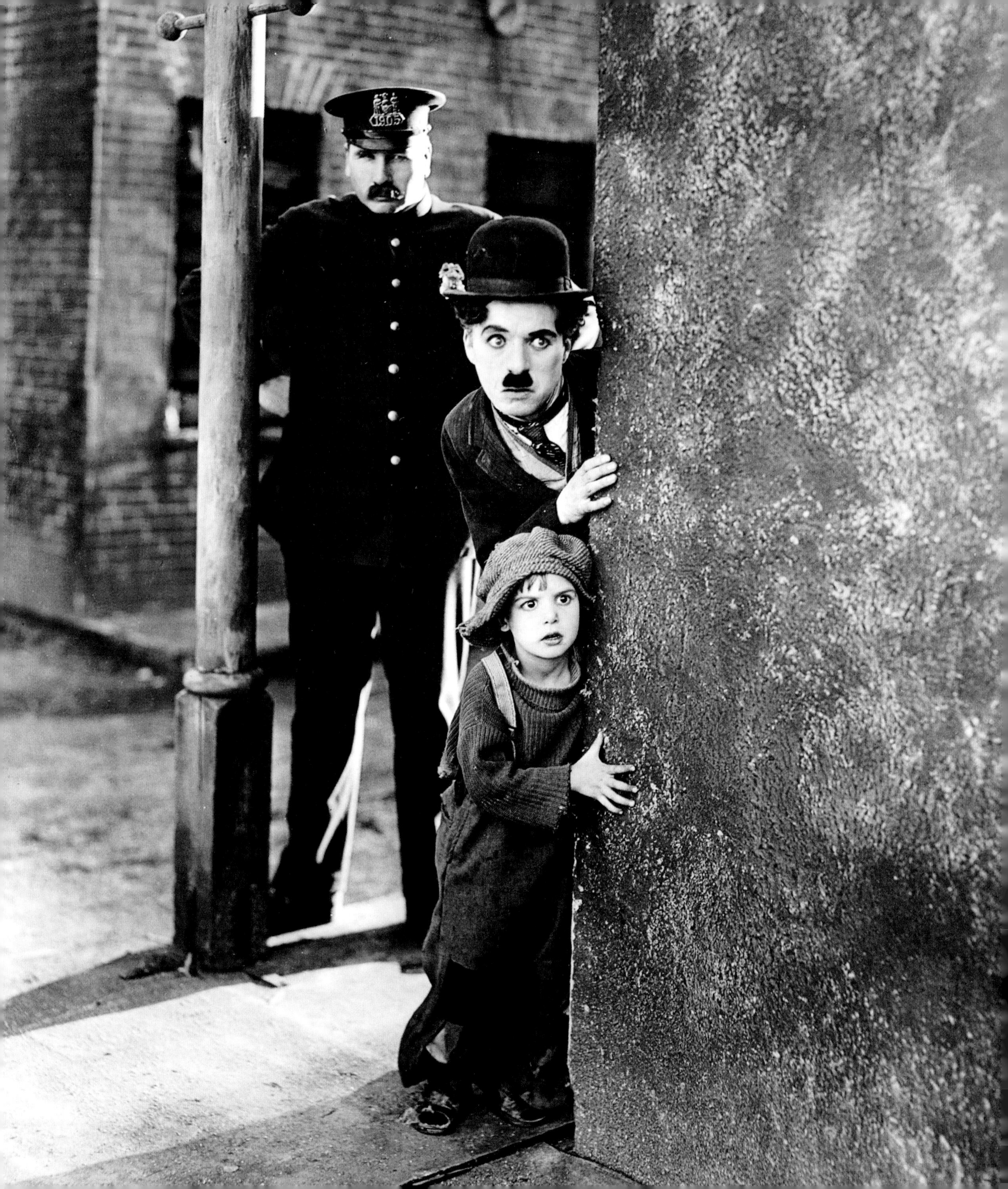

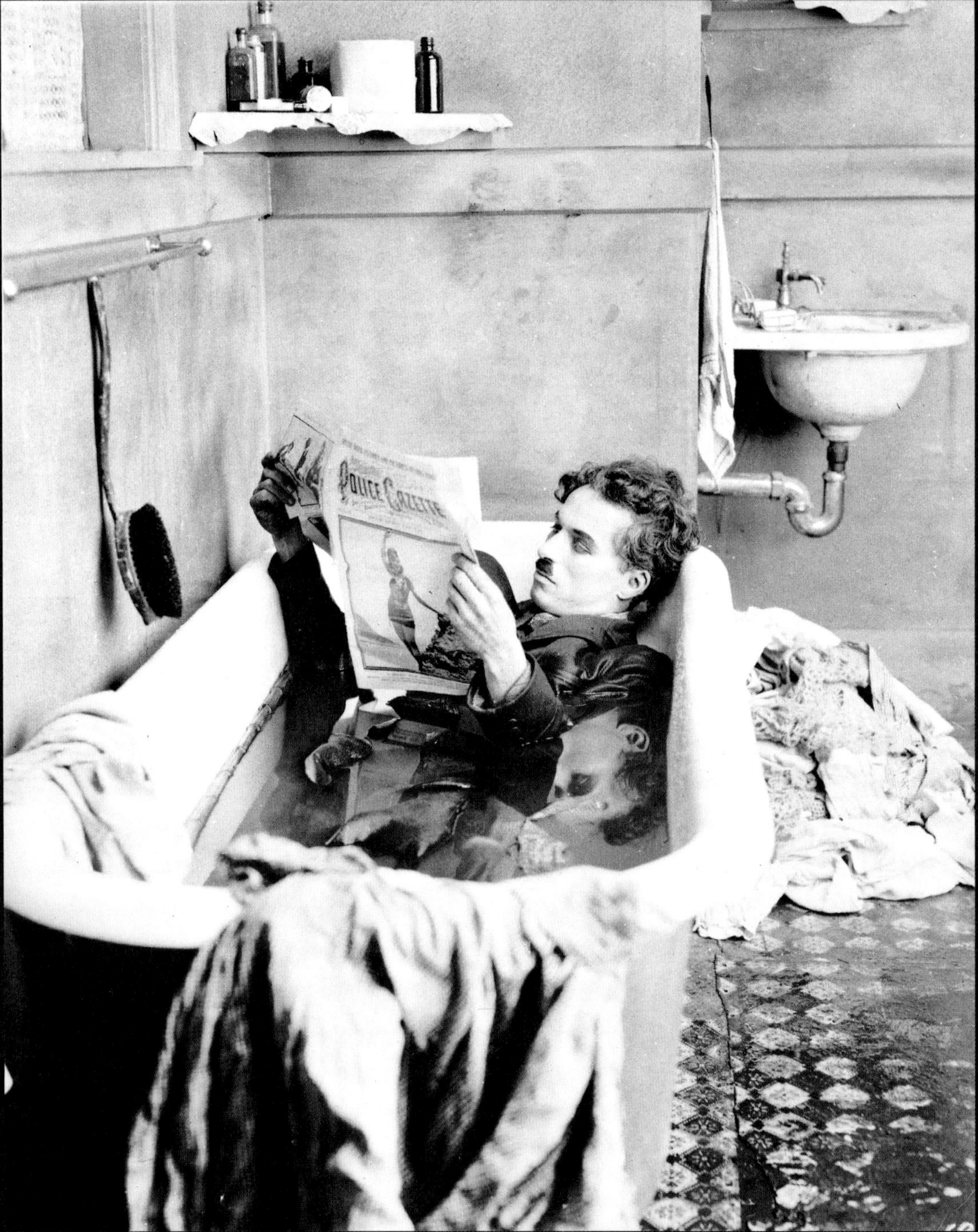

Left

Pay Day, 1922.

Opposite

The Pilgrim, 1923
Photograph by
James Abbe

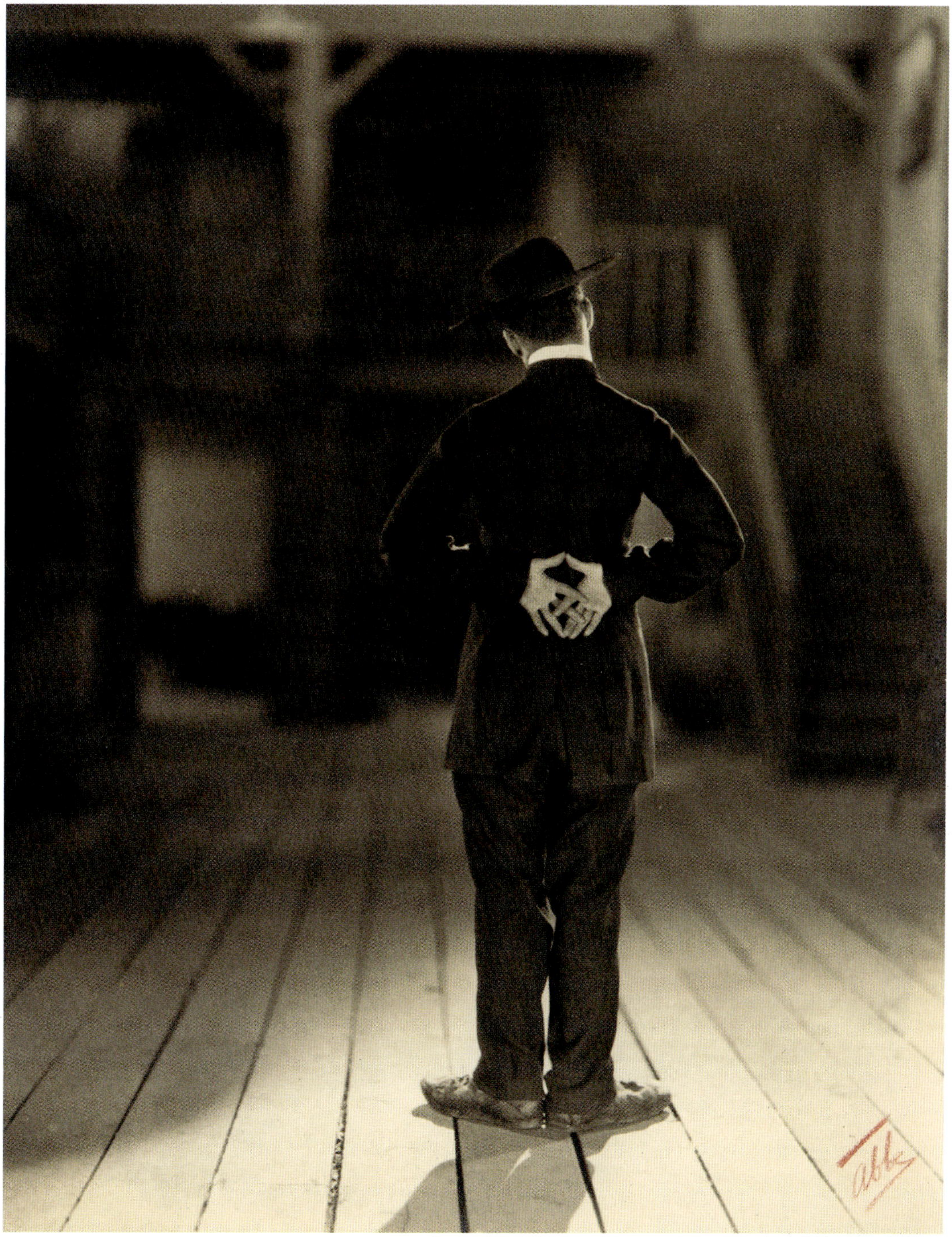

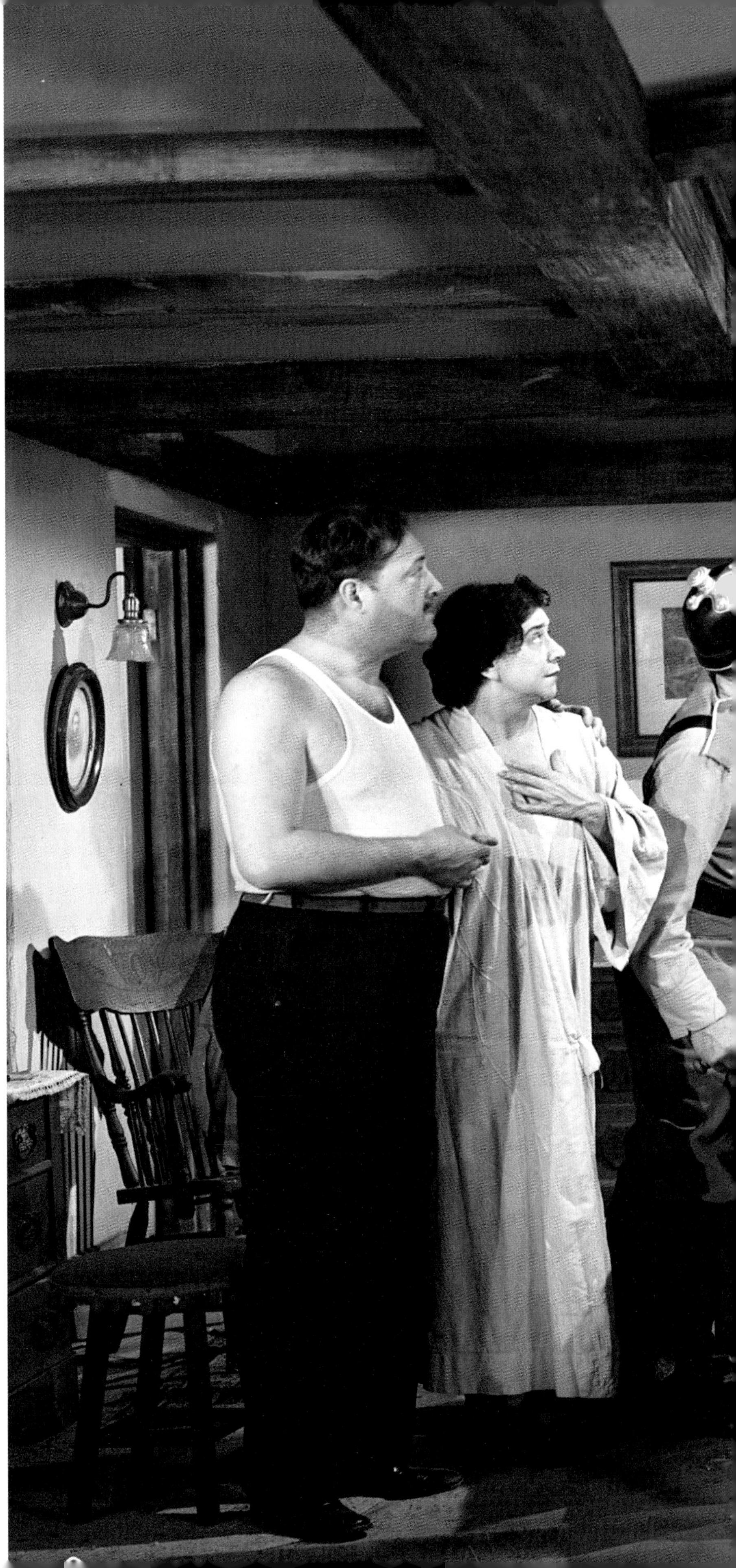

Right

The Jewish barber captured in *The Great Dictator*, 1940.

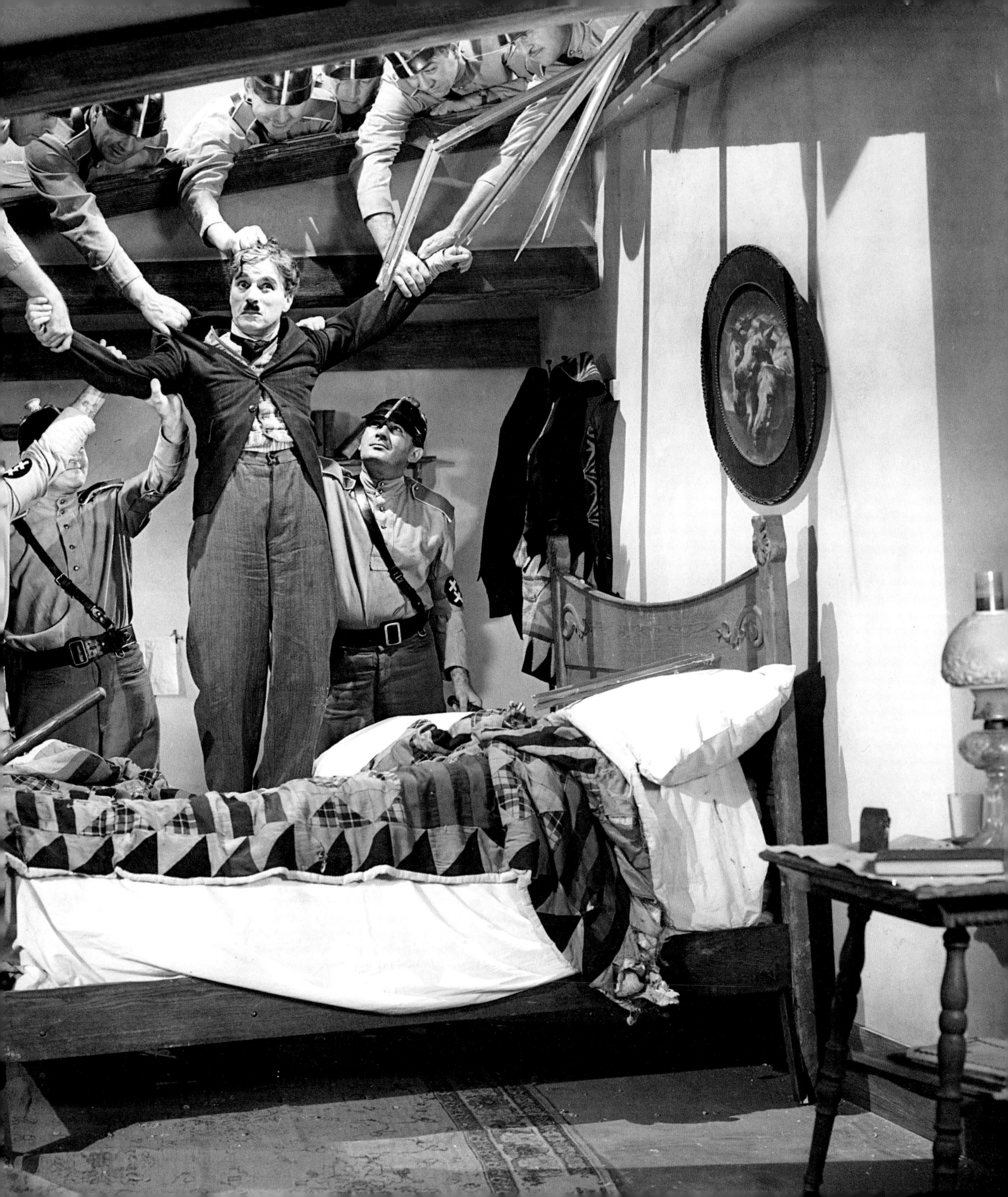

Dan Kamin

Visual music

Your comedy is balletique, you are a dancer.

NIJINSKY TO CHAPLIN, 1916

It all started with the costume, a misfit motley that Chaplin immediately sensed how to inhabit. Rising to his full height and arching his back, he assumed a regal bearing, and with this simple postural change he established his character, a man who looks poor but acts rich. Everything about his appearance reinforced the contrast between poverty and wealth: the fussy, carefully trimmed mustache was set off by the mop of unruly hair, which in turn was barely contained by the neat bowler hat; the ridiculously oversized pants seemed to flow out of the undersized swallowtail coat; the elegant wing collar was adorned not by a bow tie but a skimpy long tie. And then there were those battered big shoes, comically contradicted by the twirling bamboo cane of a dandy.

Con men and tramps wearing shabby dress clothing had been staples of literature and popular entertainment for centuries, of course. And at first he did the same things every other male comic on the Mack Sennett lot was doing—flirting with women, getting drunk, fighting with other men and running frantically from cops.

What made him stand out was the way he found of making everyday actions funny.

For example, he brought his oversize shoes into play by turning his feet out like a ballet dancer, leading to a walk that was only the first of many signature comic trademarks. All the movements that we take for granted—turning a corner, lighting a match, tossing away a cigarette—became grist for his comic mill.

Many of his comic actions grew from parodying the formalities of polite behavior. Thus, he lifts his hat straight off his head with mechanical precision, or snaps it up and down like a box lid. He's forever tipping it both to people and to the objects he may have offended by tripping over. As a corollary, he often treats people as if they're objects, running or walking over their prone figures or tapping cigarette ash into their hands.

People loved the audacity and kinetic brio of these bits, and the proof is the dozens of songs and hundreds of cartoons that appeared in 1915 trumpeting Chaplin's

Opposite

The Rink, 1916.

appearance and characteristic comic actions. In just a year he had become the funniest and coolest guy on the planet. Part of the appeal was that his signature comic moves were easy to imitate, and soon there were songs, cartoons, and jokes about people imitating him as well.

But nobody could do the moves as well as he could, because one of the things that made them so funny and appealing was the crisp precision with which he executed them, a precision that was as dancelike as his mock-balletic stance.

Many people since Nijinsky have called Chaplin's films balletic, and there's certainly some truth to the notion. He occasionally quotes from the ballet repertoire for comic effects, such as when he incongruously breaks into entrechats in *The Floorwalker* and *The Cure*, or does arabesques as he throws big switches in *Behind the Screen* and *Modern Times*. And of course, the paradoxical gracefulness of his personal movement, with its interlocking circular

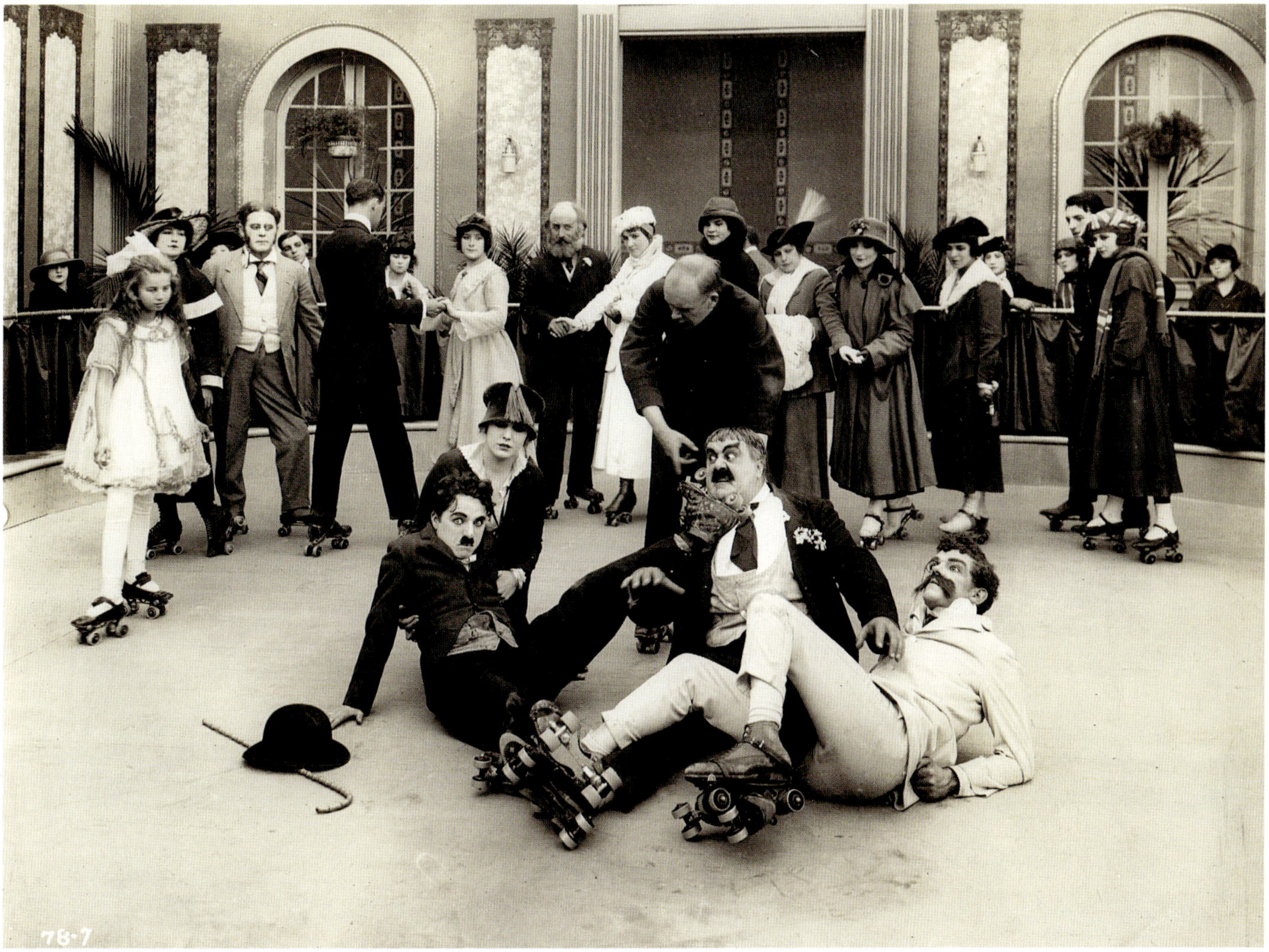

patterns, also suggests ballet. But to call his films balletic is to limit them, for Chaplin's comedy goes far beyond the formalized movement vocabulary of ballet.

To take just one example, ballet dancers create the illusion that they can loosen gravity's bonds, becoming ethereal creatures that can float through the air.

Chaplin turns this notion into a joke.

At the beginning of *The Pawnshop* he creates a comical illusion of weightlessness by hoisting himself onto the curb by the seat of his pants. At first glance this gag seems like a pleasant non sequitur, since there's no one else on the street to witness it. But it actually sets the tone of the film, because right before this shot we see his boss pacing back and forth inside the pawnshop; Charlie, as the film's first subtitle tells us, is "Late, as usual!" So it's funny to see him strolling jauntily across the street, twirling his cane as if he hasn't a care in the world, and then taking a moment to share his little private gravity joke with us. The boss may be weighed down by care, but Charlie isn't. He *defies* gravity, both literally and metaphorically, something he'll continue doing throughout the film.

The joke is funny and also pleasurable to watch because of Chaplin's great mimetic

Right

Chaplin in bathing suit in *The Cure*, 1917.
Caught in a changing room by two of his pursuers, Chaplin prepares to execute a few leaps to escape them.

Opposite

Chase around a wooden fence in *A Dog's Life*, top, and in the department store manager's office in *The Floorwalker*.
The flight and the chase are recurrent motifs in Chaplin films. They call on a relatively limited repertoire of gestures.

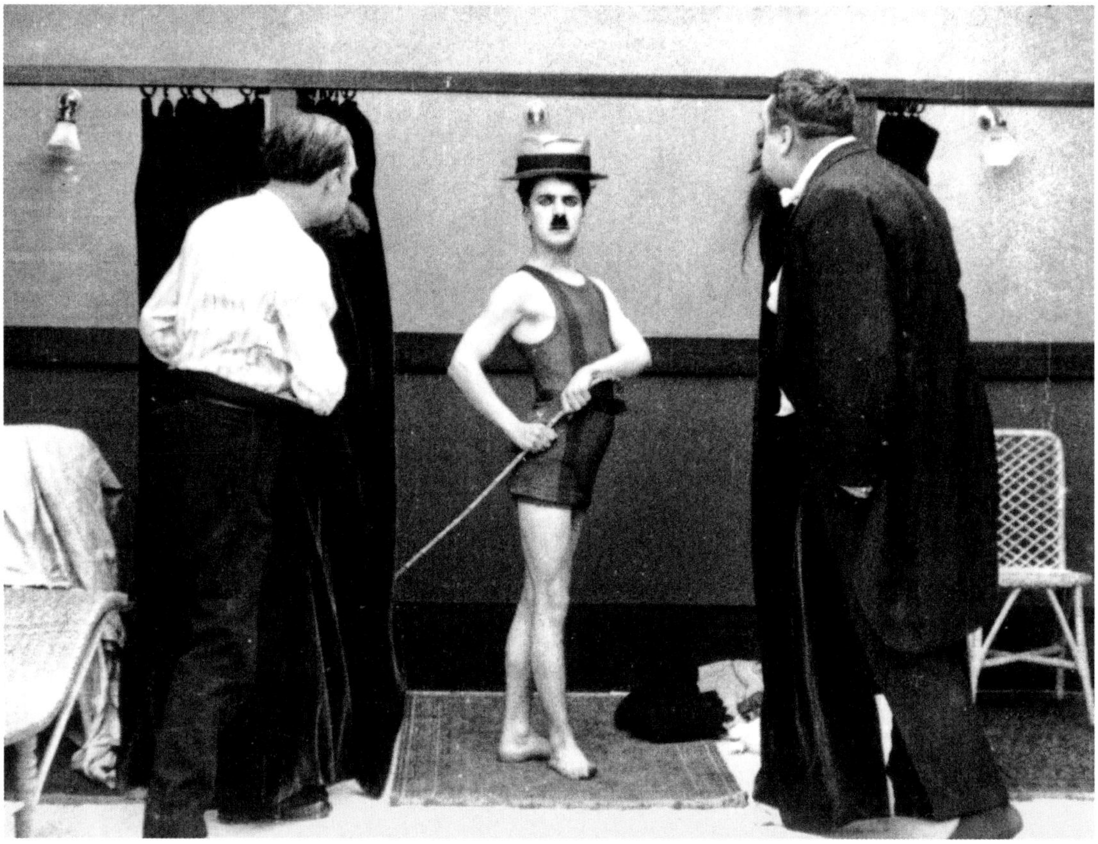

skill. Such inventive play with a fundamental element of the physical world is one of the qualities that give Chaplin's films their visceral appeal and staying power.

Call it visual music.

Chaplin also finds rich comic possibilities in the law of momentum. A kick, a revolving door, or a fall is an excuse for a display of visual and acrobatic pyrotechnics. In *The Cure* he is spun by a revolving door into the lobby of a health spa, creating the improbable effect of falling up a set of stairs and rocketing from room to room until he plummets into a pool.

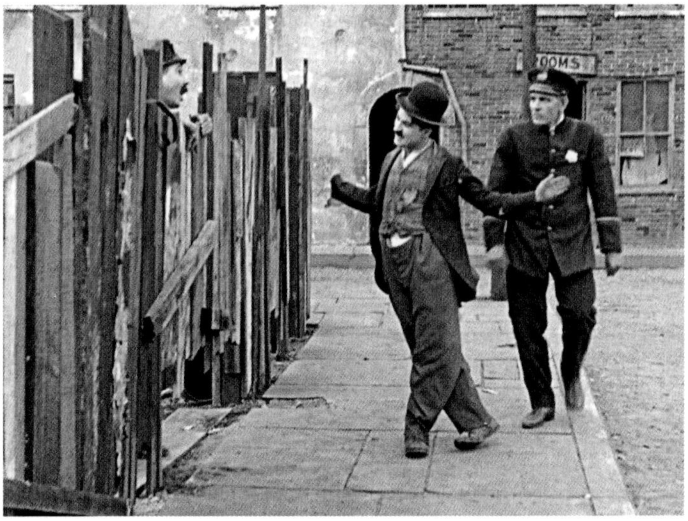

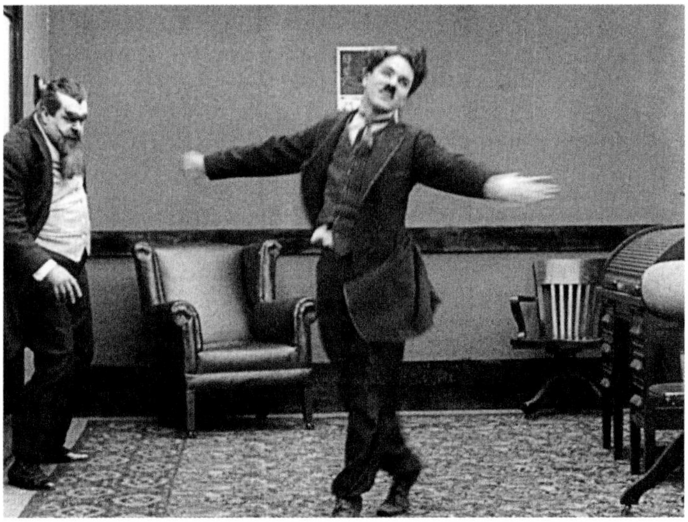

But no element of movement was more important to Chaplin than rhythm.

In his famous essay "Laughter," written three years before Chaplin's film debut in 1914, French philosopher Henri Bergson asserted that people become funny when they act like machines, because blindly repeating motions often leads to mishaps and disasters. Bergson must have been thrilled with the Tramp, who repeatedly proves his dictum.

Thus, Charlie begins dusting the back room of *The Pawnshop* but immediately goes on automatic pilot, maintaining a steady rhythm as he indiscriminately dusts shelves, a co-worker and an electric fan, which creates a feather snowstorm. When Charlie finally notices that his duster has been shredded he looks directly at the camera and laughs, once again "defying gravity."

Chaplin's most rhythmically sophisticated film is *A Dog's Life* from 1918, in which rhythmic play is at the heart of every major comic sequence. Charlie, asleep in a vacant lot, is awakened by the tempting smell of hot dogs wafting from the other side of a wooden fence. He filches one, but before he can take a bite a cop catches him in the act, and the chase is on. The cop runs through a door in the fence, but Charlie simply rolls under it through a gap, then back as the cop circles around. Charlie reaches under the fence to untie one of the cop's shoes, and when the cop pauses to tie it he unties the other. For good measure Charlie sticks him with one of those straight pins that always seem to be conveniently attached to his vest.

The camera cuts from one side of the fence to the other as the chase accelerates. Finally, the cop tries to squeeze under the fence, giving the agile Charlie the chance to run around and boot him soundly in the butt a few times. They round the fence a couple more times, and Charlie, feeling safe and a bit cocky with the fence between them, offers his adversary a mocking bow, only to find his outstretched hand touching the badge of a second cop. He rolls under the fence and dashes through the gate a last time, eluding them both.

Charlie's standard flight from the cops is here presented with such choreographic

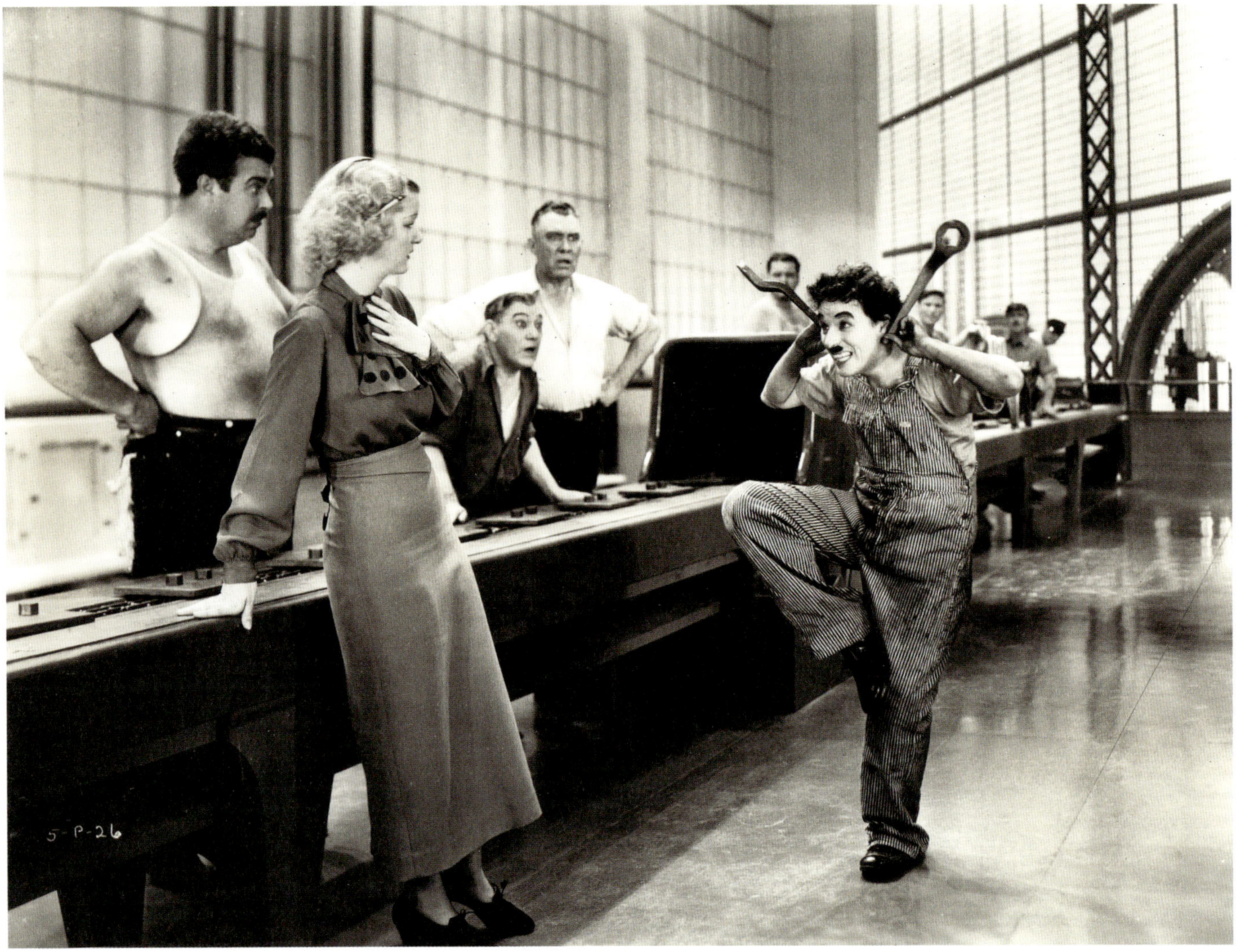
5-P-26

Left

Chaplin, having just danced like a fawn, imitates a donkey in *Modern Times*, 1936. Photograph by Max Munn Autrey.

ingenuity and compelling rhythmic variety that one can practically hear the opening crescendo as the sequence begins, the tempo quickening as the chase accelerates, the percussion accents as Charlie kicks and jabs the cop, and finally the explosive release as he makes his escape. It's a comic chase scene, and it's also a dance. There's no longer any difference. Without quoting a single ballet movement Chaplin has married comedy with choreography. In addition, Charlie's ease and clear enjoyment as he taunts and mocks his way through the sequence make him something more than a vagrant eluding a cop; he's a performer who can't resist showing off a bit.

Charlie's hunt for a means of survival leads him into a second rhythmically rich scene. As he strolls past an employment center a sign on the blackboard proclaiming "Men Wanted for Brewery," for some reason, attracts a crowd who had been indifferent to one asking for "Strong men for Sewer work." Charlie dashes into the office first and sits expectantly on a bench. But when the window opens, just as he reaches it one of the other men slips in front of him. He returns to his seat. It happens again. As he's going back to his seat a second window opens and he goes for it, but someone gets there first too. Charlie's pace accelerates steadily as he tries to reach one of the windows, but somehow, someone's always there just ahead of him. He overshoots and slams into a wall, enabling yet another man to slip past. By the time it's over ten men have gotten jobs, and Charlie is running full tilt from window to window. Each of the windows slams shut as he reaches it, decisive percussive BANGS that conclude the sequence. One of the clerks emerges and Charlie skids into him. When Charlie asks for a handout the clerk looks at him contemptuously, as though to say, "Why don't you get a job?" Of course, we've just seen why. Charlie is a vagrant because he *can't* find work in his world.

The bravura window sequence is shot in one continuous take, and it's thoroughly convincing. None of the men seem to rush to get ahead of Charlie, they're just *there*. Only Charlie rushes, faster and faster as it goes along. The sequence, for all its speed and apparent spontaneity, is choreographed with such painstaking precision that it unfolds with almost stately inevitability.

And so it goes, a different rhythm dominating each scene and providing its structural underpinning, just as the bass line in a musical piece underscores the more obvious melody line.

The rhythms percolating through *A Dog's Life* impose a playful quality to what is actually a surprisingly grim and uncompromising depiction of the desperate fight for survival in the slums. It was a giant step in storytelling for Chaplin as he sought to infuse serious content into his films while not stinting on the comedy.

The next time you see it in a crowded theater listen carefully. Henri Bergson's laughter might still be echoing off the walls.

Below

Sheet music, 1915.
In 1915 the Tramp's image spread around the world. His walk became the source of inspiration for foxtrots and one-steps. Sheet music bearing his image circulated and certain songs directly mentioned the Tramp in their titles and lyrics.

Opposite

Raoul Artez, poster for *A Day's Pleasure*, 1919.

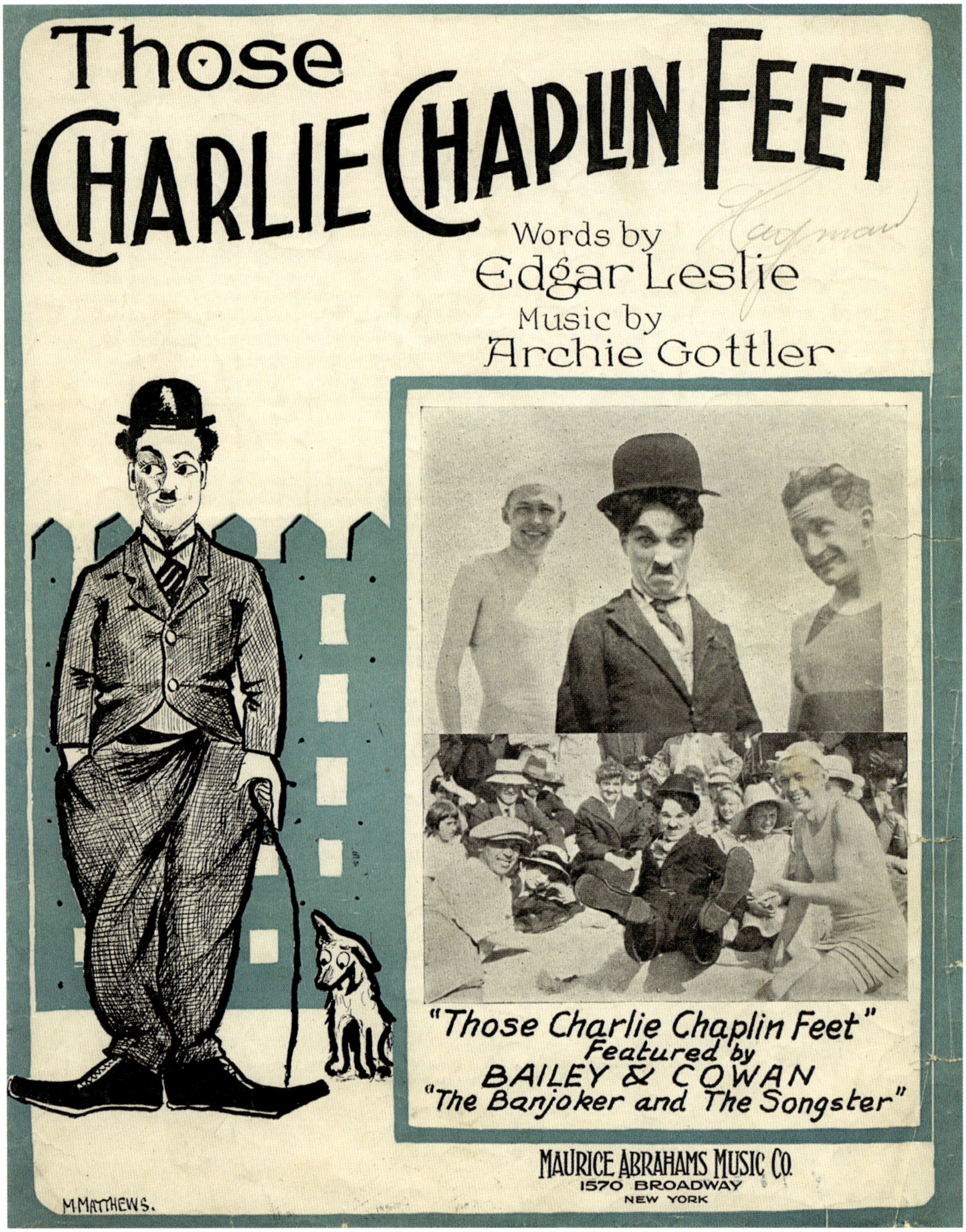

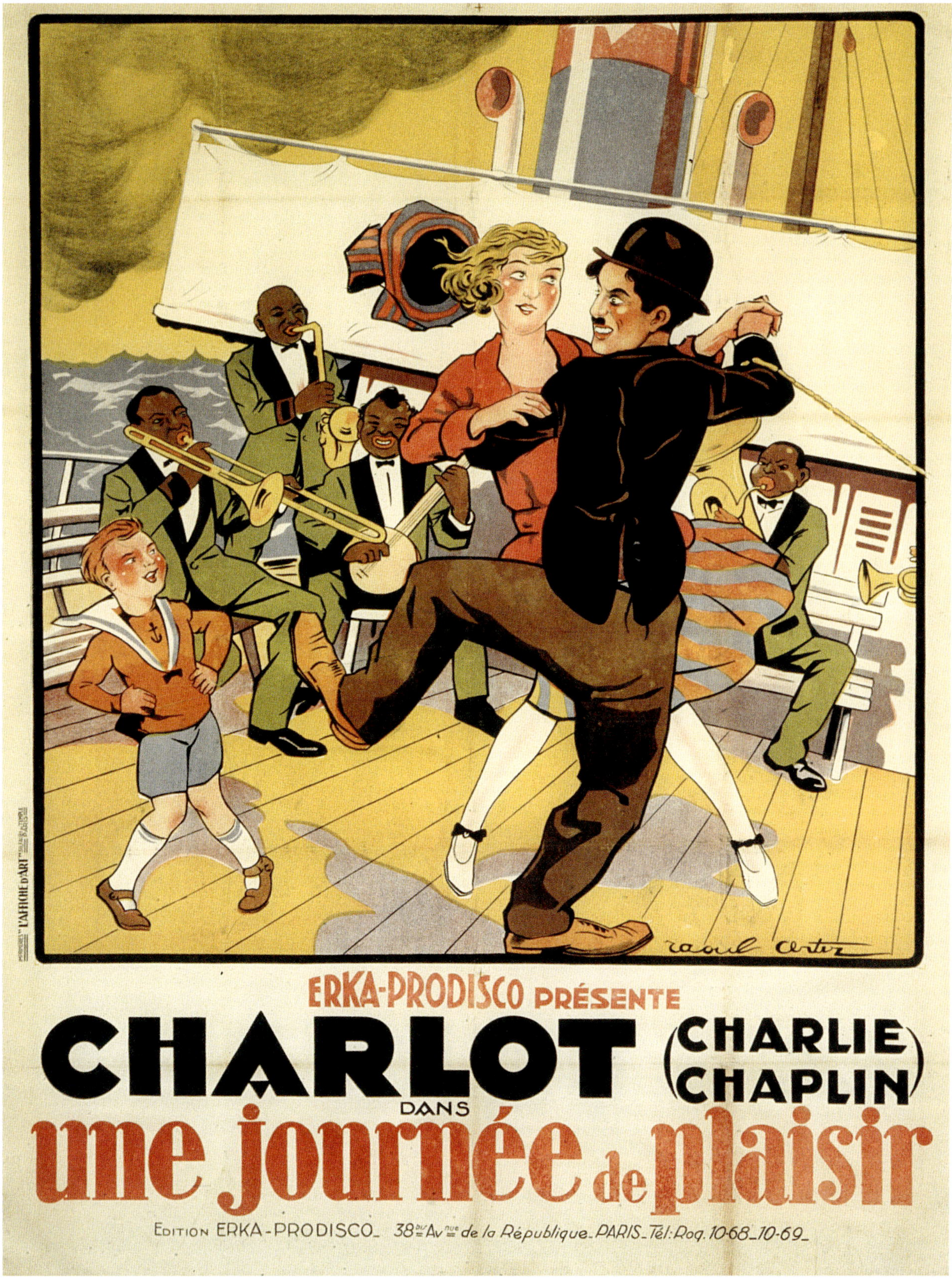
ERKA-PRODISCO PRÉSENTE
CHARLOT (CHARLIE CHAPLIN)
DANS
une journée de plaisir
EDITION ERKA-PRODISCO_ 38bis Avnue de la République_PARIS_Tél: Roq. 10-68_10-69_

Kate Guyonvarch

Chaplin and Nijinsky

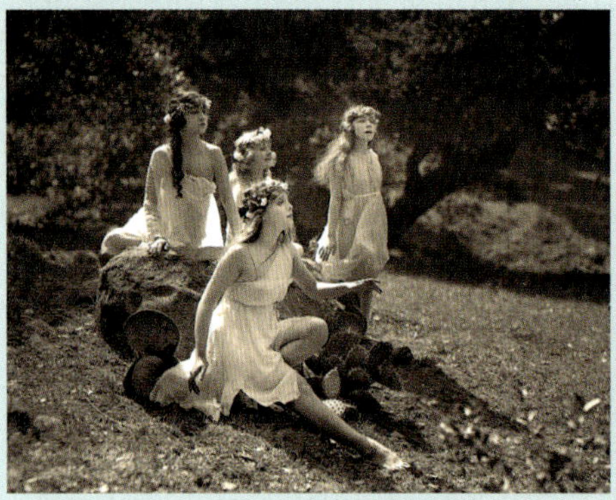

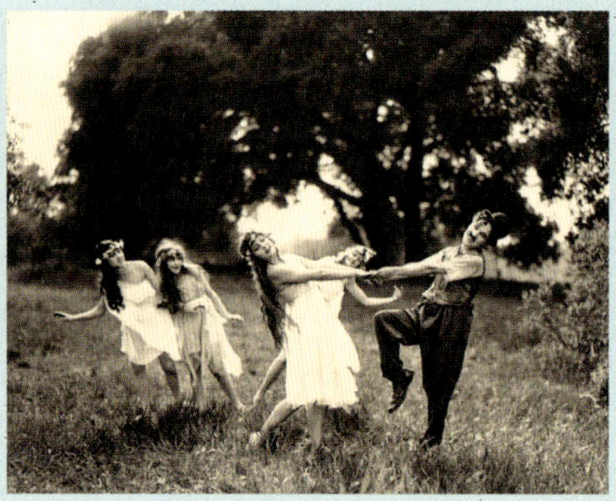

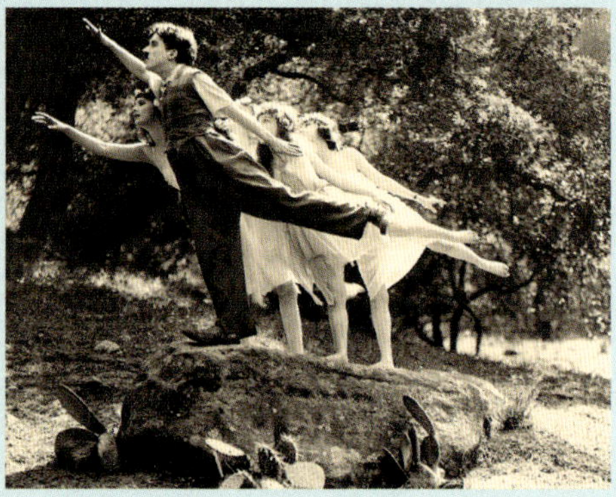

"Nijinsky, with members of the Russian Ballet, came to the studio [in 1916]. He was a serious man, beautiful-looking, with high cheekbones and sad eyes, who gave the impression of a monk dressed in civilian clothes. [. . .] He sat behind the camera, watching me at work on a scene which I thought was funny, but he never smiled. Although the other onlookers laughed, Nijinsky sat looking sadder and sadder. [. . .]

No one has ever equalled Nijinsky in* L'Après-midi d'un Faune*. The mystic world he created, the tragic unseen lurking in the shadows of pastoral loveliness as he moved through its mystery, a god of passionate sadness—all this he conveyed in a few simple gestures without apparent effort.

MY AUTOBIOGRAPHY, CHARLES CHAPLIN, 1964

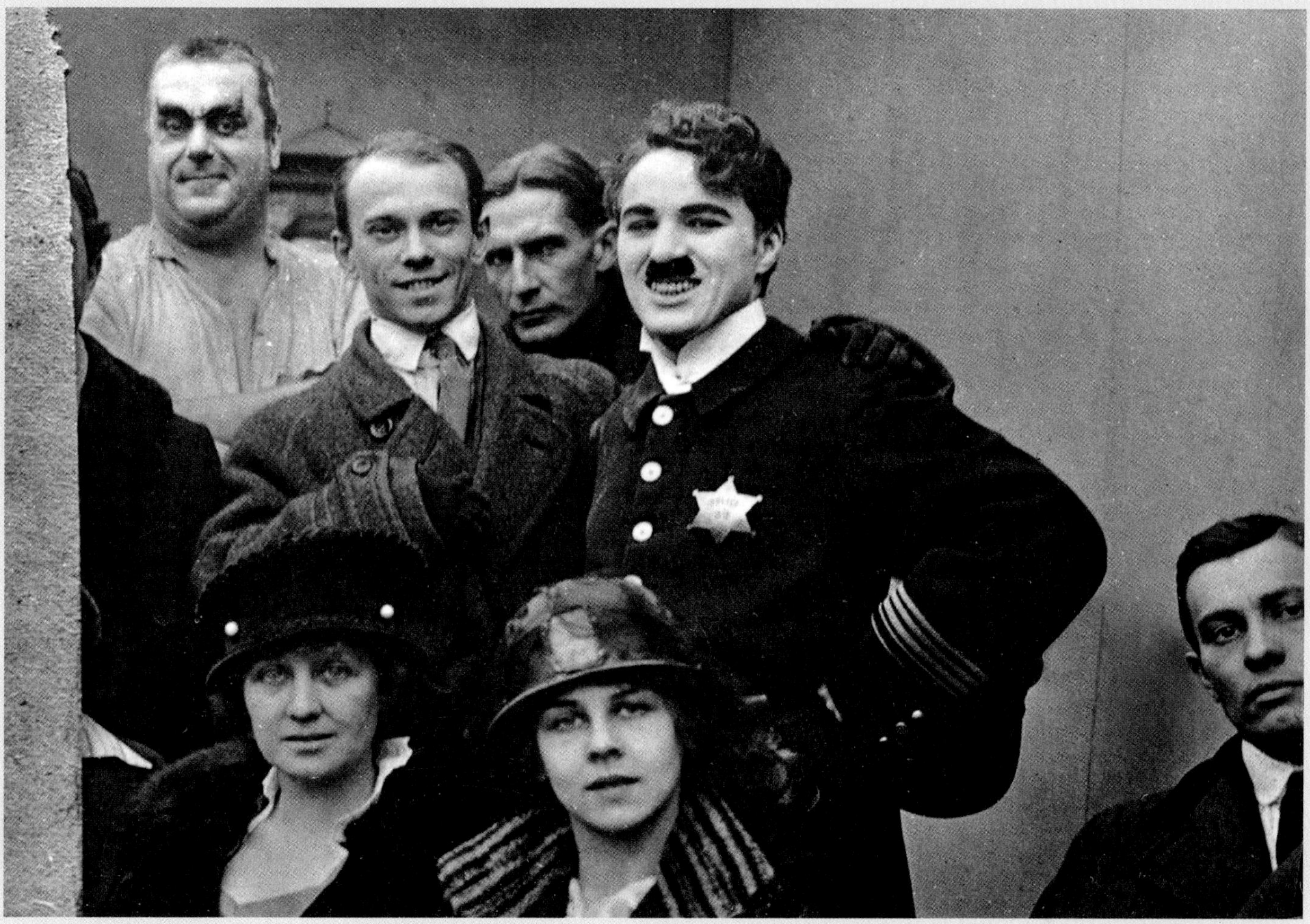

Left

Chaplin and the nymphs in *Sunnyside*, 1919.

Above

Chaplin and Nijinsky with the team filming *Easy Street*, December 1916.

As noted by Dan Kamin in his essay "Visual music," Nijinksy called Chaplin's comedy "balletique." Perhaps with this in mind Chaplin created a dance scene in *Sunnyside* (1919) in which the sleeping tramp dreams of gambolling in the meadows with four lovely nymphs. Their dancing is however far from the seriousness of the *L'Après midi d'un faune* nymphs—more comical skipping than balletic—forming a veritable, sweet, comic dance sequence, the comedy of which was emphasized by the deliberately unballetic music Chaplin composed to accompany the scene almost sixty years later.

Chaplin's thoughts of Nijinsky did not stop with *Sunnyside*, in particular because news of his schizophrenia became public soon after they met. This would have particularly affected Chaplin, whose mother lost her mind when he was a child and who for years worried her madness might be hereditary. Over several years he worked on various storylines for a screenplay about the tragic existence of a genius ballet dancer, named Tamerlain, or Neo, but more often "Najinsky." "Suggestions: In *Après Midi d'un Faune*, the close-ups are to be beautiful compositions in half light, of Najinsky and the three nymphs photographed from the waist up. Najinsky in the foreground is immobile, but for the occasional flick of his eyes and the quiver of the hand."

In some notes, the descriptions of the lonely, genius ballet dancer could be of Chaplin himself: "Najinsky was a simple, shy, inarticulate man. Born in humble circumstances he had not the advantages of an academic education. This he thought was an insurmountable obstacle that kept him from fully expressing himself. That was why he sought an escape, work hard at his dancing for in that medium he was articulate and able to bring to life the fruits of his imagination." Perhaps the notes began during his marriage to and later divorce proceedings from Lita Grey? "After all, our work—call it what you like, art, or anything else—is but a love letter addressed to someone, and when you've nobody to write to life becomes very lonely."

In nearly all the versions of the story, the protagonist has reached an age where he fears being unable to dance as before. "Dissolve into a scene of montage showing Tamerlain making his entrance with a leap, going through an exciting solo dance of grace and elevation. Then dissolve into shots of the audience applauding, the curtain descended, and into the Bacchanale dance which dissolves into the moonlight sonata. The finale of this dance is a leap over the wall landing T. on the other side, prone with exhaustion. He is picked up and carried to his dressing room." All the notes are undated, but Chaplin definitely worked on the idea in the 1930s, since a dancer in one script is called Paulette—he met his future wife Paulette Goddard in 1932.

Chaplin eventually shelved this ballet scenario, but those who know *Limelight* will have recognized the similarities.

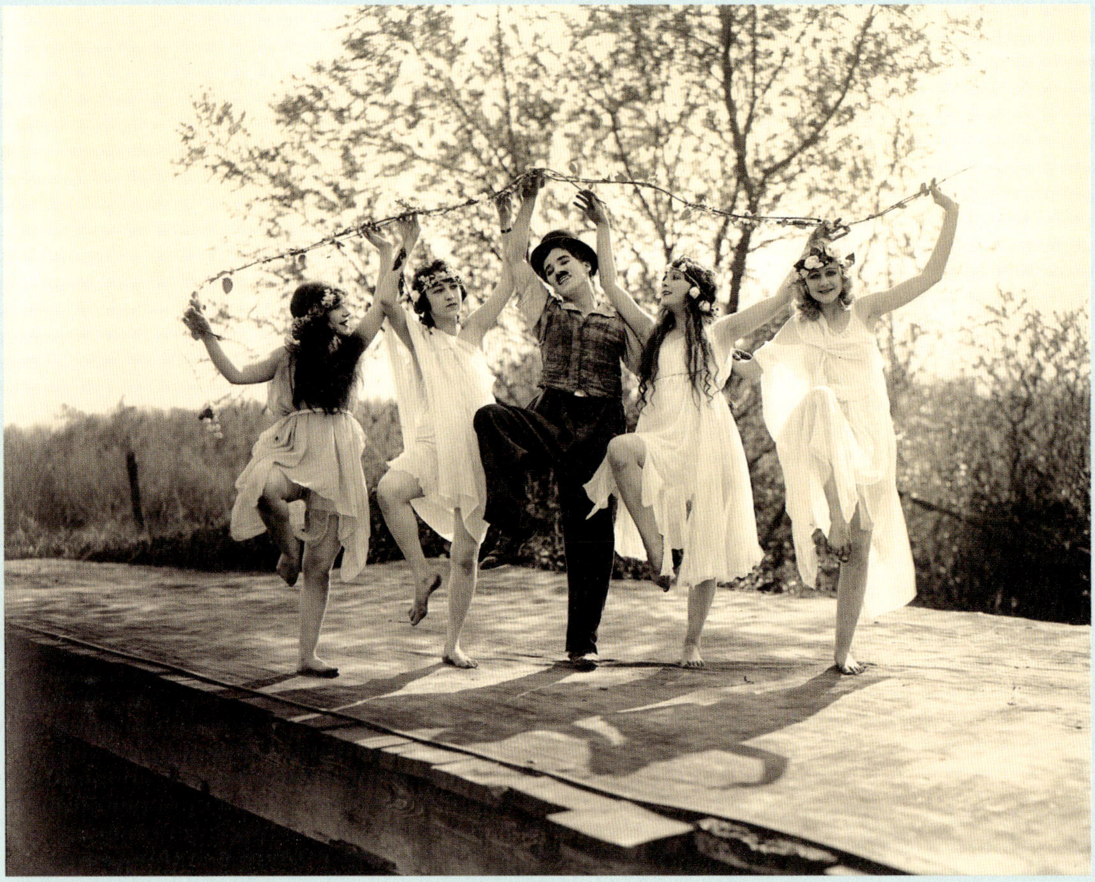

Left

Chaplin and the nymphs in *Sunnyside*, 1919.

Opposite

Poster for *Sunnyside*, c. 1925.

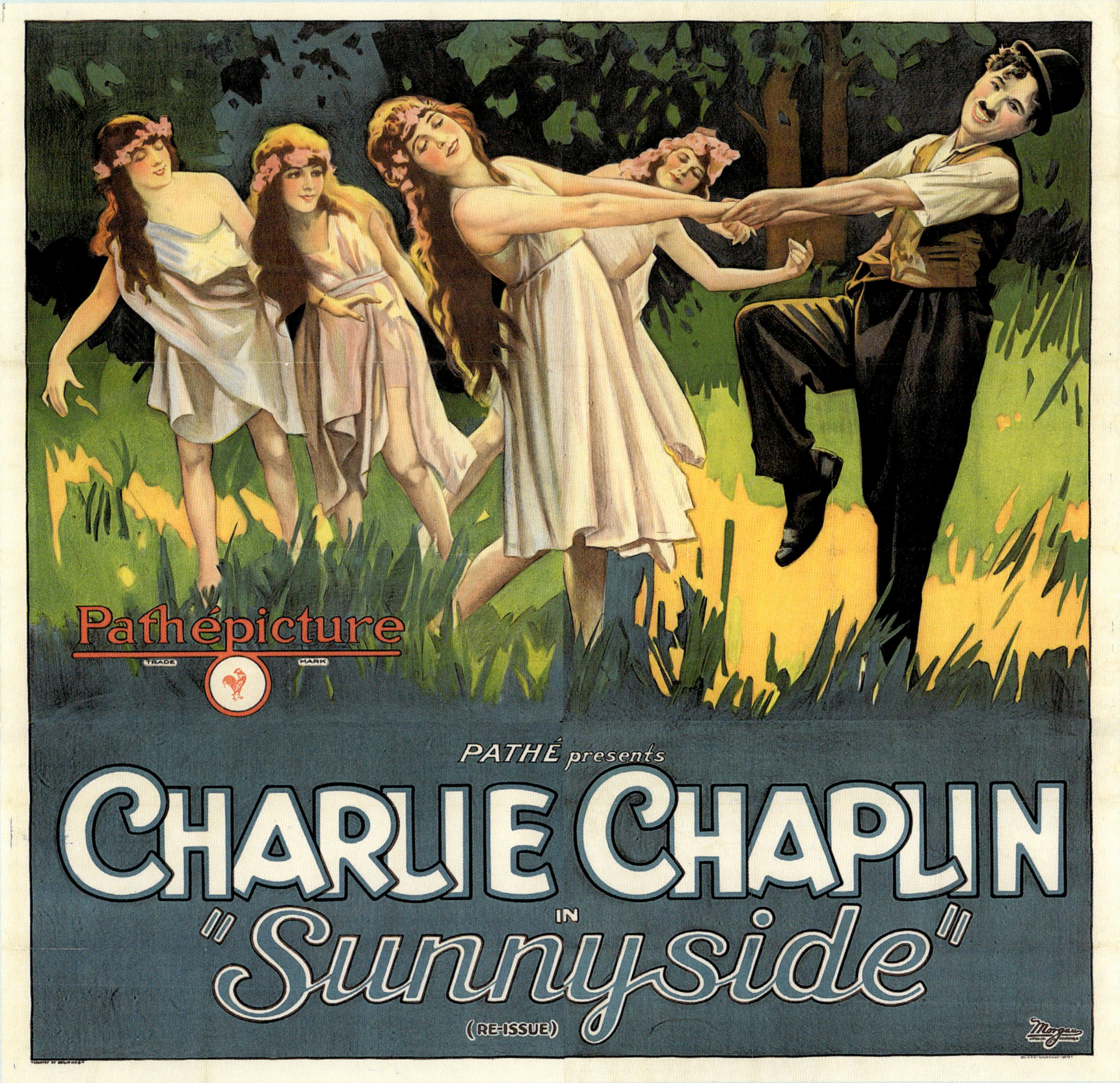
Pathépicture
TRADE MARK
PATHÉ presents
CHARLIE CHAPLIN
IN
"Sunnyside"
(RE-ISSUE)

Ariane Coulondre

"Emperor of cubism" and "mobile image"

Charlot through the eyes of Fernand Léger

"I'm interested in Charlie Chaplin because he is the only one to have become a 'mobile image' on screen," wrote Fernand Léger in March 1923, in response to a survey of cinema by René Clair (*Le Théâtre et Comœdia illustré*). Very soon, his fascination with the Tramp figure, shared by a good number of avant-garde artists (Varvara Stepanova, Erwin Blumenfeld, Marc Chagall), converged with his explorations of ways to express movement. Chaplin's popular and visual art corresponded perfectly with Leger's way of looking at his era, particularly with the observation he made, well before *Modern Times* (1936), of the new position of man and art in the face of the mechanical acceleration of a world transformed by urbanization, industrialization, and World War I.

Léger's encounter with the Tramp and the ensuing aesthetic shock were inseparable from his experience of World War I. Mobilized at the front, he traversed those painful years fluctuating between torpor and idleness. In the summer of 1916, in a Montparnasse movie theater, he discovered the adventures of the little man armed with a bowler hat and a cane, shown between newsreels from the trenches. "Apollinaire took me to see the Tramp when I was on leave from the front, we thought that everything happened 'up there,' that life was concentrated in 'the lines,' that behind the lines was trouble and death. Apollinaire told me, 'There is something though, come see.' I saw THE TRAMP; indisputably, it was something, since it held up against the enormous show that I had just left for seven days."[1] Emerging from his memory in capital letters, the figure of the Tramp gave substance to his pictorial preoccupations. The mischievous tramp with his quick, jerky gestures embodied the pulsating, contrasting, and fragmented modernity that Léger translated visually in his Cubist paintings. Described as "a type of, dry, mobile, black and white living object," his was an ever-moving body image totally free of psychological burdens. The ex-music hall actor with extraordinary talent as an acrobat, mime, and dancer revealed the essence of the nascent seventh art that Léger preferred to theater, to his mind encumbered by literature and sentiment. Passionate about films, and friends with several filmmakers, he proclaimed that "cinema began with Charlie Chaplin." A member of the first movie club in Paris, founded in 1921 by Ricciotto Canudo, Léger rubbed shoulders with Abel Gance, to whom he presented poster designs for

1 Fernand Léger, "Sur Charlie Chaplin," *Les Chroniques du jour* 7–8 (December 31, 1926): 243–44. All the quotations from Léger reproduced here without a reference come from this article.

Right

Fernand Léger, *Cubist Charlie Chaplin*, 1924.

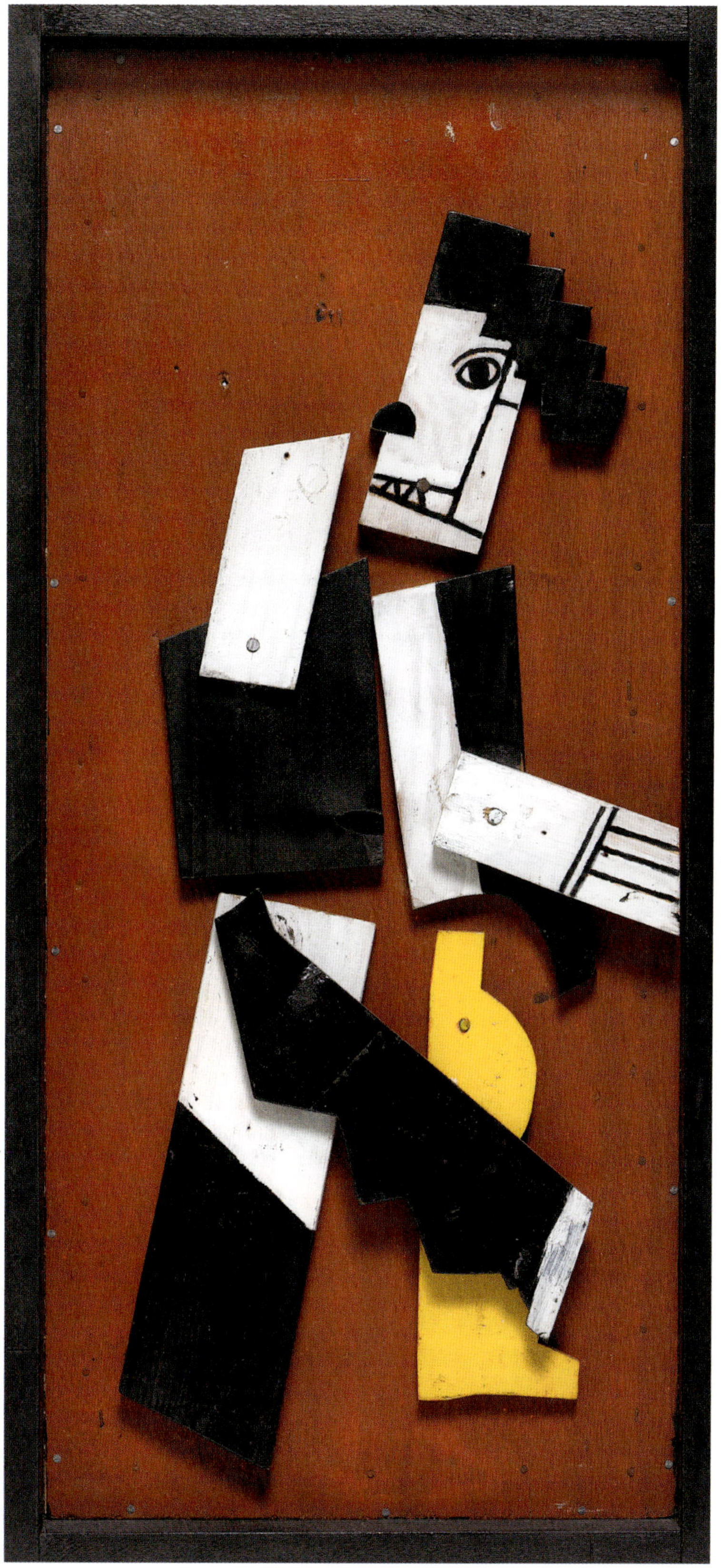

La Roue (1921), and Marcel L’Herbier, who commissioned sets from him for his film *L’Inhumaine* (1923). He later maintained a friendly correspondence with Sergei Eisenstein, himself a friend of Chaplin’s.

In the 1920s, when Léger’s painting favored mechanical forms and urban landscapes, it was not surprising to see the Tramp appear as a Cubist figure in some of his works. He is the hero of four pen-and-ink drawings for the book *Die Chapliniade* by Léger’s friend the poet Yvan Goll (1920, Dresden). The following year, the French version of the text appeared, “La Chapliniade ou Charlot poète” (*La Vie des lettres*, no. 5, July 1921), and later with the title “La Chaplinade” in the anthology *Le Nouvel Orphée* (1923, Éditions de la Sirène). Dadaist in spirit, the “cinematographic poem” recounts the tragicomic adventures of a Tramp who has come down from his poster to become a poet. Contrary to the caricatural portrait by Hans Blanke on the cover of the German edition, Léger reduced the character to a flat, graphic figure, made up of a heap of geometric forms. He played on the effects of dispersal and contrast, theorized before

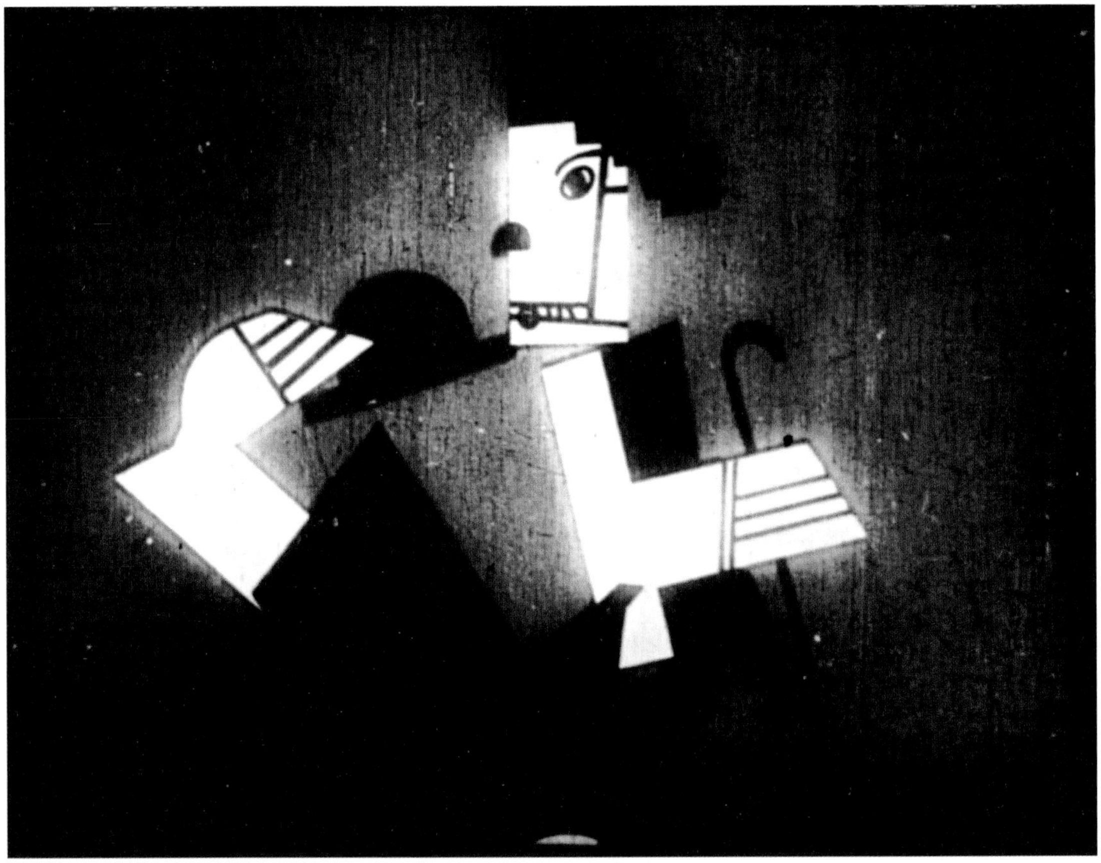

Right

Fernand Léger and Dudley Murphy, *Le Ballet mécanique*, 1923–24.

Opposite

Fernand Léger in front of his Cubist Charlie Chaplin (montage of pieces of wood), 1926. The American photographer Thérèse Bonney took several portraits of artists in their studios, including Raoul Dufy, Léonard Foujita, and Kees van Dongen. Here, she captured Fernand Léger in front of one of the versions of his *Cubist Charlie Chaplin*. The photograph was published in *Der Querschnitt*, a German avant-garde magazine founded by the gallery owner Alfred Flechtheim and active between 1921 and 1936.

the war: "Present-day life, more fragmented and faster moving than life in previous eras, has had to accept as its means of expression an art of dynamic divisionism."[2] The straight lines contrast with the curves, the roundness of the bowler hat contrasts with the waves of the hair, the black flat tints contrast with the whiteness of the paper. Scattered, what the subject loses in legibility, he gains in dynamism and visual power. The fragmentation even affects the letters of his French nickname Charlot ("CHA," "OT"), written in capitals in keeping with the style of contemporary advertisements. In the composition of the Tramp on the telephone, the typographical finds are reminiscent of his collaboration with Blaise Cendrars for *La Fin du monde filmée par l'ange N.-D.* (1919), a novel conceived as a screenplay. As modest as they seem, these drawings led him to several projects.

In the early 1920s, Léger wrote a short screenplay for an animated film, *Charlot cubiste*, which remains little published.[3] While it appears to be a variation on and a response to the comic film *Rigadin peintre cubiste* (Georges Monca, 1912), which mocked the pretentiousness of avant-garde artists, Léger's screenplay makes the Tramp a painter, i.e. his fictional double. The editing and framing directions in this text, nearly as whimsical as that of Yvan Goll, reflect Léger's own visual considerations: "His cleaning lady enters, round in shape, with one gesture he transforms her into a square, the same goes for the objects in the studio. Increasing speed. Close-ups. Delirium. The Tramp emperor of cubism. Intensity. White or black close-up." The animated film remained unfinished, except for the first sequence ("projection of a cubist Tramp, in dispersed fragments and reconstitution—then he takes his leave and disappears, shrinking"), shot using a marionette made by Léger. Made up of painted wooden planks, this contorted Tramp takes on the silhouette of *La Chaplinade*. Endowed with his inevitable attributes, the bowler hat and the cane, the body-puzzle enabled the game of taking the geometric formed figure apart and putting it back together. In 1924, Léger used these rushes in his *Ballet mécanique*, the "first film without a screenplay," which served as a manifesto. In the manner of a ringmaster, the Tramp introduces, and appears at the end of, an extraordinary collage of images, in which successive repeated sequences juxtapose the human body, the machine, and abstract shots. Three nearly identical versions of his marionette are known, one which belonged to Yvan and Claire Goll (Musée Pierre-Noël,

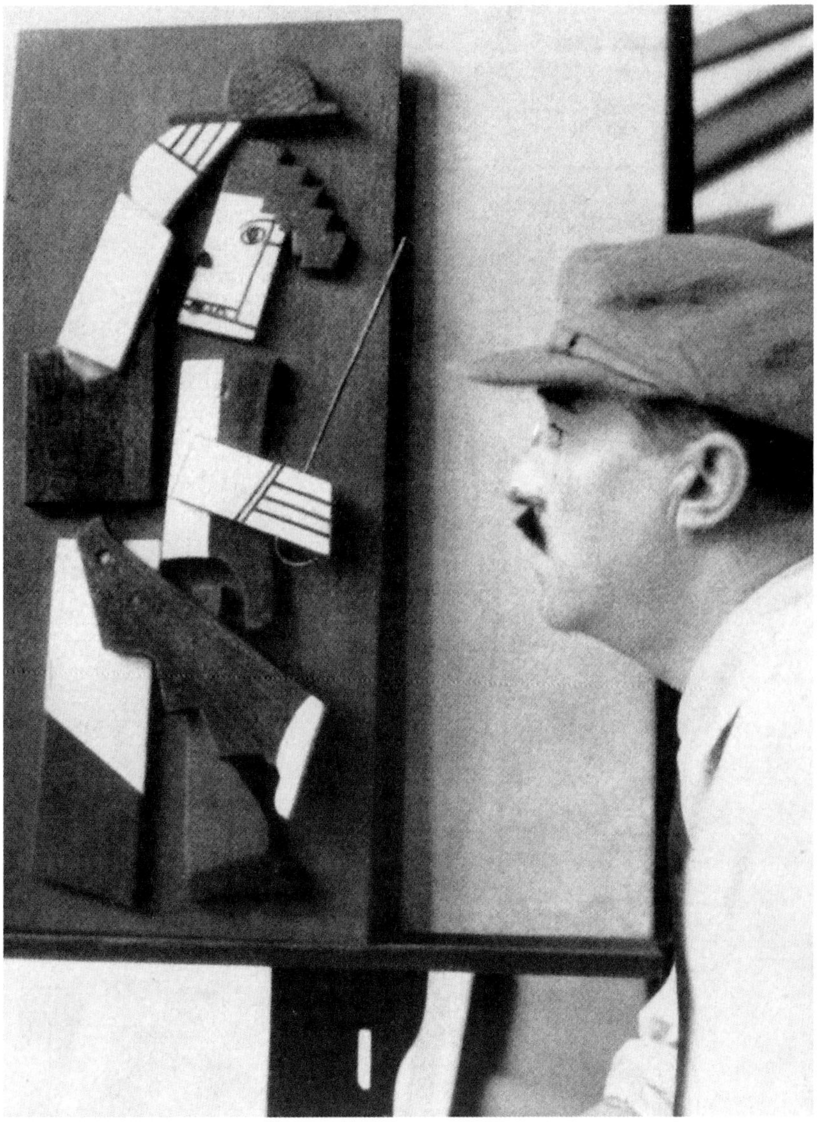

2 Fernand Léger, *Functions of Painting*, trans. Alexandra Anderson (New York: Viking Press, 1973), 8.

3 François Albera, "Deux scénarios inédits de Fernand Léger," *1895* no. 81 (spring 2017): 125–26.

Opposite

Fernand Léger, illustrations for *Die Chapliniade* by Yvan Goll, 1920.

Saint-Dié-des-Vosges), and another to the Brazilian painter Tarsila do Amaral, Léger's pupil in the 1920s (private collection). Kept by Léger throughout his life before joining the Musée National d'Art Moderne collections, the Tramp filmed for *Ballet mécanique* appeared in a photograph by Thérèse Bonney (*Der Querschnitt*, no. 8, August 1929) in which the puppet's profile smiles from ear to ear in front of the inexpressive painter. This series tends to give credence to the hypothesis of a commercial "modern toy" project, mentioned in a message from Léger reproduced in Cendrars' memoirs: "To kill time, I painted a big Charlie Chaplin . . . . I am going to have it sawn out and mounted on strings like a puppet. It will be very funny. One could mass-produce them in different sizes. And make a lot of money!"[4] Making good use of the first international movie star, this modulable and multiple Tramp reflects Leger's desire to ensure the mass distribution of his oeuvre. The project was not pursued.

But, in the same way as in his films, the Tramp does not go out of shot when he is chased out of the frame, the hero of *La Chaplinade* continued to circulate in Léger's works. Was it the retrospective organized in Zürich in 1933 that prompted him to look back at his past? Or was it Claire Goll, publisher of May Reeves's memoirs, *Charlie Chaplin intime (NRF Gallimard, 1935),* who reminded him of the comedian? Whichever it was, ten years later his Cubist Chaplin figure reappeared in a humorous photomontage titled "La Joconde amoureuse de Charlot," sent by the painter to Christian Zervos's magazine, *14 rue du Dragon* (no. 1, March 1933). Side by side with reproductions of the *Mona Lisa* and the *Venus de Milo*, he again embodied modernity in the face of symbols of classical art with a view to maximum contrast (masculine/feminine, stylization/illusionism, high art/popular art). The illustration directly refers to the animated film project that Léger was then reworking in a longer, color version.[5] Picking up the thread of his first screenplay, sketches present the Tramp trained at the Cubist academy visiting the Louvre, being hit on by the Mona Lisa, who literally burns with love for him, then attending her funeral. Is this a nod to the silent film *Un tragique amour de Mona Lisa* (1912), with a screenplay by Abel Gance? In any case, the meeting between these icons of art parodies the great Renaissance tradition, disparaged by Léger: "The Tramp left, the Tramp did not give a damn," he wrote. In late 1935, passing through New York for a lecture and the screening of *Ballet mécanique*, Léger sent the screenplay of his animated film (letters now in the Norton Simon Museum, Pasadena) to the Los Angeles artist and art dealer Galka Scheyer. Mentioning that he had been working on it for two years, he asked her to help him obtain the right to make the film using Charlot's name. Through her intermediary, Chaplin turned down the request, bringing this long-term project to a definitive end. No doubt disappointed, Léger showed little interest in Chaplin's films thereafter. Surprisingly, he thus barely mentioned *Modern Times*, which he saw on its release in a Broadway cinema, as attested by one of his letters to Simone Herman (February 14, 1936). The Tramp returned, however, as though for a final farewell, in a small gouache painted for the book prefaced by his friend André Maurois (*Sur champ d'azur. Les douze grandes dates du cinéma,* Festival International du Film, Cannes, 1949). Black-rimmed eyes, hat, cane, and baggy pants mark the permanence of the figure, which had become a symbol in Léger's imagination.

4 Blaise Cendrars, *The Astonished Man*, trans. Nina Rootes (London: Peter Owen, 1970), 183.

5 Pierre Descargues, *Fernand Léger* (Paris: Cercle d'art, 1955), 17–18.

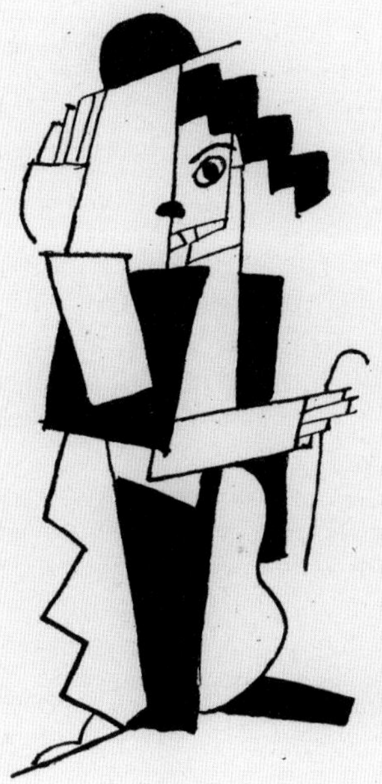

9

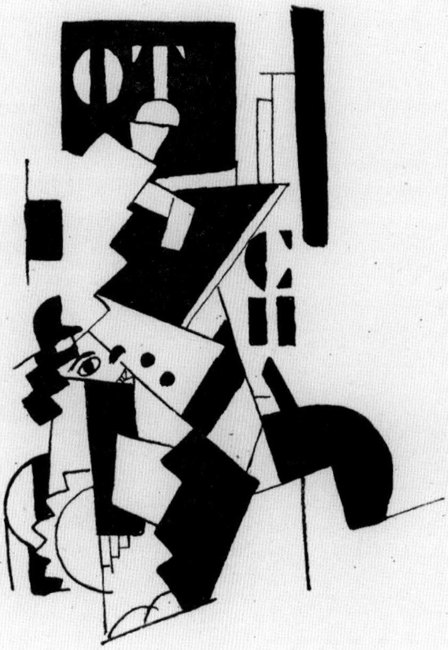

15

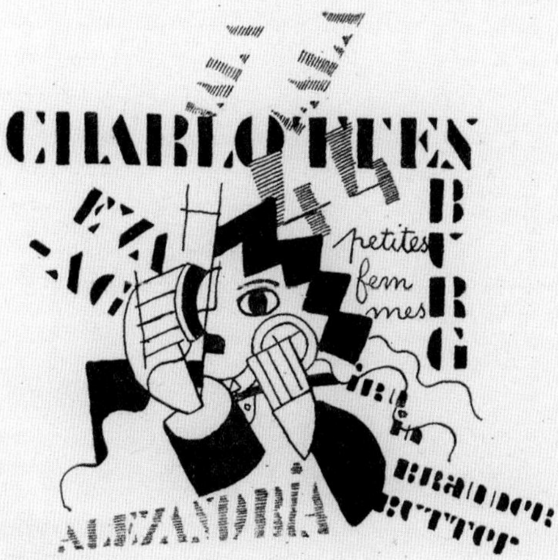

31

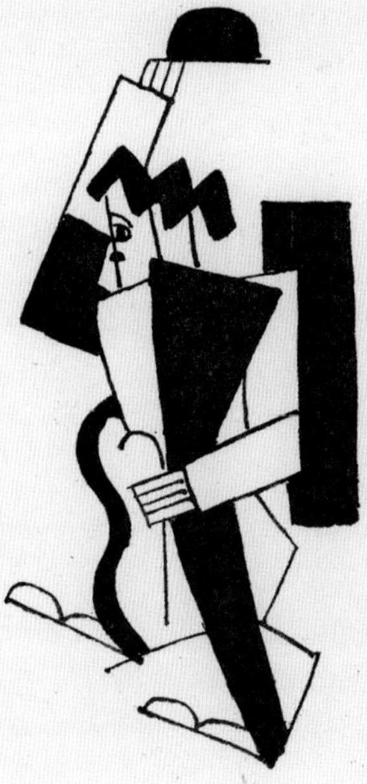

37

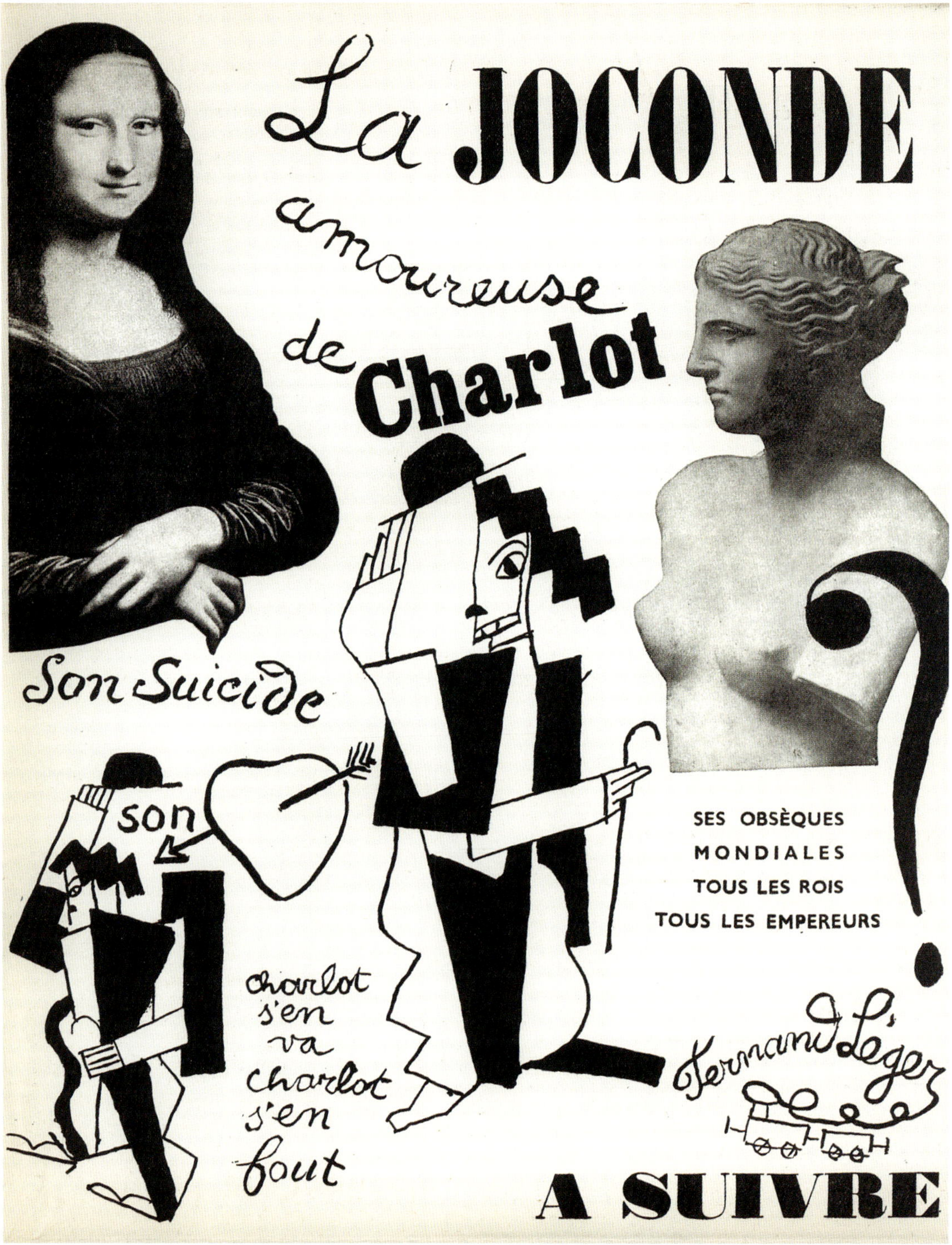

Left

Fernand Léger, *Mona Lisa in Love with the Tramp*, in the Éditions Cahiers d'Art review, *14, rue du Dragon*, no. 1, 1933.

Fernand Léger

The Cubist Tramp[1]

Under the title projected on the screen, projection of a cubist Tramp, in scattered fragments and reconstitution—he takes his leave, disappears, and becomes smaller.

Beginning of the film

The Tramp in his room, in bed. Close-ups. He is bored, yawns, and leafs through magazines that do not interest him. Suddenly discovers reproductions of cubist paintings. Astonishment—enthusiasm—admiration. He jumps out of bed and tries to transform curved objects into an impossible straight line (his gas pipe becomes curved once again).

Dreamily he goes out, goes down the large staircase, stops, starts again, he thinks. In the street he walks dreamily, absent-minded. Accident. He bumps into objects, falls, gets up, steps on the tail of a dog that bites him, enters a urinal and cannot get out of it (the Tramp's footwork seen in the lower section of the urinal). He moves around without being able to get out. He leaves and finds himself in front of a store. Above it is written "CUBIST ACADEMY." The Tramp's joy, gesticulations (the Tramp seen from the back). He enters the Academy.

Lesson in cubism. Quite slow comic scene. Timid, awkward. Beginning of cubist deformations of objects and himself. He goes out, his hat, which he had been holding, has become square. The Tramp tries to make it round again. The smoke rings from his pipe become square, objects in the street transform themselves. The nervous Tramp goes back home, sits in his armchair, and falls asleep.

The Tramp's dream. (High point of the film.) He has become an easel. Large canvas—the Tramp as an artist, tall (hair?), wide-legged pants—large gesture—he is an authoritarian master, he draws lines, fights with curves. Pursues them in the studio. He works furiously, a ball enters through the window. The Tramp's fury. He chases after the ball and bursts it.

His cleaning lady enters, round in shapc, with one gesture he transforms her into a square, the same goes for the objects in the studio. Increasing speed. Close-ups. Delirium. The Tramp emperor of cubism.

Intensity. White or black close-up. The Tramp wakes up in his armchair. It was only a dream. As he wakes, objects take on their usual form. The Tramp's disappointment. He takes his leave (becoming smaller) and disappears.

End.

1 Manuscript text from 1923, untitled. Reproduced in François Albera, "Deux scenarios inédits de Fernand Léger," *1895. Mille huit cent quatre-vingt-quinze*, https://doi.org/10.4000/1895.5287.

Fernand Léger

The Cubist Tramp[1]

Screenplay for an animated film.

1. The Tramp in a bed. Close-up. He sleeps. Pieces of the Tramp scattered around the room.

2. Wakes up. Sitting on his bed. Reconstitution of the fragments.

3. Chair. Cubist magazine.

4. Discovery of Cubist paintings.

5. Surprise.

6. Compares objects and paintings.

7. He stares at a curved gas pipe.

8. The pipe timidly becomes a straight line.

9. The Tramp gets up. Complicated. Reconstitution of the pieces of the Tramp once more. He mistakenly puts his arms where his legs should be. Difficulties for the hat that, every now and then, becomes square.

10. The Tramp walks, entirely reconstituted.

11. He opens the door.

12. Goes down the large staircase. Interminable. His feet become square. Stops. Starts again. Falls. Picks up the pieces.

13. In the street.

14. Houses, cars, people.

15. Cubist deformations.

16. Cubist Academy. Entrance of the Tramp.

17. Lesson in cubism. Timidity. Awkwardness.

18. He leaves, enthusiastic, and becomes agitated in the street.

19. Cane play. Cubist deformations around him.

20. Transformations of objects.

21. The Louvre. The Museum. Entrance.

22. Leaves cane at the cloakroom.

23. Stroll through the Museum.

24. Disdains the representative canvases.

25. Admires the Egyptians, the Aztecs, the Negros, the Middle Ages, and the High Renaissance.

26. The encounter with Mona Lisa. Silence. Stops. Observation.

27. Mona Lisa has a crush on the Tramp.

28. He looks at her and creates a few Cubist deformations of her face. They do not last.

1 Text from the early 1920s. Reproduced in Pierre Descargues, *Fernand Léger* (Paris: Cercle d'art, 1955), 17–18.

29. Disdainful, the Tramp moves away.

30. Mona Lisa is in love, follows him with her frame under her arm and declares that she burns with love for him

31. He turns around and warms his hands in her flame.

32. She declares her flame to him. He wants to extinguish it and blows on it.

33. The flames become square.

34. He moves away.

35. Furious, Mona Lisa swallows her flame and kills herself.

36. Mona Lisa's suicide. She catches fire.

37. Choir of panic-stricken security guards. The Curator.

38. Fire! Telephone. The fire brigade.

39. The Institut and the École des Beaux-Arts arrive. (March of the École and the Institut.)

40. Fight against the fire.

41. Mona Lisa's funeral. Grandiose.

42. All the kings and emperors follow the cortege.

43. The Tramp on a huge blue horse plays the violin and precedes the hearse. Funeral march.

44. Mona Lisa in the arms of Venus de Milo goes toward the cemetery.

45. A magnificent Rolls Royce follows, carrying Mona Lisa's heart pierced with an arrow.

46. Cemetery. Grand landscape. The Tramp-Hamlet alone, backlit. Stormy sky. Silence.

47. Heavy thought. Melancholy. The blue horse disappears in the distance. The Tramp moves away alone.

48. Return. Large staircase.

49. The Tramp goes to bed, falls asleep.

50. The Tramp's dream and nightmare.

51. He is the emperor of Cubism.

52. He works furiously. Delirium of curves, straight lines, fragments. Infernal orchestra. The fight against curves and curved objects. Appearance of the Mona Lisa. Disappearances. Obsession. Everything gradually calms down. The Tramp wakes up. He falls back asleep.

END

F. L.

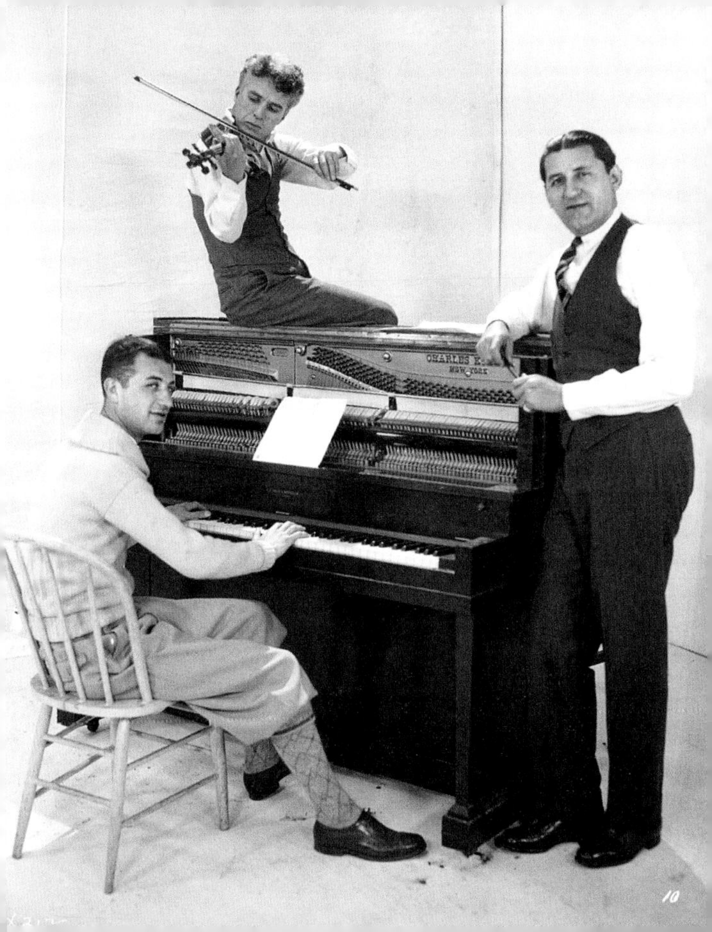
NEW YORK
10

CHARLIE CHAPLIN COMPOSER

Left

Chaplin playing violin, Gus Arnheim playing piano, and Abe Lyman, c. 1925.

A real one-man band, Chaplin rigorously oversaw all the stages in his film production as director, actor, editor, and producer. Thanks to the invention of sound cinema, he was not only able to take control of the music in his films but also to compose it. He learned the violin, cello and piano by ear and at one point dreamed of becoming a professional musician. To transcribe into scores the melodies he came up with, he employed different arrangers and, from *City Lights* (1931) to *A Countess from Hong Kong* (1967), experimented with different musical formations, from the jazz ensemble to the symphony orchestra.

Despite the variety of sources—his compositions draw on a strongly dramatic classical repertoire and on popular songs—Chaplin's music is immediately recognizable. In particular he maintained a principle inherited from his years with Fred Karno: the music should not compete with the comedy of the image but be "a counterpoint of grace and charm." He developed a style that can now be qualified as "Chaplinesque," making extensive use of strings and bold phrasing. His lack of academic training allowed him to ignore conventions and he did not hesitate to change meter regularly in order to fit the action on screen more appropriately.

An internationally renowned filmmaker, Chaplin won an Oscar in 1973 for the music of *Limelight*.

Jim Lochner

The musical DNA of Charlie Chaplin

Charlie Chaplin was born with music in his DNA.

As the son and nephew of English music hall performers, he grew up in Walworth, a subsection of London, among what author Barry Anthony called the "lesser lights" of the music halls.[1] "As a baby," his Aunt Kate remembered in an interview with *Pearson's Weekly*, "[Charlie] would stop playing with his toys the instant he heard music of any description, and would beat time with his tiny hand and nod his head until the music ceased."[2] Legendary is the story of Chaplin's first stage appearance at age five when he went on for his ailing mother, singing the cockney song "'E Dunno Where 'E Are." But it was at Kennington Cross where, he said, "music first entered my soul."[3]

"I was just a boy, and its beauty was like some sweet mystery," Chaplin wrote in *My Trip Abroad*. "I did not understand. I only knew I loved it and I became reverent as the sounds carried themselves through my brain *via* my heart." The sound of a harmonium and a clarinet playing "The Honeysuckle and the Bee" "was played with such feeling that I became conscious for the first time of what melody really was. My first awakening to music."[4]

At age sixteen, as soon as he was able to afford them, Chaplin bought himself a violin and cello. The cello "was the instrument I think he loved best," Kate remembered, "'because it was so plaintive', he said. I took a delight in watching his changing expression and his small hand quivering as he touched the cords. It was almost a caress."[5] While on tour in the US with the Fred Karno sketch troupe, he bought a cello from a store in Los Angeles for twelve dollars. "I remember carrying the 'cello in my hand naked, as it were, for it had no case, and boarding a car for home," Chaplin told journalist Konrad Bercovici. "So anxious was I to hear its sound that I plucked its strings while in the car. I wonder what people thought of the bleary-eyed boy plucking the strings of that instrument! . . . I had to wait another week before I had money to buy a bow and a piece of rosin."[6] On the set of *The Gold Rush*, Chaplin

1 Barry Anthony, *Chaplin's Music Hall: The Chaplins and Their Circle in the Limelight* (London: I. B. Tauris & Co. Ltd., 2012), 6.
2 *Pearson's Weekly*, September 24, 1921, quoted in Barry Anthony, *Chaplin's Music Hall*, 65.
3 Charlie Chaplin, *My Trip Abroad* (New York: Harper and Brothers, 1922), 62.
4 Ibid.
5 Anthony, *Chaplin's Music Hall*, 65.
6 Konrad Bercovici, "Making a Picture with Charlie Chaplin," *The Royal Magazine*, 1925, 490.

Opposite

During his first American tour with Fred Karno's company, Sacramento, June 5, 1911.

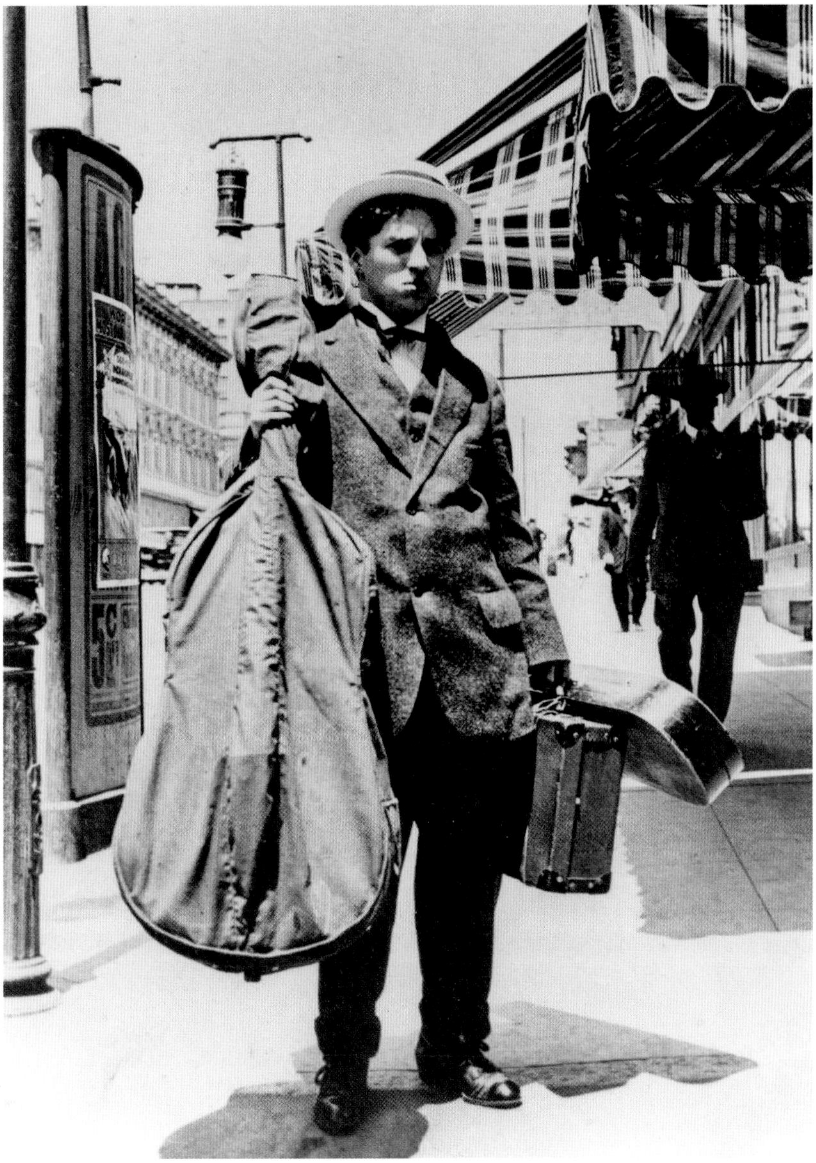

had photos taken in his Tramp costume, his legs astride a cello. “I could pose well with it,” he said in *My Life In Pictures*, “but that’s about all.”[7] But it was the early memories that still stung. “Because it is like a symbol of my poverty, although I am still passionately fond of the cello, I seldom play it,” he told Bercovici. “My heart sinks when I touch it.”[8]

As for his violin, Chaplin had a special instrument made that reversed the fingerboard because he felt he had greater dexterity in the fingers of the right hand. He took lessons from the musical directors of the various theaters on tour and claimed he practiced four to six hours a day. Stanley Jefferson, better known as Stan Laurel, Chaplin’s roommate on the Karno tour of the US in 1912, later told author John McCabe that Chaplin carried his violin “wherever he could . . . And he would practise for hours . . . He would always dress like a musician, a long fawn coloured overcoat with green velvet cuffs and collar and a slouch hat. And he’d let his hair grow long at the back . . . I wouldn’t call him a good violinist, but he sure as hell wasn’t a bad one.”[9]

Later, Chaplin’s press releases played up his abilities. “If you were to drop into Chaplin’s home in Los Angeles some evening, you might be surprised to find him playing a selection from *Carmen* or *La Bohème* on his violin,” read an unsigned article from Chaplin’s time with the Mutual Film Corporation. It praised Chaplin as “an exceptionally good violinist . . . Every spare moment away from the studio is devoted to this instrument. He does not play from notes excepting in a very few instances. He can run through selections of popular operas by ear and if in the humor, can rattle off the famous Irish jig or some negro [*sic*] selection with the ease of a vaudeville entertainer.”[10] But, as Chaplin said in a 1921 interview, “I used to play my violin a great deal up to a couple of years ago, but since then I’ve hardly touched it. I seem to have lost interest in such things.”[11]

7 Charles Chaplin, *My Life in Pictures* (Reprint, London: Peerage Books, 1985), 116.
8 Bercovi, “Making a Picture,” 490.
9 John McCabe, *Charlie Chaplin* (Reprint, London: Robson Books, 1992), 87.
10 David Robinson, *Chaplin, His Life and Art* (Reprint, London: Penguin Books, 2001), 215.
11 Frank Vreeland, “Charlie Chaplin, Philosopher, Has Serious Side,” in *Charlie Chaplin: Interviews*, ed. Kevin J. Hayes (Jackson, MS: University Press of Mississippi, 2005), 54.

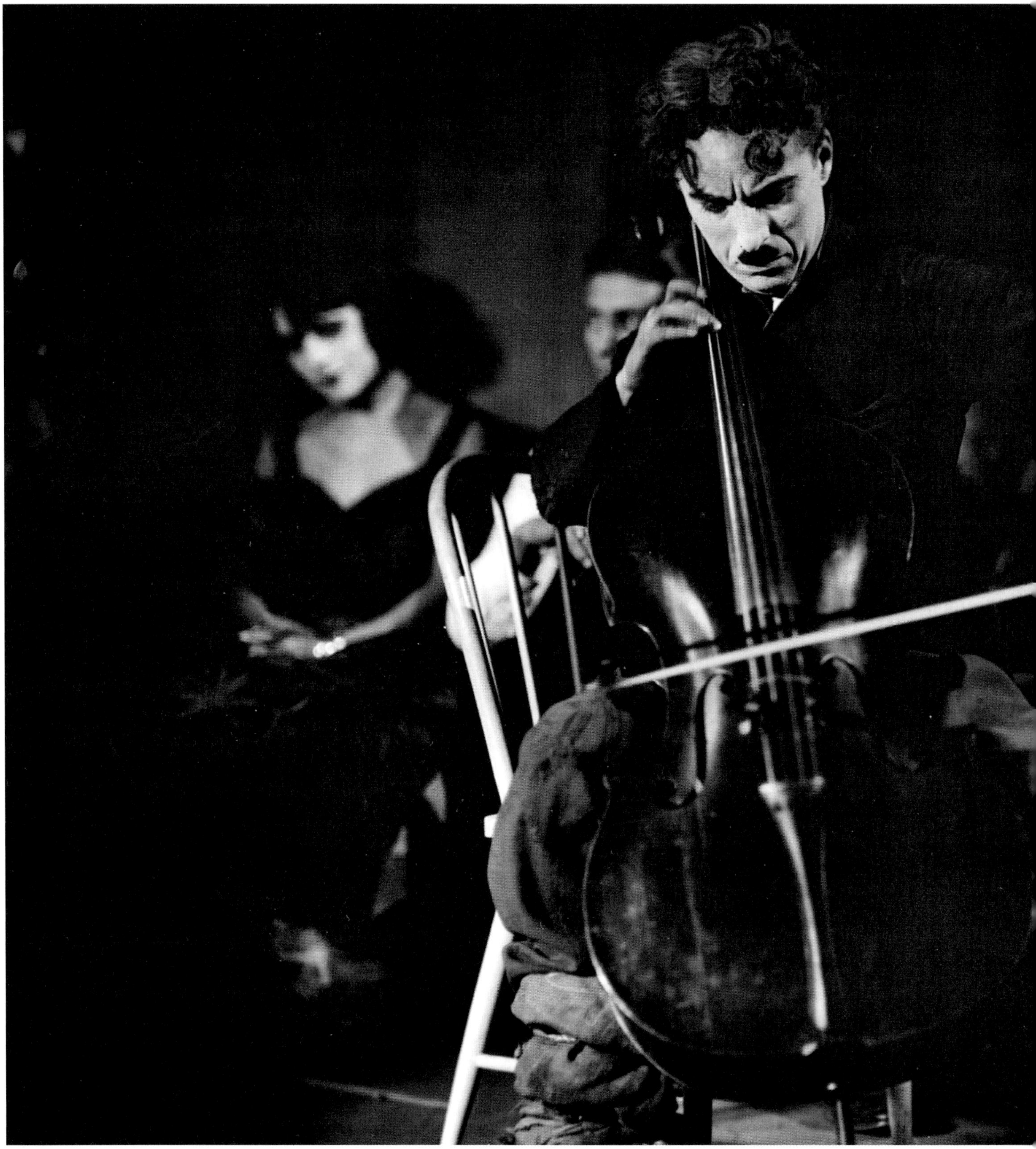

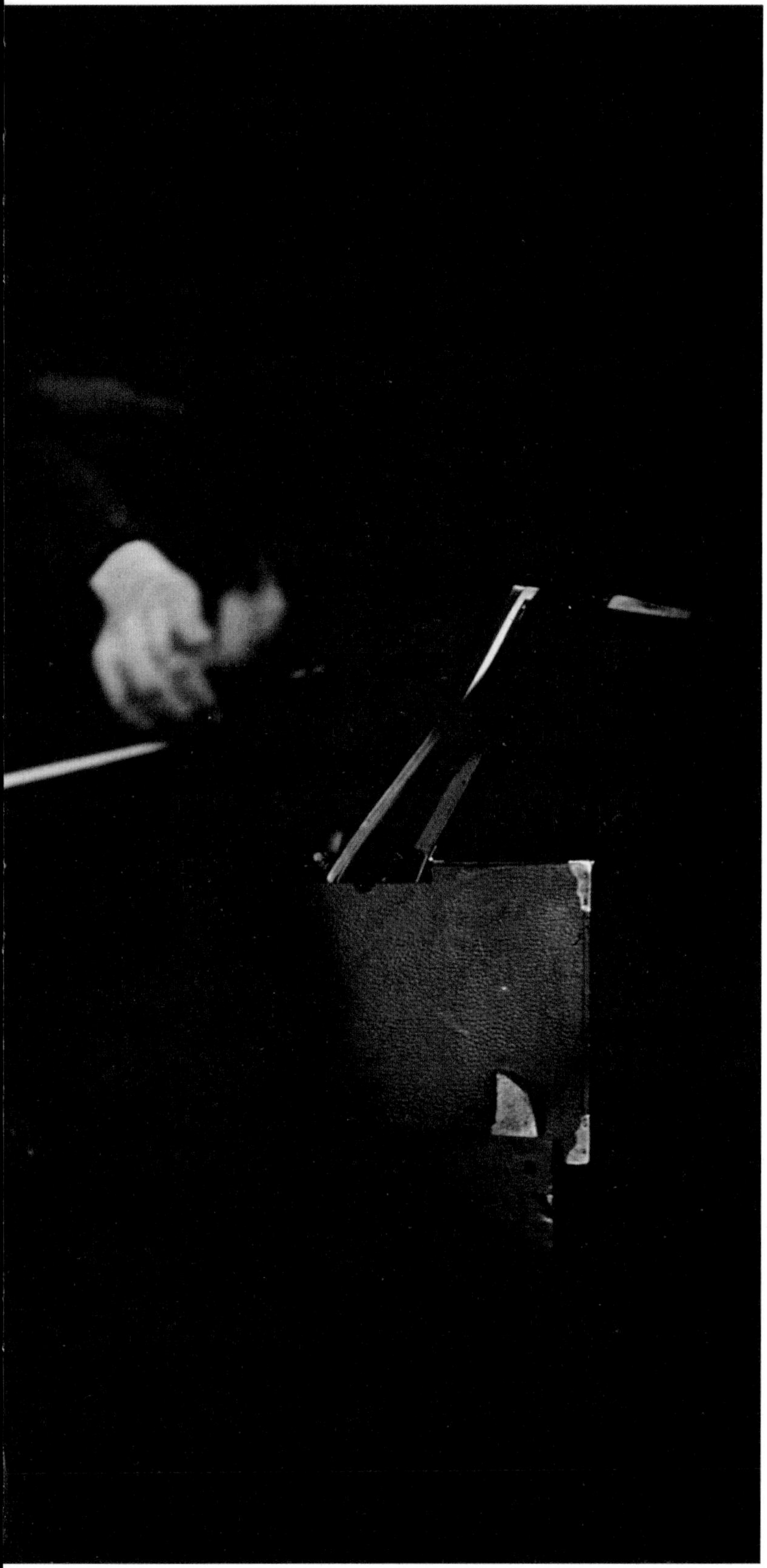

Left

Chaplin playing cello on *The Gold Rush* set, c. 1923–25.

Opposite

Chaplin playing the organ at home, 1922. Photograph by Apeda.

At home, Chaplin installed a pipe organ, which he would often play "into the small hours," Georgia Hale remembered in her memoir. "On his seven-acres estate he felt free to play the organ as late as he pleased, knowing for certain that he could not disturb his far away neighbors."[12] The organ room, which opened onto the master bedroom, was "the most mysterious one in the whole house," said Charles Chaplin, Jr., "for so my father made it appear to us."[13]

In 1918, *The Music Trade Review* reported, Chaplin bought a baby grand player-piano, which "he says he will be able to play even with his face interred in pies."[14] But, Eric James, Chaplin's music associate for the last twenty years of life, wrote in his autobiography *Making Music with Charlie Chaplin*, piano mastery "was always to elude him."[15] James "found it deeply distressing watching and listening" to Chaplin's efforts. "Even when he managed to get some sort of melody with his first three fingers of the right hand—the only ones he ever succeeded in using, in the key of F, his favorite key—the minute he started to try and use the left hand frequent discords resulted and he would curse vehemently in his frustration. Although it was his limited ability to play that resulted in my working with him, I did feel deeply sorry that he had not been able to find time to develop a talent that would have meant so much to him."[16] "What a grand piano player has the motion picture lost," proclaimed legendary pianist Ignacy Jan Paderewski. "What a great pie thrower has the music world gained in the fine Mr. Chaplin."[17]

But even before he was "a great pie thrower," musicians of note noticed a musical spark. In 1909, as a twenty-year-old entertainer performing with the Karno troupe at the Folies Bergère, Chapin was told "a celebrated musician" wanted to meet him. "The invitation was mildly interesting," he wrote in his autobiography, "for in the box with him was a most beautiful, exotic lady, a member of the Russian Ballet." When he was introduced, "the gentleman said that he had enjoyed my performance and was surprised to see how young I was." "You are instinctively a musician and a dancer," said the stranger. "Yes . . . you are a true artist." When he was told he had met Claude Debussy, Chaplin remarked, "Never heard of him."[18] But the meeting made a lasting impression. He later paid homage to the "celebrated musician" in his own scores, interpolating *Prélude à l'après-midi d'un faune* to underscore the Tramp's entrance in *Pay Day* and to accompany the

12 Georgia Hale, Heather Kiernan, ed., *Charlie Chaplin: Intimate Close-Ups* (Lanham, UK: The Scarecrow Press, Inc., 1999), 160.
13 Charles Chaplin, Jr., and N. and M. Rau, *My Father, Charlie Chaplin* (New York: Random House, 1960), 71.
14 "Charley [*sic*] Chaplin Buys Brambach Player," *The Music Trade Review*, January 26, 1918, 38.
15 Eric James, *Making Music with Charlie Chaplin: An Autobiography* (Lanham, MD: The Scarecrow Press, Inc., 2000), 101.
16 Ibid., 93.
17 Robinson, *Chaplin*, 171.
18 Charles Chaplin, *My Autobiography* (New York: Simon and Schuster, 1964), 114.

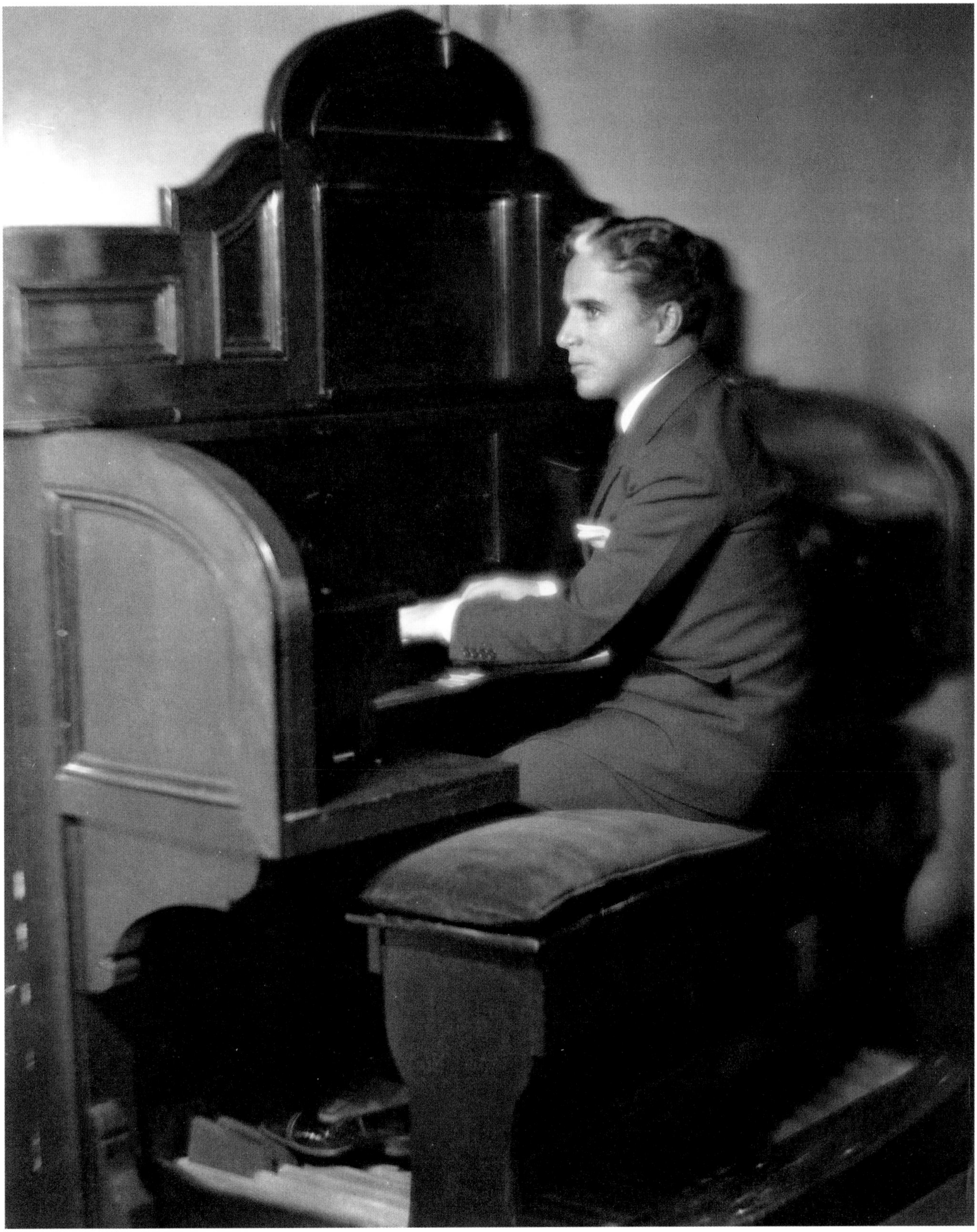

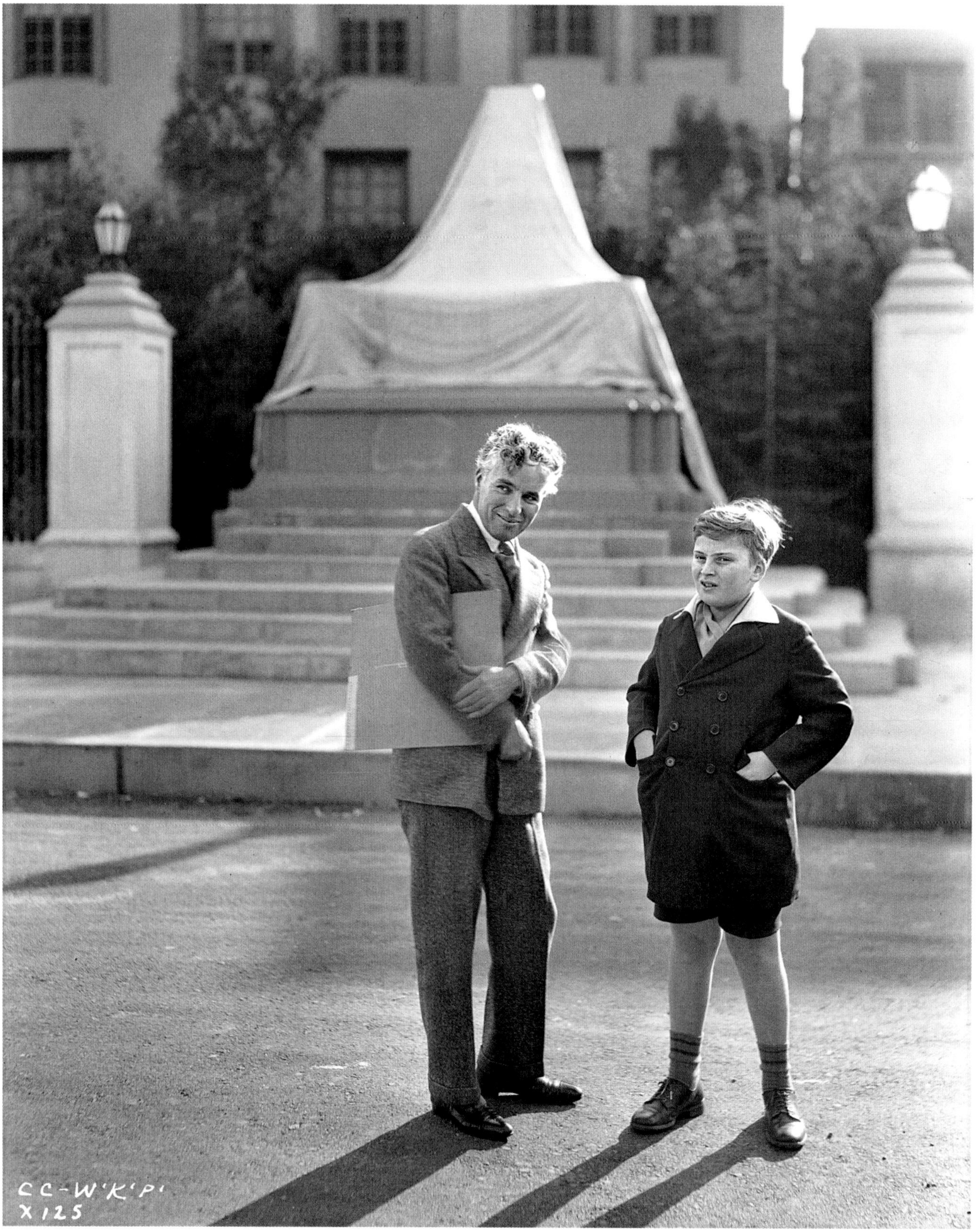

Left

Chaplin and Yehudi Menuhin during the filming of *City Lights*, February 1929.
In 1929 the young violin prodigy toured the United States before returning to Switzerland to finish his studies. He visited Chaplin's studio with his father and his teacher Louis Persinger. Chaplin interrupted work to welcome Menuhin and was so pleased by the encounter that he kept the group as long as possible, almost making them miss their train.

Below

Chaplin with Gertrud and Arnold Schoenberg, and David Raksin, c. 1935.
Before working on the arrangements for *Modern Times*, Raksin studied music with Schoenberg in Los Angeles. When he arrived at the United Artists studios, he was only twenty-three and had yet to prove himself. Working with Chaplin was not always easy: Raksin was temporarily fired by the filmmaker for daring to question his compositional choices.

dream ballet with the nymphs in *Sunnyside*. "My father has always considered those moments with Debussy one of the highlights of his career," Charles Chaplin, Jr. said. "He spoke of it often to me when I was a boy."[19]

Evenings at home after supper, Josephine Chaplin remembered, Chaplin would regularly turn off the lights, and the family would listen to records of classical music by candlelight. So it must have been particularly satisfying when some of the biggest names in music wanted to meet the man behind the bowler hat and the funny mustache. In addition to Paderewski, fellow pianist Leopold Godowsky visited the Chaplin studio, and fourteen-year-old violin prodigy Yehudi Menuhin joined Chaplin on the set of *City Lights*. Arranger David Raksin brought his composition teacher Arnold Schoenberg and his wife, Gertrude, to the *Modern Times* set. At home, Chaplin hosted Arthur Rubinstein and even claimed (perhaps apocryphally) to have played "a bit of Bach" for virtuoso violinist Jascha Heifetz over dinner.[20] Years later, Charles Chaplin, Jr. was still disconsolate he had missed a visit from Sergei Rachmaninoff—"Imagine it! Rachmaninoff at my father's house!"[21] Once Chaplin moved to Switzerland in 1952, he continued to entertain a host of celebrated musicians, including Isaac Stern, Rudolf Serkin, Leonard Bernstein, Pablo Casals, Clara Haskil, and Petula Clark.

But the meetings were not always productive, especially when egos clashed. In the 1930s, Chaplin met Igor Stravinsky, who suggested collaborating on a film. On the spot, Chaplin came up with a scenario of the Crucifixion performed as the floor show in a nightclub, an idea which, much to Chaplin's surprise, struck Stravinsky as sacrilegious. By the time the composer re-approached him about working on a film together, Chaplin wrote in his autobiography, "my enthusiasm had cooled off and I became interested in making a film of my own."[22]

A backstage meeting at the Metropolitan Opera with Enrico Caruso was probably doomed from the start after the legendary

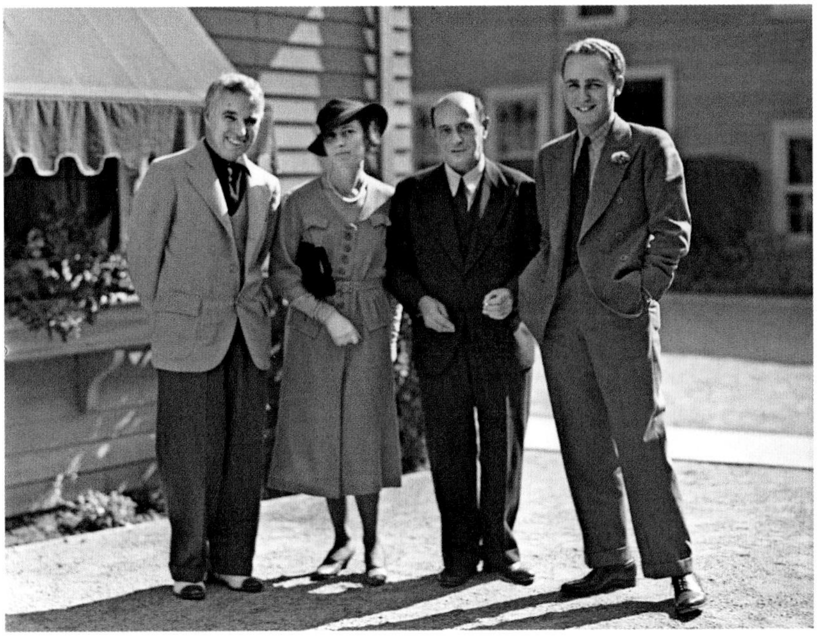

19 Chaplin Jr., Rau, Rau, *My Father, Charlie Chaplin*, 19.

20 Hale, Kiernan, ed., *Charlie Chaplin: Intimate Close-Ups*, 164.
21 Chaplin Jr., Rau, Rau, *My Father, Charlie Chaplin*, 199.
22 Chaplin, *My Autobiography*, 114.

Below

Top

Chaplin and the violinist Jascha Heifetz, c. 1920. During a party at Chaplin's house in Los Angeles, Heifetz is said to have borrowed his violin to play a piece at the request of the other guests. As Chaplin's violin was strung for a left-handed player, apparently cacophony ensued.

Bottom

Pablo Casals, Clara Haskil, and Chaplin, 1958. Chaplin often invited the pianist Clara Haskil to the Manoir de Ban. In 1961 he said: "In my lifetime I have met three geniuses—Professor Einstein, Winston Churchill and Clara Haskil . . . her touch was exquisite, her expression wonderful, and her technique extraordinary."

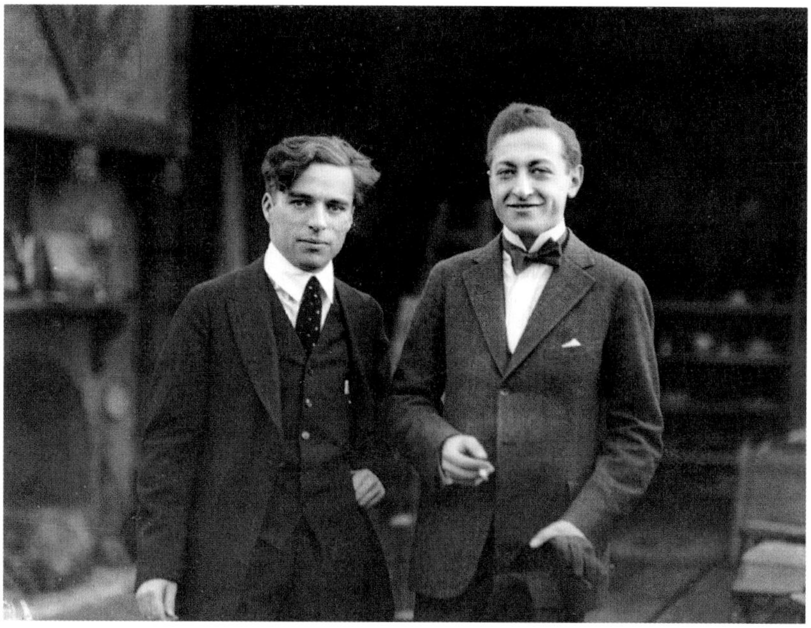

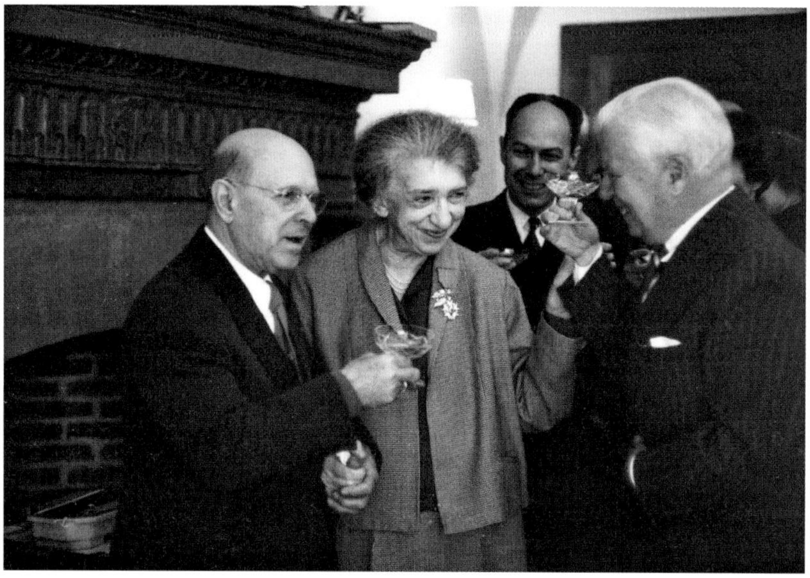

tenor called Chaplin the "Caruso of the Movies." "I was taken in the presence of the great Enrico, who not only did not receive me in state, but stood with his back toward me gluing something on his face in a mirror," Chaplin told the *New York Times Book Review and Magazine*. "The humor of the assumed superiority of a tenor over a comedian struck my funnybone instantly . . . So when, after several minutes had elapsed and my feet were getting cold and Caruso's back grew less and less inviting, I bawled out, looking over his shoulder into his face in the mirror: 'Greetings from the Caruso of the Movies to the Charlie Chaplin of the Operatic Stage!' Enrico whirled around and I got a close-up of two angry eyes. I did a quick fade."[23]

Chaplin "knew a good deal about music," David Raksin said. "And what he didn't know, he would pick up from everybody."[24] It is a DNA strand that inevitably leads back to Kennington Cross. "It was here that I first discovered music, or where I first learned its rare beauty," Chaplin said, "a beauty that has gladdened and haunted me from that moment."[25]

23 Benjamin De Casseres, "The Hamlet-Like Nature of Charlie Chaplin," in *Charlie Chaplin: Interviews*, ed. Kevin J. Hayes (Jackson, MS: University Press of Mississippi, 2005), 48.
24 David Raksin, "Interview," *Modern Times*, Blu-ray, Criterion Collection, 2010.
25 Chaplin, *My Trip Abroad*, 62.

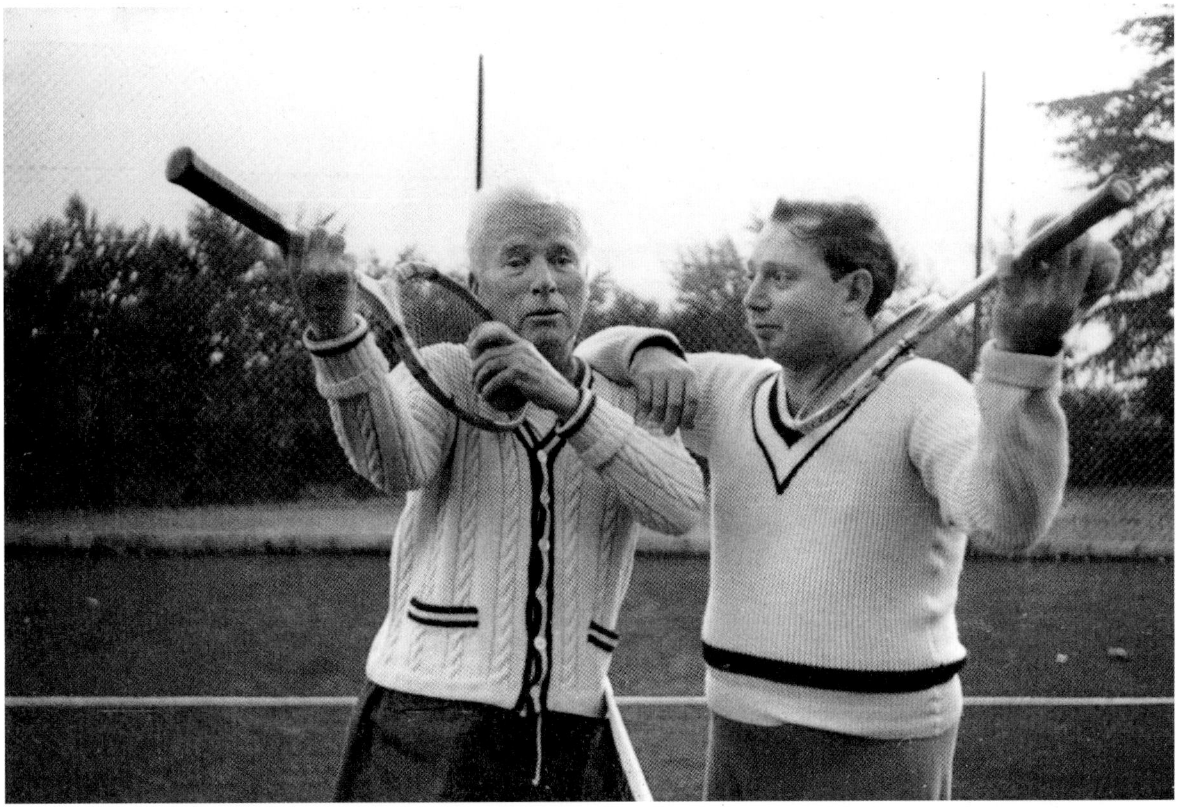

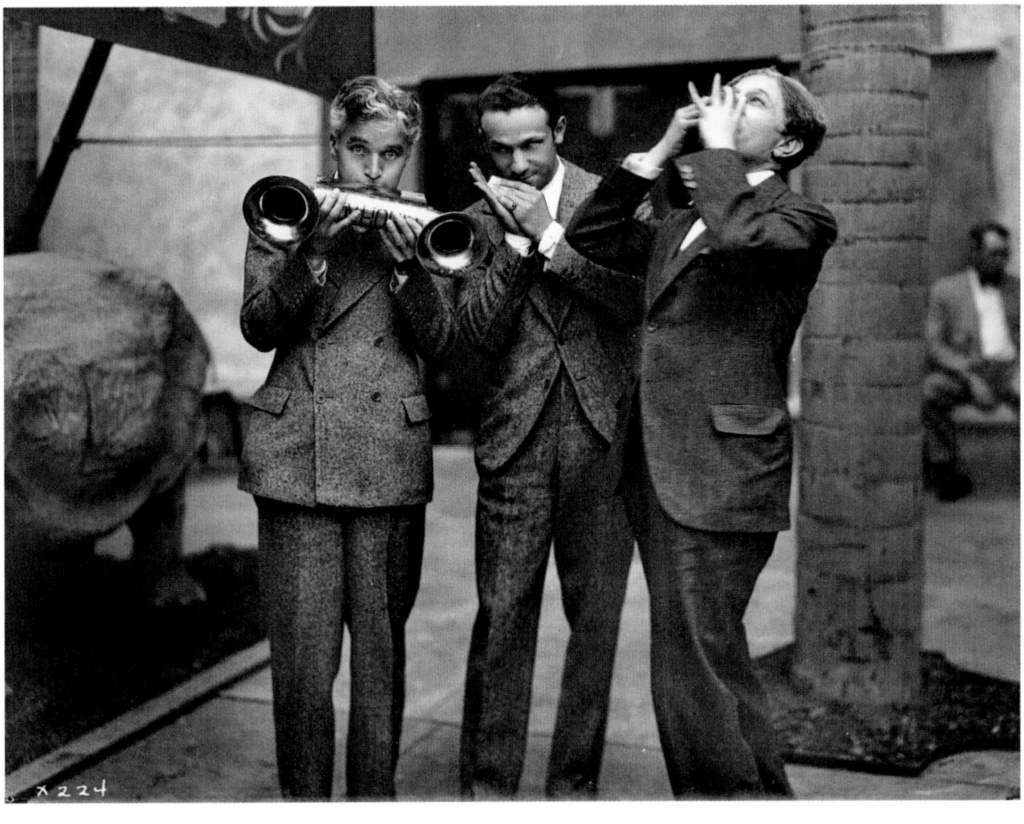

Top

Chaplin and the violinist Isaac Stern, c. 1957–58.

Right

Chaplin, Borrah Minevitch, and Sid Grauman at the Chinese Theatre, for the premiere of *The Circus* in 1928. The premieres of *The Gold Rush* and *The Circus* were organized in the movie theaters of the entrepreneur Sid Grauman. Chaplin and Grauman pose with Borrah Minevitch, actor and famous harmonica player. Here, Chaplin plays a harmonica with an amplifier.

Francis Bordat

Music for *The Gold Rush*

Chaplin's film music is immediately recognizable. Despite its variety of sources, it is striking for the homogeneity of its inspiration, which draws on a classical repertoire with great dramatic potential and on the memory of popular tunes from the filmmaker's London childhood. Yet what characterizes his music above all is the fact that it is indissociable from the images that it accompanies, even though it only arrived "after the fact" in his works of the 1910s and 1920s.

The melodies and background music of *The Gold Rush* were in Chaplin's head even before the filming of what he always considered his masterpiece. The drawings of the little prospector in the snows of Alaska illustrated the first songs he published, as though tunes and rhythms *emanated* from the images. And the film director oversaw a complete score to accompany the screenings of his film.

For cinema was never "silent." Musicians played live during screenings, and, for the most ambitious feature films, orchestras followed cue sheets distributed to cinema owners. The score for *The Gold Rush* was written by Carli D. Elinor, one of the most renowned composers in Hollywood between 1915 and 1928. This accompaniment must be seen in the tradition of the 1920s, in which music was played mainly in autonomous blocks, which began and ended according to their own melodic and rhythmic logic, with little concern for synchronizing sound and action. Like the colors of "tinted" film prints, the pieces were chosen for the ambiance that they evoked and, when repeated, for the echoes thus produced.

The 1925 compilation is in keeping with this practice, but also strays from it, borrowing from a greater number of sources (no fewer than forty fashionable tunes, classical pieces, dances, and folk songs) and based more on the interplay of leitmotifs. These motifs refer sometimes to characters, sometimes to situations and sometimes to feelings, the first mark of a style specific to Chaplin. They include the themes of "the young girl," "the storm," "sadness," "love," and, of course, the theme of the Lone Prospector, "The Bowery," a well-known tune at the time, whose dark tonalities, Jim Lochner remarked, contrast with an elegant staccato: a reflection of the central contradiction between the dignity of the tramp character and his shabby attire.[1] Georgia inspires three different pieces, depending on whether her appearance gives rise to admiration, adoration, or nostalgia.

The first version of *The Gold Rush* bears witness, moreover, to Chaplin's taste for opera. *Natoma* (Victor Herbert, 1911) was one of the main sources, as were Verdi (*Rigoletto*)

1 Jim Lochner, *The Music of Charlie Chaplin* (Jefferson, NC: McFarland, 2018), 76.

and Offenbach (*Orphée aux Enfers*). But classical music, despite a little borrowing from Beethoven's *Pathétique* and Grieg's *Peer Gynt*, is in the minority. It would occupy a more significant place in the 1942 version.

The famous dance of the bread rolls scene deserves particular attention. It is announced by an intertitle: "I'll dance the Oceana Roll." But it was not the "Oceana Roll," a hit for Roger Lewis and Lucien Denni (1911), that was chosen by Chaplin and Elinor, but an eighteenth-century Scottish popular song, "The Keel Row." According to several witnesses, however, it was indeed "Oceana Roll" that Chaplin hummed when rehearsing the scene, and it was probably the song played by Abe Lyman's band during the eleven takes he shot of the scene. So why was "Oceana Roll" not kept? Perhaps the fame of the song, known to all Americans in 1925, risked interfering with the scene by distracting the audience? Or perhaps the rights to the song were too expensive for the budget.

In 1941, Chaplin decided to rerelease *The Gold Rush*. It was an original and rather courageous undertaking because no one to date had attempted to rerelease a silent film. To adapt it to the talkie era, Chaplin removed the intertitles and replaced them with a voiceover spoken by himself. He deleted or shortened certain sequences, modified a few others, and added a musical score that had the great advantage of being recorded on a soundtrack printed on the film, thus realizing his artistic dream: the precise and definitive association of image and sound. Chaplin spent nearly a year on this operation with the editor Harold McGhean, then with the composer-arranger

Below

Chaplin rehearsing with Abe Lyman's band, 1925. To promote the release of *The Gold Rush*, Chaplin conducted Abe Lyman's band during the recording of "With You, Dear, in Bombay" and "Sing a Song." The event received a lot of media coverage. "Chaplin himself conducts the orchestra on this record and, therefore, we get a true interpretation of his fine melody," according to the British newspaper *Gravesend Reporter*, October 10, 1925.

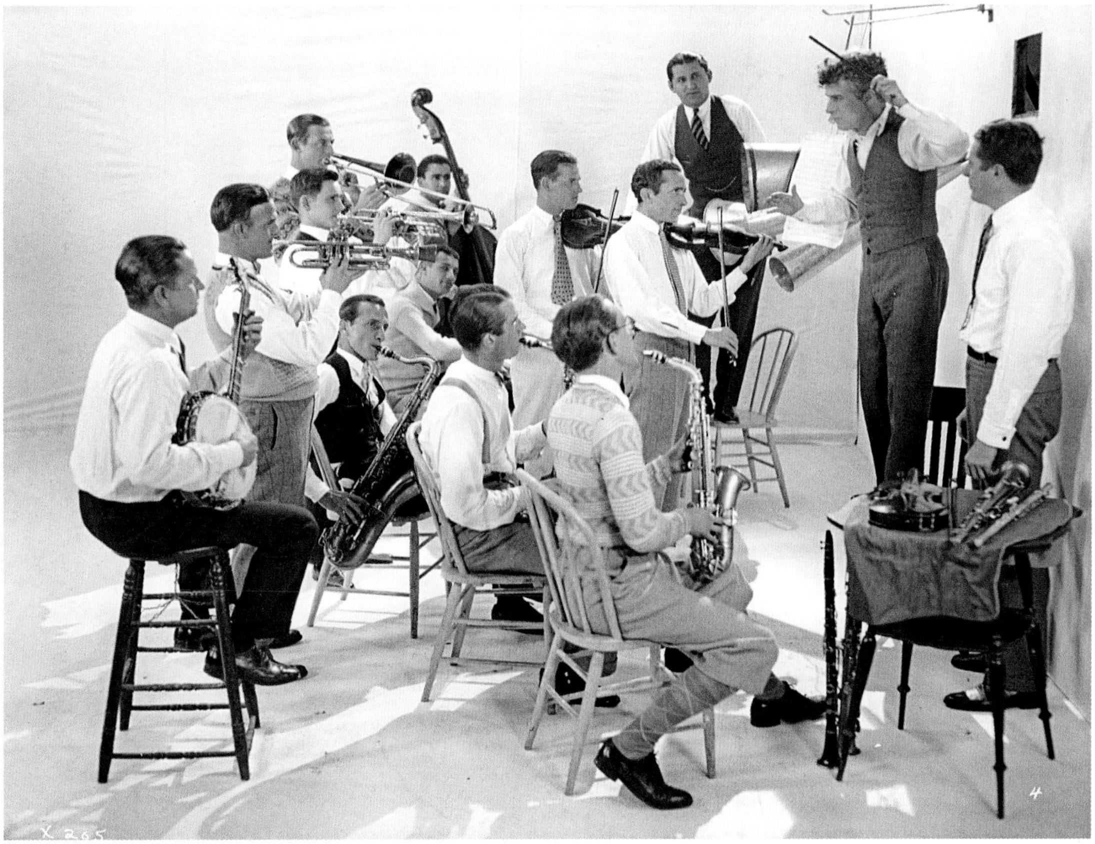

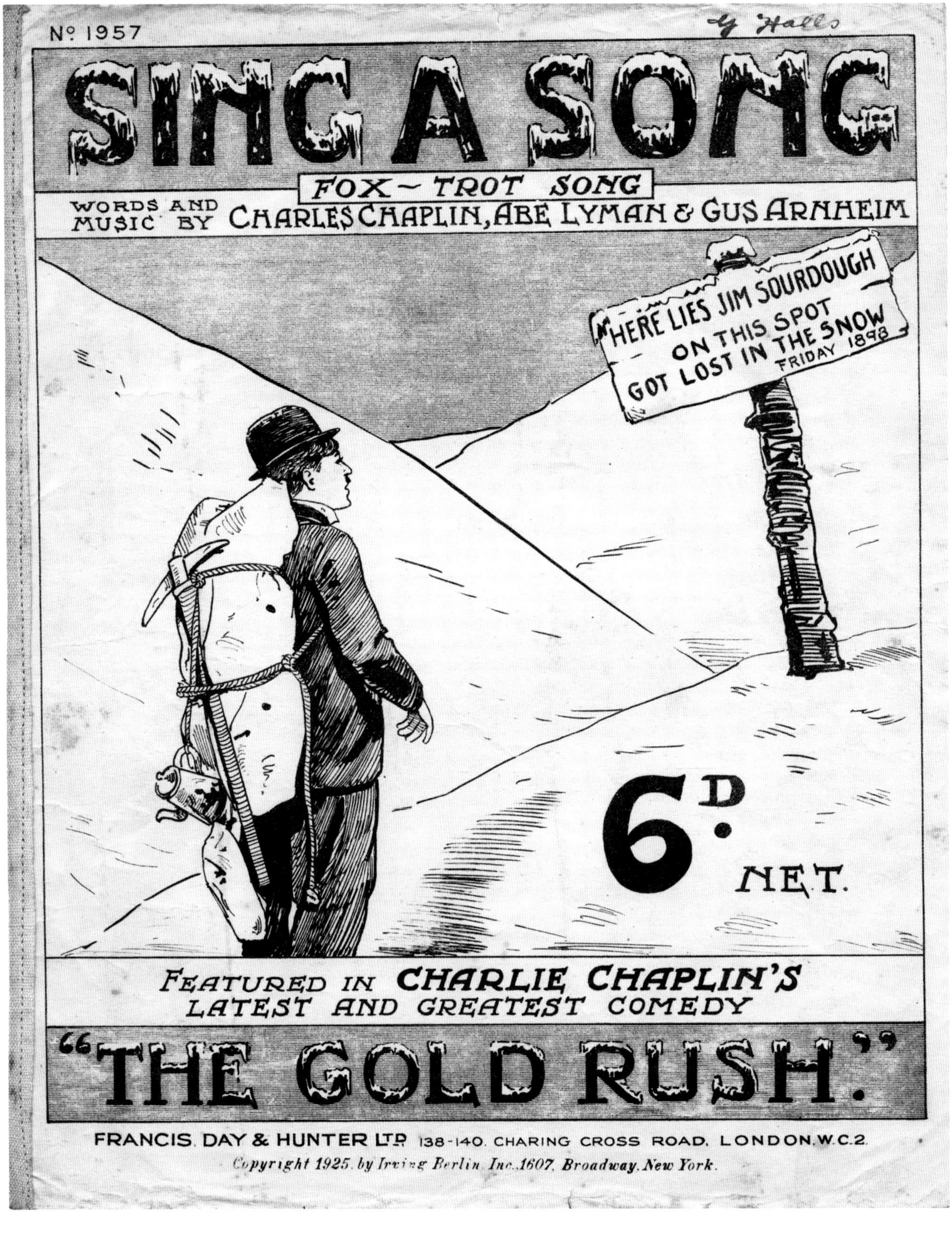
No. 1957
SING A SONG
FOX-TROT SONG
WORDS AND MUSIC BY CHARLES CHAPLIN, ABE LYMAN & GUS ARNHEIM
HERE LIES JIM SOURDOUGH
ON THIS SPOT
GOT LOST IN THE SNOW
FRIDAY 1898
6D. NET.
FEATURED IN CHARLIE CHAPLIN'S LATEST AND GREATEST COMEDY
"THE GOLD RUSH."
FRANCIS. DAY & HUNTER LTD 138-140. CHARING CROSS ROAD. LONDON. W.C.2.
Copyright 1925. by Irving Berlin. Inc. 1607, Broadway. New York.

Opposite

Sheet music for "Sing a Song," a song written by Chaplin, Abe Lyman, and Gus Arnheim in 1925. As for "With You, Dear, in Bombay," the sheet music for this song was published in 1925 illustrated with images from *The Gold Rush*, even though the lyrics have nothing to do with the film. The recordings of these songs could be played in movie theaters before or during the film.

Max Terr, assisted by Gerard Carbonara. It took him sixteen weeks to write, perform, and synchronize the soundtrack, using the working methods he had previously perfected for his three feature films of the 1930s.

Even when borrowing from classical or popular music, the choices were always Chaplin's. He added tunes that he himself had composed: he played them on the violin or piano, or sometimes contented himself with humming them, to Max Terr, who transcribed and arranged them and conducted the orchestra for the recording. The archives bear witness to this collaboration: of the sixty or so pieces that comprise the score (many more than that of the original version), forty were co-written by Terr and Chaplin. Except for two very brief interventions, Terr wrote only one piece alone, the "work" theme, which is played several times in the film, notably in the sequence in which the Tramp shovels snow to earn money. It is nevertheless in keeping with Chaplin's style, notably the glissando attacks and the irregular rhythm of the pauses—this "Chaplinism" of suspended time is also found in the arrangements of "La Violetera" (1931) and "Eternally" (1952), which speaks volumes about the filmmaker's influence over his collaborating musicians—even the most competent and creative ones.

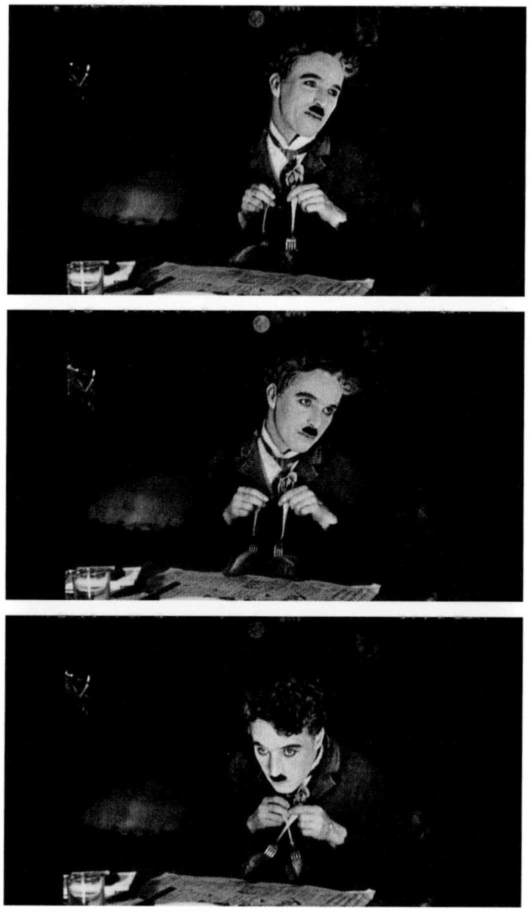

Below

The dance of the bread rolls, *The Gold Rush*, 1925.

As in *The Great Dictator*, released two years previously, classical themes, particularly from Brahms and Wagner, played an important role for the main themes. The "Love Theme" adapts for twelve bars of violin the andante of Brahms's Romance in F Major for Piano and the "Snow Theme" its Allegretto grazioso. Wagner's *Tannhäuser* ("O du mein holder Abendstern") inspired the "Hunger Theme." In the cabin, the Tramp resists the gusts of wind to Rimsky-Korsakov's "Flight of the Bumblebee," and the dance sequence with the Tramp and Georgia takes place to Tchaikovsky's *Sleeping Beauty* waltz. Finally, nine seconds of Rossini's *William Tell Overture* are perfectly in tune with the audience's laughter and suspense when the cabin is discovered hanging over the precipice after the storm.

Apart from three waltzes with tender or lively melodies and tempos attesting to the Chaplin touch ("Valse Mange," "Valse Charmante," and "Valse Élégante"), the most striking themes composed by Chaplin and arranged by Terr are "On the Trail" and "Pagliaplin": the first evoking the harshness of life in Alaska, the second expressing the Tramp's solitude faced with the hostility of nature and the indifference of men.

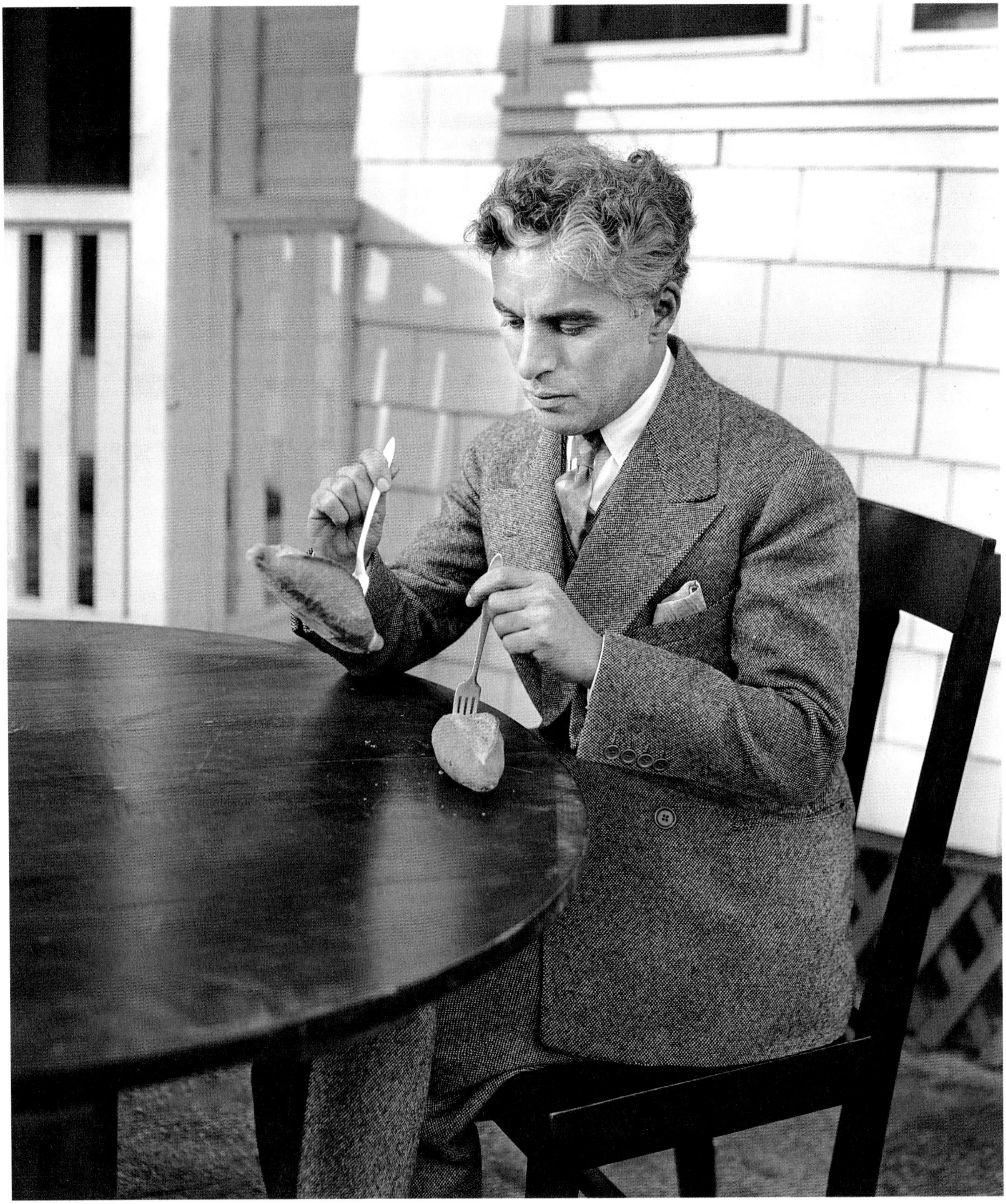

Opposite

Chaplin rehearsing the dance of the bread rolls, c. 1920–30.
"Long before he immortalized his 'dance of the rolls' on the screen, on many occasions when we lunched at Musso & Frank restaurant, Chaplin provided us with endless fun by draping a napkin round his neck like a curtain, spearing two rolls with forks and making them dance," said the journalist and filmmaker Robert Florey. This gag seems to have been a classic. In 1917, the actor Roscoe Arbuckle was the first to bring it to the screen in *The Rough House*.

Below

Chaplin and Max Terr conducting the orchestra during the recording of the music for *The Gold Rush*, 1942. Photograph by Max Munn Autrey. Meredith Willson's assistant for *The Great Dictator*, Max Terr worked with Chaplin for more than three months to compose and then record a soundtrack for *The Gold Rush*.

We should add the famous "Mother's Dance," which henceforth accompanies the "dance of the rolls." No one really knows who the "mother" of the title is: I favor Hannah, the mother of Charles and Sydney, who may have sung (danced?) them this tune. In any case, even though it was to "Oceana Roll" that Chaplin filmed the sequence in 1925, it was with music from his childhood that he chose to immortalize it.

But more than the question of sources, it is the writing that deserves attention. Without detriment to the unity of the sequences, the music of 1942 is more "fragmented" than that of 1925. It is what the Germans call *durchkomponiert*: music composed "according to the principle of permanent renewal of its substance," which develops through "short motifs repeated, twisted around, and made to measure for the action."[2] The leitmotifs are shortened, and undergo incessant instrumental and rhythmic variations in order to adapt to every situation and adventure, however short. A few bars of accordion from "Pretty Girl Milking Her Cow" accompany the fourteen seconds of famous shot in which the Tramp, seen from behind, looks through snowy windows into the dance hall. Four sforzando notes (F-D-A-F) signal imminent danger. The synchronization of image and sound is, moreover, strengthened and sometimes taken to the extreme by the practice of Mickey Mousing: a way of accompanying the action step by step, of intensifying it with crescendos and of highlighting it with sound effects. When the snow is blown into the Tramp's face through a hole in the wall, it is to the sound of a popping cork. Staccato and glissando accompany each of the hero's jumps and slides, two sixteenth notes (piccolo and pizzicato strings) each of his tips of the hat.

Inspired by the musical traditions of the silent film and of the talkie, Chaplin developed a personal style: one that best fitted his character and his adventures. No score could better serve the humor and pathos of *The Gold Rush* than that of 1942, because its aim was to make heard a music that was ever present, sewn into the fabric of the images from 1925. In his adaptation of this score to the original version of the film restored by David Gill and Kevin Brownlow in 1993, Timothy Brock has given us access to the *complete* masterpiece that Chaplin had dreamed of for his second feature film.

2 Michel Chion, *Les Lumières de la ville* (Paris: Nathan, 1989), 53.

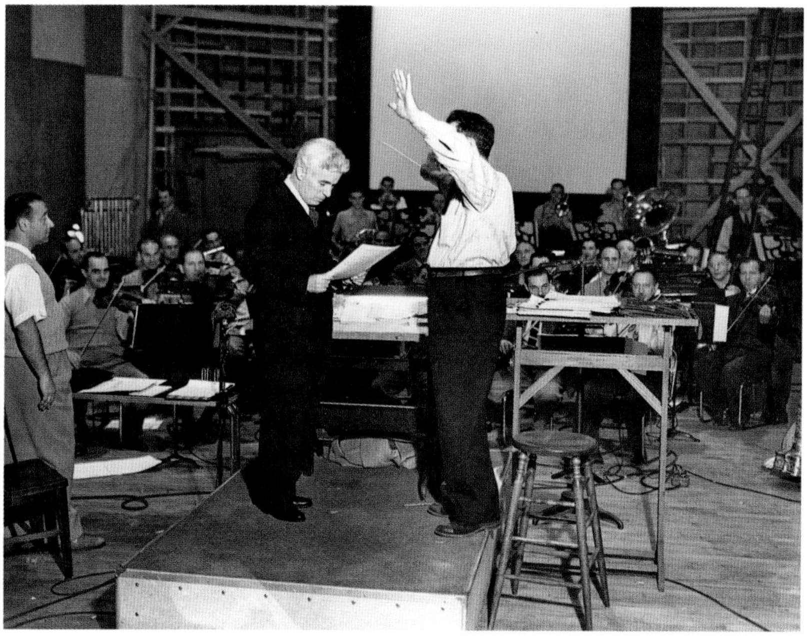

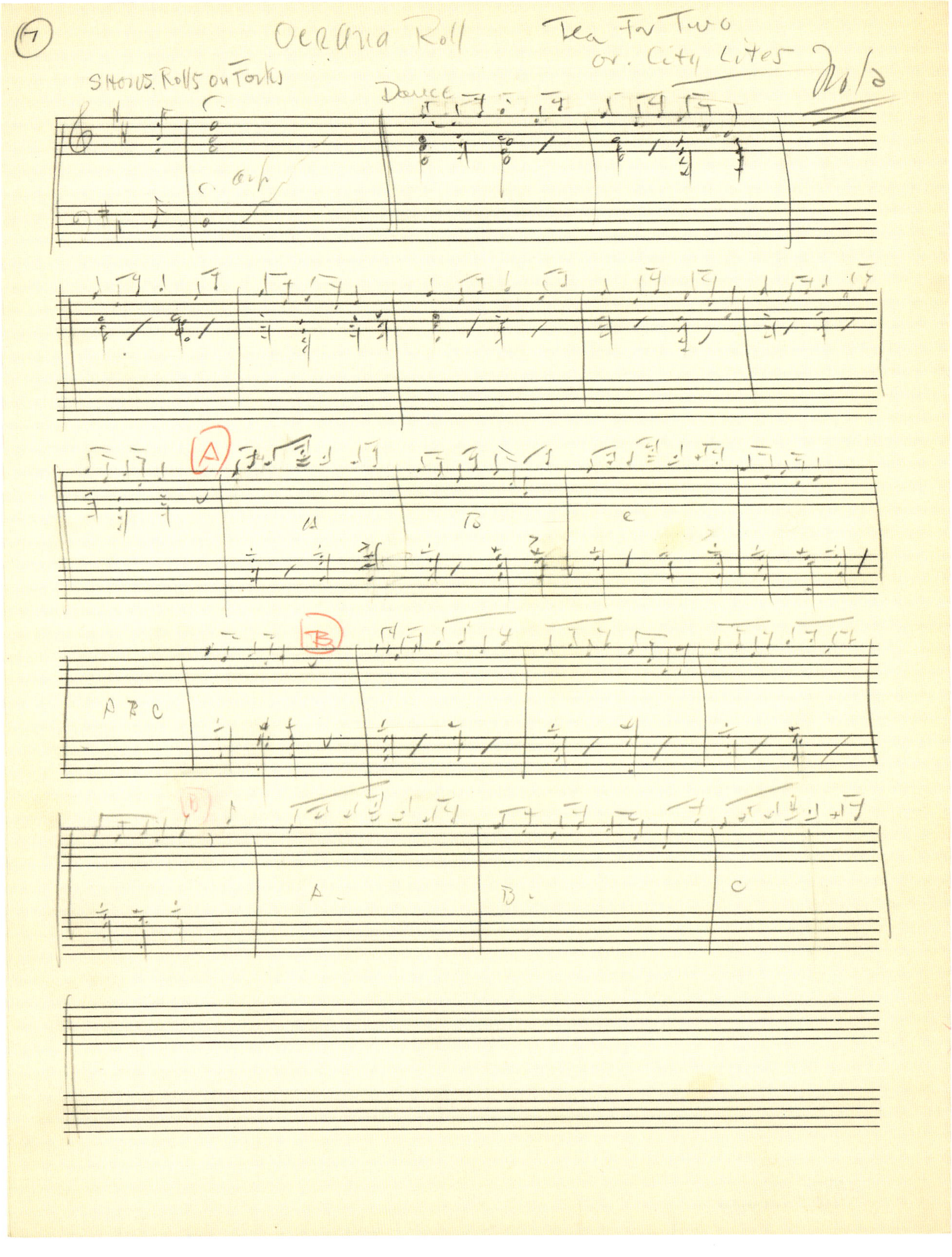

Oceana Roll
Tea For Two
or. City Lites
Shows Rolls on Forks
Dance
A
B

Left

Piano score, "Oceana Roll," 1942.
Titled "Oceana Roll" in reference to the intertitle of the silent version of the film, this score takes up the theme of "The Keel Row," a song from the popular repertoire used in the compilation for the first release of the film in 1925. Annotations at the top—"Tea for Two," "City Lites" [*sic*], and "Nola"—show that Chaplin was hesitating between several pieces of music to accompany the scene and even considered reusing themes from his previous films.

Right

Score for "Mother's Dance," 1942.
In the end, Chaplin and Max Terr composed new music to accompany the dance of the bread rolls. The original dotted eighth note-sixteenth note motifs, which seem to be a legacy of the swaying rhythm of "The Keel Row," were changed in pencil to triplets, catchier and lighter. The song's title remains unexplained: was Chaplin referring to his own mother, in memory of the acts that Hannah Chaplin put on to entertain her sons?

Following pages

Léo Kouper's poster for a later rerelease of *The Gold Rush* in the United Kingdom, 1950s.
At the release of the sound version of the film in 1942, the publicity focused on the addition of music and words to the original film. The reviews were enthusiastic. According to *Motion Picture Daily*, Chaplin, who produced, directed and wrote the silent version, composed an outstanding music score for this version, in addition to writing the narration and delivering it.

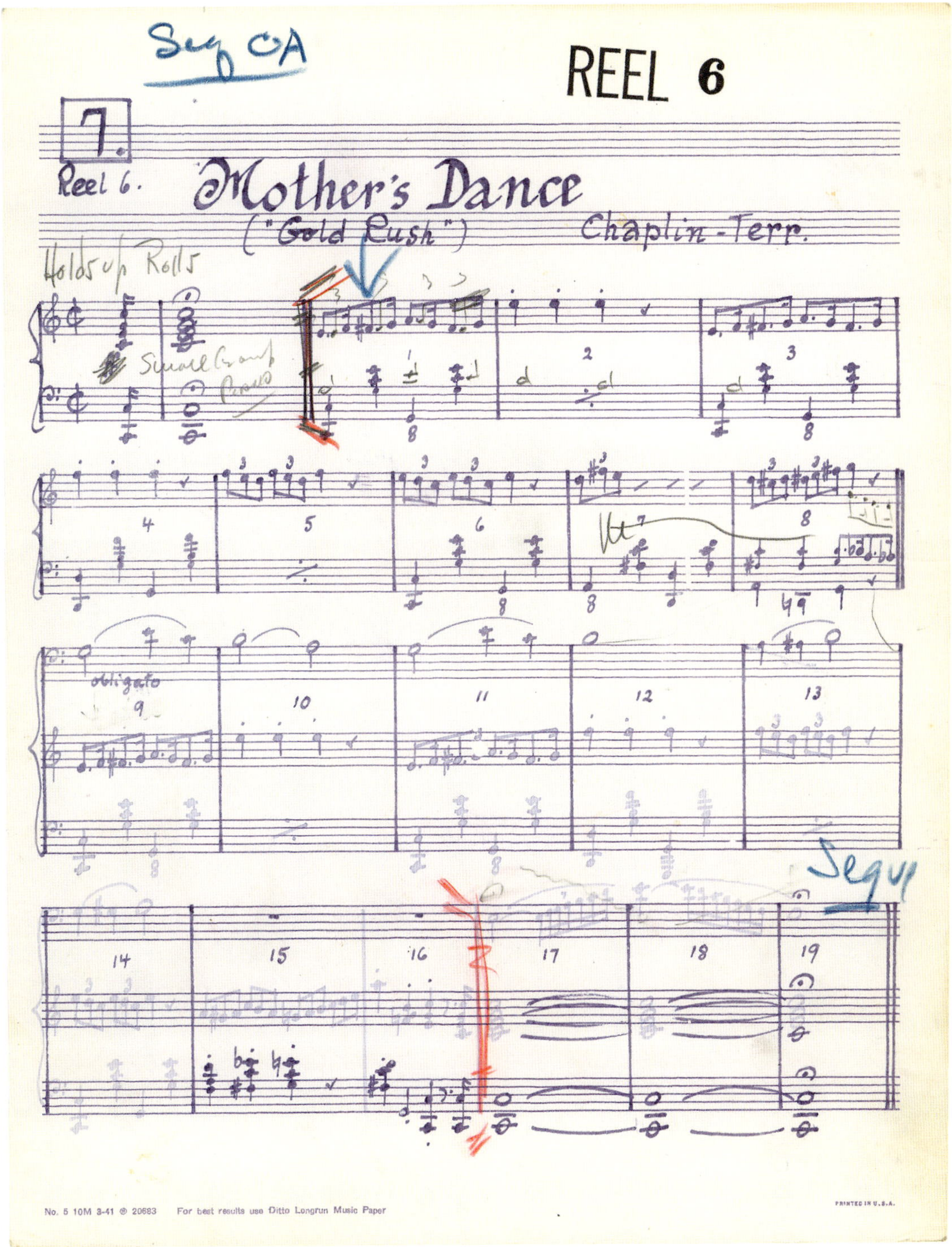

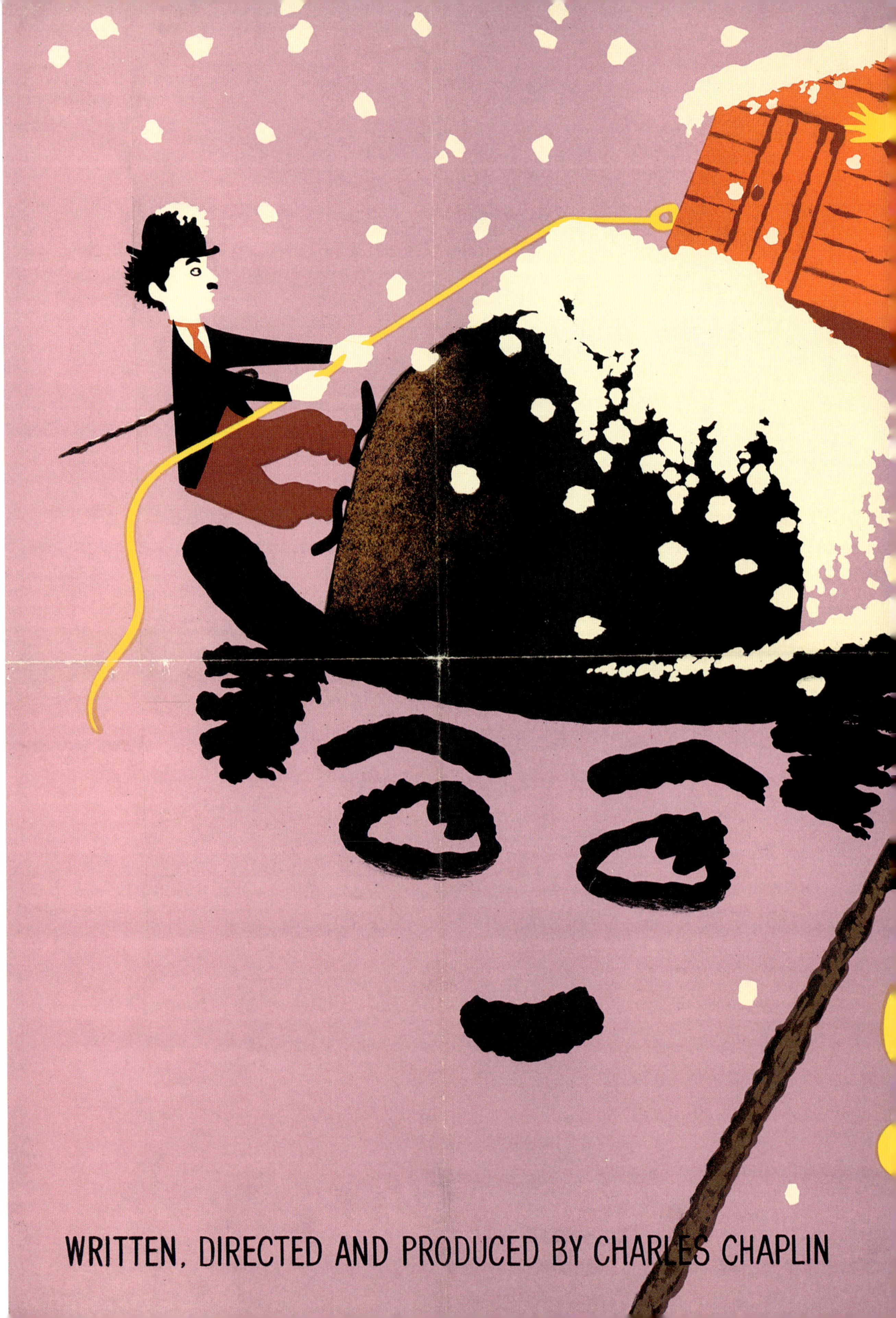
WRITTEN, DIRECTED AND PRODUCED BY CHARLES CHAPLIN

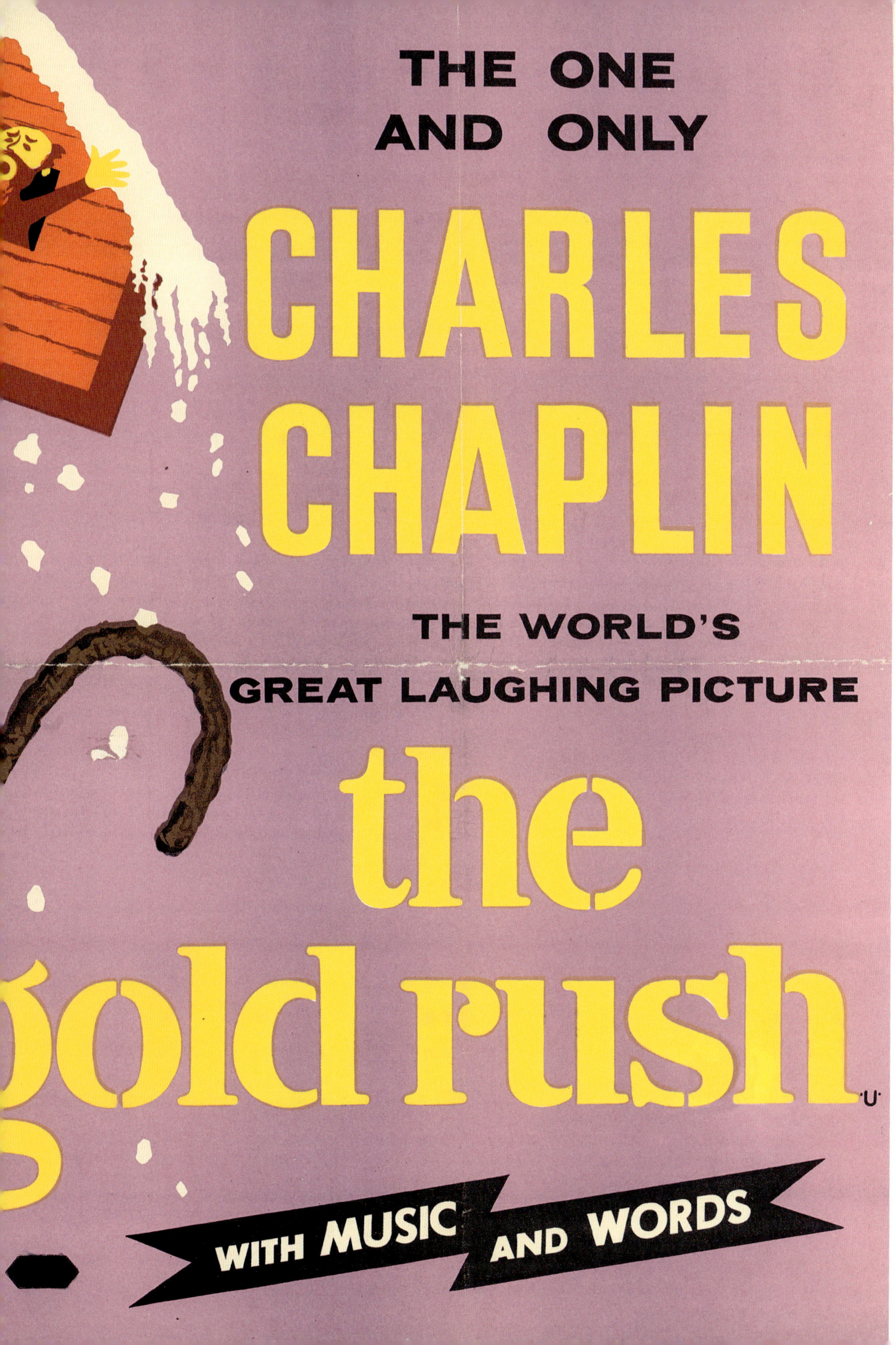
THE ONE
AND ONLY
CHARLES
CHAPLIN
THE WORLD'S
GREAT LAUGHING PICTURE
the
gold rush
'U'
WITH MUSIC AND WORDS

Charles Chaplin, Jr.

My Father, Charlie Chaplin

On composing for *Modern Times*
Though the filming of [*Modern Times*] was over, Dad still had his musical score to complete . . . Dad can't read a note of music himself, but he knew what he wanted, and when he wasn't getting it, and he wouldn't give up until it sounded right to him. He had some of the industry's top musical talent to help him.

Alfred Newman, who has won several Oscars and who at the time was under contract to Sam Goldwyn, was assigned to do the score and direct the music. David Raksin, the talented young composer who was later to make musical history with his tune "Laura," was hired, with Edward Powell, to take down and orchestrate Dad's music.

Dad wore them all out. Edward Powell concentrated so hard writing the music down that he almost lost his eyesight and had to go to a specialist to save it. David Raksin, working an average of twenty hours a day, lost twenty-five pounds and sometimes was so exhausted he couldn't find strength to go home but would sleep on the studio floor. Al Newman saw him one day in the studio street walking along with tears running down his cheeks.

But David still had plenty of resilience in him, enough to play an occasional prank on Dad by way of lightening the pressure. Dad had a recording machine similar to a Dictaphone, into which he would hum his tunes. This enabled him to work longer hours and have his ideas canned, ready for presentation when he and Raksin got together.

On composing for *The Great Dictator*
Syd and I, once again visiting the sets with our father, noticed the change in atmosphere from the old days when *Modern Times* was produced. Things had become much quieter. By quieter I don't mean calmer. The old silent-film camera, with its soft, friendly whine punctuated by faint staccato clickings, was gone. Dad felt awkward at first, acting in front of a camera that made no noise at all. It took him a while to realize that he had used the noise of the silent-film camera to establish his own rhythm. He now had to depend on his own inner timing.

[. . .]

[For *The Great Dictator*], because many of his sessions with the musicians were held at the house, I had the opportunity of watching first-hand a man who couldn't read a note and knew nothing of the mechanics of the art, work at being a composer—and drive men mad as he had Al Newman in earlier years. The musicians were actually musical secretaries taking Dad's dictation. The music was always his. He would hum or play his tune and the musicians would take it down and then play it back for him.

"That part's good," he'd say. "But there's something wrong here. Wait a minute."

He would concentrate and hum the phrase again, and the musicians would get back to their dictation. It might take a number of tries before Dad had the tune to his satisfaction.

He and the musicians not only worked long hours at home, but more long hours at the studio, where they used a Movieola so that a scene could be played, reversed and played again until the music to match it popped into Dad's head. Once he had it in its entirety he would give the musicians a description of how he wanted it scored for each scene—the tempo, the rhythm, the style. Though he knew some of the various musical forms and could correctly use a great deal of terminology such as *pizzicato*, *rubato*, *allegro* and the like, he preferred to describe what he wanted by referring to a composer's name or an instrumental label by way of illustration.

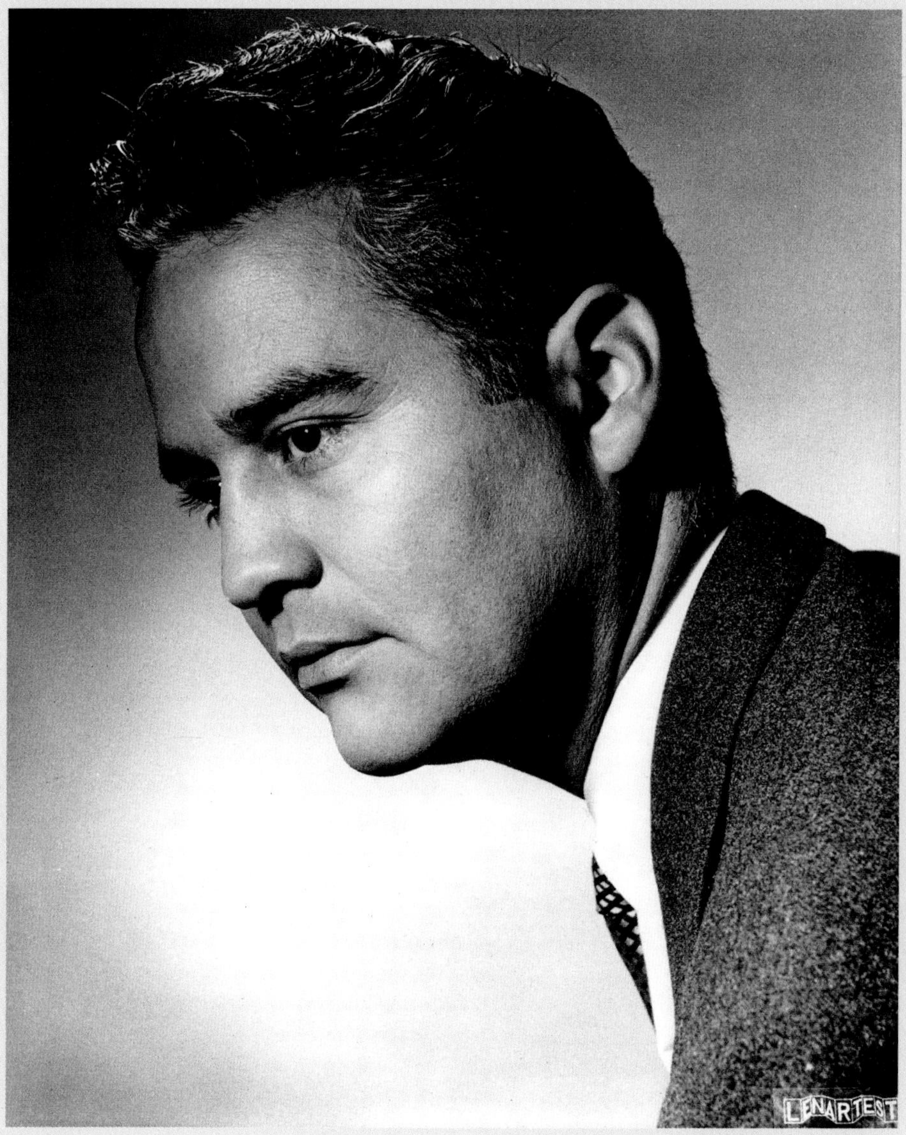

"We should make this Wagnerian," he would say, or "This part should be more Chopin. Let's make this light and airy, a lot of violins. I think we could use an oboe effect in this passage."

Sometimes when Dad described what he wanted the musicians would shake their heads, because Dad's timing of a musical phrase to suit a bit of action was sometimes so unorthodox it threw them off. They would try to explain the technical reasons for not being able to give him what he asked for.

"Well I'm not concerned about that," Dad would say. "Just put it down here the way I want it."

It was only after they'd done so that they could see that, though unorthodox, Dad's dramatic instinct as it related to music was brilliant. So phrase after phrase, literally note by note, Dad and his valiant musicians worked their way through *The Great Dictator*. The musicians turned gray and were on the verge of nervous breakdowns by the time it was over, but whatever they suffered they couldn't say that working with Dad was ever dull. He gave them a free performance at every session, because he didn't just hum or sing, or knock out a tune on the piano. He couldn't stay quiet that long. He would start gesturing with the music, acting out the parts of the various people in the scene he was working on, but caricaturing their movements to evoke a tonal response in himself. At those times his acting was closer than ever to ballet.

Excerpts from Charles Chaplin, Jr., *My Father, Charlie Chaplin*, London: Longmans Green, 1961.

Left

Charles Chaplin, Jr., in the 1950s.

Jim Lochner

Charlie Chaplin: the world's most curious composer

In a musical career that spanned over fifty years, Charlie Chaplin composed over two dozen published songs and nearly 900 minutes of film music, a remarkable achievement for someone who could not read or write music.

Chaplin's first public foray into music was the Charlie Chaplin Music Publishing Company, which he co-founded in 1916 with his old friend and former Keystone co-worker, vaudevillian Bert Clark. Located in a room on the third floor of Blanchard Hall, a now-demolished downtown Los Angeles office building devoted exclusively to music, art, and science, the company printed "two very bad songs and musical compositions of mine," Chaplin wrote in his autobiography, "then we waited for customers."[1] Once word got out, other publishers wanted a piece of the potentially lucrative pie, while newspapers and trade journals wondered if "the eminent artist whose ability to run down an ascending escalator or tap another gentleman on the coco with a billet of stove wood" was the same Charlie Chaplin listed as the composer of "Oh! That Cello," "There's Always One You Can't Forget," and "The Peace Patrol." "We do not know," said the *Music Trade Review*, "but we certainly do care."[2] Unfortunately, not enough people did. "The enterprise was collegiate and quite mad," Chaplin admitted. "I think we sold three copies, one to Charles Cadman, the American composer, and two to pedestrians who happened to pass our office on their way downstairs."[3] The office closed after a month.

As Chaplin took greater control over his films, he asserted greater authority over the music. He helped arrange the compilation scores for *The Kid*, *A Woman of Paris*, *The Gold Rush*, and *The Circus* and co-wrote two promotional songs ("Sing a Song" and "With You, Dear, in Bombay") for *The Gold Rush*. It was not until the arrival of sound and *City Lights* that Chaplin was ready to put his personal musical stamp on a film. But the task of writing eighty-two minutes of original film music was a daunting prospect, especially for an unschooled composer with unorthodox compositional methods.

Opposite

Sheet music for "Oh! That Cello," "There's Always One You Can't Forget," and "The Peace Patrol," songs written by Chaplin, 1916.

1 Charles Chaplin, *My Autobiography* (New York: Simon and Schuster, 1964), 226.

2 "Q R S Co.," *The Music Trade Review*, August 26, 1916, 15.

3 Chaplin, *My Autobiography*, 226.

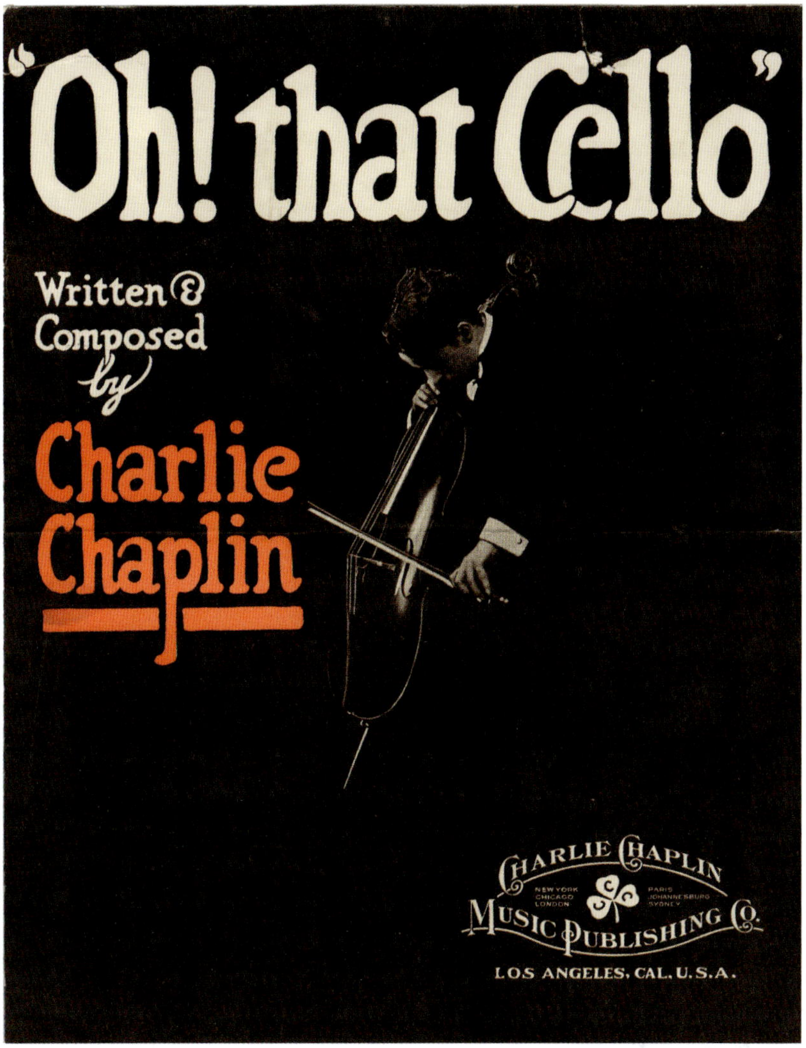
"Oh! that Cello"
Written & Composed by
Charlie Chaplin
Charlie Chaplin Music Publishing Co.
New York Chicago London
Paris Johannesburg Sydney
LOS ANGELES, CAL. U.S.A.

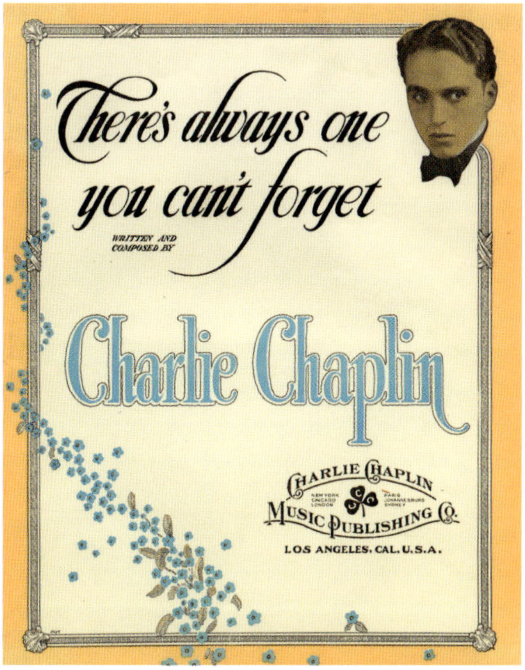
There's always one you can't forget
Written and composed by
Charlie Chaplin
Charlie Chaplin Music Publishing Co.
LOS ANGELES, CAL. U.S.A.

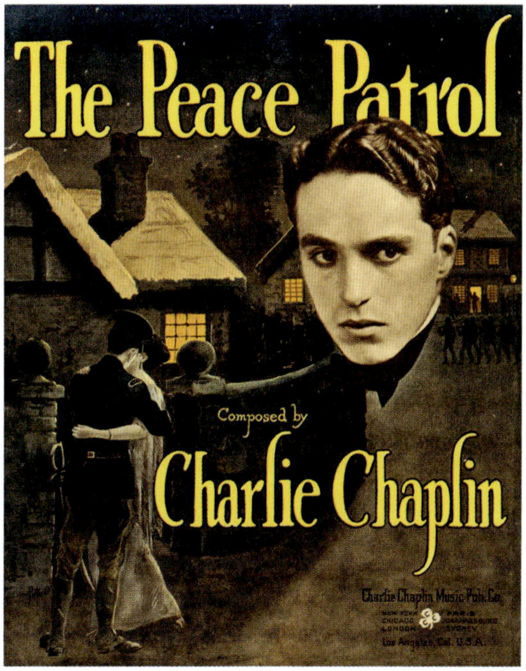
The Peace Patrol
Composed by
Charlie Chaplin
Charlie Chaplin Music Pub. Co.
Los Angeles, Cal. U.S.A.

Below

Charles Dunworth, Alfred Newman, Chaplin, David Raksin, Paul Neal, and Edward Powell during the recording of *Modern Times*, autumn 1935. Chaplin poses with his musical team: Raksin and Powell, arrangers; Newman, conductor; Dunworth, his assistant; and Neal, sound engineer. Recording lasted three weeks, during which Chaplin fell out with Newman who was replaced as conductor by Powell.

With no formal musical training, Chaplin relied on a string of musical collaborators over the years to translate his humming, singing, and amateur violin and piano playing into a cohesive score. Chaplin wanted his amanuenses, arrangers, and orchestrators to be malleable, and he often hired musicians with little or no experience when it came to the nuts and bolts of film music. Working with Chaplin was not easy and most of his music associates did not last for more than one film. "As a matter of record," said Associated Press journalist Henry Gris, who filed a lengthy report from the set of *Limelight*, "few musicians have found it possible to work with Chaplin who tolerates no contradiction. He plays by ear in one key, that of 'F,' even if he doesn't know it, but goes into a tantrum when corrected or told his tune is wrongly constructed."[4] According to Charles Chaplin, Jr., during the scoring of *The Great Dictator* he watched "first-hand a man who couldn't read a note and knew nothing of the mechanics of the art, work at being a composer—and drive men mad."[5]

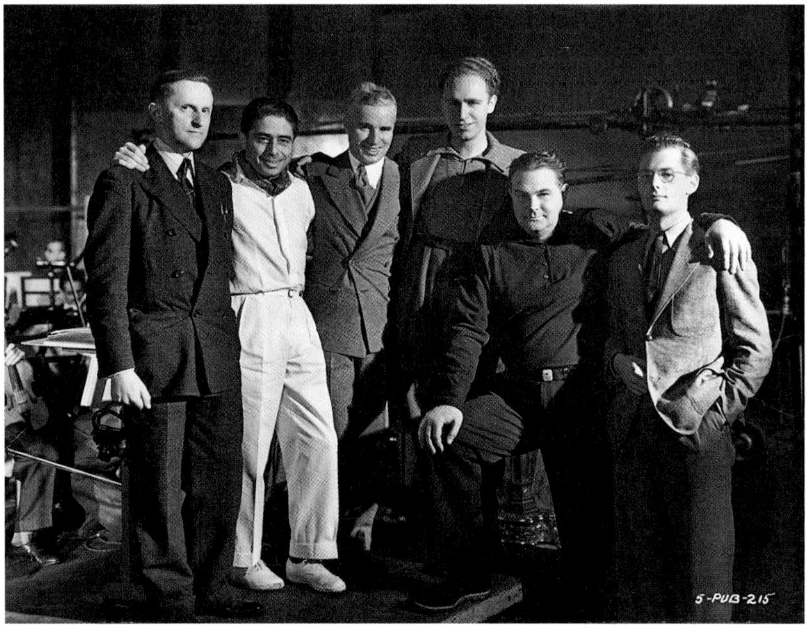

Both David Raksin, arranger on *Modern Times*, and Eric James, Chaplin's music associate for the last twenty years of his life, claimed Chaplin used only the first three fingers of his right hand to demonstrate his musical ideas on the piano. "Wrong notes would resound unceasingly while he played," James wrote in his autobiography *Making Music with Charlie Chaplin*. "My job, after listening to the . . . basic melody line, was to formulate them into an acceptable musical composition, which I would then play back to him complete with chords and harmony. Hopefully, he would accept it. If not, he would ask me to try again or to emphasize this or that aspect of the melody and harmony or to change the mood and so on. This was a tremendous challenge because his first thoughts were virtually random jottings of his melodic ideas, and bore very little or no resemblance to the finished product. An hour or more would frequently be spent on perhaps one or two bars of the music until eventually his face would light up with a smile and he would say, 'I'll buy that' (the only 'Americanism' I ever heard him use during my long association with him)."[6] James said he and Chaplin "must have presented a comic sight while at work because we would constantly be changing places at the piano. He would try to indicate with his limited playing ability what he was after and I would

4 Henry Gris, "Hollywood Chaplin," ECCI00030190, Chaplin Archive, 16.
5 Charles Chaplin, Jr., and N. and M. Rau, *My Father, Charlie Chaplin* (New York: Random House, 1960), 228.
6 Eric James, *Making Music with Charlie Chaplin: An Autobiography* (Lanham, MD: The Scarecrow Press, Inc., 2000), 64.

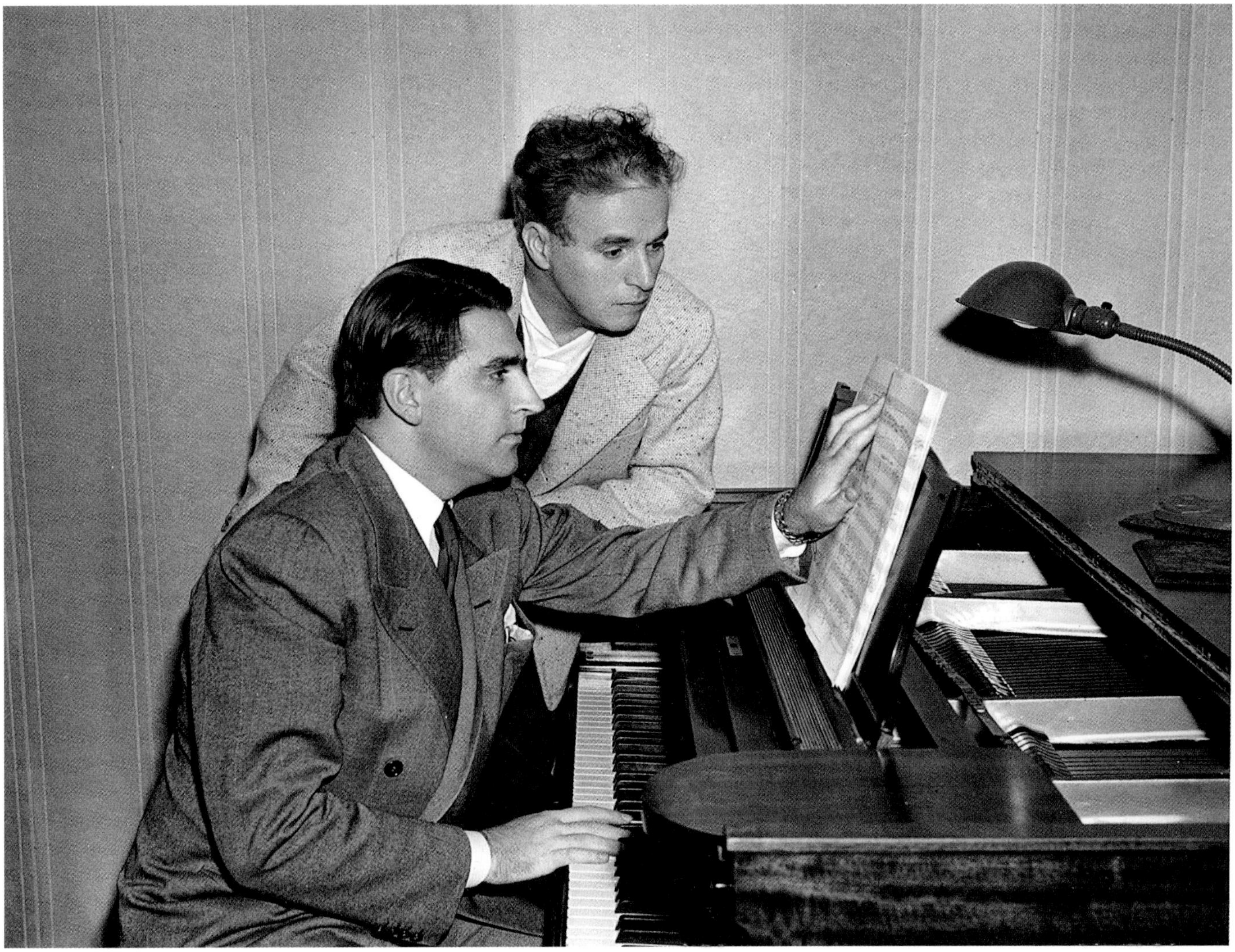

Above

Chaplin and Meredith Willson, 1940. Photograph by Max Munn Autrey. Meredith Willson was hired by Chaplin to "write, compose, orchestrate, arrange, prepare, rehearse, direct and record, and to supervise the writing, composition, orchestration, arrangement, preparation, rehearsal, direction, recordation and dubbing of, the complete musical score" of *The Great Dictator*. Willson highlighted Chaplin's perfectionism: "I have never met a man who devoted himself so completely to the ideal of perfection as Charlie Chaplin. I was constantly amazed at his attention to detail, his feeling for the exact musical phrase or tempo to express the mood he wanted."

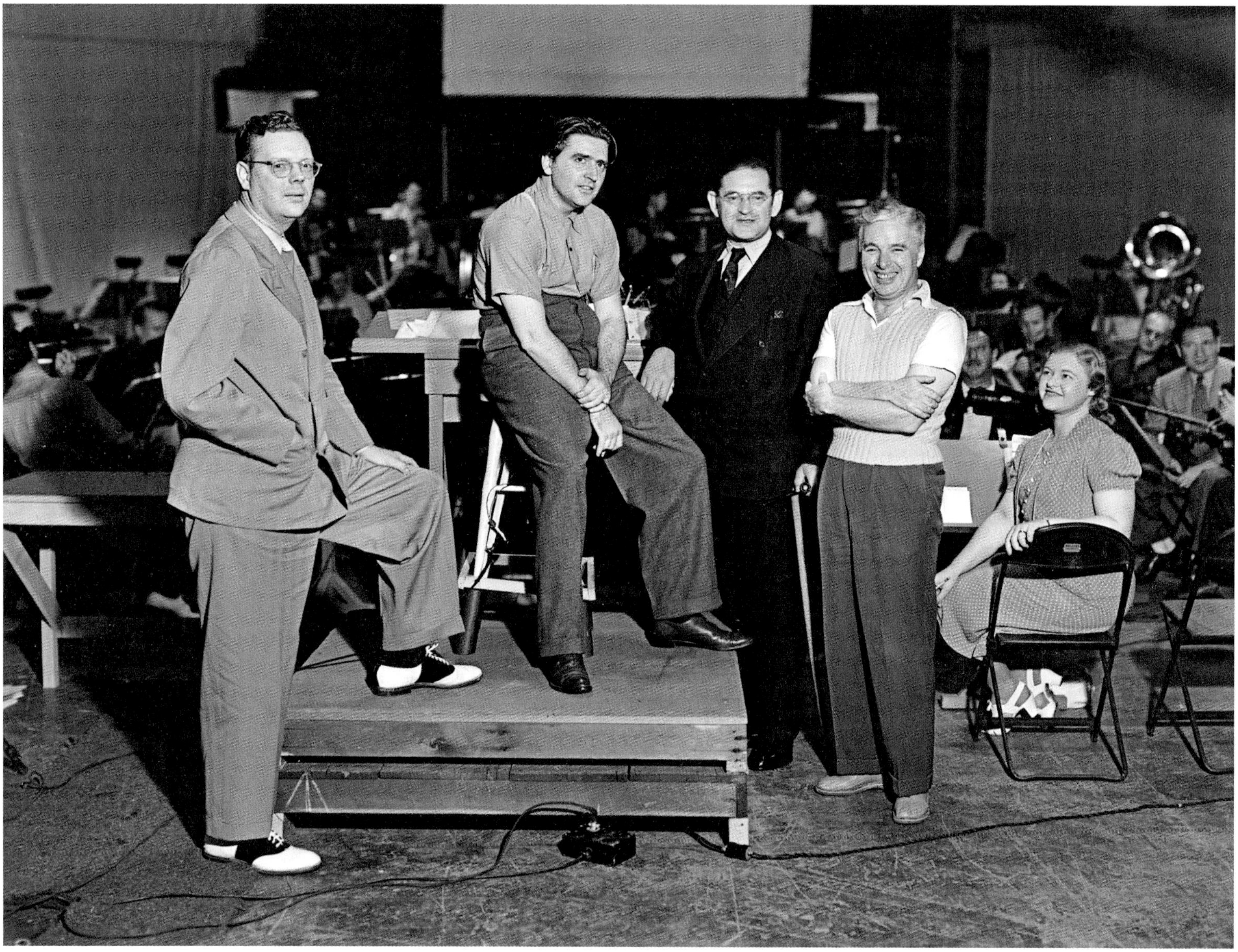

Left

Chaplin's musical team during the recording of *The Great Dictator*, 1940.

immediately change places and try to create the melody line that I felt he was searching for. It was like a game of musical chairs!"[7]

An even bigger challenge, James said, was transcribing Chaplin's singing, which was "as out of tune as his playing and I used to dread this form of composition." Chaplin also sang his melodies "far more quickly than it was possible for me to transcribe them on paper. Patience was not one of Chaplin's virtue[s] and he would frequently shout, 'Haven't you got it down yet?' My reply was always the same: 'I am a musician not a magician. I can only write music at a speed which is anatomically possible.' I usually then added, 'If you will sing a little slower I'll be able to keep up with you.' He would then apologize and we would continue on and make good progress for a while at least."[8]

Chaplin also jotted down on paper the names of famous pieces of classical music that contained the notes he required (e.g., "first two notes of Grieg's 'Morning,'" "next four notes, those in the opening bars of Liszt's 'Liebestraum'")[9] or invoked the names of legendary composers, exhorting his collaborators to "make this Wagnerian" or "this part should be more Chopin."[10] Chaplin also had definite ideas about orchestration, apportioning certain music to the violins, others to the woodwinds, an obbligato to the cello, etc., until every phrase had been allocated. "It was," James said, "the most arduous and difficult way I've ever heard of in music composition."[11]

When a melody satisfied Chaplin, "he would go over it and over it," *Limelight* arranger Raymond Rasch told *The New York Times*. "He didn't seem to care that I was just playing on a piano. He would ask for French horns in one spot: then violins and cellos and woodwinds. I just kept pounding away until he was satisfied."[12] Chaplin would stride about the room at his home humming as Rasch struggled to keep up on the piano, occasionally varying the routine by bellowing the melodies while lying stretched out on a couch. "I hear plucking," Chaplin would say. "I want something 'nasty-nice' but not disgusting."[13] "At first," Rasch said, "I was sure that I had met up with a madman. I couldn't believe that this was genius at work. He would bellow for hours at a time and all that I could hear was a senseless jumble."[14]

One day, Rasch was transcribing Chaplin's humming, and, according to the report by Gris, Chaplin was "expressing as best he could the melody that sung inside him. Before long Rasch was going through the most complicated calisthenics, trying to reproduce on the piano the instruments Chaplin had in mind. 'Now the French horns,' he ordered, 'where are the French horns?' A moment later, 'Where is the counter melody?' When he stomped, 'Where is the harp?' Rasch stopped abruptly, and looked up. 'There is no harp here,' he said, 'this is only a piano.' Chaplin shuddered and his eyes winked as though he had just been slapped. It was as if he had been mistreated by crude reality that wouldn't let a piano be anything else."[15]

7 Ibid., 65.
8 Ibid.
9 Ibid., 71.
10 Chaplin Jr., Rau, Rau, *My Father, Charlie Chaplin*, 228.
11 James, *Making Music with Charlie Chaplin*, 71.
12 Thomas Pryor, "How Mr. Chaplin Makes a Movie," *The New York Times*, February 17, 1952, 22.
13 "*Limelight* . . . with Tunes by a Man who Can't Write Music . . . !," *Bristol* (UK) *Evening World*, February 3, 1953.
14 Pryor, "How Mr. Chaplin Makes a Movie," 22.
15 Gris, "Hollywood Chaplin," 13.

"The musicians turned gray and were on the verge of nervous breakdowns by the time it was over," Charlie Chaplin, Jr., said, "but whatever they suffered they couldn't say that working with Dad was ever dull. He gave them a free performance at every session, because he didn't just hum or sing, or knock out a tune on the piano. He couldn't stay quiet that long. He would start gesturing with the music, acting out the parts of the various people in the scene he was working on, but caricaturing their movements to evoke a tonal response in himself. At those times his acting was closer than ever to ballet."[16]

"I tried to compose elegant and romantic music to frame my comedies in contrast to the tramp character," Chaplin explained in his autobiography, "for elegant music gave my comedies an emotional dimension. Musical arrangers rarely understood this. They wanted the music to be funny. But I would explain that I wanted no competition, I wanted the music to be a counterpoint of grace and charm, to express sentiment, without which, as Hazlitt says, a work of art is incomplete. Sometimes a musician would get pompous with me and talk of the restricted intervals of the chromatic and the diatonic scale, and I would cut him short with a layman's remark: 'Whatever the melody is, the rest is just a vamp.'"[17]

"The truth of the matter is that I don't know a note," Chaplin admitted in a 1925 interview. "I can't read music, and what I have learnt," he said, pointing to a phonograph in the corner of his office, "I owe to this teacher."[18] "Chaplin's musical genius is that of organized revolt against conventions combined with perfect feeling for the real thing," Raymond Rasch told Henry Gris. "[It] is closely connected with his inner hearing, the way he hears the world, his eyes closed . . . He doesn't know, just feels, but it's fabulous!"[19]

Fabulous . . . and curious.

Below

Chaplin with Ray Rasch (center) and Keith Williams (left) during the recording of *Limelight*, June 1952. Rasch was responsible for the arrangement and Williams conducted the orchestra. Rasch said the following about Chaplin: "At first I was sure I had met up with a madman. I couldn't believe this was genius at work. He would bellow for hours at a time and all that I could hear was a senseless jumble. But suddenly he would strike a note or sometimes a whole phrase and would scream at me to play it and jot down the notes.

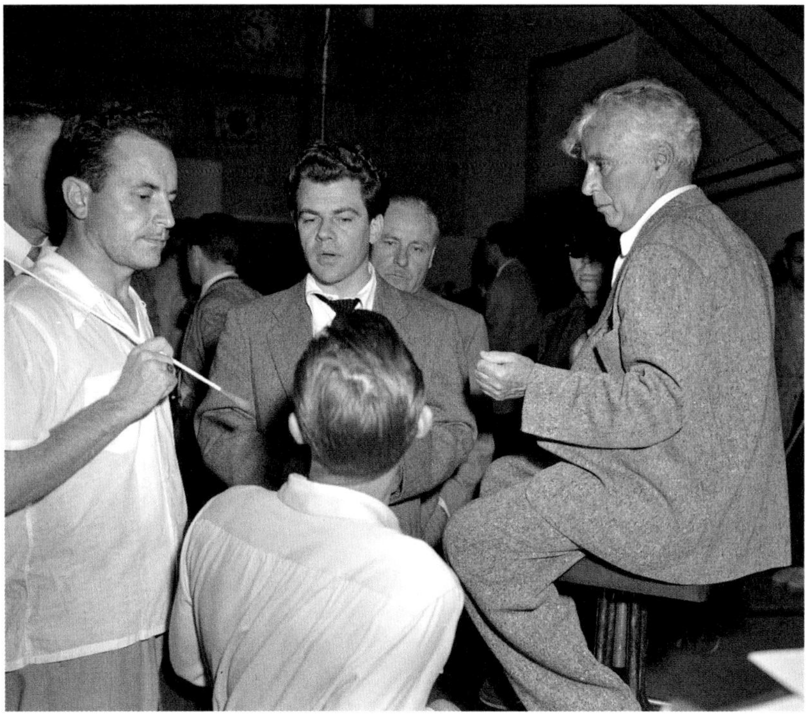

16 Chaplin Jr., Rau, Rau, *My Father, Charlie Chaplin*, 228.

17 Chaplin, *My Autobiography*, 328.

18 Konrad Bercovici, "Making a Picture with Charlie Chaplin," *The Royal Magazine*, 1925, 490.

19 Gris, "Hollywood Chaplin," 17.

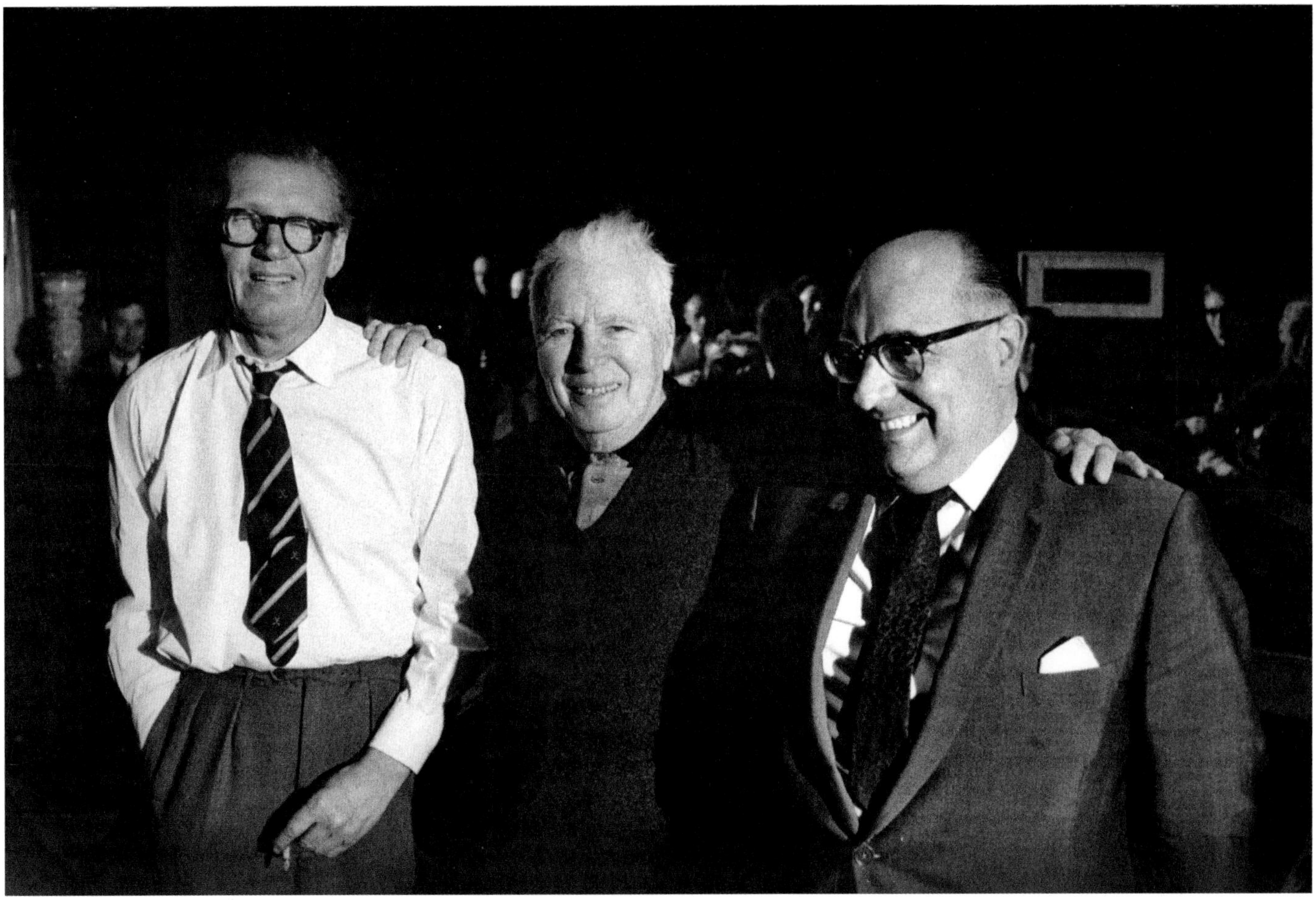

Above

Chaplin, Lambert Williamson (left), and Eric James (right) during the recording of "This Is My Song," c. 1966. James and Williamson worked with Chaplin on several films, as arranger and conductor respectively. James, who met Chaplin during the filming of *A King in New York*, worked with him until 1976 at the Manoir de Ban in Corsier-sur-Vevey. Chaplin left him progressively more latitude in the choice of compositions.

David Raksin

Life with Charlie

Charlie would usually arrive at the studio in midmorning, at which point the staff, which had been notified that he was *en route*, would spring into activity; Carter De Haven, Jr., the son of one of Chaplin's cronies (and now a film producer), would alert me. I would put aside the sketches of the previous day or so, on which I was working, and join Charlie in the projection room. Our equipment included a small grand piano, a phonograph, a portable tape recorder, a large screen for the 35 mm projectors, and a smaller one for the "Goldberg ," a projection moviola that could also back up in sync.

When he appeared, Charlie was generally armed with a couple of musical phrases; in the beginning, apparently because he thought me as an innocent, he seemed to enjoy telling me that he got some of his best ideas "while meditating [raising of eyebrow]—on the throne, you know." Innocent or not, few composers can afford to be squeamish about the *loci* of the muse, so unless one of us had some other idea that could not wait we would first review the music leading to the sequence at hand and then go on to the new ideas. First, I would write them down; then we would run the footage over and over, discussing the scenes and the music. Sometimes we would use his tune, or we would alter it, or one of us might invent another melody. I should say that I always began by wanting to defer to him; not only was it his picture, but I was working from the common attitude that since I was ostensibly the arranger the musical ideas were his prerogative.

Here it may be valuable to discuss the nature of the collaboration which Chaplin found necessary, and which has invariably been misinterpreted. For example, in an article by one of Chaplin's biographers, Theodore Huff, in the very first paragraph we read, "When *City Lights* first appeared with the credit title 'Music composed by Charles Chaplin' . . . [people] assumed that Chaplin was stretching it a bit in order that the public be certain that from him came everything in the film." The fact is that in *City Lights* as in all of his films, Chaplin was assisted by another composer; in that instance it was Arthur Johnston . . . I do not know how large a part Johnston played in that score, but I did discuss the music for *The Great Dictator* with the man who assisted Chaplin on that film.

The Great Dictator was Charlie's first real talkie; although he had used a sound track in *City Lights* and *Modern Times*, he had only been heard in the "Titina" sequence of the latter film. The composer who worked with Chaplin on *The Great Dictator* was Meredith Willson . . . an old friend who authorized me to quote him: "I know you will want to make it clear that Charlie was a very brilliant man, a very creative man. He would come into the studio they had given me to work in, and he would have ideas to suggest—melodies. After that, he would leave me alone. When he came in to see me again I would show him what I was doing, and often he would have very good suggestions to make. He liked to act as though he knew more music than he actually did, but his ideas were very good." [...]

From Meredith's account of his experience, it seems clear that he had more to do with the score for *The Great Dictator* that I had with *Modern Times*. Charlie and I worked hand in hand. Sometimes the initial phrases were several phrases long, and sometimes they consisted of only a few notes, which Charlie would whistle, or hum, or pick out on the piano. Thus far, it does not seem too different from what Willson has recounted. But here the differences begin. Where Meredith retreated to his studio to write, I remained in the projection room, where Charlie and I worked together to extend and develop the musical ideas to fit what was on the screen. When you have only a few notes or a short phrase with which to cover a scene of some length, there must ensue considerable development and variation—what is called for is the application of the techniques of composition to shape and extend the themes to the proportions . . . No informed person has claimed that Charlie had any of the essential techniques. But neither did he feed me a little tune and say "You take it from there." On the contrary; we spent hours, days, months in that projection room, running scenes and bits of action over and over, and we had a marvelous time shaping the music until it was exactly the way we wanted it. By the time we were through with a sequence we had run it so often that we were certain the music was in perfect sync. Very few film composers work this way . . . the usual procedure is to work from timing sheets, with a stop clock, to coordinate image and music.

Extracts from "Life with Charlie", published in *The Quarterly Journal of the Library of Congress*, 1983.

Timothy Brock

Chaplin's musical style

To Chaplin, music had the potential of compensating for everything sound had to offer but also lacked. His writing was so moment-specific, so tightly synchronized, that one can nearly follow a Chaplin film hearing only the score—for example, the musical portraits he paints of the tramp with the Promenade of *City Lights*, first heard in the sidewalk scene with the newsboys, or the impish Gamin music of *Modern Times* as Paulette Goddard dashes away having stolen food for her destitute family. If one could imagine the final scene of *City Lights* with dissimilar music, it would be another film entirely.

He always had an interest in the music for his feature films but not until *City Lights* did he self-compose his first score—a tremendous challenge when what people knew of his music, if anything, was a handful of songs and a few Brunswick records. The pressure of composing an eighty-two-minute score, to be heard by millions of people around the world, must have been more than great.

With all his film scores, Chaplin was aided by what he termed as a "musical associate." This was a person who, to varying degrees of participation, helped with the notation and orchestration of his compositions. Chaplin played both the violin and piano by ear, but, like many of the great popular composers of any era (Irving Berlin included), was unable to transcribe the notes on paper. Yet however constrained in his ability to notate his work, nearly every score has the indelible Chaplin mark. What is often forgotten is the degree of his involvement in nearly every step of the process: no matter who the associate, the musical structure and approach remain distinctively his own.

The term "Chaplinesque" is more and more frequently used by musicologists as a point of reference to his chordal and melodic structures, and it is certainly not by accident that all his films both look, and sound, like Chaplin. Furthermore, the soundtracks contain specific unique stylistic choices. Chaplin's violin playing style was unambiguously his own, and through the carefully transcribed annotations by his musical associates the performing string player was (and still is) compelled to mimic his specific style of playing, ever-present in the extended violin solos in each of his scores, by far the most intimate and personal portrayal of the Little Tramp he had to offer.

For *City Lights*, he developed the airs of finesse and the set pieces of light accompaniment as used by the Karno Company to serve comedy into his own tastes in score writing, along with his already established penchant for rather poignant melodies and heavy yet lively dances. Because ultimately the film was to be without dialogue, he understood that the music needed to go beyond all expectations of what a typical music soundtrack of the 1930s would accomplish. The *City Lights* score was written for an Abe Lyman-size "dance orchestra," a line-up Chaplin knew personally, and knew how to write for. The film is very intimate and the music reflects that, full of incredible delicacy in notational ornamentation and other general intricacies of the 1920s and 1930s Hollywood musician.

At an orchestra's first rehearsal of *City Lights* I point out that, like any form of period music, we shall endeavor to observe the period performance rules. We are not imitating our orchestral parentage, but rather our great-grandparentage. To this end, I have always found a somewhat guilty pleasure in asking the clarinetists to play certain passages with heavy vibrato, the vibraphonists to turn the fan speed up to "maximum," or the tuba player if he or she could play a Bell Front or Sousaphone instead of a concert tuba. This was par-for-the-course stylistically at the time, but is completely hidden to the modern player. As in era-sensitive Baroque performances, there is a specific, and unwritten, manner in which the musician is expected to perform these scores. The ever-present *portamenti* in the strings, the burnished intensity of vibrato, the way in which *staccato* marks were executed, were all standard performing procedure throughout the 1920s and 1930s.

In the modern orchestral setting, we are also confronted with specific instruments or ancillary items that no longer exist. To each upcoming Chaplin performance I personally take a set of 1924 and 1926 choke cymbals, 1929 vibraphone mallets (with inaudible attack ability), and two 1930 Solo-tone mutes for trumpet and trombone—all called for in a Chaplin score, yet none manufactured today.

Below

Chaplin posing with Abe Lyman's band, c. 1925. Chaplin regularly collaborated with Abe Lyman and his band. Musicians were sometimes present on set to help create atmosphere for the actors, notably during the filming of *The Gold Rush*. Chaplin composed his first soundtracks, such as *City Lights*, with this type of small band in mind.

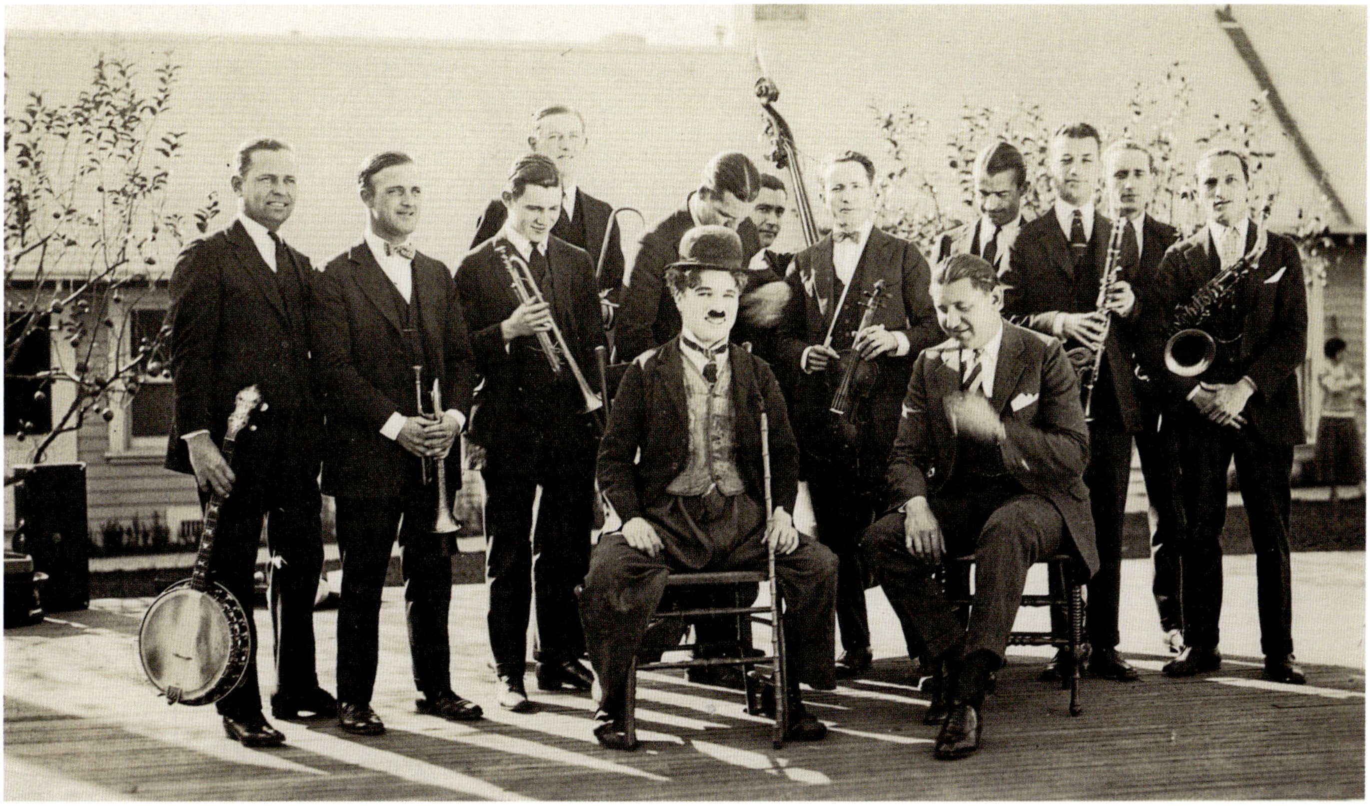

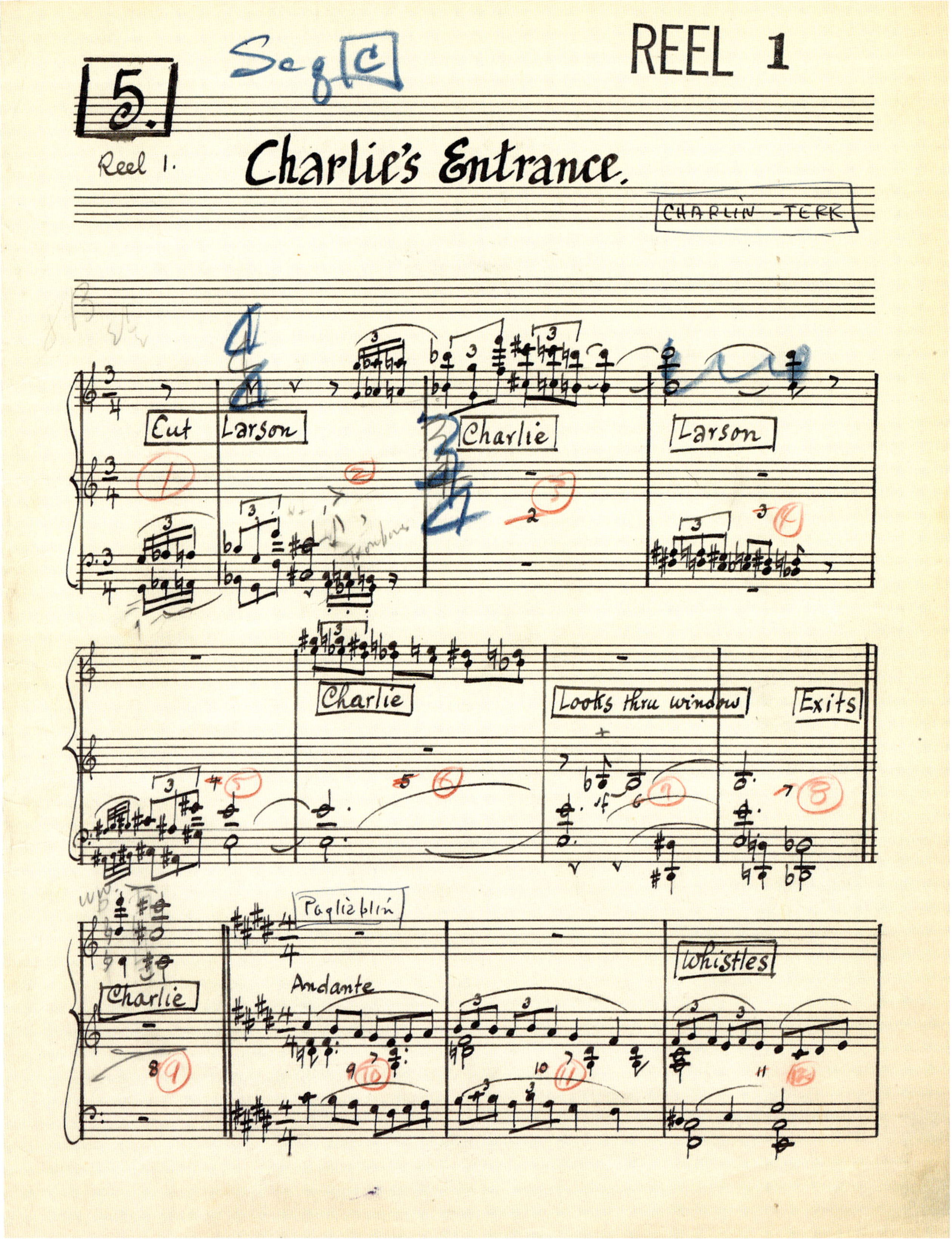
Seq C
REEL 1
5.
Reel 1.
Charlie's Entrance.
Cut
Larson
Charlie
Larson
Charlie
Looks thru window
Exits
Charlie
Andante
Whistles

Left

Score for Chaplin's entrance in *The Gold Rush*, 1942.

Below

Working notebook, 1927–30.
Example of how Chaplin did not write ideas for tunes on music staff paper but on normal paper, using the names of the notes. This is an early version of the song "Wondrous Eyes," written for *City Lights*. The song was supposed to be heard regularly in the film, as a leitmotif, whenever the Tramp thought of the flower girl. In the end, it was replaced by José Padilla's "La Violetera."

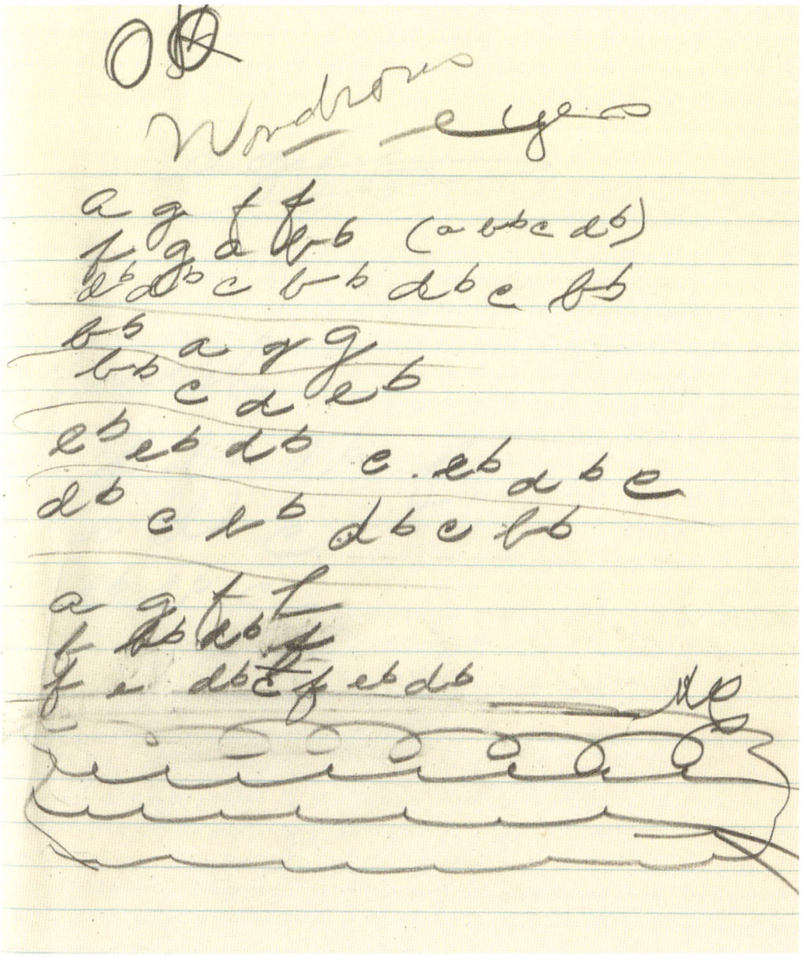

The score to *City Lights* was, and still is in every way, a success. It came out of Chaplin's love for song, dance, and tragedy, elements that permeate the rhythm of the film and read like a storybook in the score. However, the pinnacle of his composing career is most assuredly the complex and innovative score to *Modern Times* (1935–1936), marking a vast mental and practical leap from *City Lights*, fewer than thirty musicians, to symphonic proportions of sixty-four players.

As a director Chaplin was known for acting out personally all the parts during shooting to demonstrate to his actors the exact quality he sought in their performance. Equally, his ability to translate the characters' motives through music is clearly displayed in his scores—throughout *Modern Times*, for example. The Gamin music is a speed-driven and impulsive display of energetic youth, while her unemployed father's is a dark downward string motif ultimately resulting in the bleakest of chords. Charlie's murderous and burly cellmate is introduced menacingly by the lower strings and bassoon, only to be mercurially transformed by a light gavotte as he suddenly takes up his delicate needlepoint. The angry mob of the city's unemployed is characterized by five violent orchestral chords, underlined by the concert bass-drum at *fortissimo*, culminating in the shrill and expertly written orchestral "scream" of the Gamin upon seeing her dead father in the street in the aftermath of the uprising.

Chaplin's film directorial tendency was to achieve perfection by means of repetition until realization, and this too he afforded to the recording stage. Upon conclusion of a composing/orchestration session with Chaplin for *Modern Times*, David Raksin would proceed to write out the full score so the copyist could prepare the individual players' parts for the next recording. At the recordings Chaplin's displeasure with passages was noted on the full score—comments like "brighter here," "no oboe," or "add melody for cello here" riddle the various drafts.

Chaplin music serves the image not only by merely reflecting the emotional content of a scene, but also by using its properties

Right

Chaplin conducting the orchestra during the recording of the music for *A King in New York*, 1957.

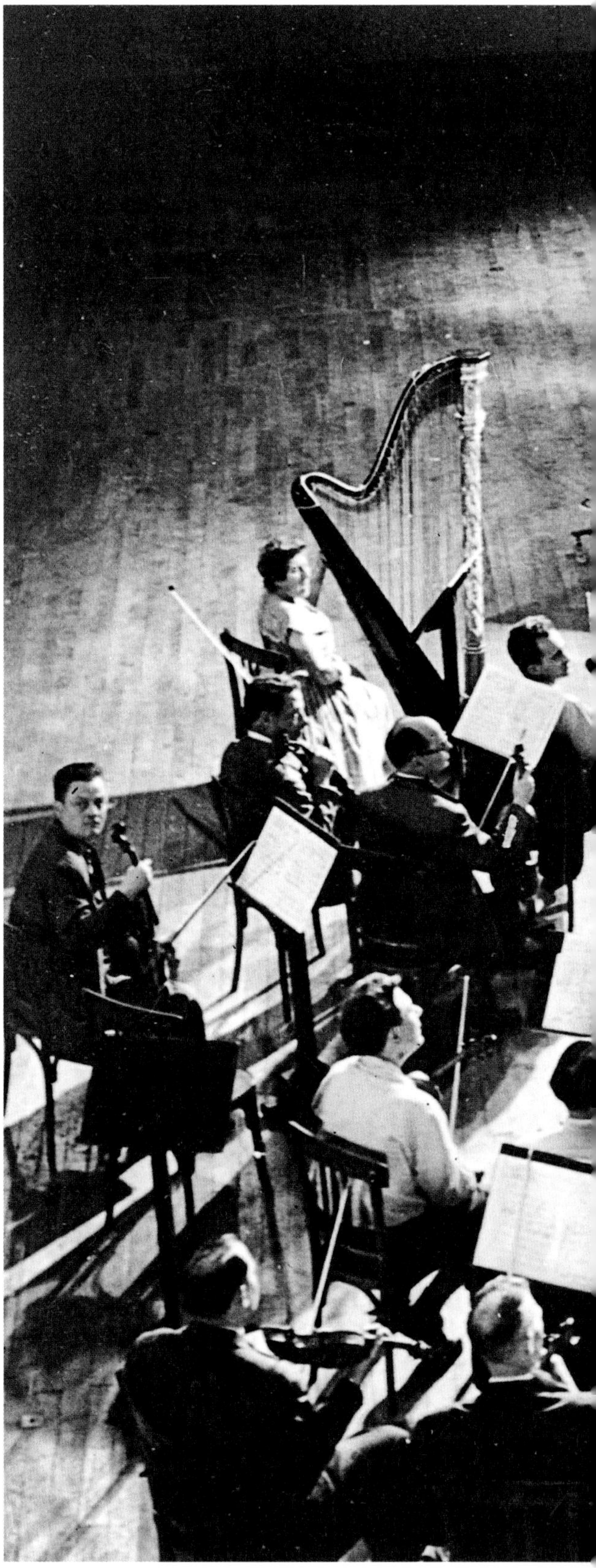

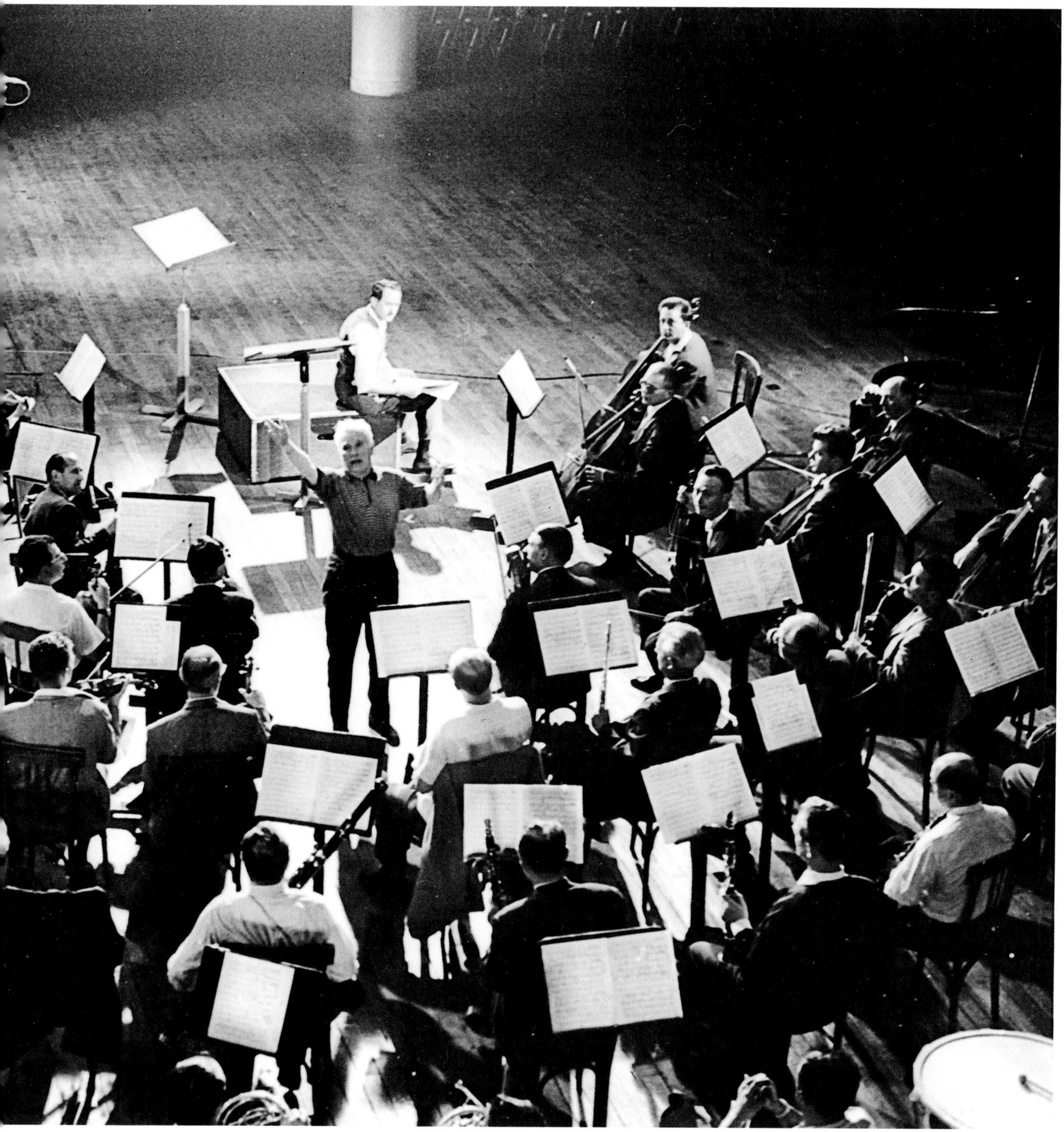

simultaneously as a film effect: the orchestra becomes the fluid line between emotion and practical response. To accompany the image of the passing construction truck that inadvertently drops its red warning flag, Chaplin employs an extremely muted version of the tune "Halleluiah, I'm a Bum" at a distant *piano*. As Charlie waves the red flag to alert the driver of his mishap, the orchestra grows louder in volume and more martial in form, and is at the full dynamic of *forte* just as the communist demonstration appears.

When Chaplin worked on the piano (as evidenced by the private recordings of Chaplin composing between 1952 and 1969), he focused primarily on melodic structure and chord progression, regardless of meter. The tune came first. This may be due to the fact that as an avid non-conventional composer he freed himself of metronomic servitude, and composed just as he heard in his head. The opening ten bars of *The Gold Rush* for example have no less than four meter changes, yet flow as naturally as any piece written in 4/4. This score contains what I like most about Chaplin's writing. It is so terribly free, and to my ears, one of his deepest and darkest scores. As in most Chaplin features, the primary function of the music was the success of the image: music that was not just simply appropriate, but charged the scene with what the content demanded. Yes, in the score to *The Gold Rush* there is storm music, fight music, love music, dance-hall music. But there is also meticulously written music for hiccups, hunger, sleep, eating, hallucinating, snowball fights, suspicion, indignity, pride, and indifference. There are the usual Chaplin musical trademarks: dark, melancholic string passages, colorful oboe and bassoon solos, the omnipresent harp and pure brute force in the brass. Yet the writing has more of a free-flowing exposition of expression and movement, and mood and character changes at a moment's notice.

The scene in reel one where the tramp stumbles upon the cabin in a storm is a prime example of this kind of writing. He knocks on the door, which causes an entire roof-load of snow to slide down and bury him at the front door. This is illustrated with a tremendous orchestral *tutti glissando*. Larson goes to the window to investigate (descending triplets in bassoon and cellos) while the tramp collects himself and searches for the door (descending *staccato* pattern in winds). Suspecting it may be the law, Larson picks up his shotgun and hides behind the door (muted horns, cellos and basses). The tramp enters hoping for refuge in an abandoned shack, only to find a dog lying beneath the bed (here the recurring lonesome string passage makes its first entrance). As he sits to wait out the storm, the walls of the shack begin to buckle from the wind (string trills) until a knothole gives way (temple block solo) and blows his hat across the room (rapid string pattern, stopped horns) to land on a pile on snow (piccolo, oboe). Annoyed, he gets up to retrieve it (limping clarinet solo in 6/8) and discovers a leg of meat, which he begins to devour (recapitulation of string passage). Larson emerges from behind the door (softened triplet *bruscamente*) and sees the tramp eating his food, which angers him (cellos, basses). Slamming the door shut (modulated triplet *bruscamente*), he yells to the tramp (orchestral *sforzando*), and forcefully asks what he is doing there (staccato triplet figure). The tramp answers (clarinet solo) and Larson orders him to get out (orchestral *sforzando*). The tramp obliges, tips his hat (piccolo, string *pizzicato*) and turns to leave. Over the course of these two minutes, the music changes character and meter over twenty times, resulting in a perfectly synchronized narration that seems to flow effortlessly.

Examples such as these make Chaplin film scores unique in their subtlety and timing. It was *Modern Times* that first introduced this kind of silent-film composition, but *The Gold Rush* was its apex.

After 1936, Chaplin abandoned the tramp in costume but musically his presence remained. *City Lights* was the starting point not only for Chaplin as a composer, but also for his musical identity. And from that time his self-portrait developed to the very end.

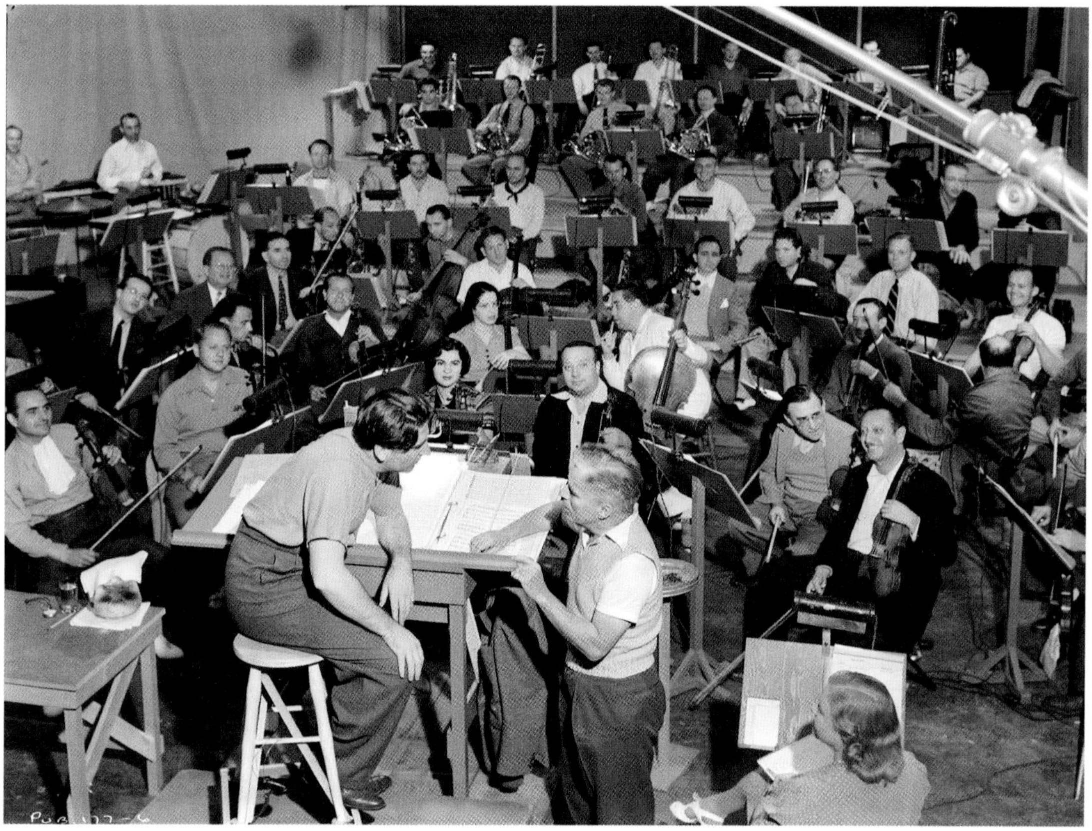

Below

Chaplin and Meredith Willson during rehearsals for the recording of *The Great Dictator*, 1940.

Mathilde Thibault-Starzyk

Quoting and borrowing

The composer and his models

Like many—if not most—film music composers, Charlie Chaplin borrowed and quoted from music composed by others in his soundtracks. While the borrowing only represents a small part of the music accompanying his films, it is frequent and varied, and thus of considerable interest. Some quotations are very well known—for example, Brahms's "Hungarian Dance No. 5" in the shaving scene of *The Great Dictator* or the reinterpretation at the end of *Modern Times* of "Je cherche après Titine," a song written in 1917 by Léo Daniderff. Others are less well known or quoted so discreetly that it is difficult for an untrained ear to hear them. To make a comprehensive list, one needs to consult the music cue sheets for each film. These invaluable documents in the Chaplin archives for all the films produced after 1931 list for the entire duration of each film every piece of music used, its composer, and the exact moment it is heard. A first reading of the cue sheets reveals that musical quotations are not used in all Chaplin film scores, but in particular in *City Lights*, *Modern Times*, *The Great Dictator*, and for the 1942 rerelease of *The Gold Rush*.

Chaplin used music by composers he liked: Brahms, Wagner, and Rimsky-Korsakov regularly feature. One can hear a few bars of Rimsky-Korsakov's *Scheherazade* in *City Lights*, his "Flight of the Bumblebee" in *The Gold Rush* with the waltz from Tchaikovsky's *Sleeping Beauty*, and the Prelude to Act I of Wagner's *Lohengrin* in *The Great Dictator*. In this last example, his choice of a composer regularly associated with the Nazi regime cannot have been a chance one, as it accompanies the scene where Hynkel plays with a globe transformed into a balloon. However, at the end of the film the piece is used against type, after the barber's speech. Chaplin thus completely frees Wagner's music from Nazi ideology by associating it with a message of peace and tolerance. While the airy melody of the bowed strings marvelously highlights the dictator's disturbing madness, it also perfectly adapts to a message of hope and rebirth.

In a radio interview, Chaplin explained: "I use music as a counterpoint, and I learned that from the Fred Karno Company. For instance if they had squalid surroundings with a lot of comedy tramps working in it, they would have very beautiful, boudoir music, something of the 18th century, very lush and grandiose, and it would be satirical, a counterpoint."[1] In 1942, for *The Gold Rush*, Chaplin once again quoted Wagner according to this method, choosing the melody of "O du mein holder Abendstern" from the opera *Tannhäuser* to accompany the complaints of a

1 "Charlie Chaplin," *The Light Channel*, October 15, 1952.

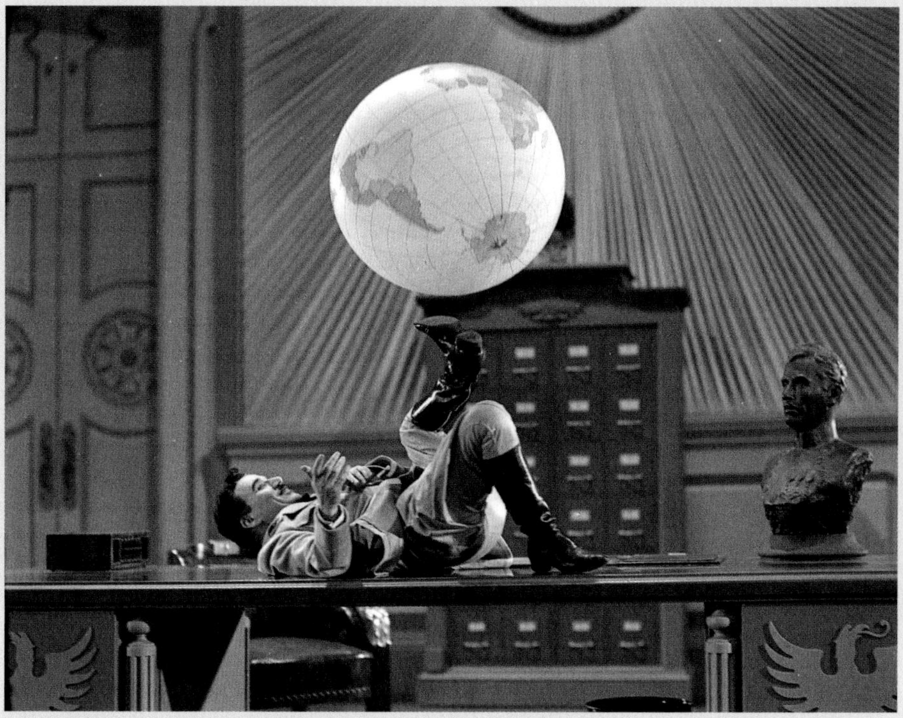

Left

Hynkel playing with a globe in *The Great Dictator*, 1940.

famished Big Jim. The delicate and ethereal melody counterbalances the triviality of the scene.

Wagner's influence goes beyond the simple quotation: Chaplin also took on his methods of composition, particularly the use of leitmotifs. For example, in *City Lights*, the theme from "La Violetera" borrowed from José Padilla is used systematically to indicate the presence of the flower girl on screen.

By quoting music composed by others, Chaplin was in keeping with a tradition established from the beginnings of the film industry: when they were screened, silent movies were always accompanied by music—played by a solo pianist or a complete orchestra—which was only very rarely composed for the occasion. It was mostly a compilation of pieces from the classical and popular repertoires. Moreover, the same musical selection went from one cinema to the next and musical accompaniment was the subject of manuals indicating what music to play for what type of scene. For the opening of *The Gold Rush*, when he appears on screen for the first time, Chaplin composed a piece entitled "Chaplin Medley," combining songs that were very popular at the time, featuring bits of "The Bluebells of Scotland," "Loch Lomond," and "Coming Thru the Rye." Although they are perhaps little known to the French public, the songs were real standards at the time for a British or American audience. During other moments of the film, "Auld Lang Syne" and "For He's a Jolly Good Fellow" are used. These songs are mentioned in manuals such as *Motion Picture Moods for Pianists and Organists* compiled by Ernö Rapée in 1924: not only did Chaplin apply the same method of compilation as for the accompaniment of silent films, but he also chose the same repertoire.

The parallel may be taken even further. In *Musical Accompaniment of Moving Pictures*, another manual published in 1920, musicians are encouraged always to have in their repertoire songs with evocative titles: the association of the theme and its title added a comic dimension to an already burlesque situation.[2] Chaplin adopted this approach when he used the song "The Near Future," written by Irving Berlin in 1919. Better known under the name "How Dry I Am," a line from the lyrics, the theme was rapidly associated with drunkenness ("dry" meaning "sober"). The song is often used in Chaplin films, present in *Modern Times* and in *City Lights* on two occasions: it is heard for the first time when the Tramp falls into the water when attempting to save the millionaire from suicide—Chaplin

2 Edith Lang and George West, *Musical Accompaniment of Moving Pictures* [1920] (New York: Arno Press, 1970), 37.

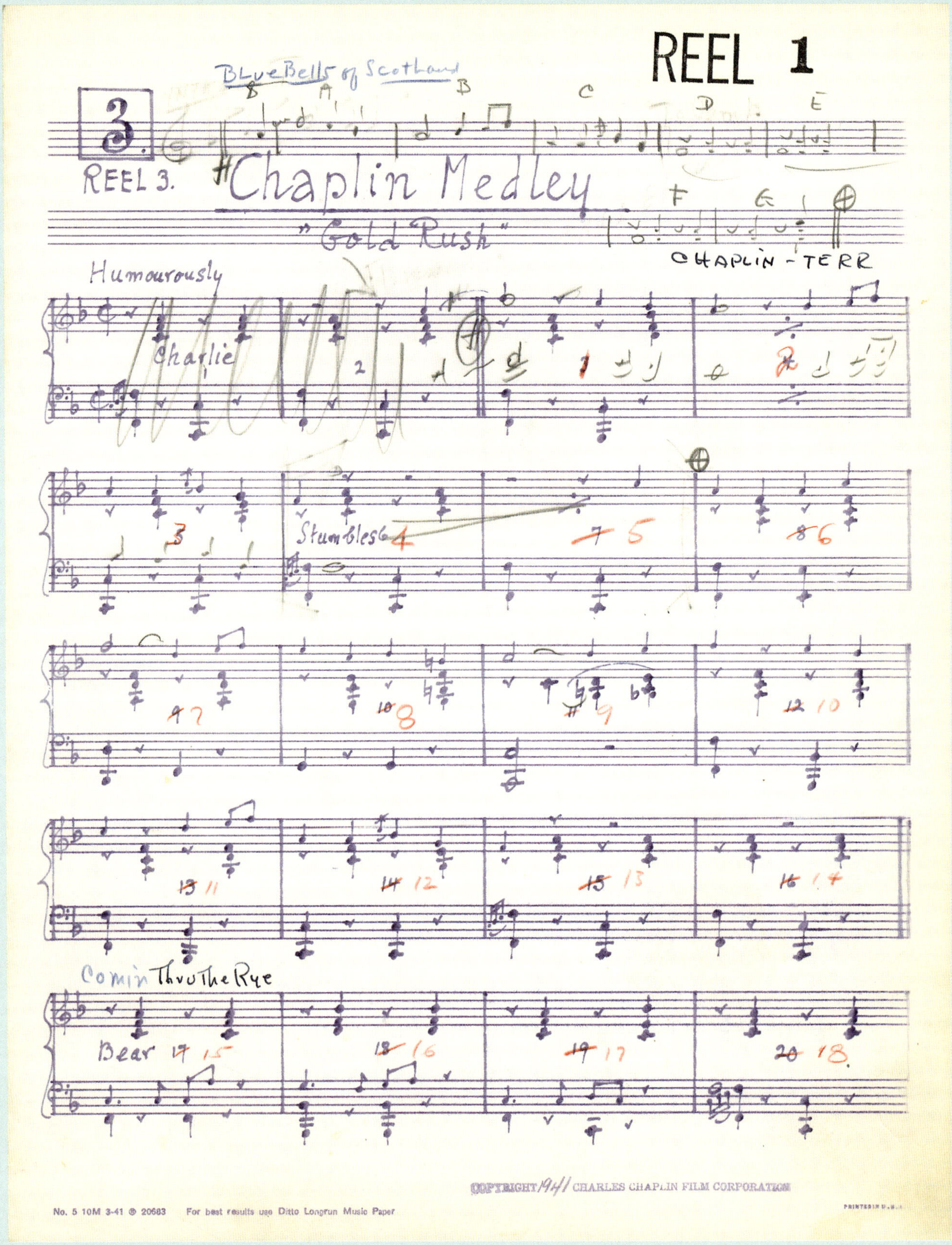
REEL 1
3.
Blue Bells of Scotland
REEL 3.
#Chaplin Medley
"Gold Rush"
CHAPLIN - TERR
Humourously
Charlie
Stumbles
Comin Thru The Rye
Bear
COPYRIGHT 1941 CHARLES CHAPLIN FILM CORPORATION
No. 5 10M 3-41 20683 For best results use Ditto Longrun Music Paper

here playing on the principal meaning of the word "dry"—and again when the two characters, drunk, stagger in front of the millionaire's house. Other borrowing of the same type can be heard in both films, such as the recurrent use of the song "Hallelujah, I'm a Bum" or "I Hear You Calling Me," a song popularized at the beginning of the century by the tenor John McCormack, who was, moreover, a friend of Chaplin's. "I Hear You Calling Me" is used in the banquet scene at the millionaire's house, when the Tramp disturbs the singer's performance with his whistle. The theme comes back repeatedly in the scene, but the guests do not have the pleasure of hearing the song performed, as the Tramp constantly interrupts the singer.

Heartfelt tribute, quest for contrast, leitmotif, or touch of humor, musical quotations are always rich in meaning and seem to serve multiple purposes in Chaplin's soundtracks. They disappeared, however, as soon as he started making talking films. The concomitance of the phenomena is perhaps a clue to understanding this. In the silent era, quoting a pre-existing tune made a scene easier to understand, or even added a level of interpretation. In talkies, dialogue took over and became the sole vehicle of communication, thus overshadowing the musical soundtrack. Perhaps it was because they carried too much significance that Chaplin did not continue to use musical quotations when he composed music for his talkies.

Left

Score for "Chaplin Medley," *The Gold Rush*, 1942.

Right

The Tramp leading a demonstration without knowing it in *Modern Times*, 1936.

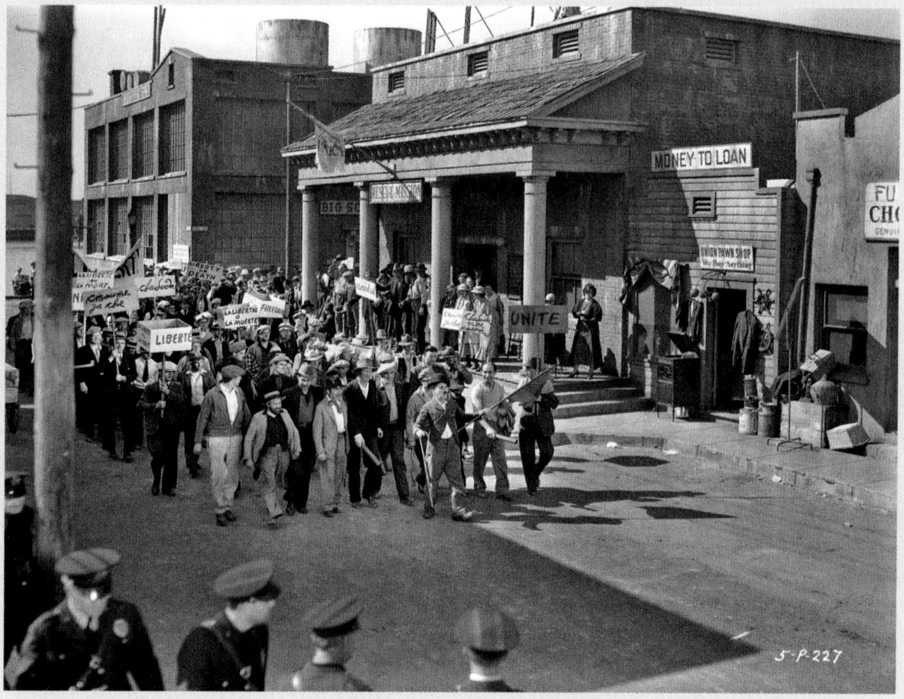

Below

Chaplin, John McCormack (to the left of Chaplin), and other visitors during filming of *The Rink*, c. 1916. A renowned opera singer, the Irish lyric tenor John McCormack recorded many popular songs in the 1910s and 1920s. "I Hear You Calling Me," recorded in 1908, was his biggest hit. In 1931, Chaplin used an instrumental version of the song on the *City Lights* soundtrack.

Opposite

The Tramp tries to prevent the millionaire (Harry Myers) from committing suicide in *City Lights*, 1931.

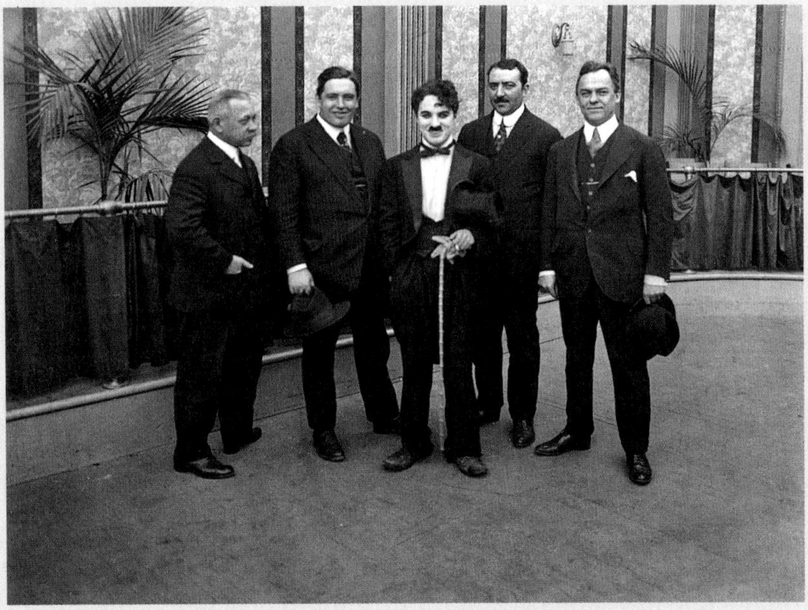

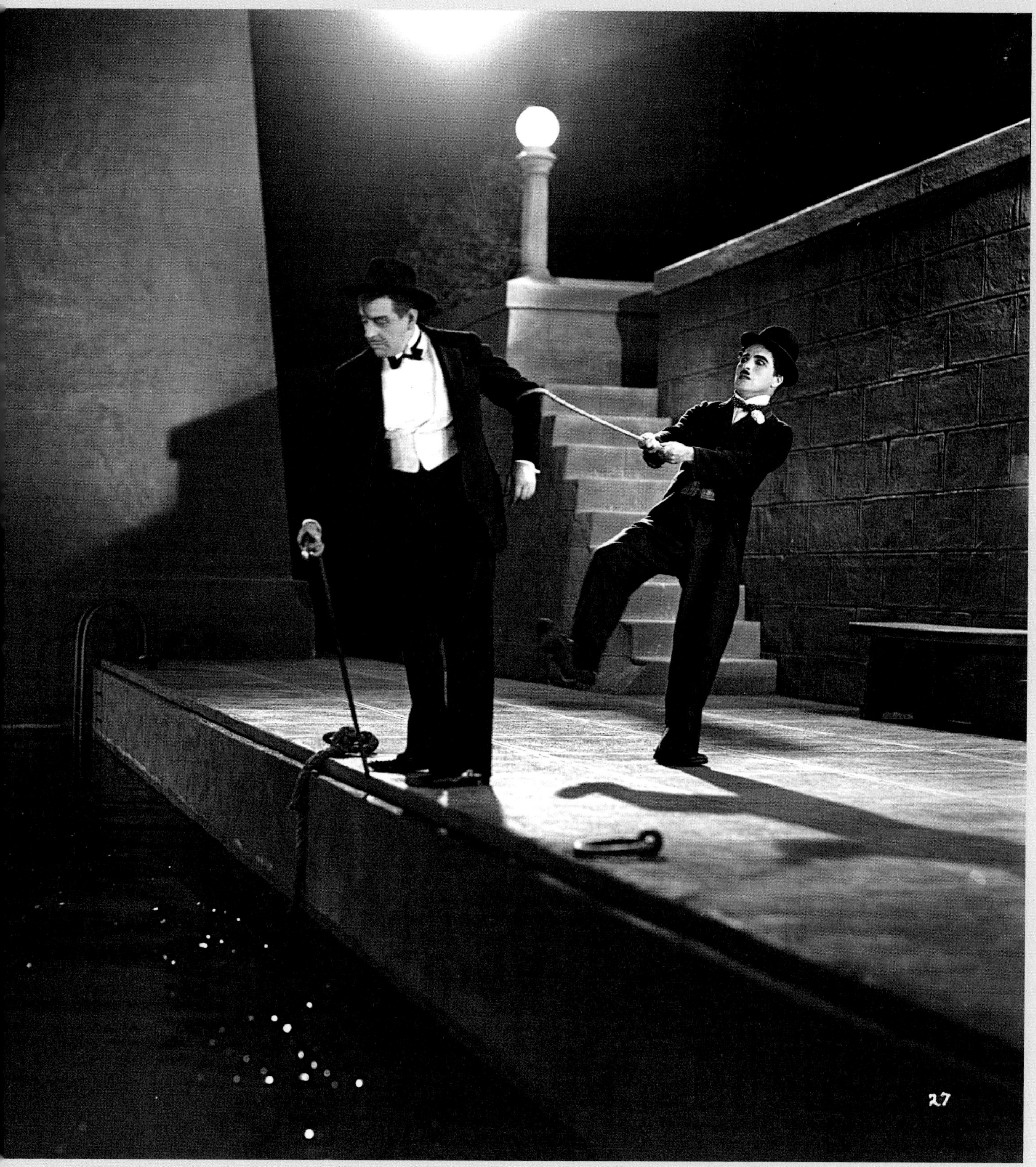
27

Carl Davis

Charlie Chaplin in concert

On April 16, 1989 we celebrated Charlie's 100th birthday with a week's screenings of *City Lights* at the Dominion Theatre, Tottenham Court Road, London, where the premiere of the film had been held in 1931. Our first night was a star-studded affair, a Royal Charity Gala, attended by Princess Diana and, bizarrely, Sir Georg Solti. Many of Chaplin's children and grandchildren came from Switzerland, Paris, and New York. I was requested to compose a fanfare to accompany Princess Diana's walk from the foyer to her seat. The evening opened with an at the time unseen rarity: *How To Make Movies*, a quasi-documentary Chaplin never finished, edited by Kevin Brownlow for the occasion.

We know Chaplin gave great attention to the scores for his films, personally supervising each premiere in Hollywood, New York, and London.

Up to the coming of sound on film, major cinemas housed orchestras to play for film screenings. With the new technology, the music would be recorded and would share space on the soundtrack with sound effects and dialogue. By the time Chaplin had completed his film in 1931, it was very clear that sound film was here to stay, yet *City Lights* had the hallmarks of a "silent," i.e., dialogue on cards. Chaplin's solution was to compose and record a score of his own and add, very selectively, sound effects. My brief was to turn the clock back and prepare the recorded score for a live performance. By 1989, I had already composed new scores for "silents" starting with Abel Gance's *Napoleon* in 1980, as well as scoring the Thames TV series *Unknown Chaplin*. But restoring an existing score to be played non-stop and synchronized to the on-screen images was a challenge. Amazingly, the original score and parts were held in an underground vault in Geneva and photocopies were dispatched. However, that wasn't enough. In many places the scores did not match the recording and no one in my team could work out why. Eventually it came out that Charlie held three weeks of sessions, continuously rewriting and pasting over the new music. The glue holding these bits and pieces of paper must have dried out; they must have dropped to the bottom of the bag and were therefore lost. It was a painfully slow, major reconstruction job to recreate Charlie's unique scoring.

Some London journalists were dubious about the week of *City Lights* at the Dominion, declaring they never found Chaplin funny. The producer/director David Gill confounded them with a live recording during the film's boxing scene in which the theater audience's laughter completely obliterated the music being performed. The shows were a great success and in subsequent years led to live versions of *The Gold Rush* and *The Kid*. The distinguished composer and conductor, Timothy Brock took up the mantle and created a magnificent realization of *Modern Times*. I continued with scoring all twelve of the "Mutual" shorts. Charlie with live orchestra is here to stay.

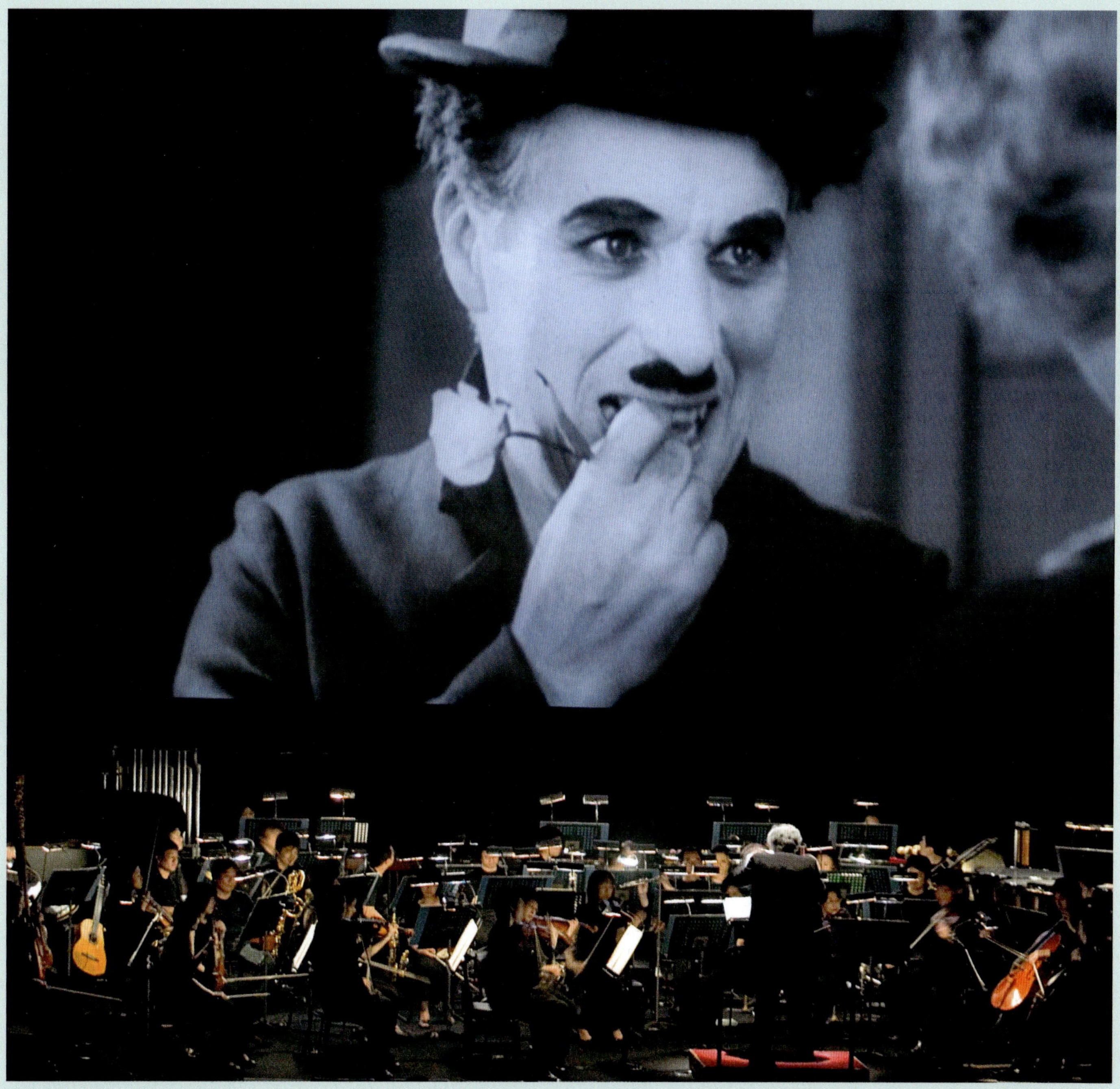

Above

Live orchestral screening of *City Lights* conducted by Carl Davis.

Mathilde Thibault-Starzyk

From the hit to the standard

When Chaplin became a classic

When Chaplin published three compositions with the Charlie Chaplin Music Publishing Company in 1916, it was a commercial failure. Ten years later, in 1925, his songs "Sing a Song" and "With You, Dear, in Bombay," which he composed and recorded to promote *The Gold Rush*, were not much more successful. In fact, it is very likely that the success of the film facilitated the sales of the sheet music as opposed to the music promoting the film. For all that, certain songs written later by Chaplin have now become classics outside their original film context, covered by other artists and reaching an extremely wide audience worldwide.

Written for the *Limelight* soundtrack, "Terry's Theme" was a huge hit as soon it was released in 1952. The piece was covered by Frank Chacksfield in 1953 and topped the charts for several weeks in the United States and the United Kingdom, opening the way to other versions by musicians such as Richard Hayman and Hugo Winterhalter. The vocal version of the piece, titled "Eternally" with lyrics by Geoffrey Parsons, was also a triumph.

In the wake of this commercial success, the Bourne Music Company teams watched *Modern Times* again in order to pick out a tune with comparable potential. Chaplin, who deemed the royalties of "Eternally" unsatisfactory, was not immediately convinced. Geoffrey Parsons was once again, alongside John Turner, asked to write the lyrics for the chosen theme—that of the final scene in which the tramp and the girl set off towards a better future. Titled "Smile" and popularized by Nat King Cole in 1954, it traveled around the world and became a true standard, performed by more than 150 artists, from Judy Garland to Michael Bublé, via Céline Dion, Eric Clapton, and Plácido Domingo. It has been adapted to all styles of music—including gospel, jazz, folk, metal, and pop—and to all occasions: said to be Michael Jackson's favorite song, it was played by a symphony orchestra and sung by Jermaine Jackson, the pop star's brother, during his funeral.

When Chaplin was working on the music for *A Countess from Hong Kong*, he looked for a theme that could be released in parallel with the film. He first thought of the waltz entitled "The Countess from Hong Kong" and regularly repeated in the soundtrack, but in the end it was another theme, "Neapolitan Love Song," far less frequently present on screen, that was chosen. Chaplin wrote the lyrics for what was to become "This Is My Song"

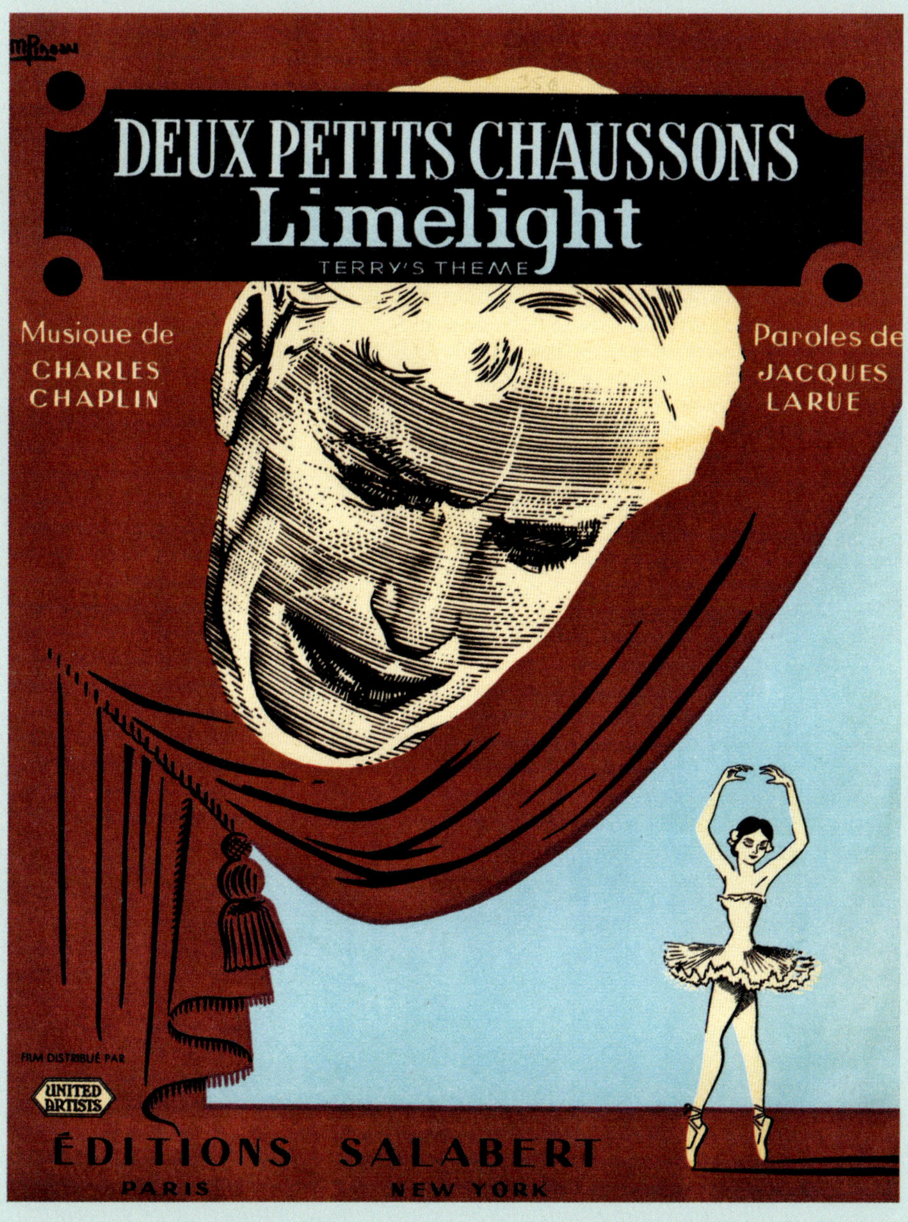

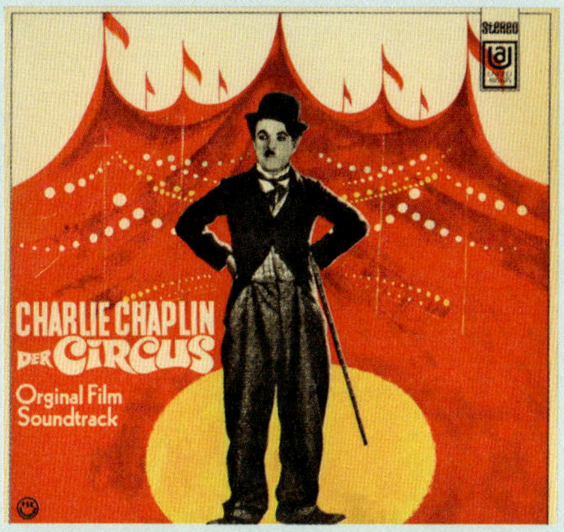

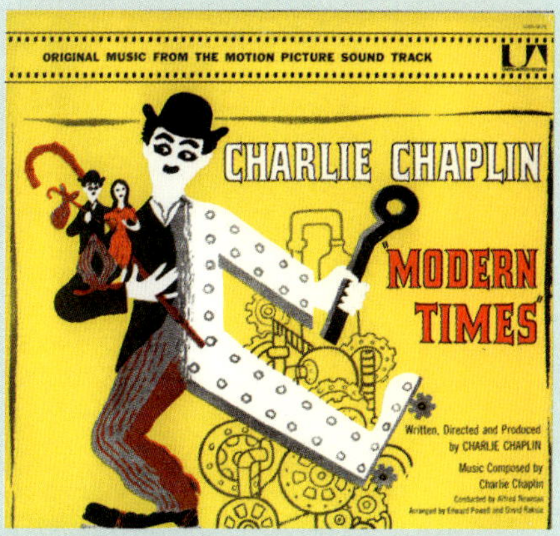

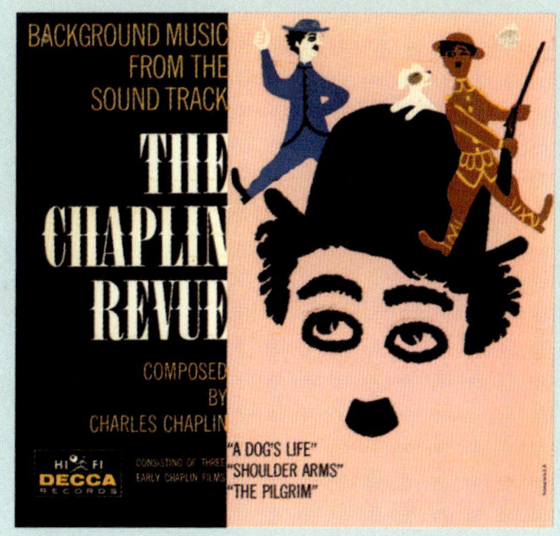

Above

Sheet music for "Deux petits chaussons," the French version of the *Limelight* theme, 1952.

Right

Album covers, *The Circus* soundtrack, 1969; *Modern Times* soundtrack, 1959; *The Chaplin Revue* soundtrack, 1960.

and Petula Clark was asked to perform it. Skeptical at first, she finally agreed to record the song in English, French, German, and Italian. By April 1967, two million copies of the song had been sold around the world. Although *A Countess from Hong Kong* was a flop, the profits from the sales of "This Is My Song" on their own were enough to recuperate the production costs of the film. Chaplin was once again under the spotlight, no longer for his talents as a filmmaker but for his music.

Chaplin's music thus began to be recognized for its own qualities in the 1950s, twenty years after he began composing for his films. It was not until 1989 that there was a real turning point and the music became truly appreciated—not only certain isolated songs, but his composition in general. Thanks to the cinema screenings with live orchestra initiated by Carl Davis and greatly developed by Timothy Brock, Chaplin film soundtracks are now recognized as works in their own right.

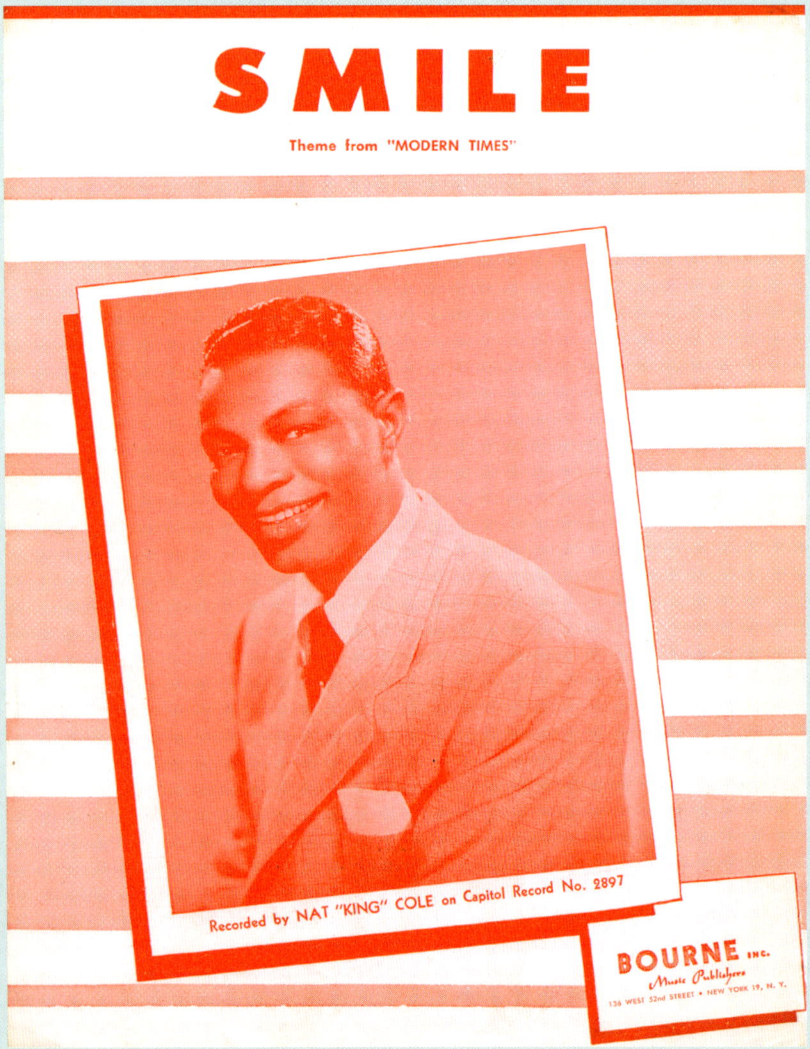

Left

Cover of the sheet music for "Smile," sung by Nat King Cole, 1954.

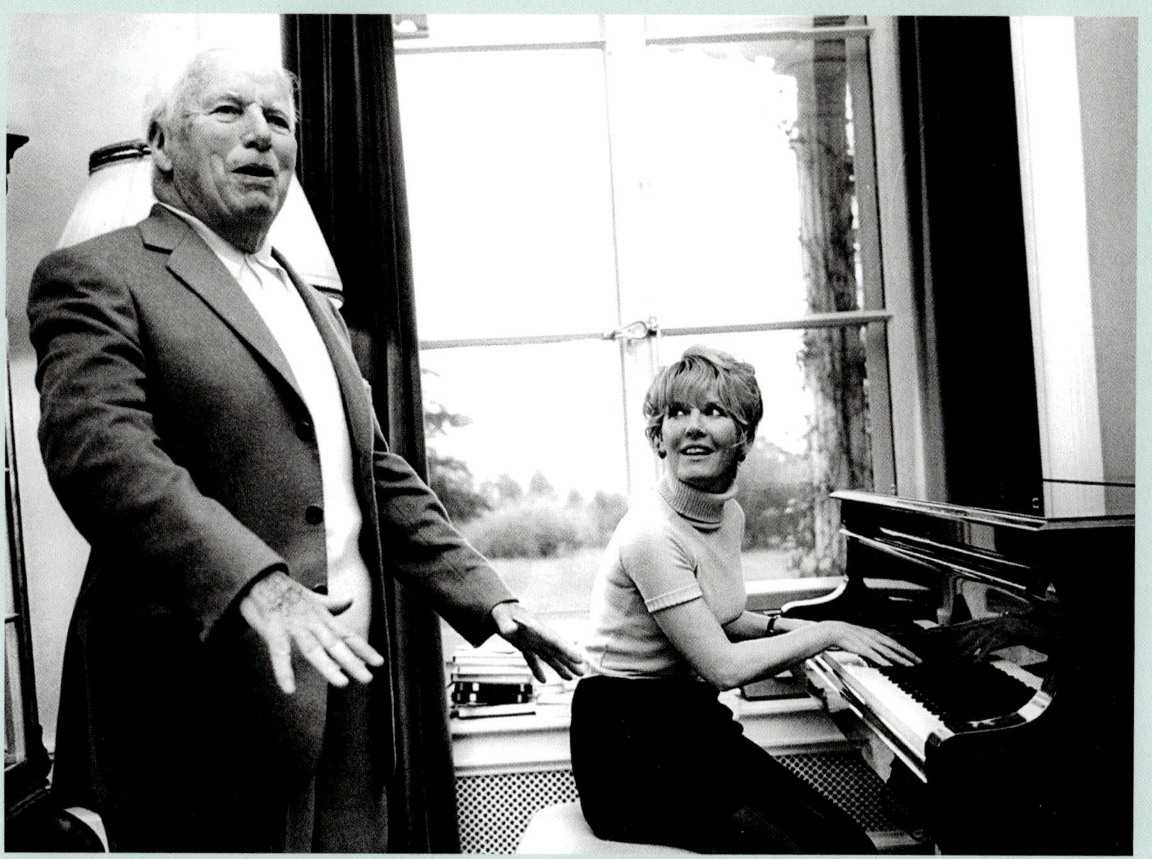

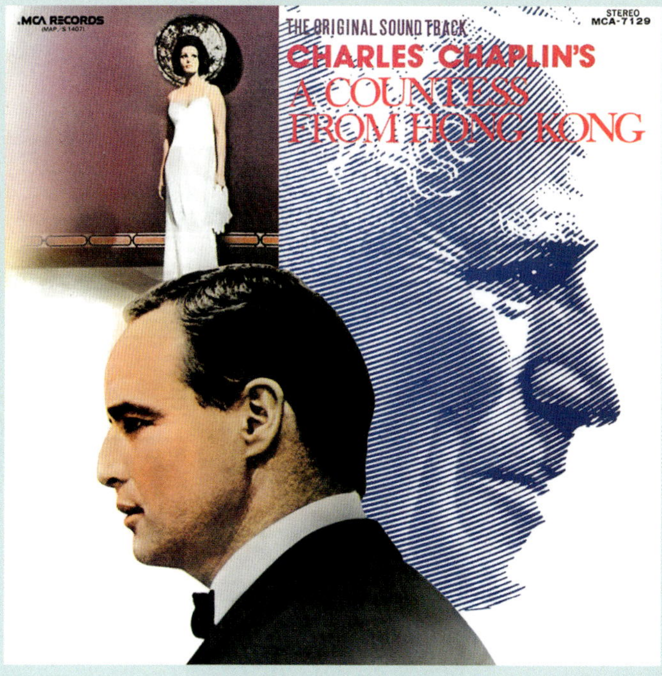

Above

Chaplin with Petula Clark, Manoir de Ban, April 22, 1967. Photograph by Bernard Hermann. The French version of "This is My Song", "C'est ma chanson," was the biggest hit of 1967 in France.

Left

Album cover, *A Countess from Hong Kong* soundtrack, 1968.

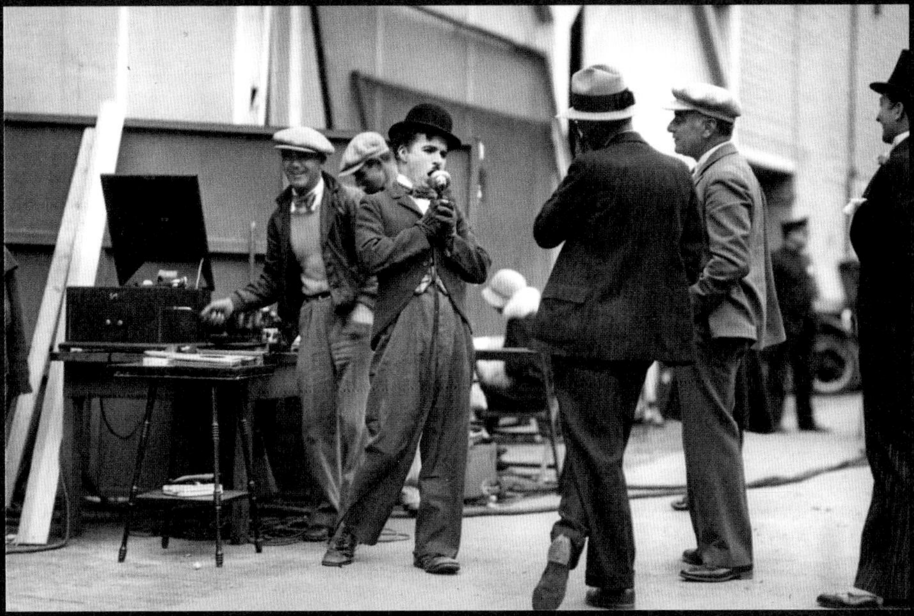

4.

SPEECH

In 1927, with *The Jazz Singer*, the visual art of cinema also became an art of sound. Aware that his comedy was universal because it was based on non-verbal communication, Chaplin resisted the talkies. It thus took him three films and nearly ten years to introduce dialogue into his work. *City Lights* and *Modern Times*, without dialogue but nevertheless sound films, made good use of the new possibilities offered by technological advances and introduced genuine reflection on the spoken word by parodying speeches and dialogues. Refusing the talkies was a means for Chaplin to maintain his position as icon of a popular culture that resisted, and was insubordinate to, the powers that be.

At the end of *The Great Dictator* (1940), Chaplin is prompted: "You must speak." Speech seemed to be the result of a historical emergency. With the little Jewish barber's final words Chaplin removes the mask of the Tramp and the filmmaker himself delivers a passionate message of peace and hope. However, Hynkel's harangue at the beginning of the film shows that Chaplin maintained an ambivalent position with regards to speech. From the mimed sermon in *The Pilgrim* in 1923 to the communist-accented logorrhea of the character played by Michael Chaplin in *A King in New York* in 1957, Chaplin never stopped questioning the impact and the limits of words as opposed to pantomime.

Left

Chaplin holding a microphone on the set of *City Lights*, c. 1929–30.

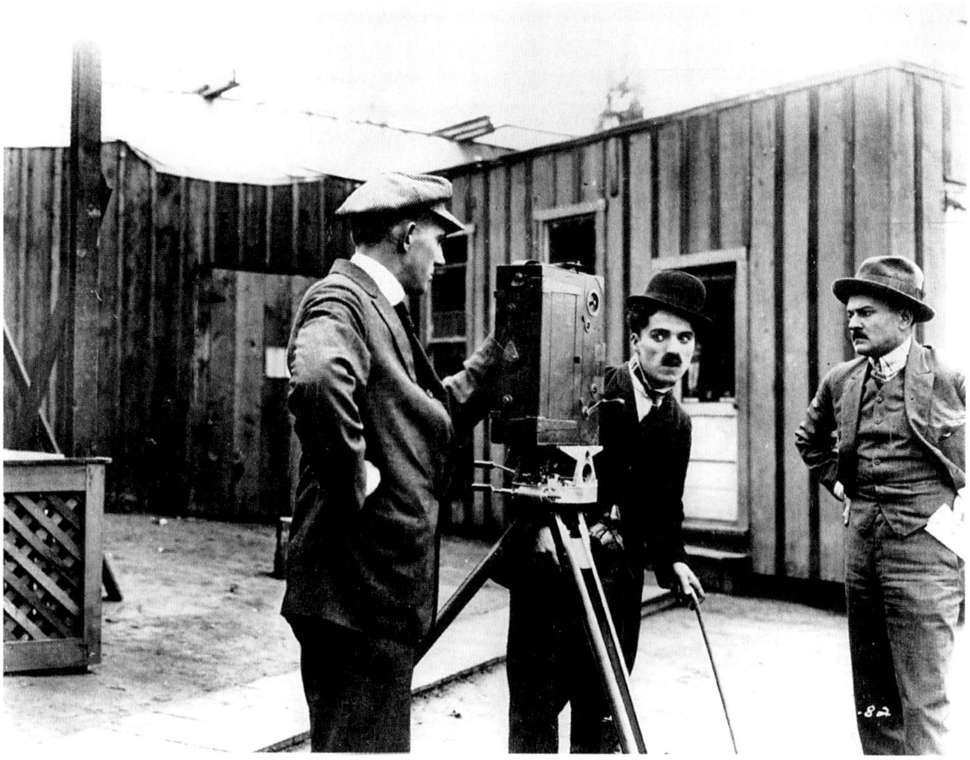

Left

Kid Auto Races at Venice, Cal., February 1914.
In this title, in which the character of the Tramp was in front of the camera for the very first time, he disrupts the filming of a race. The camera in the film is a Prestwich, fairly widely used at the time. Compact and made with high-quality, robust materials, it was particularly suited to filming outdoors.

Opposite

During the filming of *How to Make Movies*, 1918.

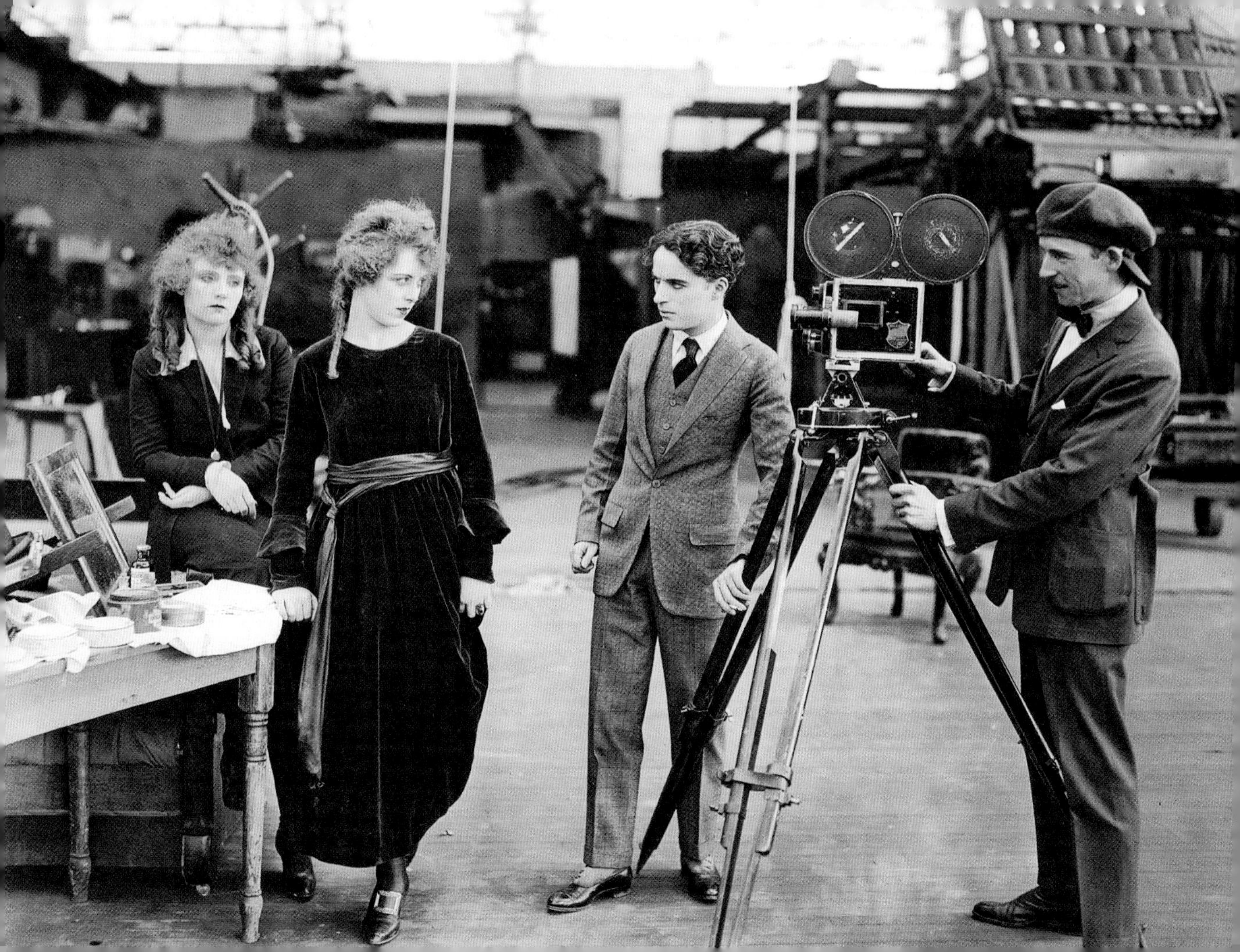

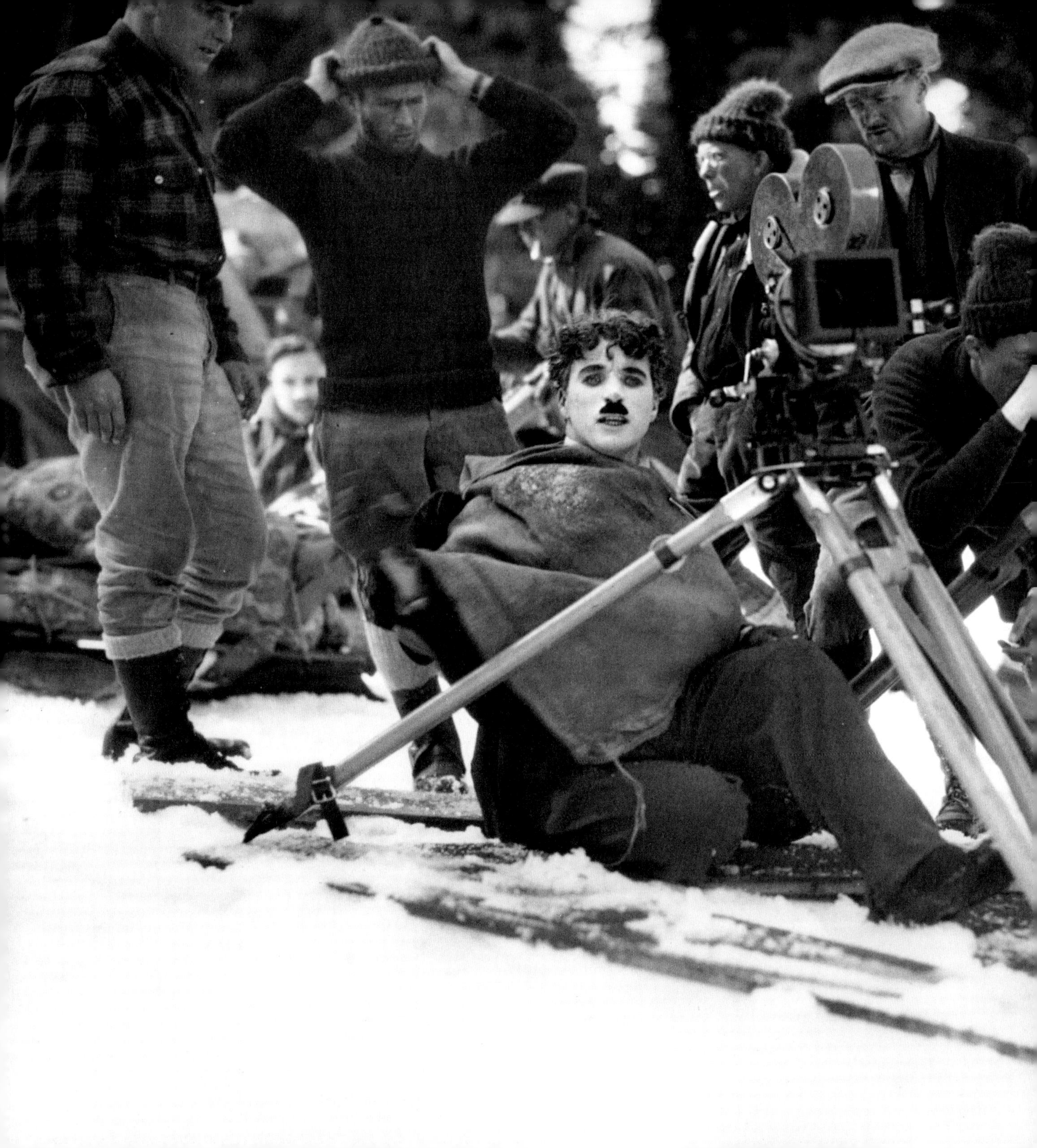

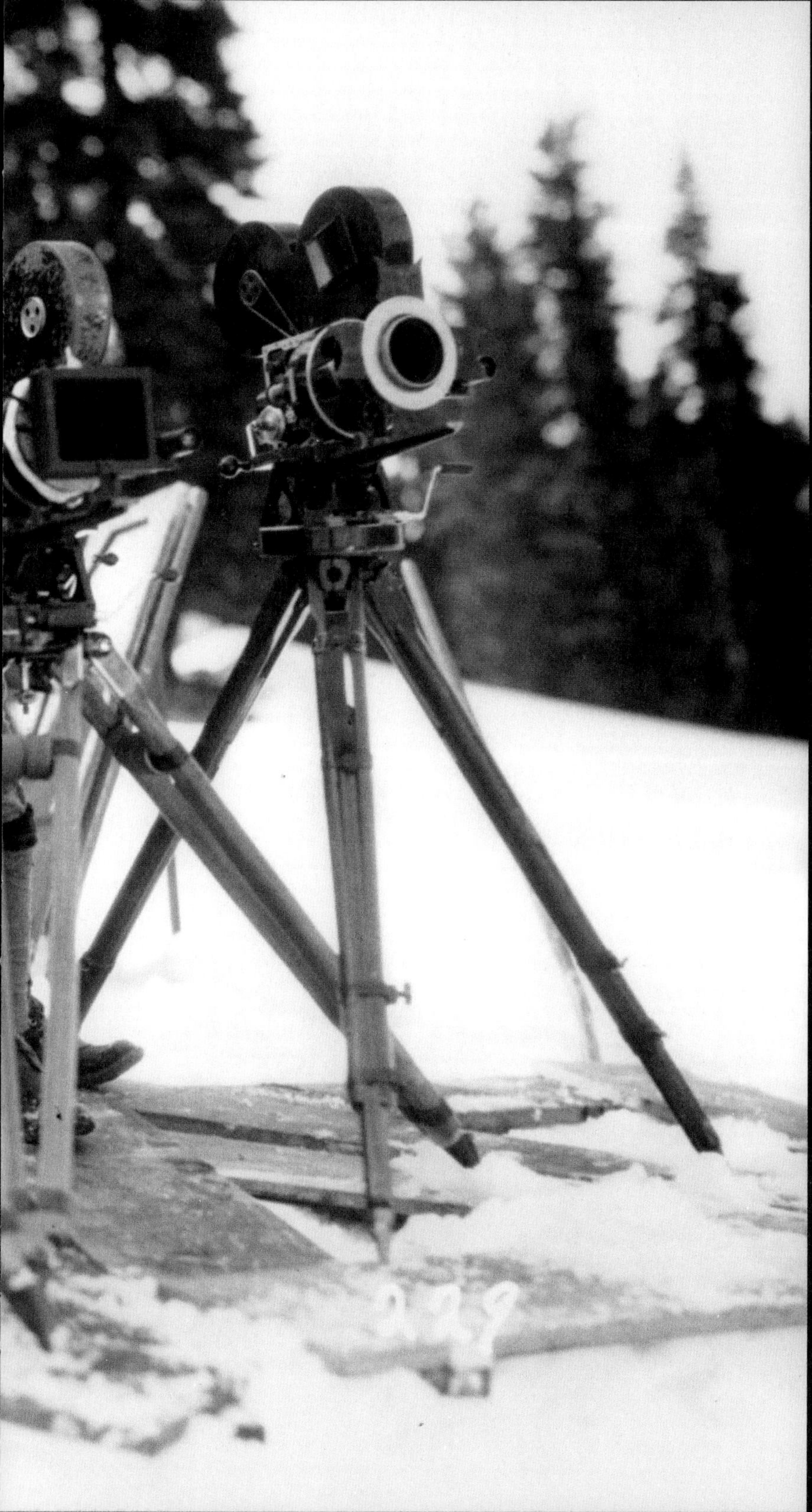

Left

Chaplin during the filming of *The Gold Rush* in Truckee, 1924. Like many silent-film directors, Chaplin shot with several cameras, which allowed him to obtain several negatives for the same film, at a time when the printing of many prints from a single negative gave less than satisfactory results. The framing of shots could thus vary slightly from one copy to another.

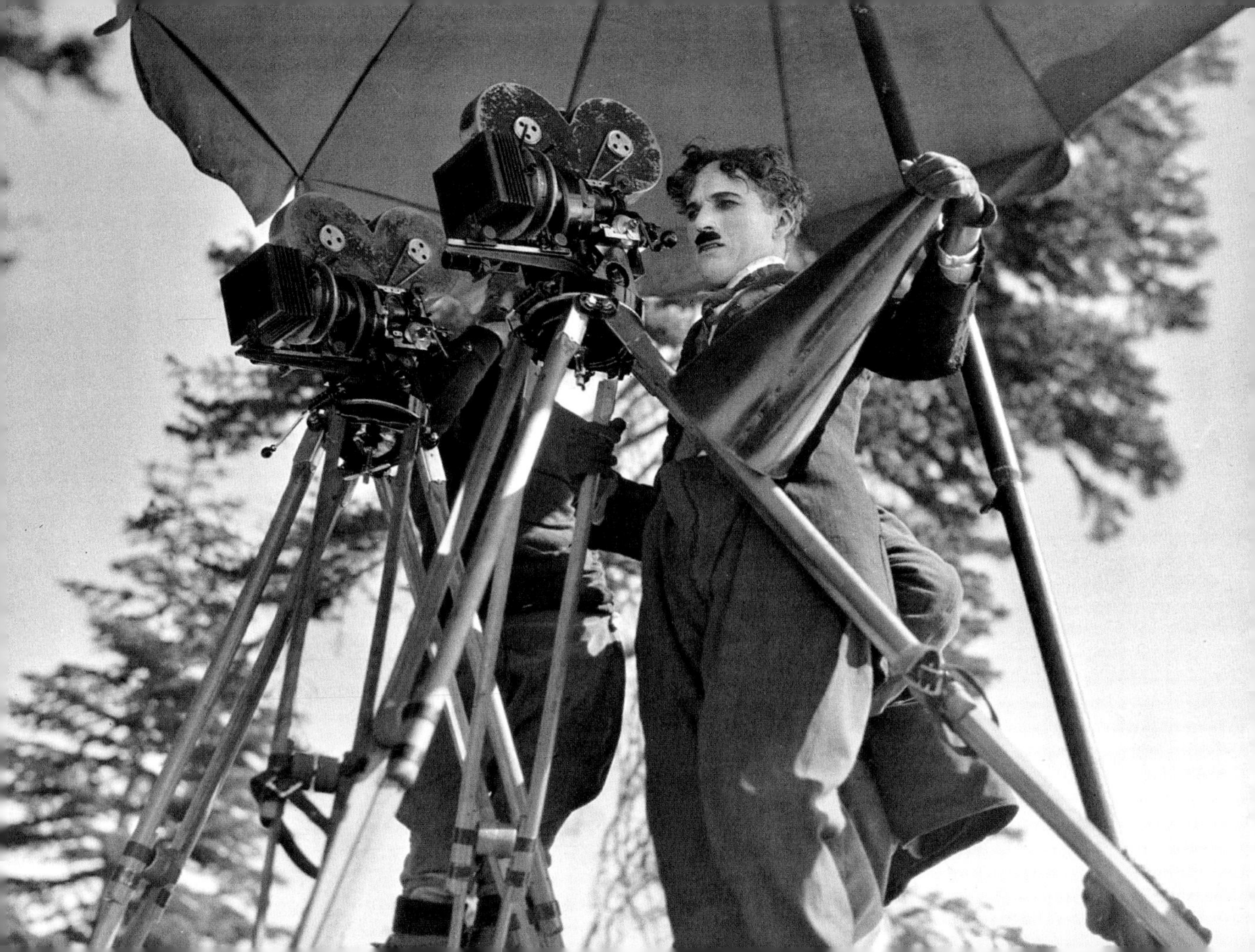

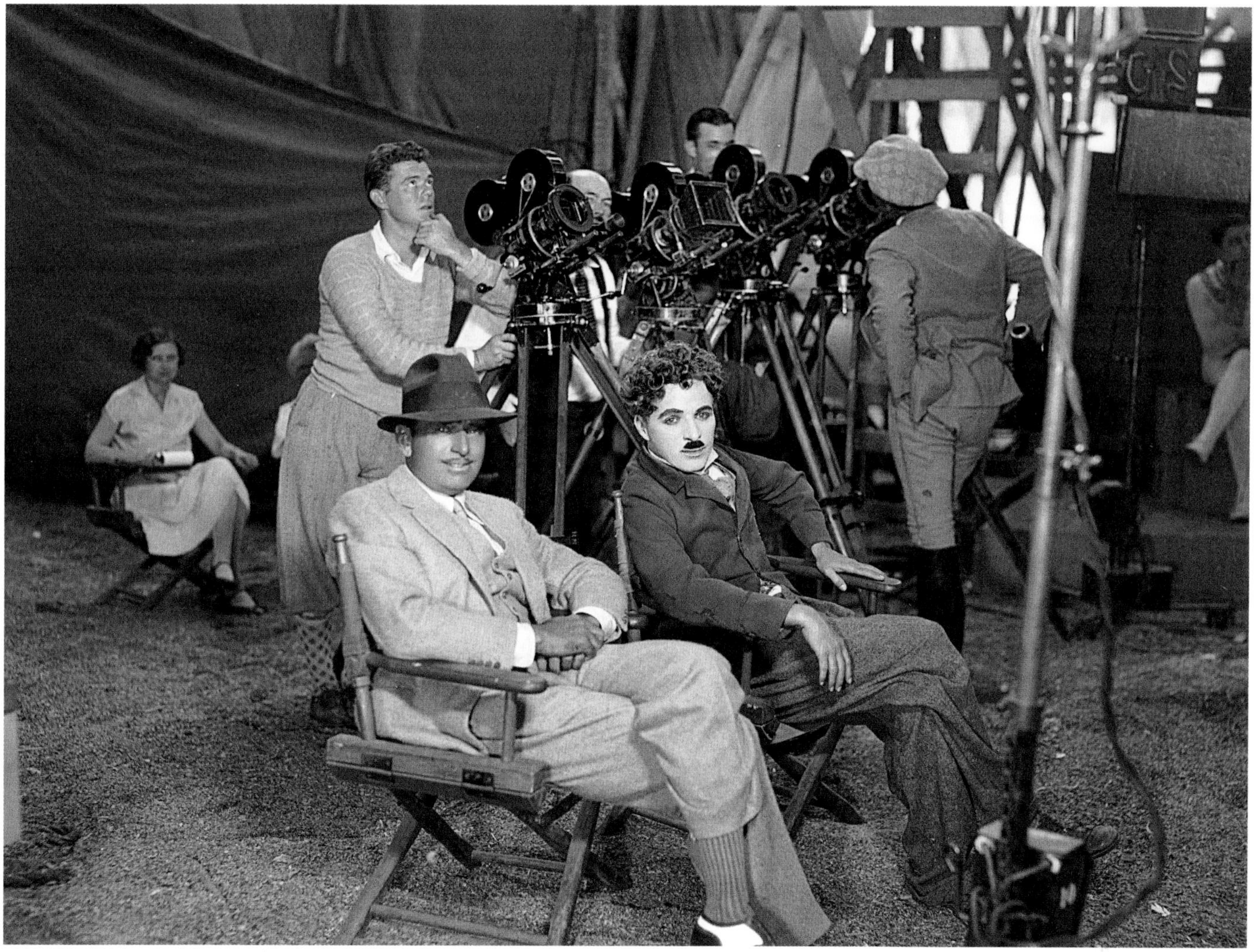

Left

Chaplin behind the camera during the shooting of *The Gold Rush*, 1923–25. Chaplin holds the emblematic accessory of silent-film directors: the megaphone, which enabled communication with teams all over the set. As there was no recording, filmmakers could give instructions even if the camera was running.

Above

Douglas Fairbanks and Chaplin during the filming of *The Circus*, 1926-1927.

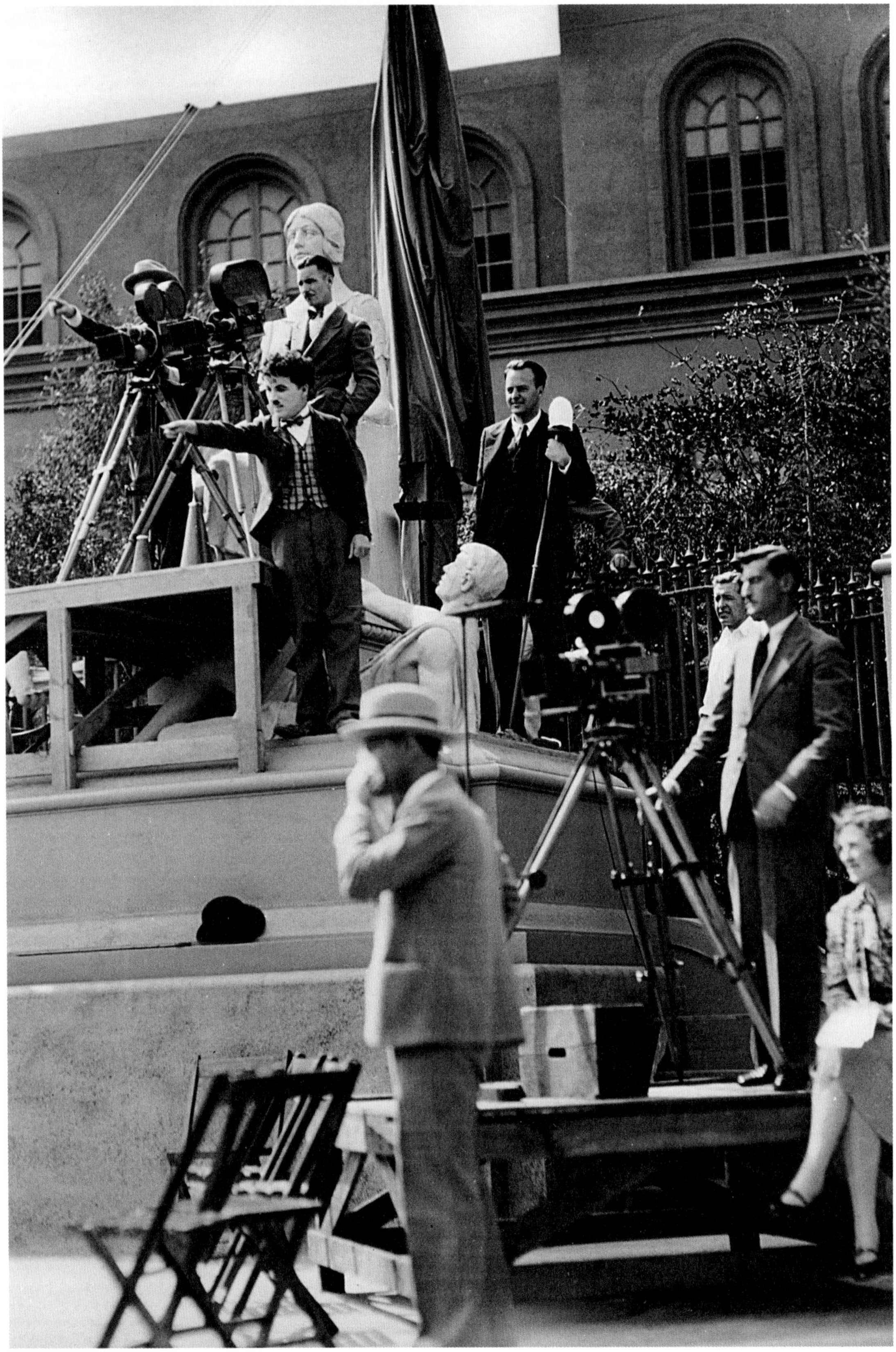

Left

During the filming of the opening scene of *City Lights*, c. 1930.

Opposite

Chaplin giving instructions by megaphone on the set of *Modern Times*, c. 1935–36.

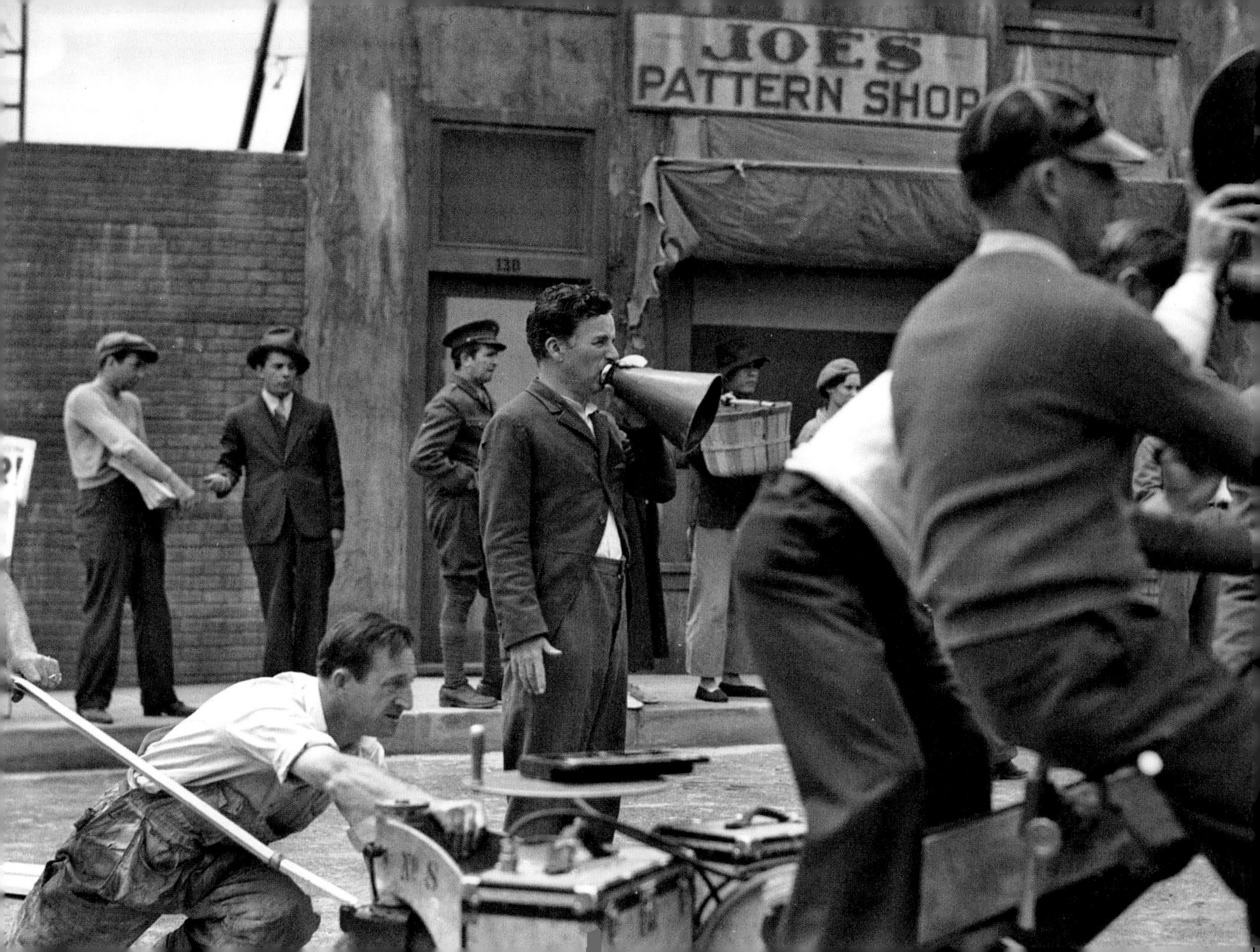

JOE'S
PATTERN SHOP

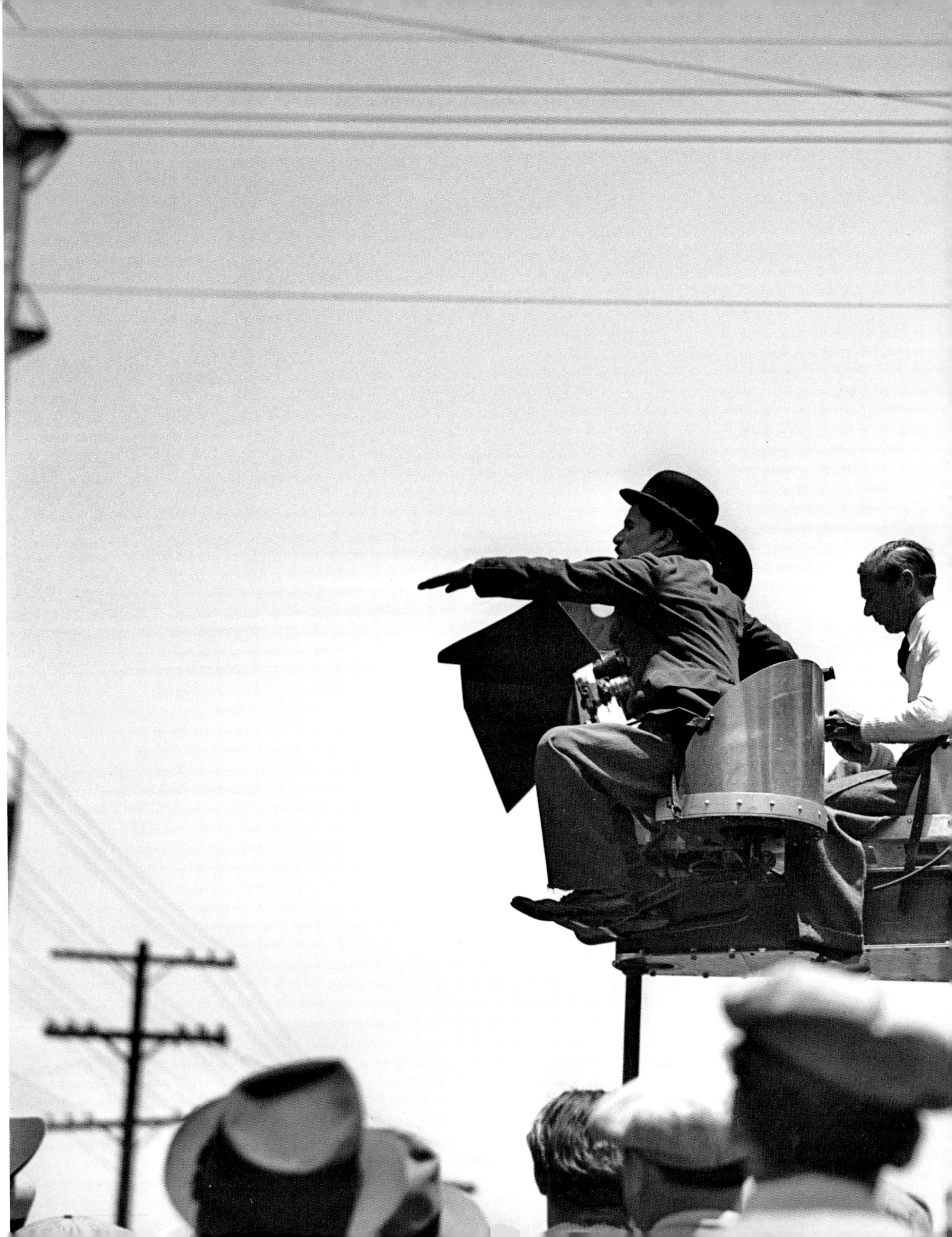

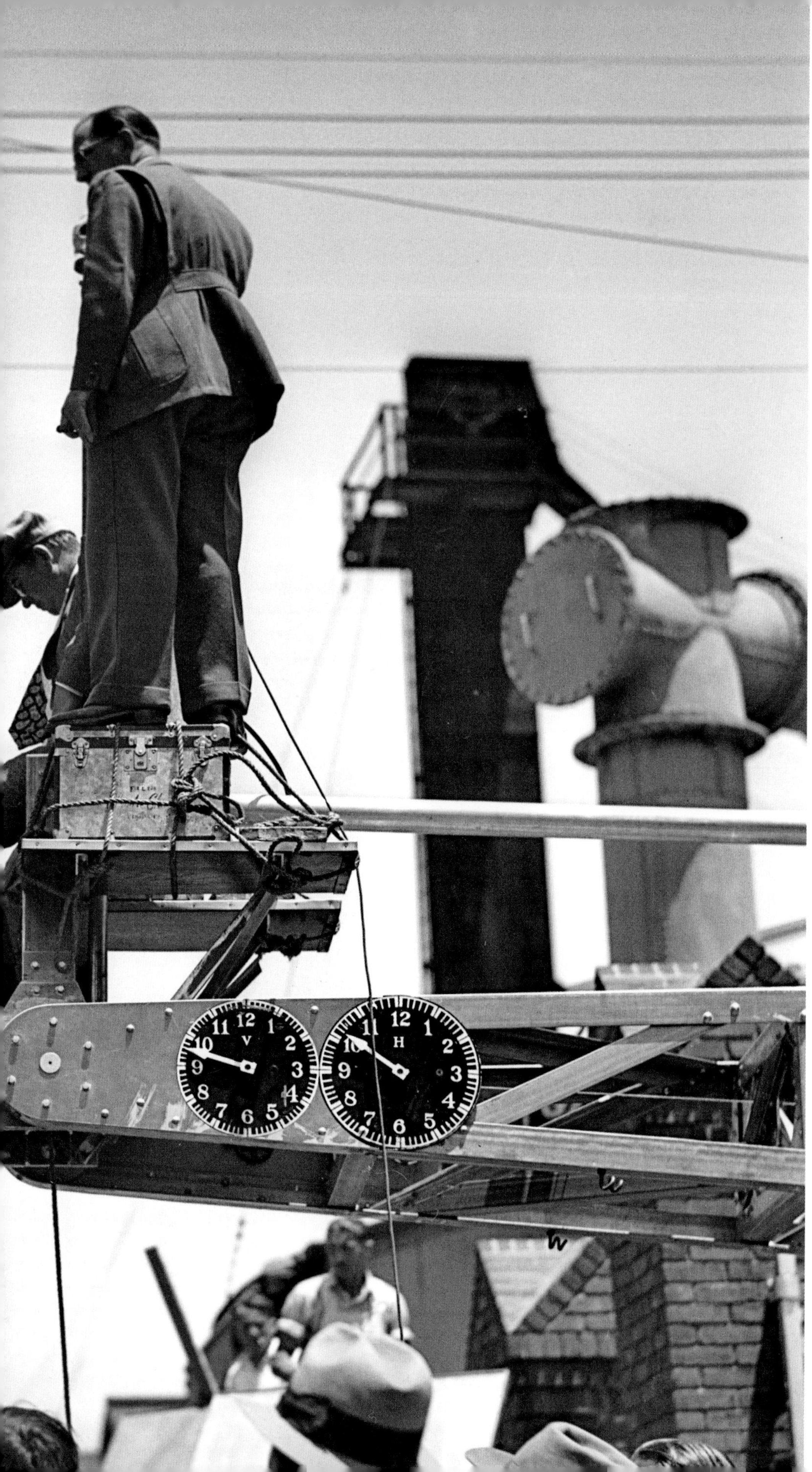

Left

In his Tramp outfit, Chaplin directs his actors from the top of a crane during the filming of *Modern Times*, c. 1935–36.

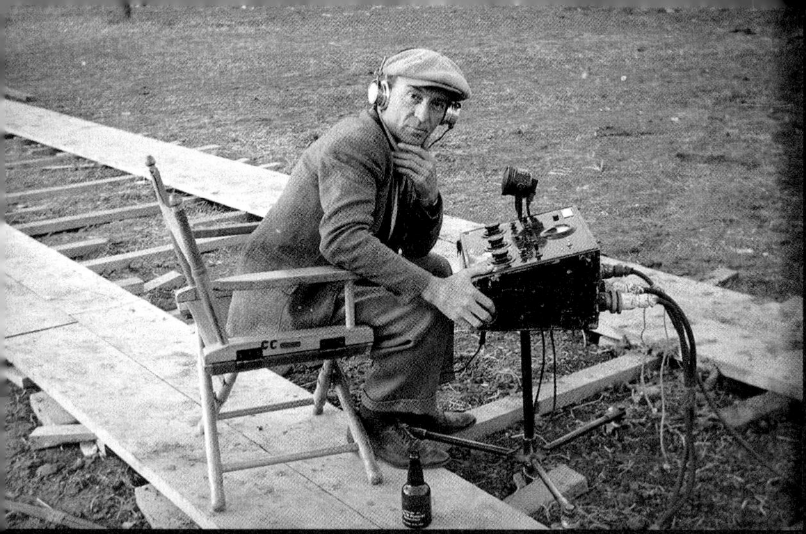

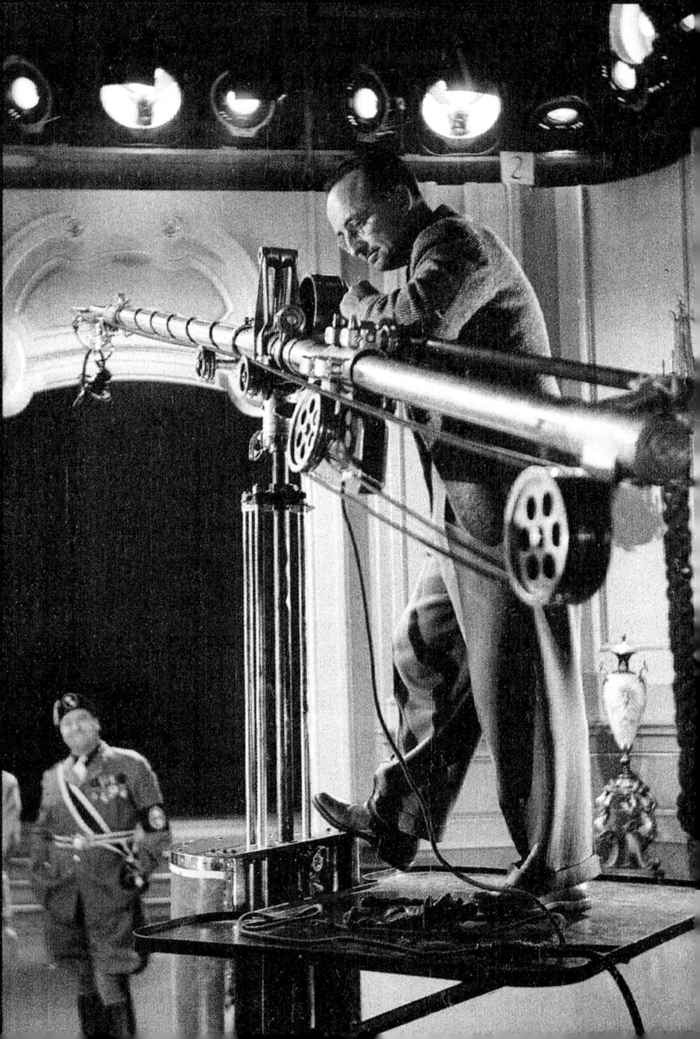

bove

'he sound engineer
luring the filming of *The
Great Dictator*, c. 1939–40.
Photograph by Dan James.
The Great Dictator was
Chaplin's first real talkie.
For the shoot, the studios
were soundproofed, which
ook a month. The arrival of
sound was a real revolution
or Chaplin: while he had
previously alternated
phases of writing and
ilming, he then had to
write the entire screenplay
and dialogue before the
beginning of shooting.

Right

Boom operator at work
luring the filming of *The
Great Dictator*, c. 1939–40.
Photograph by Dan James

Opposite

Paulette Goddard on the
ghetto street set, *The
Great Dictator*, c. 1939–40.
Photograph by Max
Munn Autrey

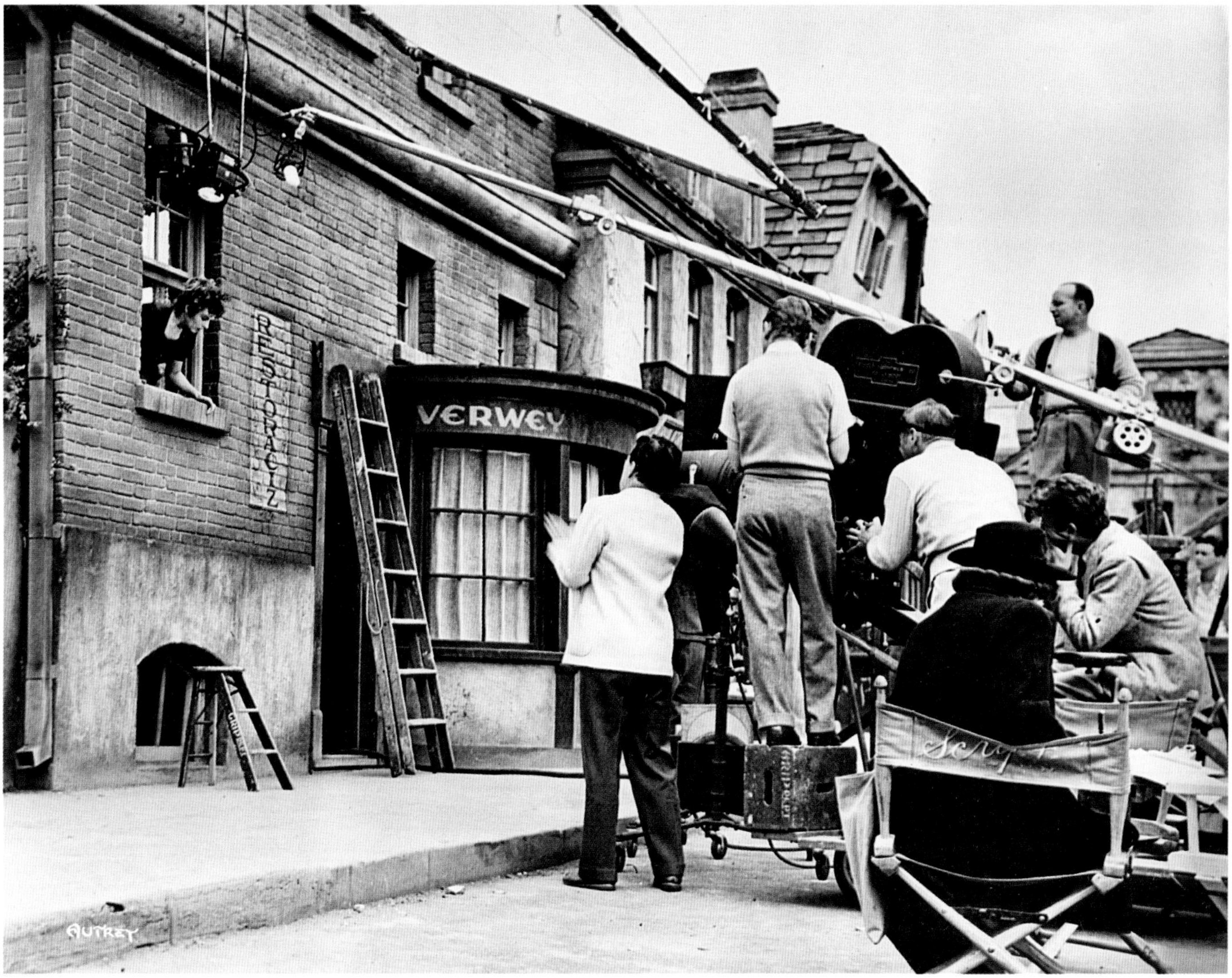
RESTORACIZ
VERWEY
AUTREY

Right

Chaplin behind the camera during the filming of *The Great Dictator*, c. 1939–40. The noise of the motor of the Mitchell NC camera that Chaplin had chosen to shoot his film disturbed the sound recording and called for the use of a blimp: a soundproofing case that covered the camera. At the time, cameras with integrated blimps already existed but they were perhaps too advanced for Chaplin and his team.

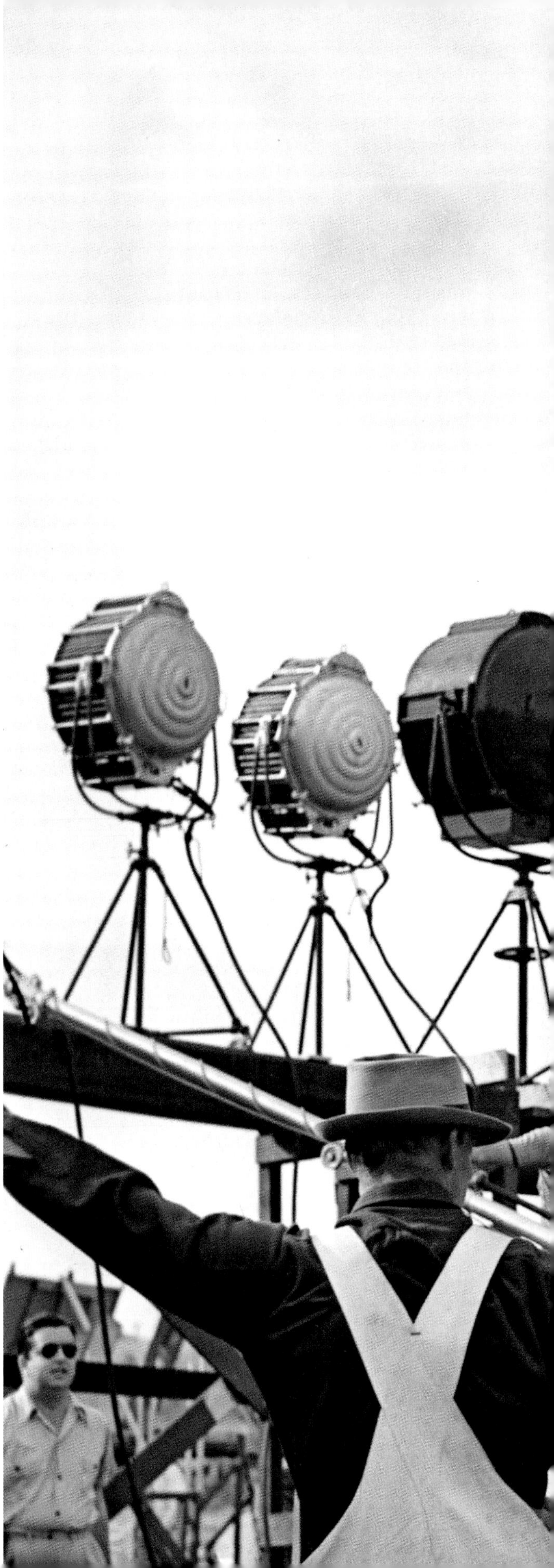

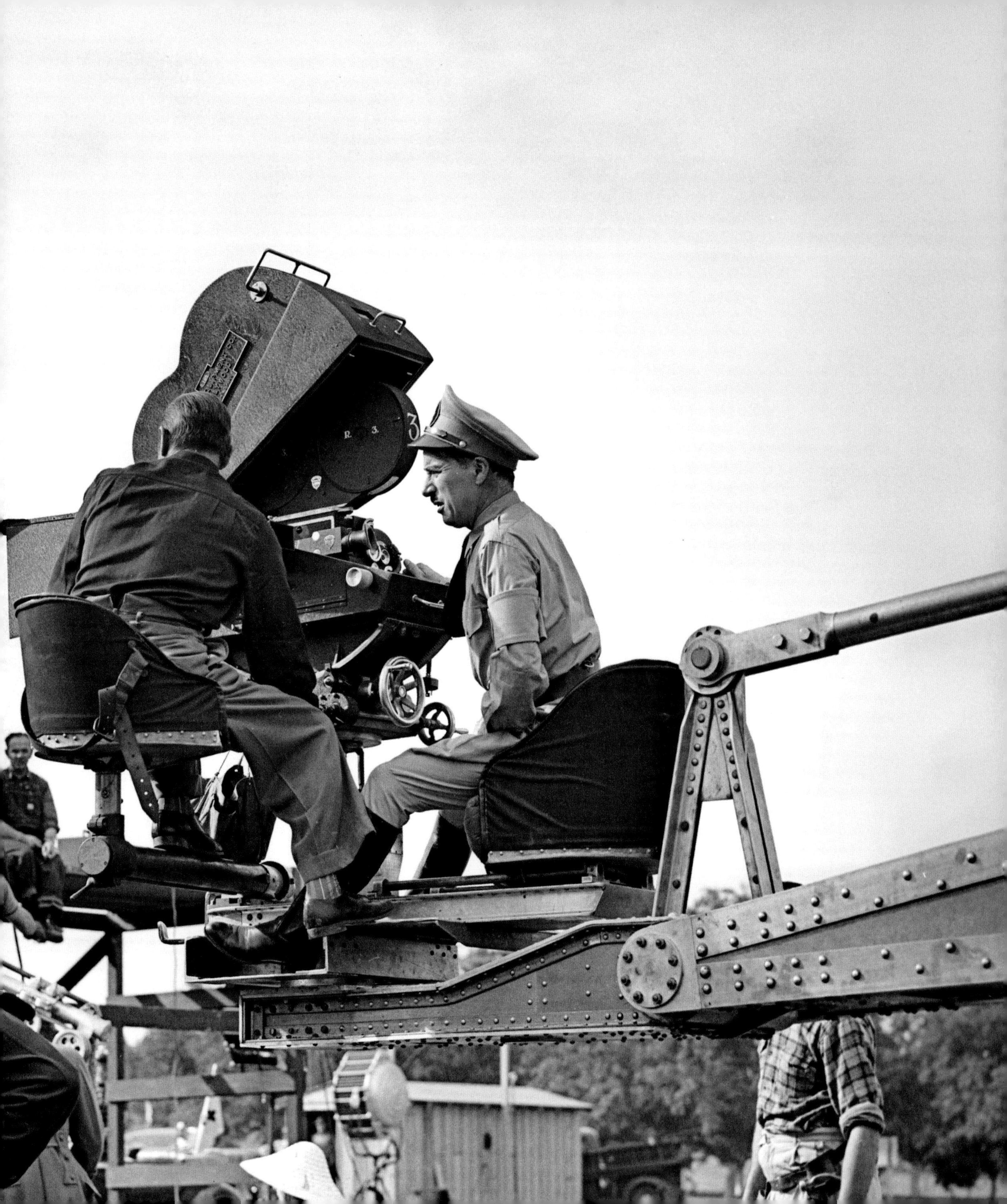

3
R. 3.

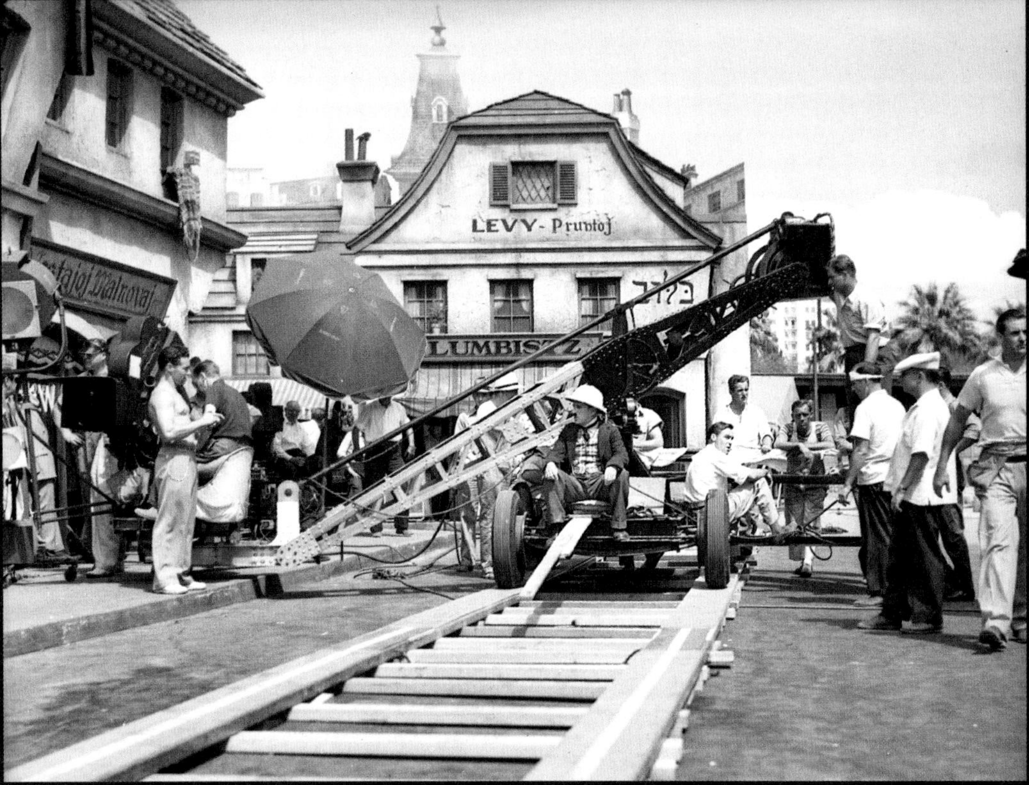

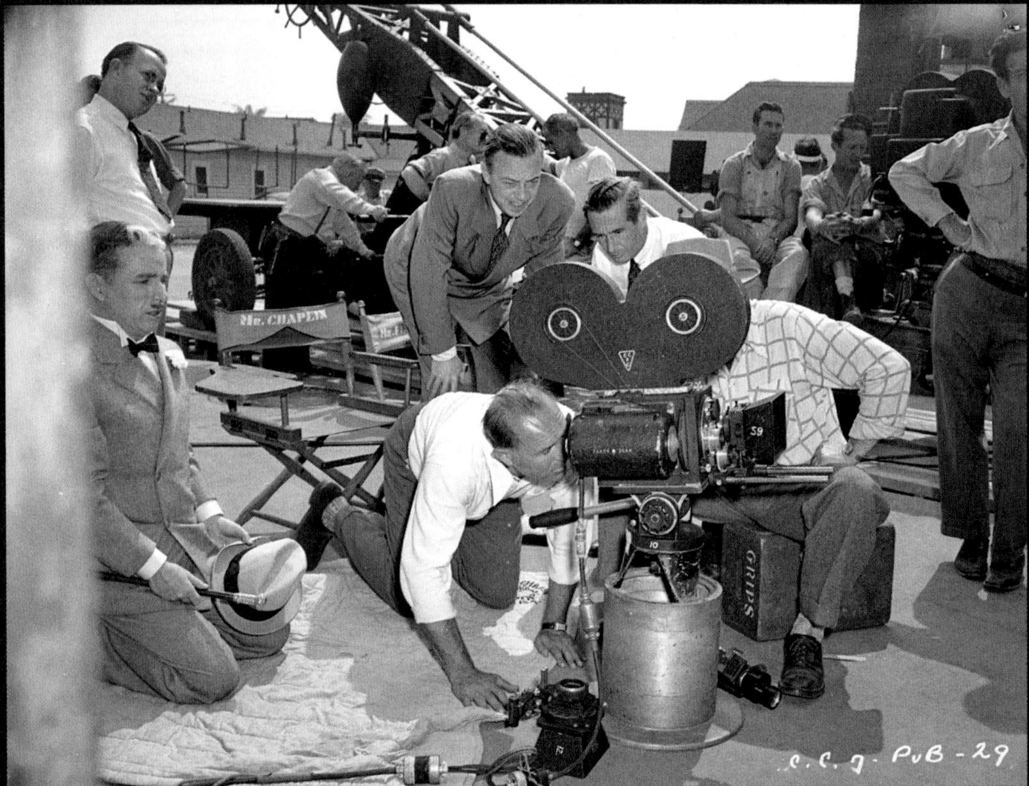

Top

Filming a ghetto scene for *The Great Dictator*, 1939–40. Chaplin is sitting on a crane, installed on the rails of the dolly. Filming techniques and equipment had changed greatly since Chaplin invented the Tramp in 1914. His early films, with their frontal sets and static cameras, show that he was above all interested in the acting, but his way of working evolved alongside cinema itself.

Left

Chaplin and Robert Florey (standing, behind the camera), during the filming of *Monsieur Verdoux*, c. 1947.

Opposite

Chaplin and his team (Robert Aldrich and Rollie Totheroh are behind him) pose with the camera during the filming of *Limelight*, c. 1951–52.

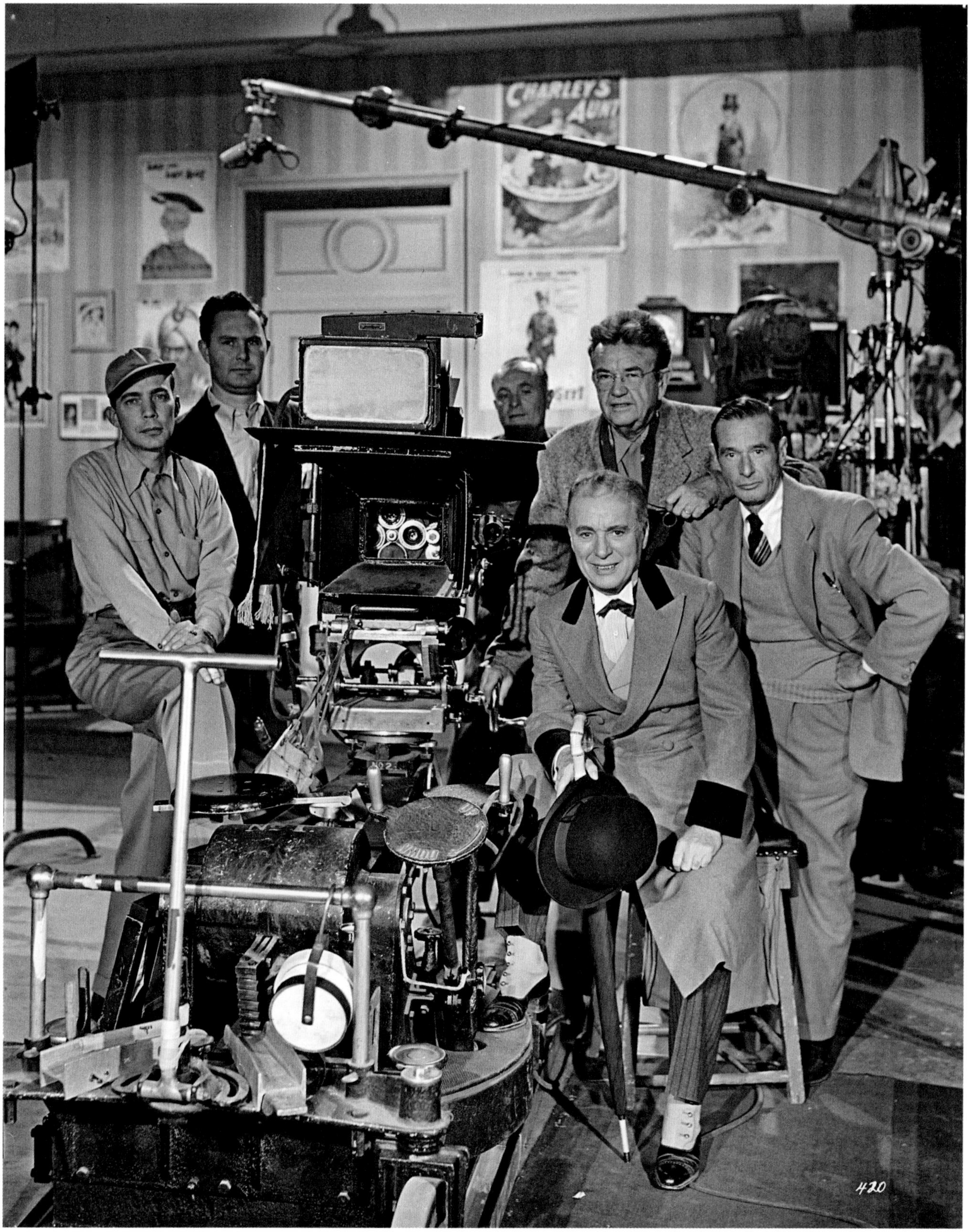
CHARLEY'S
AUNT
420

Cecilia Cenciarelli

The sound of silence

Or hearing, his eyes closed

Sometime in 1937, Igor Stravinsky suggested he and Chaplin should do a film together. In his autobiography, Chaplin describes the grotesque and irreverent musical he invented for the Russian composer: "Christianity," a Passion play, as the floor show of a night club, with groups of people watching the crucifixion of the Savior with little interest, some ordering meals, others talking business, while the mob, the High Priests, and the Pharisees shake their fists at the Cross. Chaplin's intention was—in his own words—ultimately to reveal "men's greed, hypocrisy and ruthlessness."

Contrary to the shared belief that Chaplin might have fashioned this intriguing anecdote to embellish his memoir, several penciled notes and a three-page typed treatment preserved in the Chaplin archives stand as evidence of a missed opportunity: a film by Charlie Chaplin scored by Igor Stravinsky.[1]

The great wealth of documentation preserved in the Chaplin archives reflects, in multiple directions, the core components of Chaplin's artistic and working process. The amount and variety of music and sound-related material—spanning the late 1800s to his last days in the late 1970s—is impressive, and includes a vast collection of music hall programs (collector unknown), music-related correspondence, agreements, music break-downs, cue sheets, logs, lists of sound effects and song lyrics. Chaplin's notes are always very detailed, suggesting different cues, alternate orchestration or even spotting a wrong note in the performance. Photos with the likes of Leopold Godowsky, Arnold Schoenberg, Clara Haskil, Hanns Eisler, or Pablo Casals are only a partial testimony of some of the great musicians he befriended. All in all, this generous wealth of records unequivocally shows how deeply music permeated and informed Chaplin's formative years, creative choices and, ultimately, his whole artistic vision and output.

Years before he composed his first score, Chaplin was already *perceived* as a talented musician: whether he intentionally tried to shape this specific narrative or not, his musicianship became part of the press conversation. Charlie's musical talents became a recurrent feature in the British press around the release of *The Gold Rush*: since the film was preceded at the London Tivoli by a short documentary on a famous composer—Wagner in September and Verdi in October—several newspapers titled *Chaplin and the Music Masters*. The specialized press too reported Chaplin's views on scoring for cinema: in October 1925, the *Musical News and Herald* featured a lengthy editorial on "Musical Progress in Cinema," discussing the opportunities offered to music by cinema

1 In 1937 the magazine *Life* published a series of very curious shots taken by King Vidor at Chaplin's home in Beverly Hills, featuring Igor Stravinsky rolling around Charlie's "health hoop" in the garden.

in relation to the forthcoming release of *Der Rosenkavalier*, Richard Strauss's opera directed by Robert Wiene. According to the editorialist, "Strauss's recognition of cinema as an art with which a serious musician may associate himself is bound to have a considerable influence." Chaplin's opinion on the matter was offered to support the writer's argument: "You cannot emphasize too much the importance of orchestral scores for pictures. I believe that the score should be made as the picture is made, and not that people should spend a year making a film and then have a score written in a week. It is as though Pavlova were to say 'I shall dance—and, oh, yes we will have some music, too,' at the last minute."

Chaplin's statements and interviews, quoted and reprinted extensively for half a century, have certainly contributed to reinforcing a rather monolithic interpretation of his attitude toward sound, which actually went hand in hand with the development of his musical mind. "Chaplin's genius is closely connected with his inner hearing," said Ray Rasch about him, "the way he hears the world, his eyes closed."

While he was one of the few prominent filmmakers who continued making silent films well into the mid-1930s, his experimentation and innovation with sound and music and his contribution to exploring its vast expressive potential have often been overlooked. Hence the misconception, until relatively recently, that the films he made during the decade following the sound revolution were, to a certain degree, nothing more than silent films with synchronized scores and effects.

With *City Lights*, Chaplin successfully proved that having dialogue would not only have been repetitive but also

Right

The millionaire (Harry Myers) and Chaplin in the cabaret scene, *City Lights*, 1931. In *The Count* (1916), Chaplin had already exploited the comic potential of spaghetti. He added a sonic dimension in *City Lights* with unrealistic sound effects for the sequence, with a glissando produced by a slide whistle. The scene resembles a circus act or cartoon.

Following double page

Letter sent by Eugène Lauste to Chaplin on December 9, 1918. Long before Warner Brothers' Vitaphone, the Frenchman Eugène Lauste registered a patent for the recording of sound on film in 1906. For lack of funding, his invention could not be marketed on a large scale. In 1918, he wrote to Chaplin about his discovery.

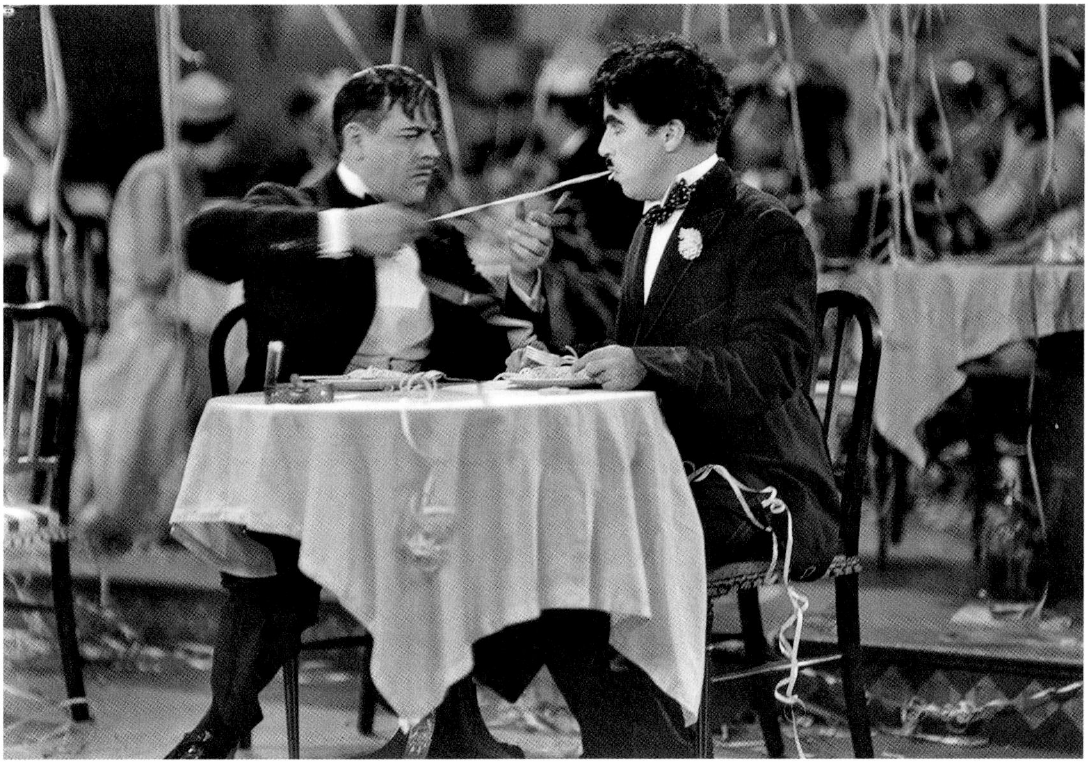

EUGENE LAUSTE
PRIVATE OFFICE
441 West 22nd Street
NEW YORK CITY

(1

New York 9th. December 1918

Lauste

To Mr. Charlie Chaplin,
California Studio,

Dear Sir,

I have just returned from England, and at my arrival I heard that you have started a new moving pictures studio on your own, for which I am very pleased to congratulate you as a wonder artist who by your cleverness and your ingenuity you have been able to conquer the whole world. I am myself one of your admirer at the time that you have been engaged with Fred. Karno Since that time, you have rapidly progressed with enormous success, so, let me take the liberty to present to you my most hearty congratulations for the great achievement you have already done in the history of the cinematograph.

My self, I am an inventor, I was firstly working with Mr. T. A. Edison, at his private laboratory at Orange N.J. for many years. Then in 1894, I had design, build, and exhibited the first projecting moving pictures machine, called the (Eidoloscope) so I claim that I was the first one who bring out this great invention, which it is not my last one. However, I am very plea-se to say that my invention has been favorable to you, and my other one, if you are interested in it, would bring to you an enormous fortune.

At present, the object of my letter is not to make any propositions of my in vention, but I will explain to you after. I must also mention to you that I have been appointed Managing Director of the American Biograph and Mutoscope Co. Limited for France, at Paris, which probably you will remember this wonderful machine who has been on exhibition for many years at the Palace theatre in London. After several years with this company, I decided to return to London, to start on my own a new experimental laboratory, for Scientific researchs, and also to work especially on the above invention which I kept in my mind for many years.

Now I will come to the conclusion of the object of my letter. I want to introduce to you a friend of mind Mr. E. A. J. Siron, who have just for-med a new company for the exploitation of films, and apparatus for Belgium, with British capital. Mr. Siron, he his one of the best man you could meet and very clever in cinematograph business, he his also, Redactor of two good papers in Europe, (Le Film de Paris,) and the (Cinema revue de Bruxelles,) so you will see by your self that his a man on which you could depend and trust. He wrote to me few days ago, to asking me if I could find the possibility to see you to make some arrangement to get your exclusive right of your produc-tions for Belgium, which I think will be of a great success for your mutual interest. So I will be very pleased if you could make some kind of proposi-tions for the above country which from your answer I will submit to him. Now the war is over, which certainly will make Belgium, a new territory to be exploited for the cinematograph, consequantly I do not think you will find a better man who his already very well known in that country.

His temporary address in London is 28 Aigburth's Mansions, Chapel Street and at Brussels,42 Rue de Laeken (Centre) The title of the Company is (The General Cine-Film).

I will be very pleased to hear from you as soon as possible regarding this matter so I will write to him at once, then after you will communicate directly with him.

Hoping your reply will be satisfactory,

I am dear sir,

Yours Faithfully,

E. Lauste

P.T.O.

2

Referring to my invention, kindly allow me few seconds of your attention to explain the great future of it. As you know, the present machines will in a short time, come at end. For years and years, the public want to see the realism, that means the real talking pictures which up to now has never been accomplished pratically and commercially. Many inventors they have already tried to synchronize the gramophone or phonograph in connection with the cinematograph, which has been a failure, and always will be?. The only way which that could be done satisfactory, is my own principle on which I have working on, for over 25 years.

I do not want that you think I come to you and bring to you an invention which is an imaginary or dreaming idea which is in the air, but the truth. So before I will engage myself with a party which I have in view, I like to give you the opportunity to take in your hands this wonderful discovery which I believe you will be surprise to hear that a such machine was in existence. The fact, that I had giving in London, several demonstrations to the press, and also to scientists experts, which their opinions was very satisfactory from their reports which I will prove to you by the originals.

In few words, I will explain the principle of my invention, which after his completion will certainly revolutionize the cinematograph industry. The idea which his alresdy accomplished, is to photograph pictures and sounds simultaneously on the same film, and in one operation, and reproduced same without any contact on the film, or the use of a gramophone or phonograph. The sounds is absolutly clear, no scratching whatever or distortion in the voice or music, I am certain that you will be very surprise to hear it.

However, if you think you will be interested, let me know as soon as possible, then I will send to you more particular regarding same, and also a copies of the reports and documents.

My invention has been already described in some French and British papers, also in this country. If you like to have a copy of the Scientific American, in which an article has been writing, I will be very please to send you one at once.

Awaiting your reply, which I trust may be favorable,

I am dear sir,

Yours faithfully,

E. Lauste

counterproductive. In an early draft of the story, he had imagined a "dialogue" between the blind girl and the tramp (here "The Duke") via a record player:

> Phonograph Episode: the blind girl shall own a phonograph which she operates at her flower stand. Her favorite record shall be "Bright Eyes" or some other semi-jazzy number. The Duke becomes haunted by the melody and whistles the tune as he strolls. In a Penny arcade he seeks the number and listens to it through the old-fashioned ear receivers . . . This means is also suggested for a lovemaking scene between the Duke and Girl, through his answering her song with another of significance.[2]

Music and sounds not only had to serve the story but also the Tramp's universe, the way Chaplin had shaped and populated it for years. In that regard, the opening of *City Lights* features a signature theme for Chaplin, the target of his satire being authority, the bourgeois and the representatives of law and morality. He had already proved he had a unique, extraordinary body for comedy—now sound offered him a new opportunity to explore how to perform with his voice.

Over the course of ten years Chaplin elevated the use of noises, voices, words, and sounds to a level of virtuosity. In *The Great Dictator* (1940) he turned verbal communication into a tool of domination and forged a speech blending together gibberish, snarls, and English-based macaronic German, which Deleuze defined "the false language of nonsense and terror, sound and fury that Chaplin has the genius to invent and put into the mouth of the tyrant."[3]

In Chaplin's 1936 *Modern Times*, human voice is recorded, filtered, amplified, and constantly delivered through a modern machine—intercoms, loudspeakers, record players—with a dehumanizing effect.[4] By the same token, the magnificent symphonic score that Chaplin composed for the film, considered by many as his musical pinnacle, is not only tightly synchronized to the action, but manages brilliantly to convey and reinforce the very premise of the film: the factory and automated work strip individuals of their humanity, and they are lost among giant corporations, indifferent bureaucracies, and the impersonal forces of markets and money. This merciless metronome mark, intentionally set by Chaplin, is so fragile, so on-the-very-edge-of-collapse, that the listener is compelled to identify with the frantic Charlie on the verge of his mental breakdown.[5] In the end, the only natural voice we hear in *Modern Times* is the Tramp's, and his last chance to make a life for himself and the Gamin is ironically dependent on his *singing*. Like in *commedia dell'arte*, he is forced to improvise his performance, and although nobody can understand his song—a *grammelot* full of macaronic and onomatopoeic sounds—his number is a delight to the audience proving that "acting, dance, pantomime and music can tell a story better than voiced words."[6]

Chaplin's full-spectrum exploration translated into a range of aesthetic and expressive uses of sound: from the more

2 *City Lights* treatment (undated), preserved in the Chaplin archives.

3 Gilles Deleuze, *Cinema I: the Movement Image* (London: Continuum, 1992), 172.

4 In his essential *Chaplin cineaste* (Paris: Éditions du Cerf, 1998), Francis Bordat was one of the first scholars not to look at Chaplin's body chronologically but rather focusing on his contribution to filmmaking. The chapter 'La bande sonore' (pp. 267–299) provides a very thorough analysis of Chaplin's relationship with sound and words.

5 Timothy Brock, "The Score to Modern Times," in Christian Delage and Cecilia Cenciarelli (eds.) *Modern Times* (Recco: Le Mani Editore), 263.

6 Aner Preminger, "Charles Chaplin Sings a Silent Requiem," in Laurence Howe, James E. Caron, Benjamin Click (eds.), *Refocusing Chaplin: a Screen Icon through Critical Lenses* (Lanham: The Scarecrow Press, 2013), 176.

Below

On the set of *The Circus*, 1927.
Musicians and instruments were often present on silent-film sets to help render the atmosphere of a scene. On set that day, the journalist A. L. Woodridge said that Chaplin started playing the harmonium to calm the lion, to make shooting the scene in which the Tramp is locked in the sleeping feline's cage easier.

Following double page

The minister's wife (Mira McKinney) and the Tramp in prison, *Modern Times*, 1936.
The comedy of this scene mainly resides in the sound effects: the actors let nothing appear on screen but the soundtrack is enriched with sounds of gurgling and dogs barking, which give the scene a schoolboyish tone.

realistic, sometimes Mickey Mousing gun shots, clashes and dog barks (*City Lights*) to the surreal use of the human body as a sound box for whistles, amplified stomach rumbles (*Modern Times*), and clinking coins (*The Great Dictator*). In the prison scene of *Modern Times*, he pushed innovation further and used the sound of birds tweeting to suggest that the Tramp is happier and freer in prison than he would be among the hungry and unemployed outside. The use of sound here is "non-synchronous and incongruous with the site of the action," allowing Chaplin to "express himself cinematically and without words."[7] With a similar intent (yet in a diametrically opposed way), he also explored the narrative potential of attracting the audience's attention to the *lack* of certain sounds, developing audio gags in the same way he used visual jokes.

One of the most brilliant examples of this, analyzed in great details by Aner Preminger, is the lion cage sequence in *The Circus* (1928), where the Tramp's main concern is to avoid all noises that could awaken the lion. The slamming of the gate between the two cages, the last-minute grabbing of the lion's water bowl to prevent it from hitting the floor and the dog's barks: all the sounds—observes Preminger—are, here, 'the source of mortal danger' and each of the obstacles in the sequence 'hinges on sounds that the audience does not hear'. Having led his audience to imagine a whole spectrum of sounds and noises, Chaplin conceives the perfect climax: as we *see* that the dog is barking more and more fiercely, we laugh at the Tramp covering his ears, as if, by doing so, he could shield the

7 Ibid., p. 174.

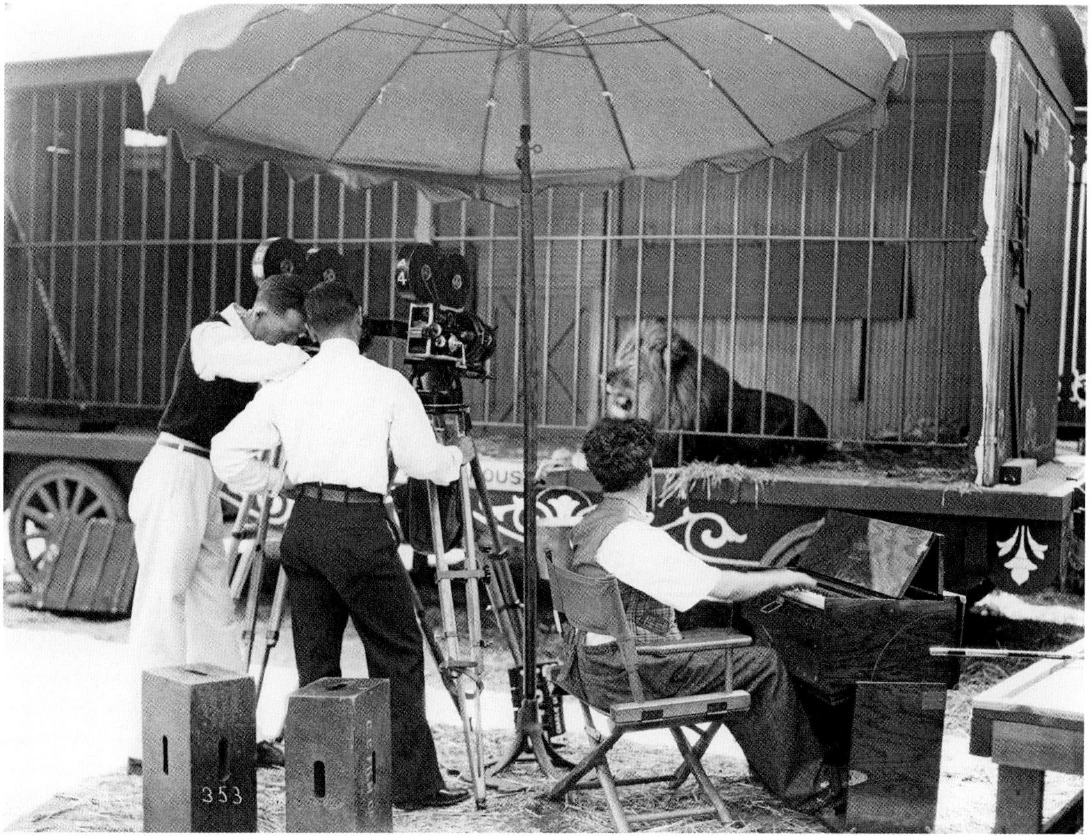

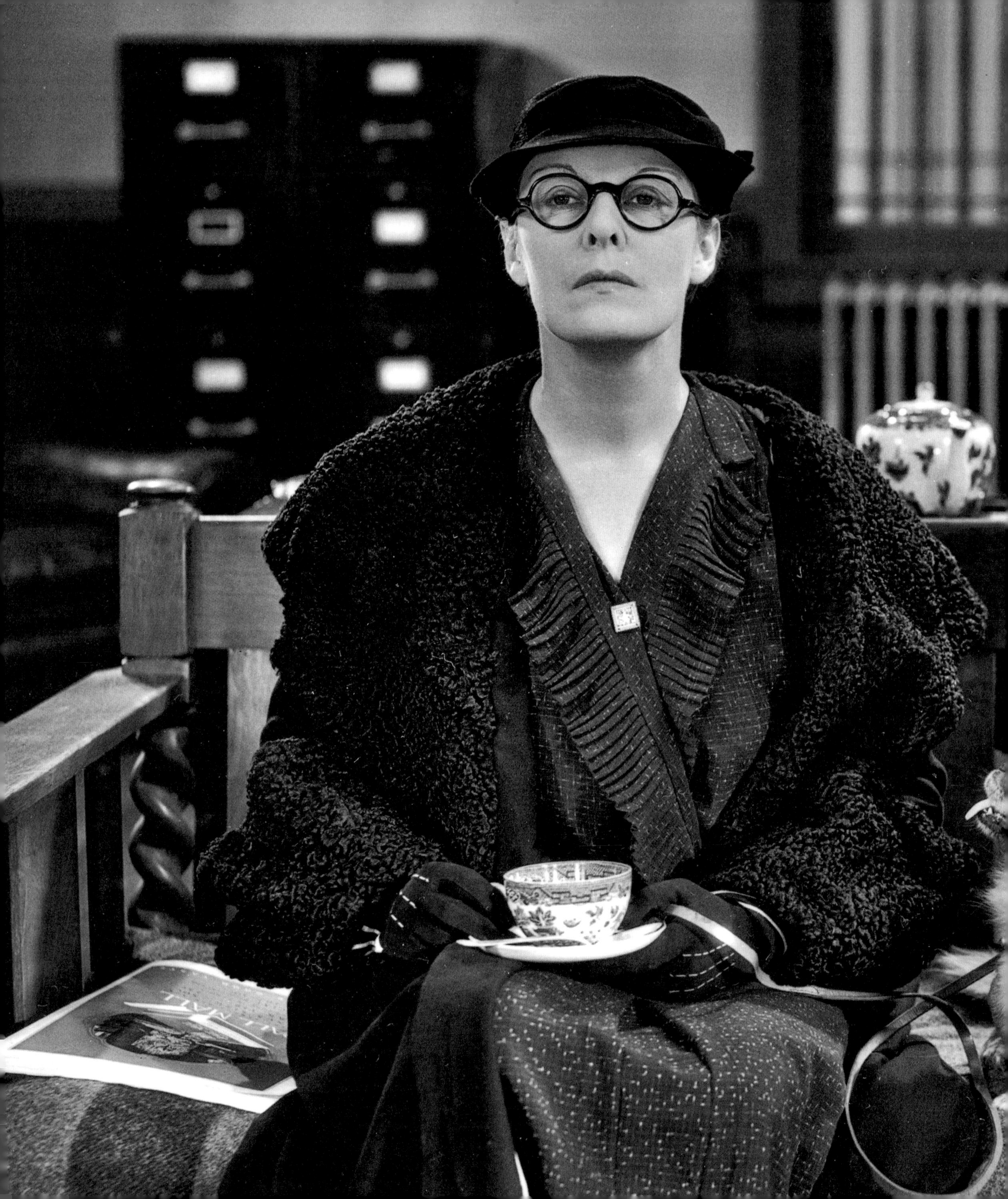

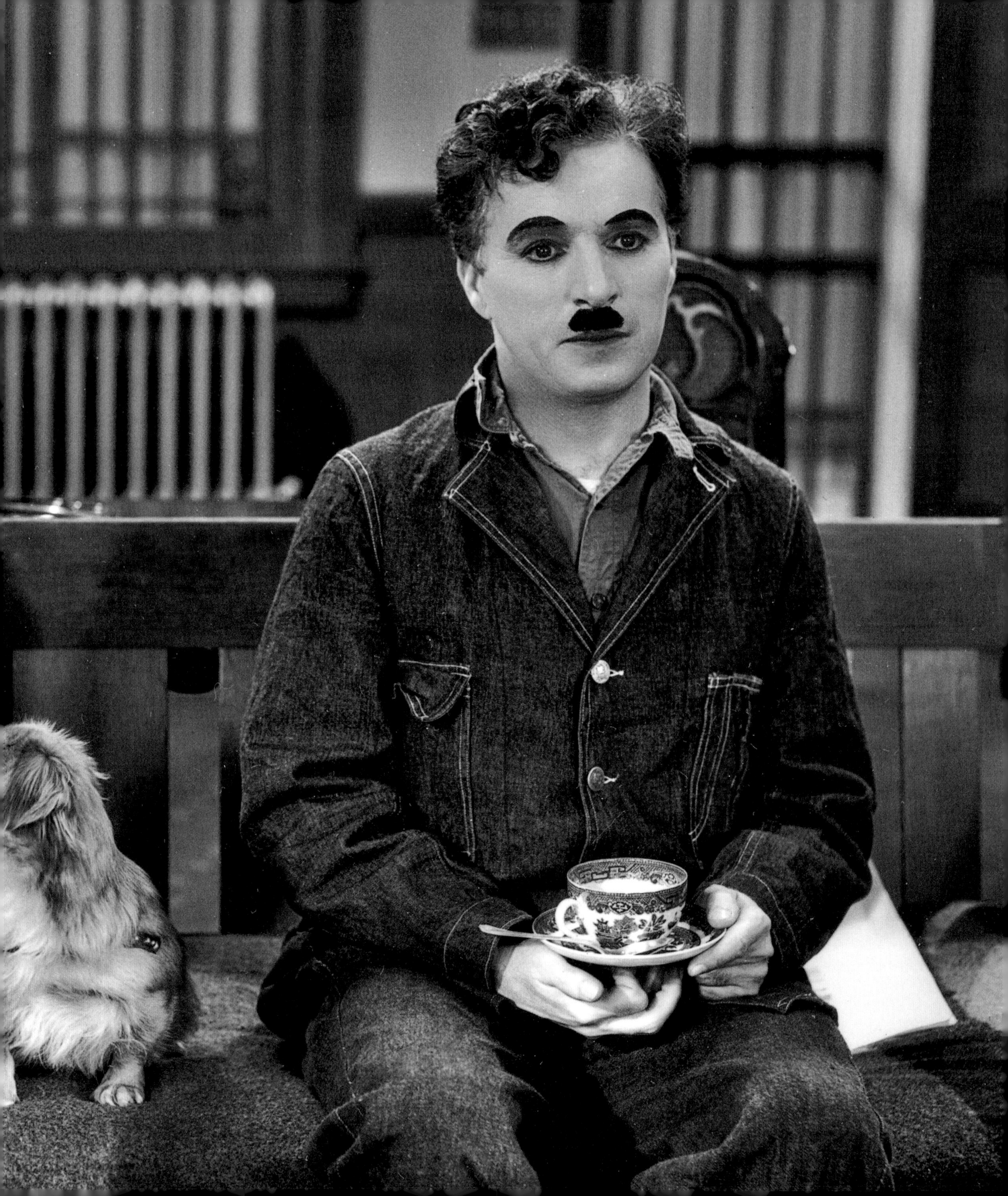

Opposite

Scene of the first encounter between the Tramp and the flower girl (Virginia Cherrill) in *City Lights*, 1931.
Chaplin dedicated several weeks to shooting the key scene of the film.

lion's ears too. "At this early stage of talking movies, Chaplin chooses not to apply the new technology, yet he is not ignoring it."

A similar principle comes into play in *City Lights* soon after the Tramp and the Blind Girl have met for the first time:

> Scene 66 – Long-shot at flower stand. Limousine standing at curb by flower stand. C.C. stands in front of flower stand. Flower girl standing up, rose in her hand. She extends it to him, says: "Please take it." C.C. pushes her back and says "That's for you". She says: "Take the money", extending left hand with money. He pushes her hand back as gentleman from park enters scene and goes up to limousine. Man enters car and slams door. Girl hears door slam. Car drives away. Girl stands back, sits down, says "Good-bye," waves hand, thinking that C.C. has left. C.C. watches her then tip-toes away and into park entrance.[8]

The scene is very cleverly shot, with the camera panning left—showing the Tramp looking at the man stepping into the car—then right, as he looks at the flower girl, and finally left again—as they both look at the departing car. The rhythm of the music, as well as the Tramp's tiptoeing away, help reinforce the assumption regarding his identity: the action unravels effortlessly, the audience relying on the Blind Girl's enhanced hearing to tell the difference between a limousine and a more modest car and therefore believing with her that the Tramp, of all people, can be mistaken for a millionaire.

Unlike the lion cage sequence in *The Circus*, where sounds are evoked to serve a specific comic moment unrelated to the narrative of the film, the "silent door slam" in *City Lights* performs a subtler, yet more significant function: while it expresses a precise artistic choice (Chaplin could have opted for sound for the entire film, or for a sound effect for the car door closing), it also sets the narrative premise for the entire film. At the end of *City Lights*, probably one of the highest moments in film history, the Blind Girl realizes that her benefactor is not a wealthy man but a destitute tramp. The production notes reveal that Chaplin had this idea in mind almost from the start, and yet he searched for a long time before finding the cause of the girl's misunderstanding in a noise that is seen but not heard.

8 Original shooting report of February 5, 1929, preserved in the Chaplin archives.

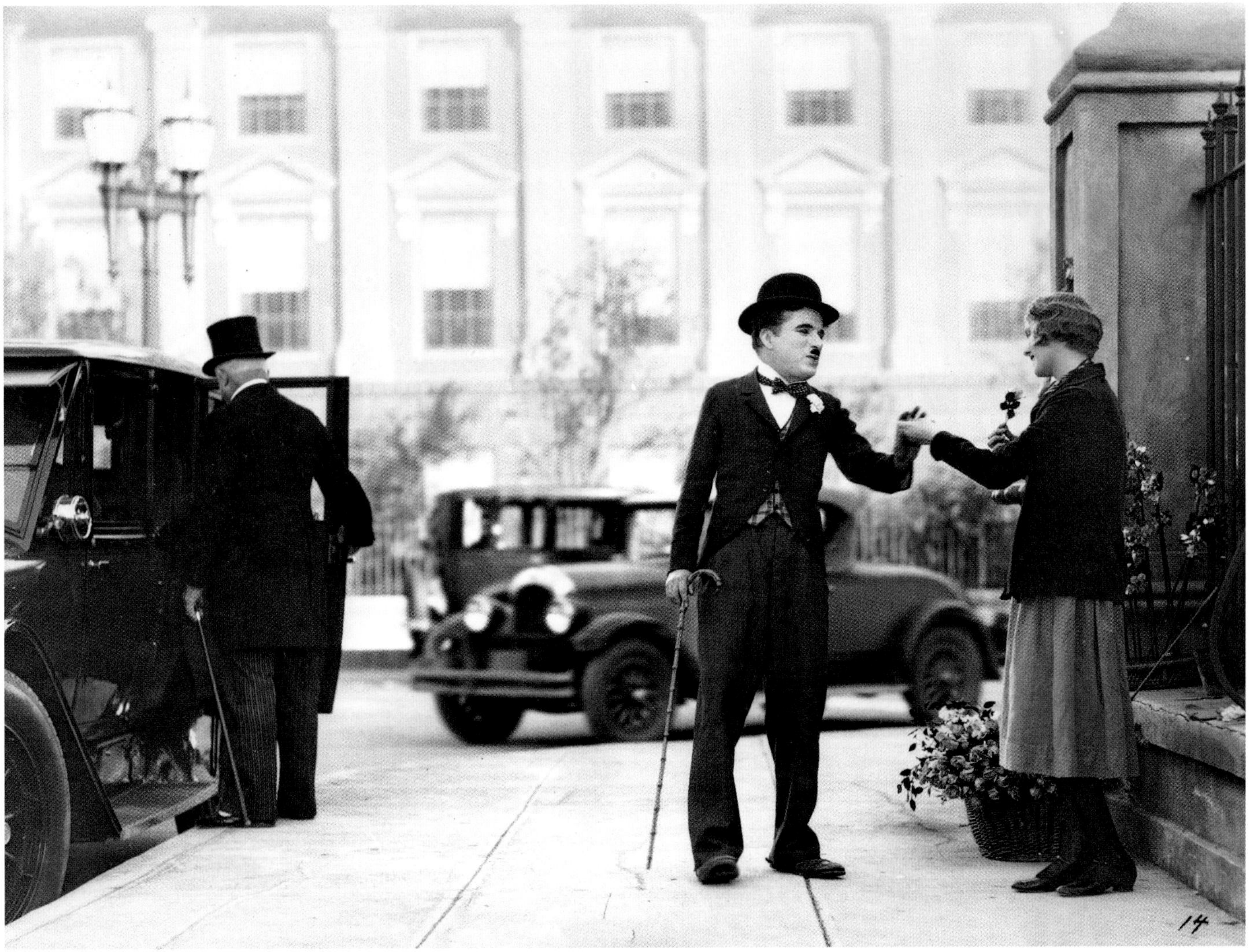
14

Kate Guyonvarch

Chaplin and the dilemma of sound

In 1931 the press was full of Chaplin's protests that silent film was the best form of cinema. Already in a 1929 interview for *Motion Picture Magazine*, Chaplin had commented that talkies were "spoiling the oldest art in the world—the art of pantomime," "ruining the great beauty of silence" and "defeating the meaning of the screen," and, even though more sophisticated technology soon put an end to the necklace-rattling, tinny dialogues of early talkies,[1] Chaplin released *City Lights* as a silent film.

We know, though, that he believed in words. Sculptress Clare Sheridan, after days with him in 1921, wrote: "I have heard him make empassioned speeches to imaginary crowds. He has harangued the sand dunes."[2] And Paulette Goddard recounted: "Charlie was a great talker. He loved an audience and would hold forth on every subject in the world . . . That's what Charlie liked to do . . . talk, talk . . . but of course with great charm."[3]

We also know he had a fantastic ear, and could be very funny, in words. Actress Constance Collier told how "he would be ridiculous and make me laugh until I was ill. He would pretend to be a German or a Frenchman or an Italian and invent an imaginary language, and keep it up so wonderfully that he really looked like the part he was assuming."[4] His brother Sydney wrote: "He made a set of prominent teeth with a piece of orange peel and gave me an impromptu conversation between the couple [we had just seen]. If he would only do it for the talkies, it would be worth a fortune. I have never laughed so much in my life."[5]

However, having decided that his character would not speak in *City Lights*, Chaplin had to defend this choice against all odds. He claimed to embrace sound film technology only for music and effects, and underlined this: "In so far as the talkie has hastened production of specially composed and synchronised scores, it has justified its existence. Music like pictures is a universal language, everywhere understandable. Hence a familiar tune, a catchy air, becomes a background for the action of a film story almost as important as the pantomime itself."[6] "*City Lights* is not silent, it is simply a non-talking film with synchronized sound."[7]

Of his own admission in his autobiography, Chaplin had worked himself into "a neurotic

Opposite

Chaplin holding a microphone on the set of *City Lights*, c. 1929–30. On April 4, 1931, the journalist Kathlyn Hayden wrote in *Picture Show*: "During one of the usual interminable waits while the electricians were charging the lights Charlie ordered the radio turned on. (It seems he always has a loudspeaker on the set—to amuse him during the waits.) . . . Instantly Charlie sprang to his feet, struck a theatrical posture, and began to sing."

1 "Dialogue pictures are not melodious; they are merely tinny. They bring out all the crudities" [Chaplin quoted in the *Daily Mail*, April 2, 1930]
2 Clare Sheridan, *My American Diary* (New York: Boni and Liveright, 1922), 347.
3 Quoted in Julie Gilbert, *Opposite Attraction* (New York: Pantheon Books, 1995), 66.
4 Constance Collier, *Harlequinade* (London: The Bodley Head, 1929).
5 Letter to Jim Minney, March 9, 1932.
6 *United Artists Distributors' Handbook*, brochure for movie theater owners, reproduced in numerous newspapers, for example, "Silent Films to Come Back: Art of Pantomime and the Screen," *Oxford Mail*, November, 12, 1931, and Charlie Chaplin, "Après les "Lumières de la ville," "Pourquoi je préfère les films muets," *Le Soir*, February 9, 1931.
7 Ibid.

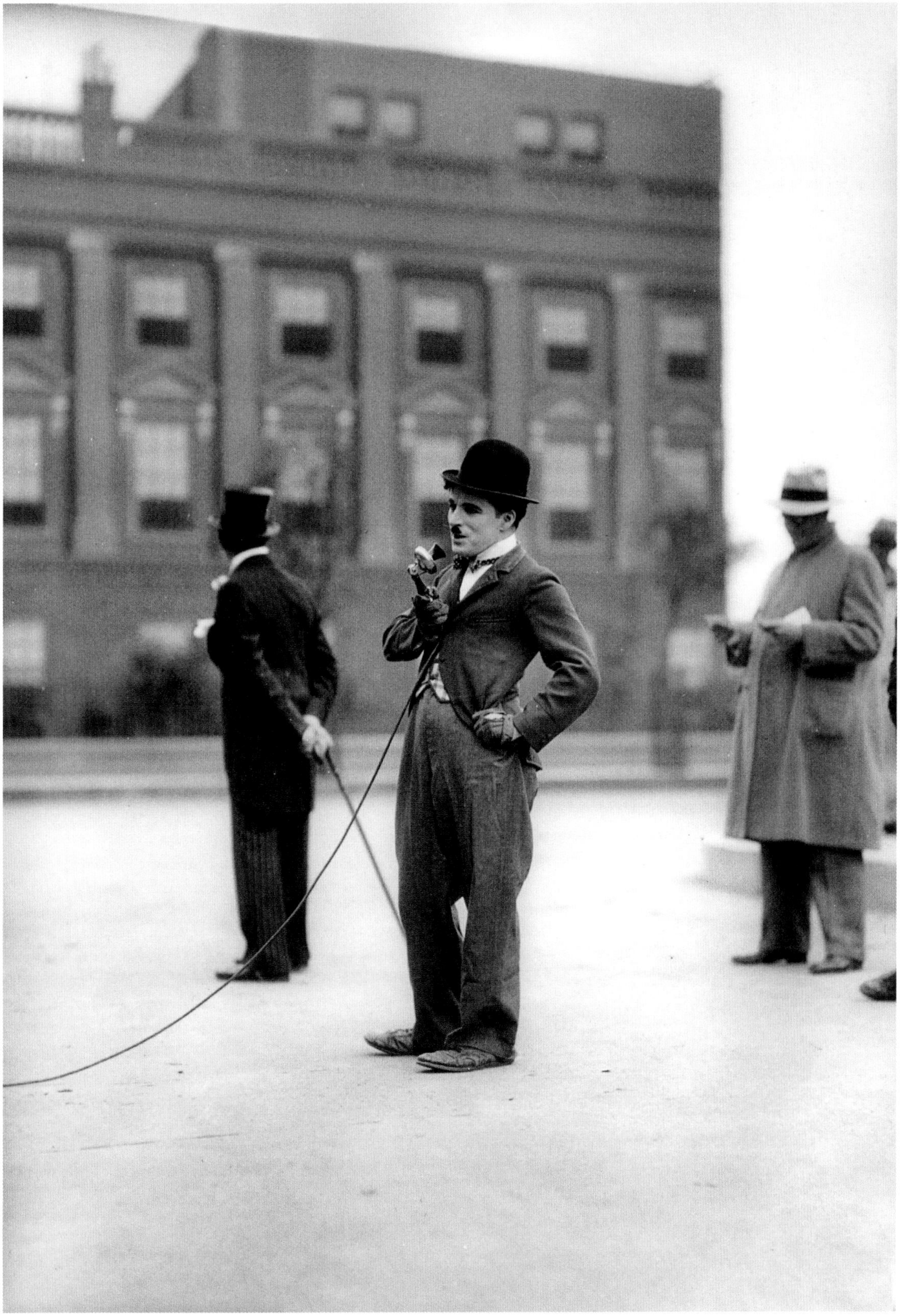

Below

"Pour Vous 1929, revue de Noël... film parlant, chantant, dansant," *Pour vous*, December 1929.

Opposite

Chaplin with Al Jolson, c. 1920.
Al Jolson made history as the actor of the first widely distributed talking film, *The Jazz Singer*, in 1927. Diametrically opposed, Chaplin and Jolson's positions on talkies were widely reported by the media.

state of wanting perfection"[8] on *City Lights*, in a climate of financial insecurity (the 1929 crash) and huge professional uncertainty (sound). The Charles Chaplin Film Corporation Board meeting minutes reflect the anxiety. On December 19, 1928, "it was discussed at length that the talking or sound innovation in the motion picture business had caused a great delay in the current picture; that it was necessary to progress slowly in order to ascertain the pulse of the public, insofar as its appreciation and acceptance of the so called 'talking motion picture' was concerned; that because of this fact, the cast and organisation necessary for the making of the current picture had been on salary since May of 1928 but that it had not yet been definitely decided whether or not it was safe to proceed without a talking edition of the current picture, and if the talking edition were necessary it would mean a further delay and an additional expense because of the peculiar and special equipment required." The minutes of the October 4, 1930 meeting report that "the current picture *City Lights* being brought to a successful close, [the President (Chaplin)] stated that inasmuch as the picture was not a talking motion picture, there was considerable doubt in his mind, as well as the minds of others engaged in the motion picture business to whom he had talked, as to the reception with which a silent motion picture would be received by the theatre going public."

8 Charles Chaplin, *My Autobiography* (London: Penguin Modern Classics, 2000), 324.

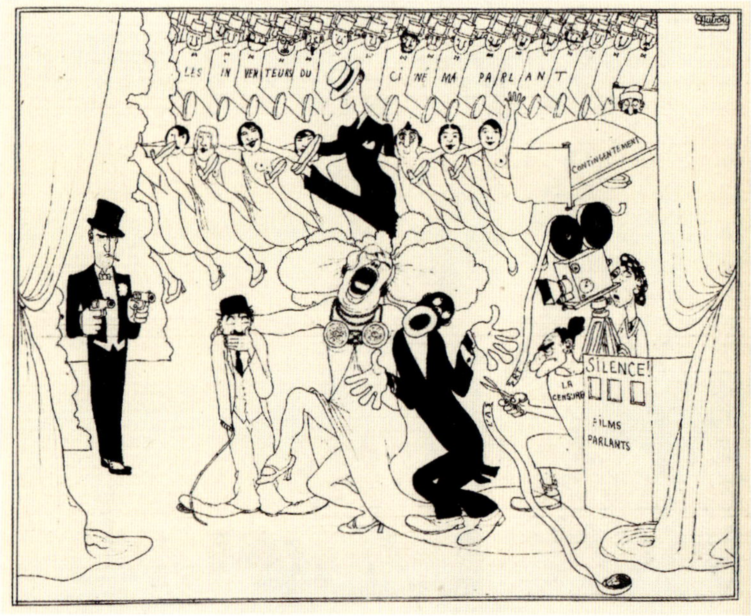

The Board decided Chaplin should attend the premieres in major cities worldwide, and publicize (defend?) his film. The first defense came in the shape of statements in the *United Artists Exhibitors' Campaign* book, describing *City Lights* as "Charlie Chaplin's gamble on the desires of the ever-fickle amusement seeking public" and declaring "after a careful study of what was going on, Chaplin reached the conclusion that the talkie was an inferior medium for the screen, one without a true art form." Chaplin is quoted as saying "silent or non-dialogue picture has been temporarily pushed aside in the hysteria attending the introduction of speech" and "talking pictures are not motion pictures, but a poor excuse for a genuine stage play. I consider my silence more eloquent than my voice and that I can give superior entertainment in the old medium, to what I consider inferior entertainment in the new medium."

Chaplin's declaration (see page 186) was reproduced worldwide.

He later published a further article, continuing: "I am confident that the future will see a return of interest in non-talking production because there is a constant demand for a medium that is universal in its appeal—the word element might be better—and I believe the medium of presentation should also be a universal rather than a restricted one . . . After all, pantomime has always been the universal means of communication. It existed as the universal tool long before language was born. Pantomime serves well where languages are in the conflict of a common ignorance."

There of course is the rub: the universality of the little tramp character. With a single sentence, millions of cinema-goers would be lost. "Charlie is the only picture actor left in the world with all nations for an audience and all countries for his market," wrote George Gerhard in the *Evening World*, February 7th 1931. And it was a highly lucrative market.

Thus it is understandable that Chaplin became even more emphatic in his denigration of sound film, declaring that "the mere sight of a microphone and a robotesque recording apparatus is positively nauseating. The cold blooded efficiency of the sound studio appals me."[9] English newspapers reported[10] that he placed dialogue films on the same level as "scent" films in which "vamps will be attended with exotic perfumes. Breakfast will be accompanied by the fragrance of sausages and coffee."

Such statements, like the absurd hyperbole in the exhibitors' book about details of the film's production,[11] are perhaps best ignored. In his 1966 interview with Richard Meryman, Chaplin was more honest. "When the talking pictures came I knew it was much easier for me to pantomime, than it was to talk—and I knew very well in talking, a lot would disappear."[12] Also, "I wouldn't know what kind of voice [to give the tramp]—how he put a sentence together—how it would be. So he had to go."[13]

In retrospect, another obvious reason for Chaplin's reluctance to accept sound was summed up by Rollie Totheroh. "When it came to talking pictures, naturally a third more in speed [was needed] for the sound to reach the ear. Instead of 16 [frames per second] it went up to 24 frames. Well, it would slow his comedy down. The tempo

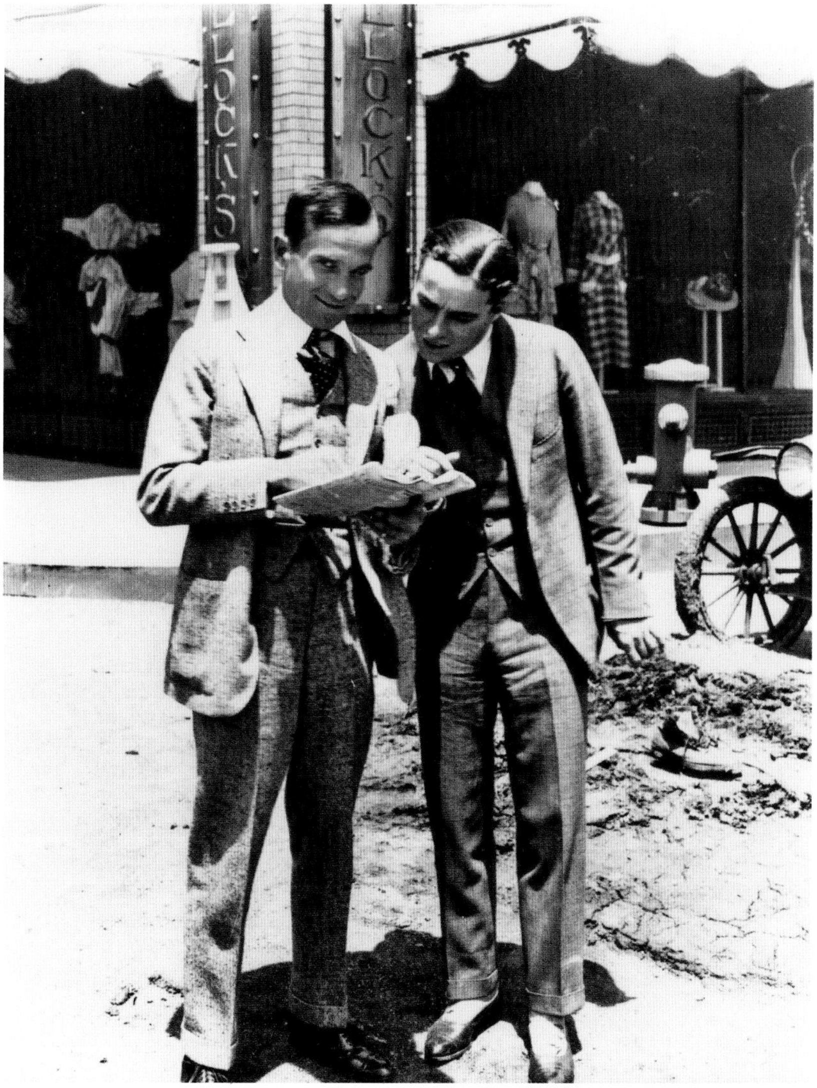

9 For example, in the *Newcastle Evening World*, February 11, 1931.
10 See also Charlie Chaplin, "I Detest These Talkies," *Evening World*, February 19, 1931.
11 For example: "All through the making of *City Lights* Chaplin has been submerged by correspondence from every portion of the world lauding him for his stand against talking pictures. From individuals and organizations representing the deaf, the comedian has had several hundred thousand letters alone, praising him for his loyalty to pantomime." Not one of these letters survives in the Chaplin archives. And where in the film do we see the "thousands of pleasure automobiles, taxi cabs and other public conveyances" they say were used during production, including "10,000 or more pedestrians"?
12 Charlie Chaplin, interview with Richard Meryman, 1966, Chaplin archives.
13 Ibid.

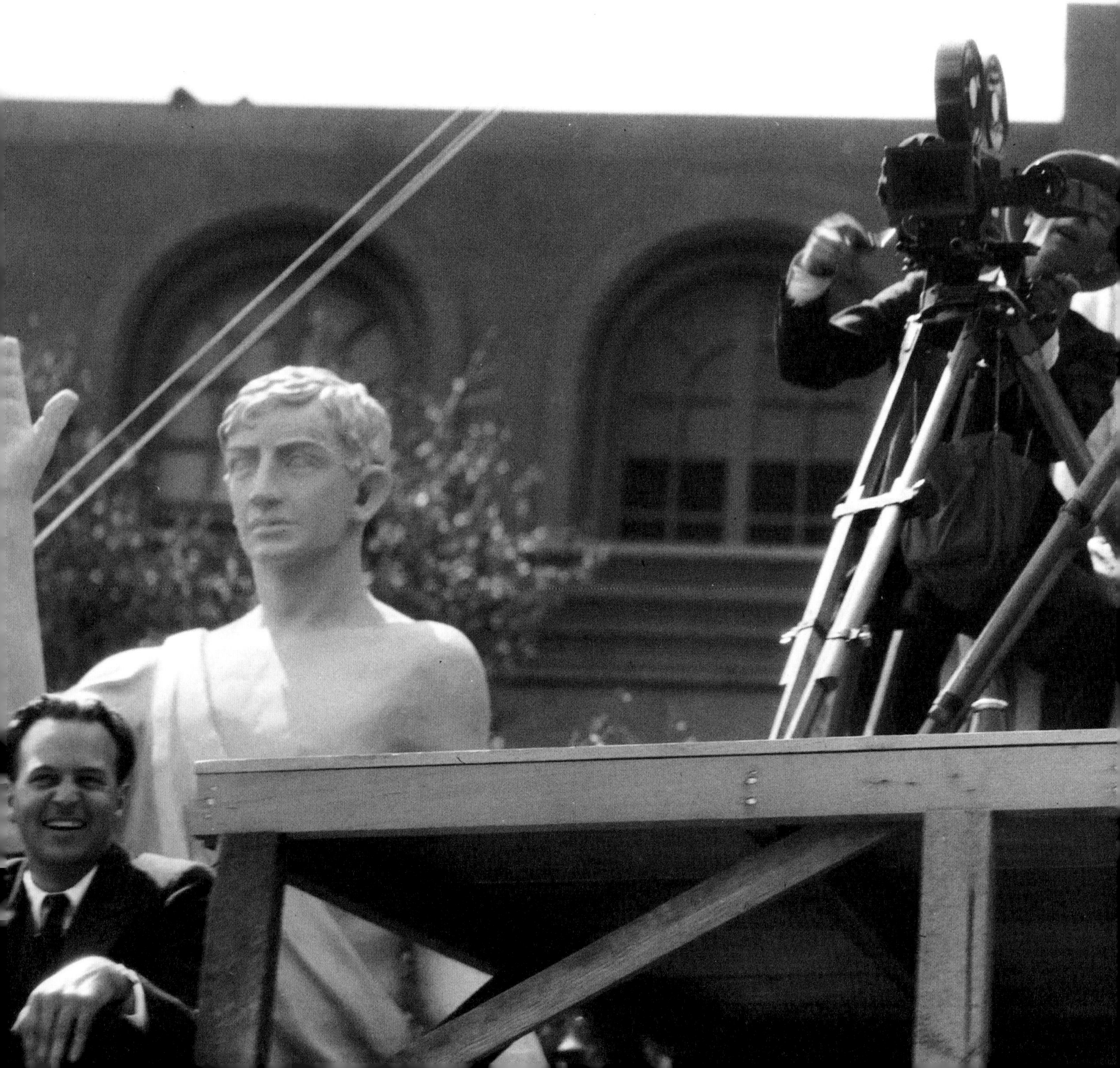

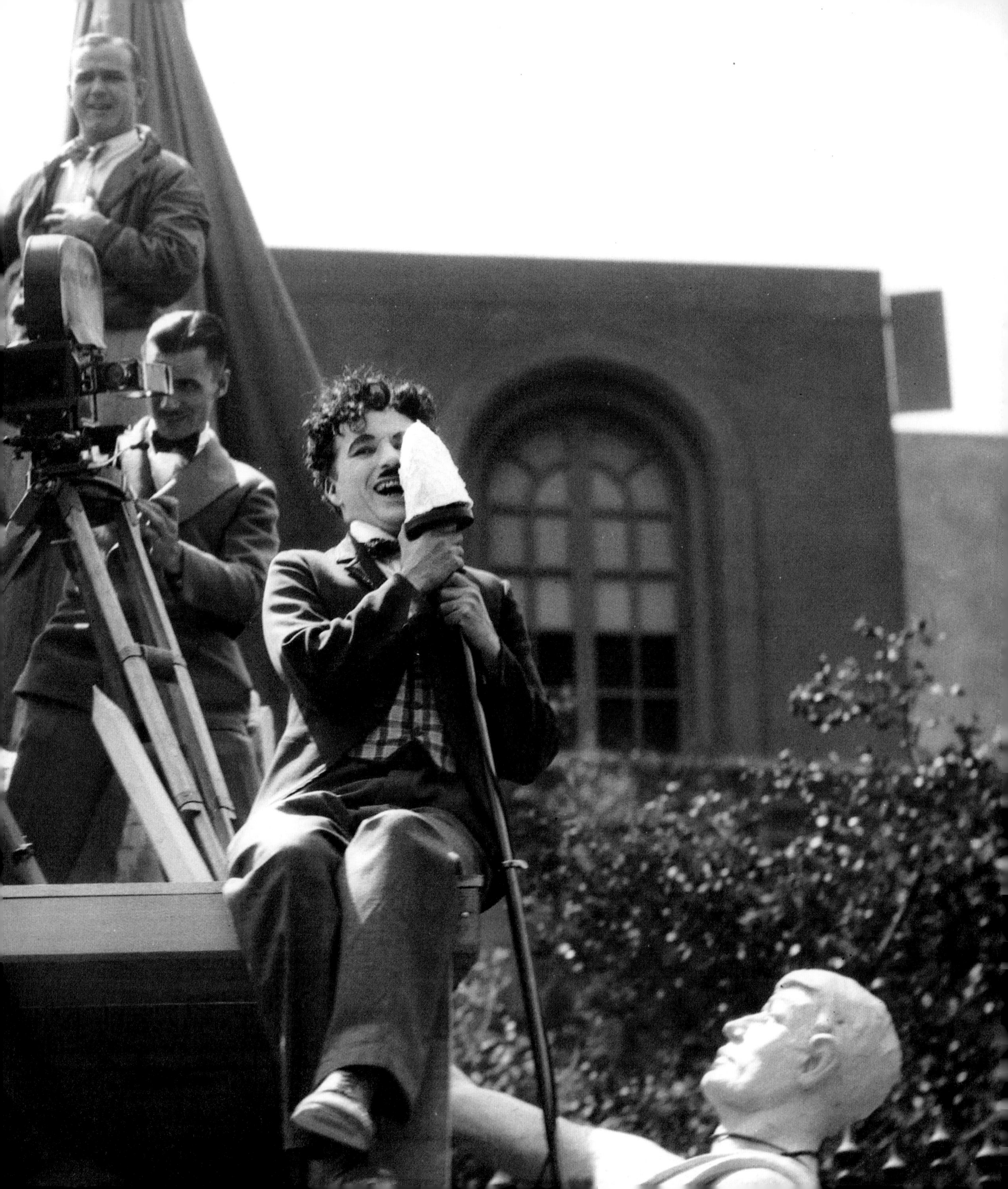

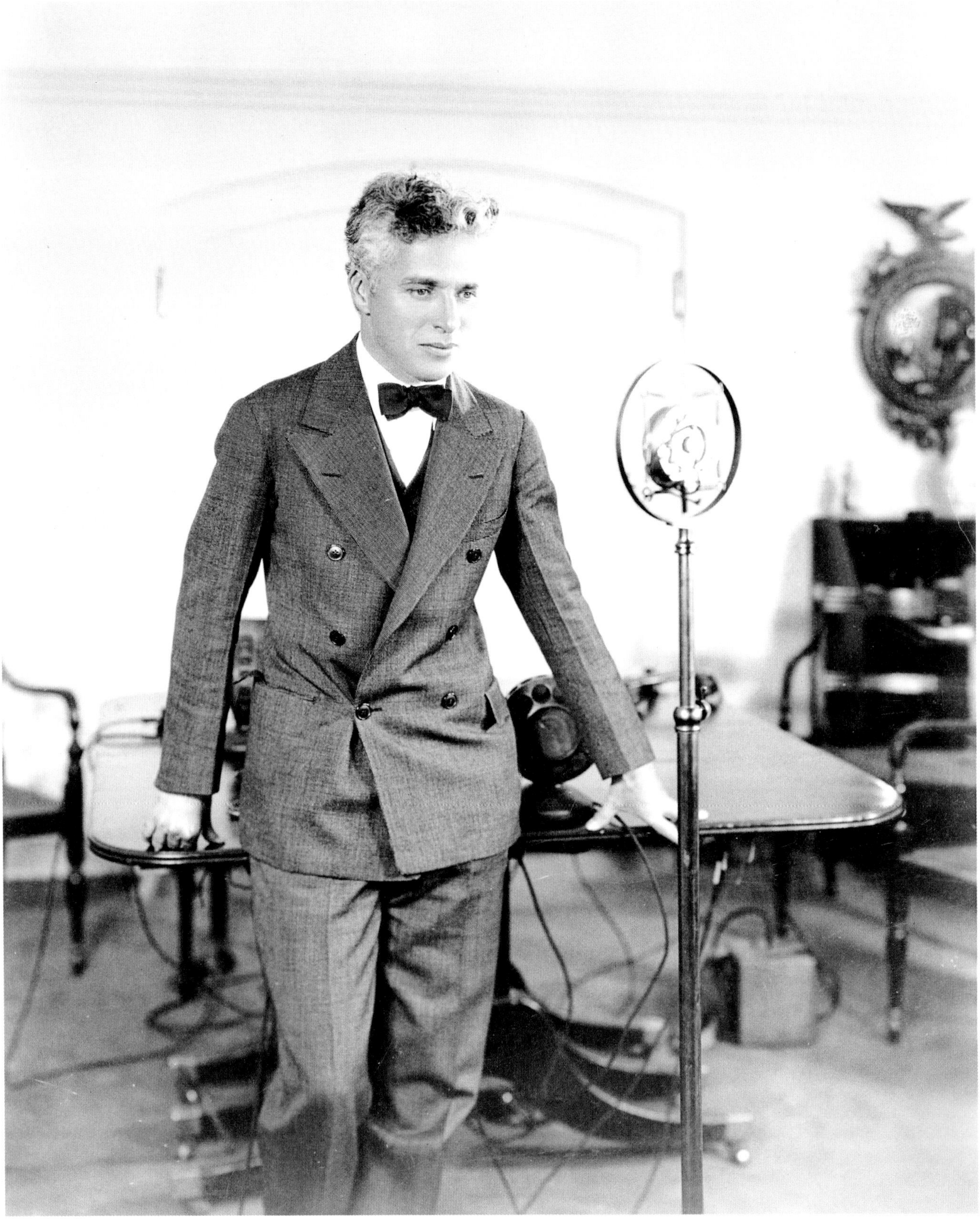

Preceding double page

Opening scene set, *City Lights*, c. 1929–30.

Left

Chaplin behind a microphone, 1930.

wasn't there, if you had to talk."[14] Not only would a talking tramp lose millions of fans, but there was also the possibility that he might not be able to make those who did understand his language laugh as before.

The Meryman interview reveals another reserve that Chaplin had about dialogue, which happily he managed to overcome for *The Great Dictator, Monsieur Verdoux, Limelight*, and *A King in New York*. "The voice is a beautiful thing, most revealing, and that's another thing—I have a sort of shyness. I didn't want to be too revealing in my art because, it may show a limitation. There are very few people with voices that can reach or give the illusion of great depth, by their voice."[15] Chaplin gave one reason for his final acceptance of talkies: actors could no longer perform as he wanted. "The actors that I had—they couldn't pantomime. Oh, they could talk all you like—have their arms loose, and relax, and yap all the time, but they couldn't—pantomime. "On that point, you turn and look," and it was so hard, so difficult—you see in the old days, everything was all pantomime. They knew what pantomime was. And when the talking came in, they stopped all pantomime, and just talked. Got these glib comedians who just yapped and talked all the time. Their timing wasn't right."[16]

He was also concerned with his own performance if he had to memorize lines. "When I started talking I knew very well I lost a lot of eloquence," he said. "Something would happen to other very important situations. In the old days, I didn't have to remember anything. Just a question of practicing a dance, as I call it, saying, you turn, and I take your hand, you take my hand—you turn, and this, that, the other."[17]

After *City Lights*, Chaplin, not known for his love of holidays, spent eighteen months in Europe and the Far East, in despair as to what he could do next. "If I did make a talking picture, no matter how good I was I could never surpass the artistry of my pantomime. I had thought of possible voices for the tramp; whether he should speak in monosyllables or just mumble. But it was no use. If I talked I would become like any other comedian. These were the melancholy problems that confronted me."[18] Happily for us, he returned to Hollywood, and made one more non-dialogue film as late as 1936, *Modern Times*, which, like *City Lights*, was a huge public success. Chaplin was right—"entertainment is entertainment, and if it is good the public will go to see it."[19]

Not until *The Great Dictator* did he finally accept dialogue. The film proved that he was definitely not just "any other comedian," but it finally laid his silent little tramp to rest.

14 Interview conducted by Dan and Steve Totheroh, December 1964.
15 Charlie Chaplin, interview with Richard Meryman.
16 Ibid.
17 Ibid.
18 Charles Chaplin, *My Autobiography*, op. cit., 360.
19 "Comedian Returns – an Economist," *Los Angeles Times*, June 17, 1932.

Charles Chaplin

Why I favor silent screen

Why did I continue to make non-dialogue films? The silent picture, first of all, is a universal means of expression. Talking pictures necessarily have a limited field, they are held down to the particular tongues of particular races.

I am confident that the future will see a return of interest in non-talking productions because there is a constant demand for a medium that is universal in its utility. It is axiomatic that true drama must be universal in its appeal—the word element might be better—and I believe the medium of presentation should also be a universal rather than a restricted one.

Understand, I consider the talking picture a valuable addition to the dramatic art, regardless of its limitations, but I regard it only as an addition, not as a substitute. Certainly it could not be a substitute for the motion picture that has advanced as a pantomimic art form so notably during its brief twenty years of story-telling. After all, pantomime has always been the universal means of communication. It existed as the universal tool long before language was born. Pantomime serves well where languages are in the conflict of a common ignorance. Primitive folk used the sign language before they were able to form an intelligible word.

At what point in the world's history pantomime first made its appearance is speculative. Undoubtedly it greatly antedates the first records of its part in Greek culture. It reached a highly definite development in Rome and was a distinct factor in the mediaeval mystery plays. Ancient Egypt was adept in its use, and in the sacrificial rites of Druidism and in the war dances of the aborigines of all lands it had a fixed place.

Pantomime lies at the base of any form of drama. In the silent form of photoplay it is the keynote. In the vocal form it must always be an essential because non-visual drama leaves altogether too much to the imagination. If there is any doubt of this, an example is radio play.

Action is more generally understood than words. The lift of an eyebrow, however faint, may convey more than a hundred words. Like the Chinese symbolism, it will mean different things according to its scenic connotation. Listen to a description of some unfamiliar object—an African wart-hog, for example—then describe it; observe a picture of the animal and note the variety of astonishment.

We hear a great deal about children not going to the movies any more, and it is undoubtedly true that hundreds of thousands of prospective film patrons, of future film-goers, young tots who formerly thrilled to the silent screen, do not attend any more because they are unable to follow the dialogue of talking pictures readily. On the other hand, they do follow action unerringly. This is because the eye is better trained than the ear. There is nothing in *City Lights* that a child won't follow easily and understand.

I am a comedian and I know that pantomime is more important in comedy than it is in pure drama. It may be even more effective in farce than in straight comedy. These two differ in that the former implies the attainment of humor without logical action—in fact, rather the reverse—and the latter achieves this attainment as the outcome of sheer legitimate motivation. Silent comedy is more satisfactory entertainment for the masses than talking comedy because most comedy depends on swiftness of action, and an event can happen and be laughed at before it can be told in words. Of course, pantomime is invaluable in drama, too, because it serves to effect the gradual transition from farce to pathos or from comedy to tragedy much more smoothly and with less effort than speech can ever do.

I base this statement on recent observations: the sudden arrival of dialogue in motion pictures is causing many of our actors to forget the elements of the art of acting. Pantomime, I have always believed and still believe, is the prime qualification of a successful screen player. A truly capable actor must possess a thorough grounding in pantomime. Consider the Irvings, Coqueleins, Berhardts, Duses, Mansfields, and Booths, and you will find at the root of their art, pantomime.

My screen character remains speechless from choice. *City Lights* is synchronized and certain sound effects are part of the comedy but it is a non-dialogue picture because I preferred that it be that, for the reasons I have given.

Text "Chaplin Favors Silent Screen" published in the *Exhibitors Handbook* for *City Lights* (1931)—sent by United Artists to movie-theater owners giving them ideas for how to publicize the film.

Adolphe Nysenholc

Chaplin speaks

The dream of every artist is to have a universal audience. Painters, musicians, dancers are perceived straightaway everywhere they are shown, played, or produced. But writers, limited by language, need to be to be translated. In the art of narrative, Chaplin was the most widely understood artist in the world because he combined all the arts in his "*cinémime*."[1]

1 Élie Faure, *Fonction du cinéma* (Paris: Plon, 1953).

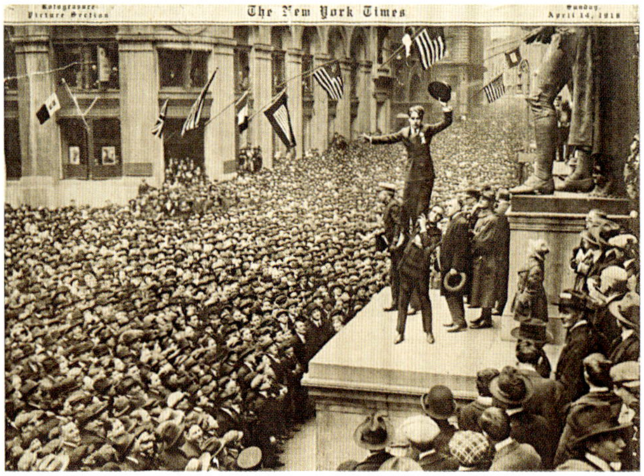

Trained as a child actor in the theater, the kingdom par excellence of speech, he adapted marvelously to the silent cinema, with a well-defined silhouette and highly expressive gestures—a "silent melody"[2]—to return to his first love in the talkies of his maturity.

Throughout the Tramp cycle, which stretched from one world war to another, Chaplin never stopped "speaking" to say what he thought of his time. From social criticism (*The Kid*, 1921) to political diatribe (*The Great Dictator*, 1940), the Tramp's saga was perceived as the *legend* of the century.

Chaplin, a great communicator, spoke to his contemporaries, first in silence, then through the talkie (see in particular his anti-McCarthyist satire, *A King in New York*, released in 1957). He was said to be a pacifist during World War I with *Shoulder Arms* (1918), in which he ridicules the Kaiser, taken prisoner by the Tramp. But, during the same period, he agreed—with his friend Douglas Fairbanks—to tour the big cities of the United States, and made stirring speeches to huge crowds to raise funds for the war industry. In 1918 he directed *The Bond*, a war propaganda film that contradicted the anti-bellicist thesis. A quarter century later, the final speech of *The Great Dictator*, in front of a crowd comparable to those of times past, is in keeping with the patriotic action of 1918: his enthusiastic words encouraged soldiers to go "fight" for freedom against those who were a global danger to democracy. Facing the camera, he addresses his immediate audience, non-interventionist America, to convince them, like in *The Bond*, to go save Europe.

2 René Schwob, *Une mélodie silencieuse* (Paris: Grasset, 1929).

It was, however, not the first time that the Tramp found himself in a situation in which he had to speak. In *The Pilgrim* (1923) he plays a pastor in disguise who risks being unmasked and is obliged to deliver a sermon. He transposes it into a music hall pantomime, parodying the verse in which David beats Goliath with his sling. On New Year's Eve, in *The Gold Rush* (1925), when his guests ask him to make a "speech,"[3] he likewise expresses himself with a puppet show, the roll dance—a French cancan in homage to his Georgia, a saloon dancer. In *Modern Times* (1936), hired to replace a cabaret singer, he loses the lyrics written on his celluloid cuffs, and cornered between silent and talking cinema, he invents words, a trial run before his grammelot performance as Hynkel parodying Hitler's German.

At the end of *The Great Dictator*, mistaken for the dictator, conqueror of Osterlich, a speech to the world is expected from the Tramp. It was a question of life or death. He had said in 1928, at the advent of talking

3 "I can't," he says (Chaplin's self-mockery).

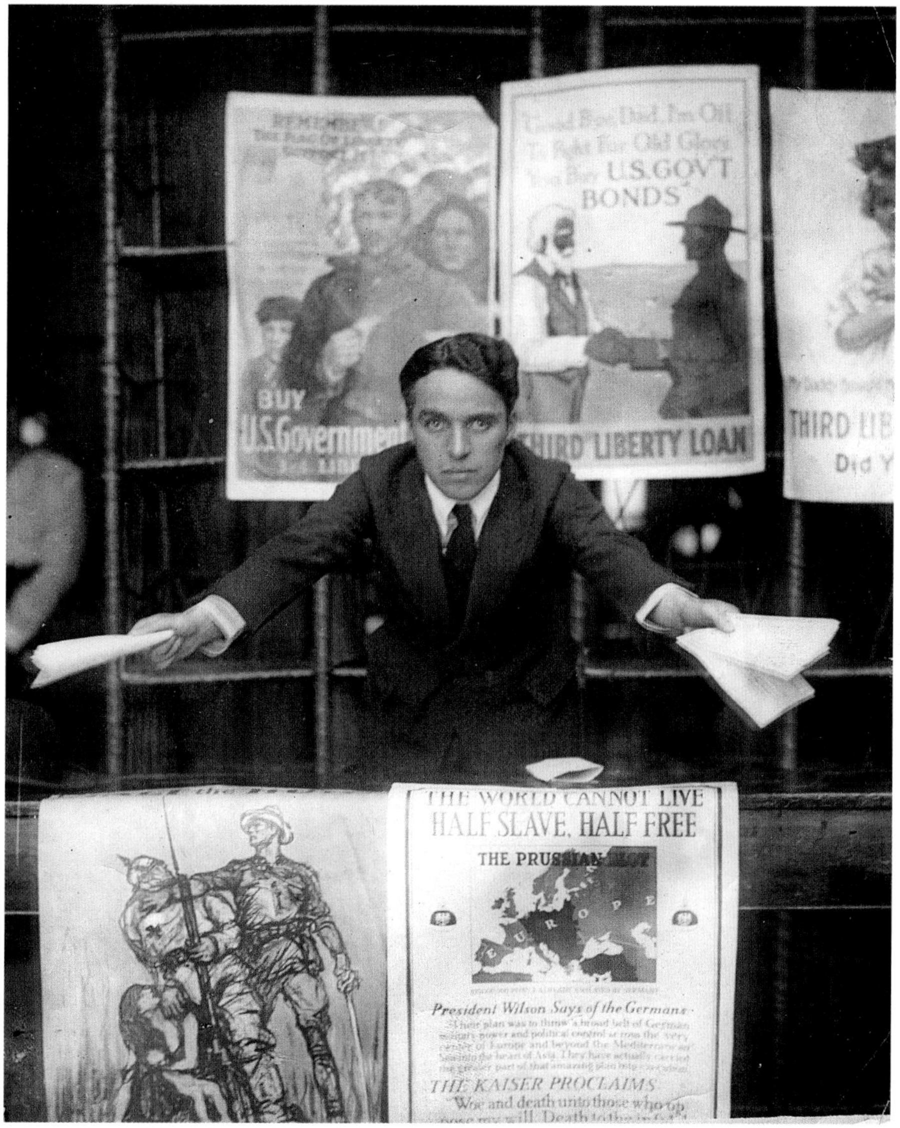

Left

Chaplin's speaks in New York to promote Liberty Bonds, April 1918. Mary Pickford, Douglas Fairbanks, Chaplin, and most other stars of the time took part in fundraising tours to support the soldiers sent to the front in Europe. The reception was triumphant and Chaplin struggled to make himself heard while he made his speech. The crowd went wild when Chaplin climbed on Douglas Fairbanks's shoulders.

Right

Chaplin promoting Liberty Bonds, April 1918.

cinema, that as soon as the Tramp opened his mouth, he would cease to be. Thus, Chaplin is showing us, in his philippic at the rostrum, the *end* of the Tramp. This speech has often been criticized by people with no understanding of the logic of the entire cycle: he who had been image without speech for a quarter of a century could only disappear as speech without image. This chiasmus gave coherence to the myth.

In *Monsieur Verdoux* (1947), condemned to defend himself in court, the accused is in fact an eloquent hero, launching into a paradoxical indictment of his century, which was capable of two world wars with genocides into the bargain: "As a mass killer, I am an amateur by comparison."

Below

Rupert Macabee (Michael Chaplin) speaks to the members of the Atomic Energy Commission in *A King in New York*, 1957, the first film that Chaplin made after his forced exile from the United States. He used the character played by his son Michael to dramatize—without officially taking position—the witch hunt of which he was the victim.

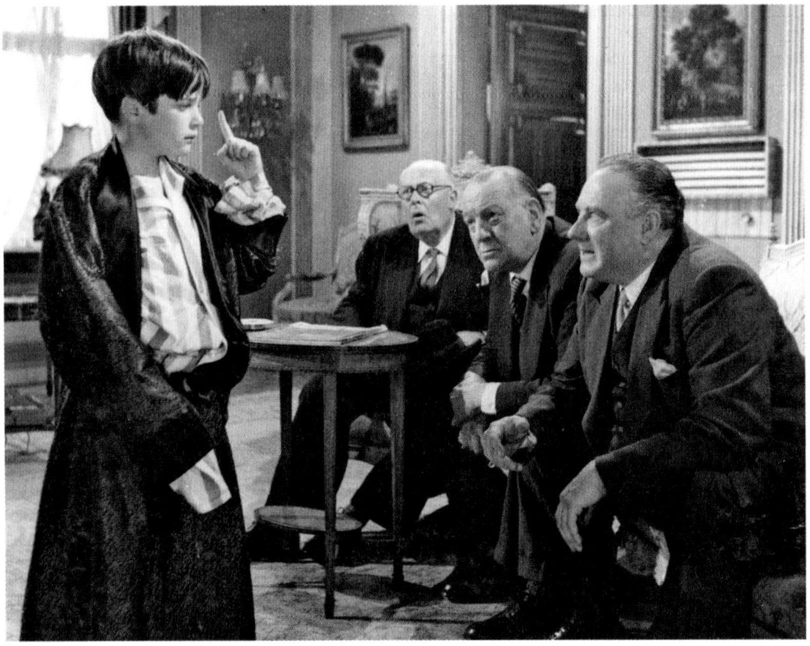

Of course, the Tramp barely spoke. He generally reacted to situations, as if he were outside speech or preceded it. Mute, the man-child reinforced his *infans* (he who does not speak)[4] side.

An exception: *The Bond* is based on a play on words, "bond" signifying "tie" and "certificate issued by a government or a public company" (there is the "bond of friendship" says an intertitle; the "bond of love" says a second, and there is "the liberty bond," to be bought to keep the arms factories running, guarantees of victory). This short film with its pronounced ideology was made in the language of its target audience, something that Chaplin tended to avoid in his films destined for worldwide distribution.

Nevertheless, he often made jokes based on expressions in his mother tongue without the comprehension of audiences around the world suffering. In *The Kid*, we see the Tramp gamboling with a beautiful woman in "Dreamland" like a goat. There are several other examples.[5] The spirit of the gesture makes us laugh, even if we do not understand it to the letter.

The arrival of talking cinema on the market in 1928 sounded the death knell for Chaplin's art. Would he move into talkies? Speech would not have added anything to the bread roll dance, he wrote.

For a decade, the former London stage actor, who had become the master of silent cinema, resisted what appeared to be a sort of hybrid of filmed theatre, and parodied it with biting irony.

Producing *City Lights* (1931), a silent film in which the Tramp meets a blind flower girl, talkies are mocked in the inaugural speech made by officials for a monument (using

4 Adolphe Nysenholc, *Charles Chaplin. L'âge d'or du comique* [1979] (Paris: L'Harmattan, 2002), 51–69.

5 Adolphe Nysenholc, *Charles Chaplin ou la légende des images* (Paris: Méridiens-Klincksieck, 1987), 49–68.

squeaks from a saxophone mouthpiece). At the millionaire's society party, the singer, ready to "speak" a noble language in music, launches into an inspired song, while the Tramp, having swallowed a whistle, heckles him (despite himself, with his hiccups).

Five years later, for *Modern Times*, he seemed to give in, and wrote dialogues, which he then renounced. While he conceded that people could speak in the film, it was in mechanical, neutral, dehumanized phrases, broadcast through modern media—record player, TV, radio—equivalents of the talking cinema that he mocked. Thus, the inventor of the feeding machine praises his device through a record on a gramophone player while remaining silent, arms crossed, crazy, *mute*. The factory boss scolds Chaplin via a closed audiovisual circuit that projects his flashy Big Brother image on a giant screen. The wife of the prison chaplain makes weird rumbling sounds (origins of the garbled song "Titine") illustrating despite herself, by her "voice-over," an advertisement for digestive pills broadcast behind her on the radio. The film ends, conversely, with Chaplin's voice heard live for the first time. Torn between his fundamental attachment to the art of pantomime and the need to evolve with cinema, he succeeds by parodying the spoken word through distortion, combining different idioms like at Babel as though, citizen of the world—the man who was understood everywhere without speech—he were recreating an Esperanto.

In *The Great Dictator*, Chaplin disparages one language, in the person of Hynkel, whose odd speech has to be "translated" in voice-

Below

The sermon in *The Pilgrim*, 1923.
In this film, Chaplin succeeds in telling the story of David and Goliath without words, miming the two characters in turn and playing on their difference in height.

Following double page

The Tramp rehearsing "Titine" before going on stage, *Modern Times*, 1936. The character played by Paulette Goddard wrote the song lyrics on his cuffs for him, but the Tramp loses them while dancing and has to improvise in a pantomime number worthy of the music hall. The words are incomprehensible but this was the first time that the worldwide film-going audience heard Chaplin's voice.

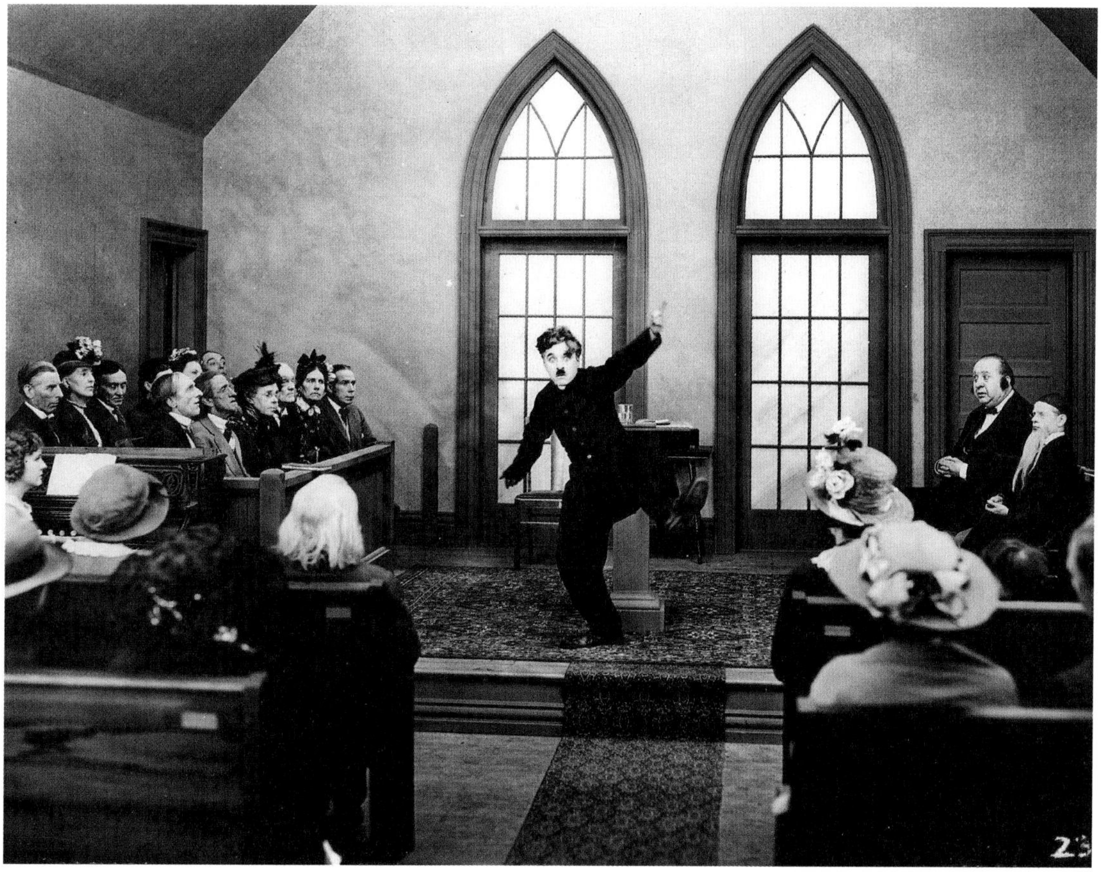

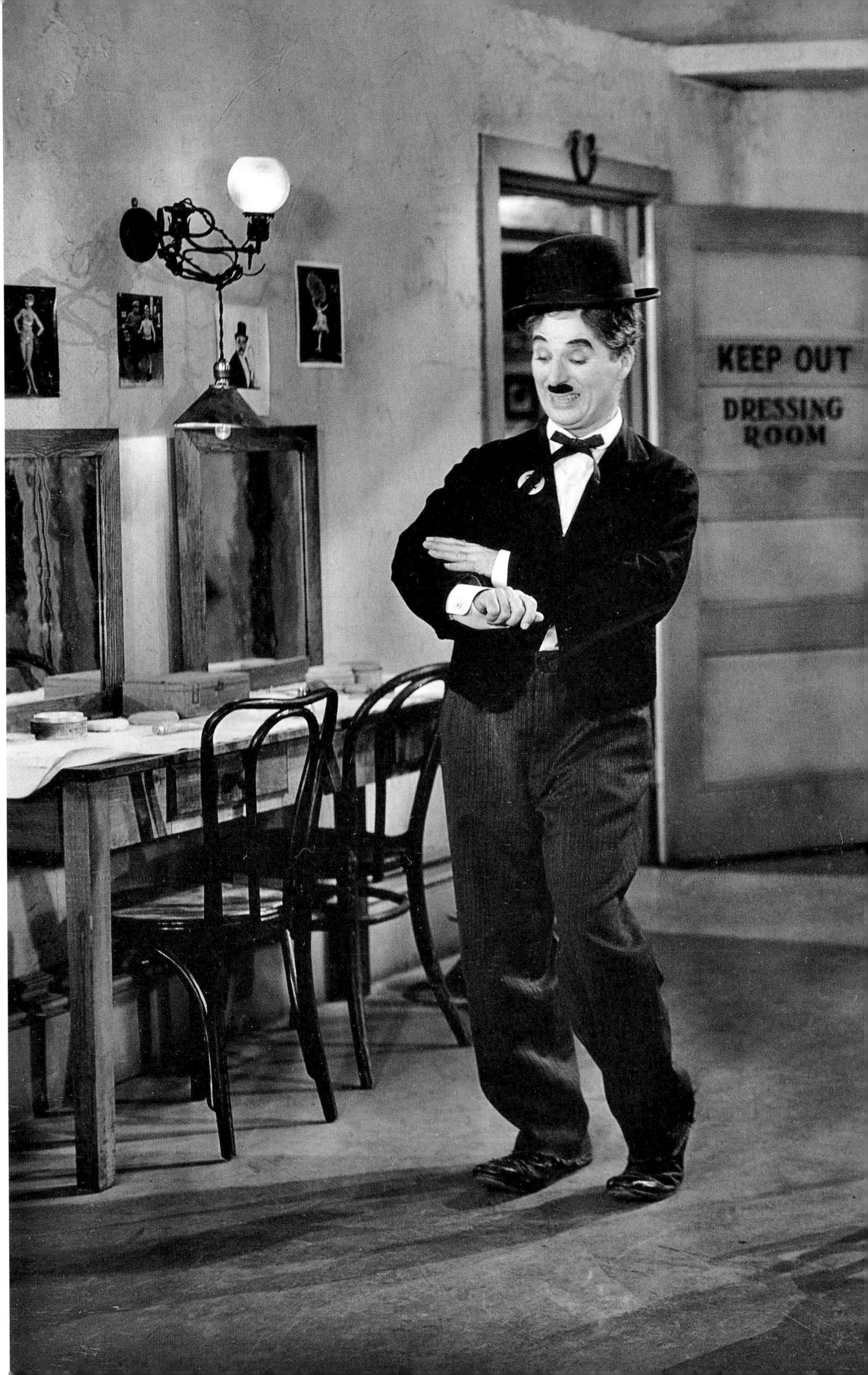
KEEP OUT
DRESSING
ROOM

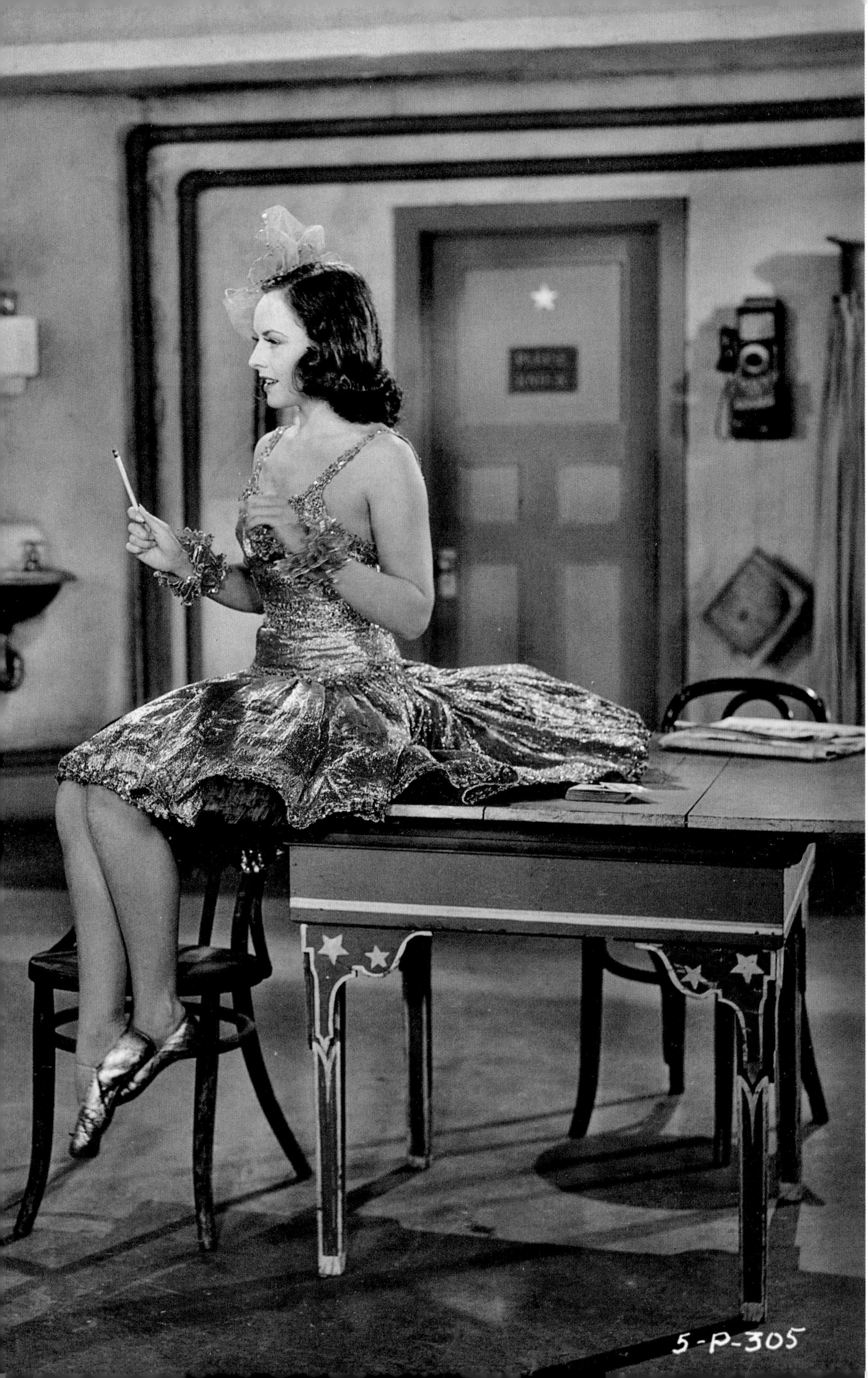
5-P-305

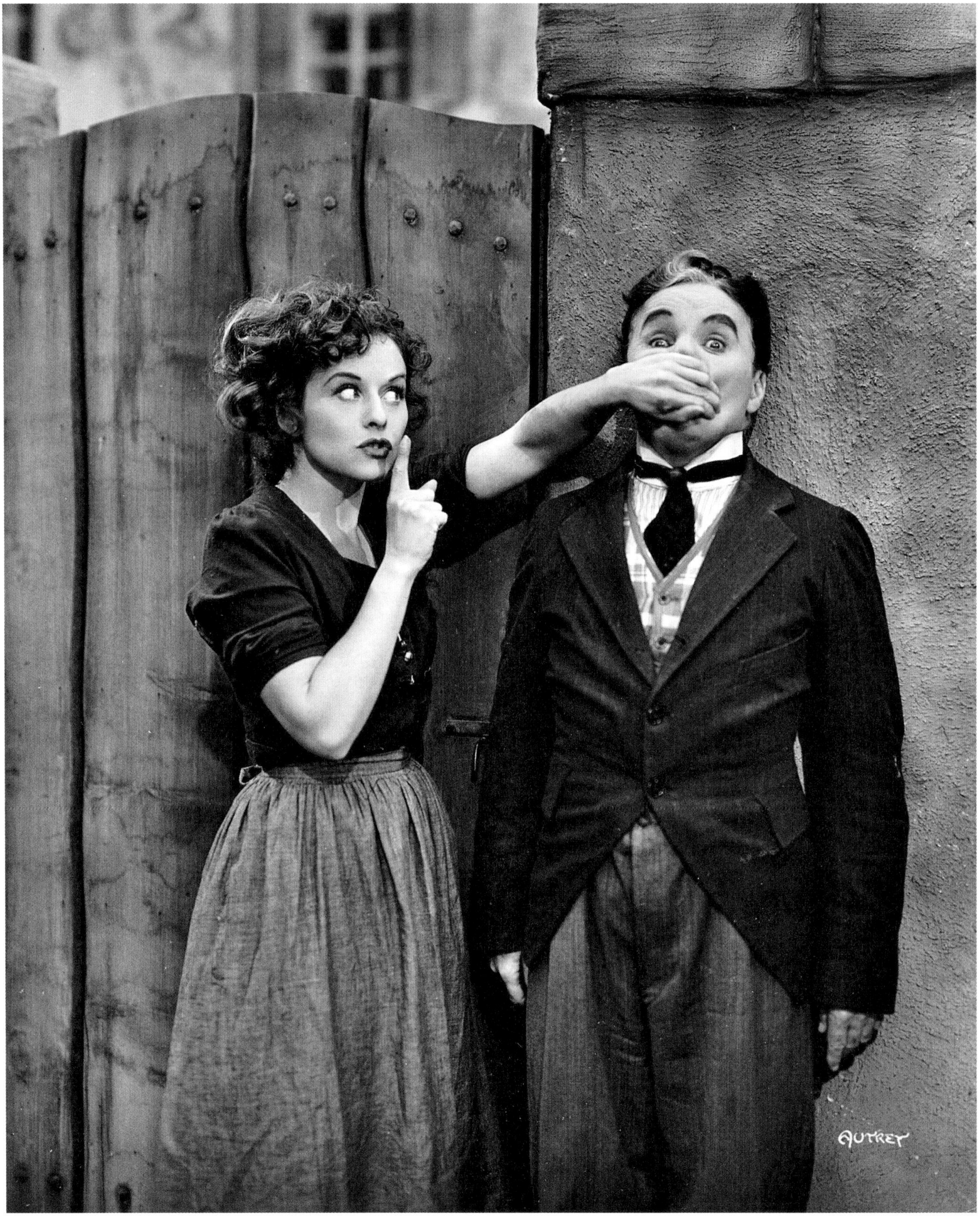
AUTREY

Left

Hannah (Paulette Goddard) prevents the barber from speaking in *The Great Dictator*, 1940. Photograph by Max Munn Autrey.

Below

City Lights set, 1929. On July 4, 1929, an extra told his story in *Cinémonde*: "Chaplin climbs onto the rostrum. He takes the place hitherto occupied by Henry [Bergman] to show him how he would like the role of the mayor to be played . . . He exaggerated all the gestures. He swayed from left to right, from right to left. What he said wasn't important. Chaplin knew that words were only worth something if there was thought behind them."

over by a radio announcer.[6] Competing with a hyper-loquacious Groucho—particularly as president of Freedonia in *Duck Soup* (1933), which is one of the sources of *The Great Dictator*—he takes over, and proves that he could be just as fun and talkative.

In the ghetto and in the palace of this film, everyone around the Tramp and Hynkel talks, but the Tramp—who attempts to remain as faithful as possible to his original character—only utters a few words. Thus, he lets Hannah believe that he has warned Schultz of the danger, despite the fact that, in his panic he could not get a word out. When he wants to reply when Hannah compliments him on his spirit of resistance, she puts her hand over his mouth (so that Hynkel's soldiers, whom he fought, cannot hear him). That is Chaplin's irony: when the Tramp finally wants to say two words, somebody shuts him up. His fate is to remain mute even during the sound era. (Chaplin is infinitely creative in his attempts to keep the Tramp silent.) In the end he dies through speech, being nothing more in the final image than a mere word borne through the air by radio waves. Behind the silent

6 See "Transcript of Adenoid Hynkel's speech in *The Great Dictator*" by Maximilien Theinhardt on page 202.

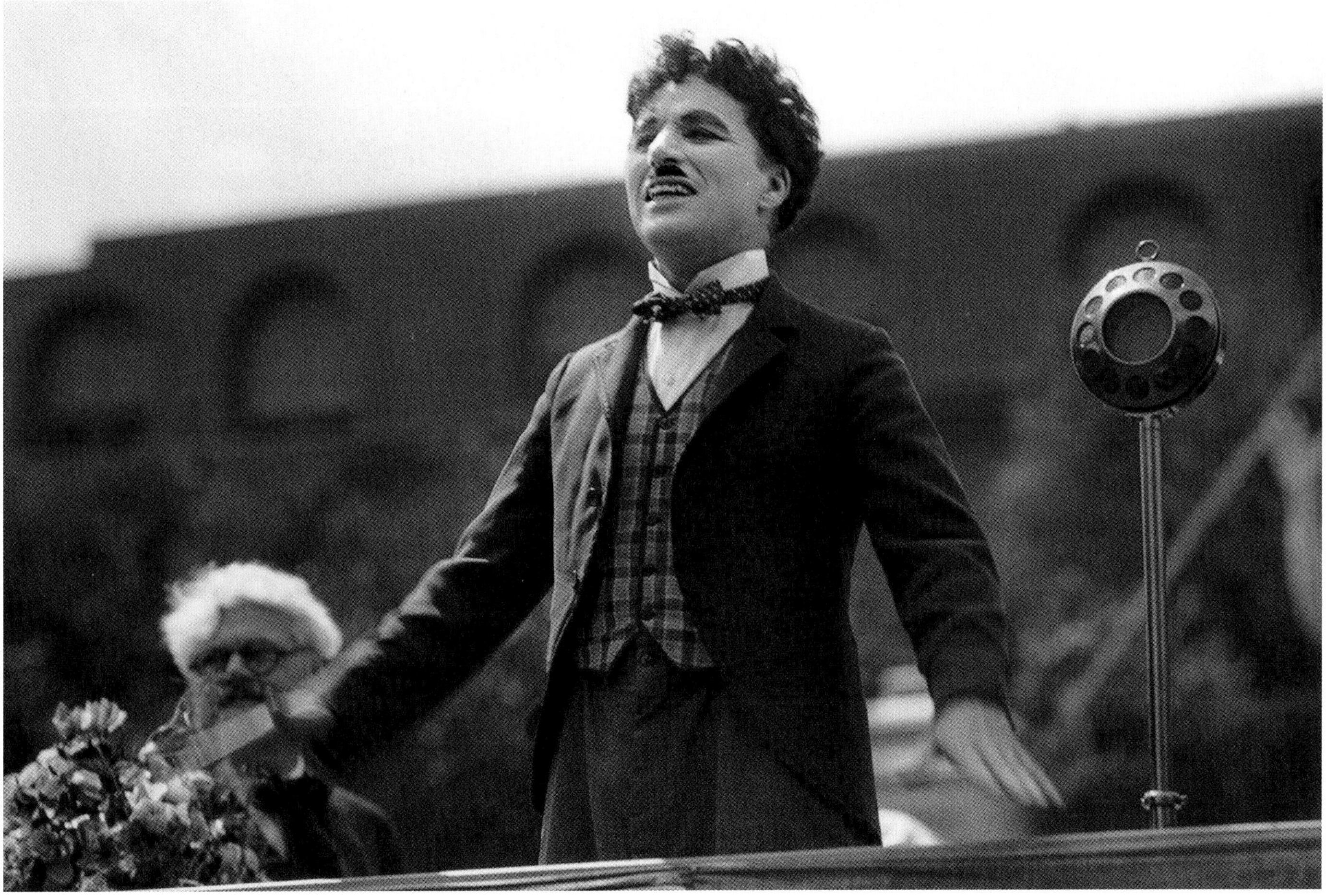

character, there was an author who spoke.[7] Chaplin's first speech was the creation of his costume in 1914, and the extremely famous silhouette said it all from the start: a gentleman on the top half, a tramp on the bottom half, carrying within him all of society and its contradictions. His second act of speech was to demand that Mack Sennett allow him to write his own scripts; they expressed the tension of the social classes that he carried within him, original screenplays in which the tramp often found himself in high society—it suffices to cite *City Lights*—as though he were developing the possibilities of his costume.

Chaplin has been called a self-made myth.[8] He was indeed the creator of parables, of fabulous words. (He was even tempted to play a Jesus Tramp, to rival the inventor of the parables of our civilization, the Master who taught with gestures and symbolic acts.) In fact, the profound speech of Chaplin, as the Tramp, showed on his face. It could be read on his forehead like an open book. Chaplin loved words.[9] His photogenicity translated a word made flesh. He never ceased speaking volumes, the spokesperson of his times.

Right

Trial scene at the end of *Monsieur Verdoux*, 1947. While the barber was forced to speak at the end of *The Great Dictator*, the character that Chaplin played in his following film was very talkative indeed. He launches into long anti-military speech, a barely veiled criticism of the position of the United States during World War II.

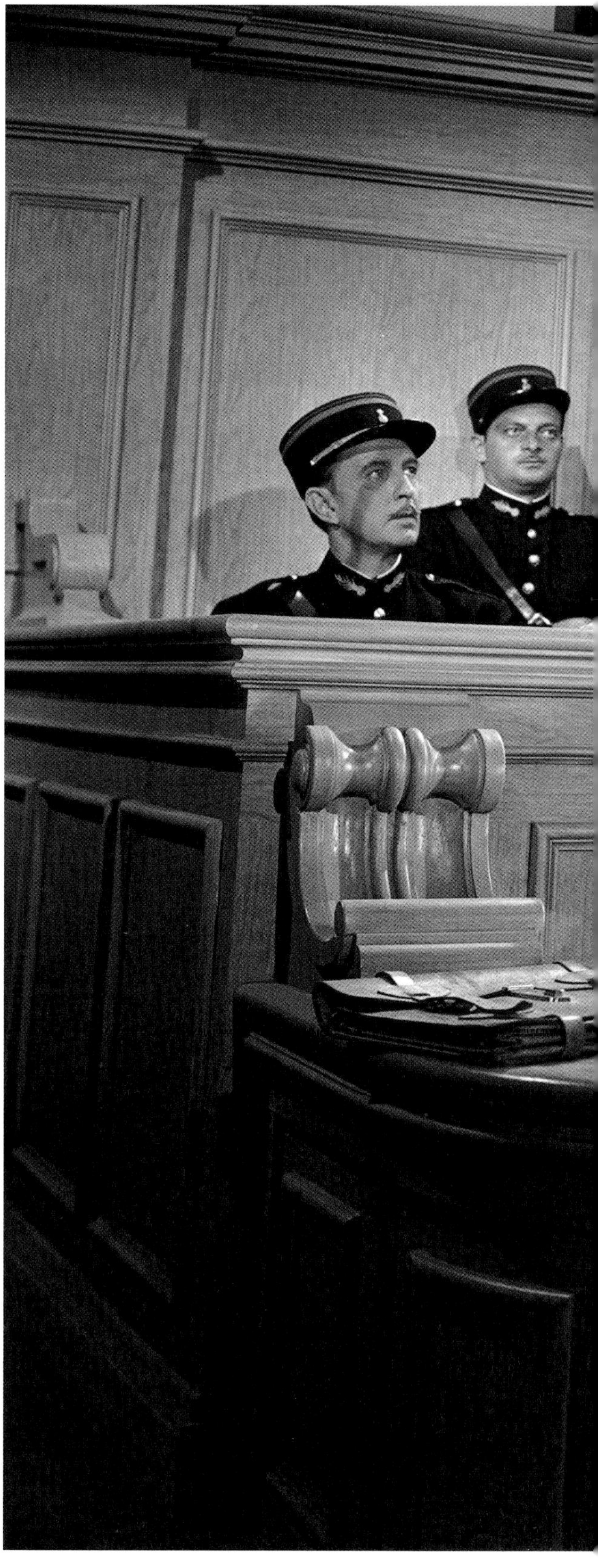

7 René Clair was the first to express this idea (*Vu*, 1931).
8 José Augusto França, *Charles Chaplin, O "self-made-myth"* (Lisbon: Inquerito, 1954).
9 David Robinson, *Chaplin: The Mirror of Opinion* (Bloomington: Indiana University Press, 1983), 1.

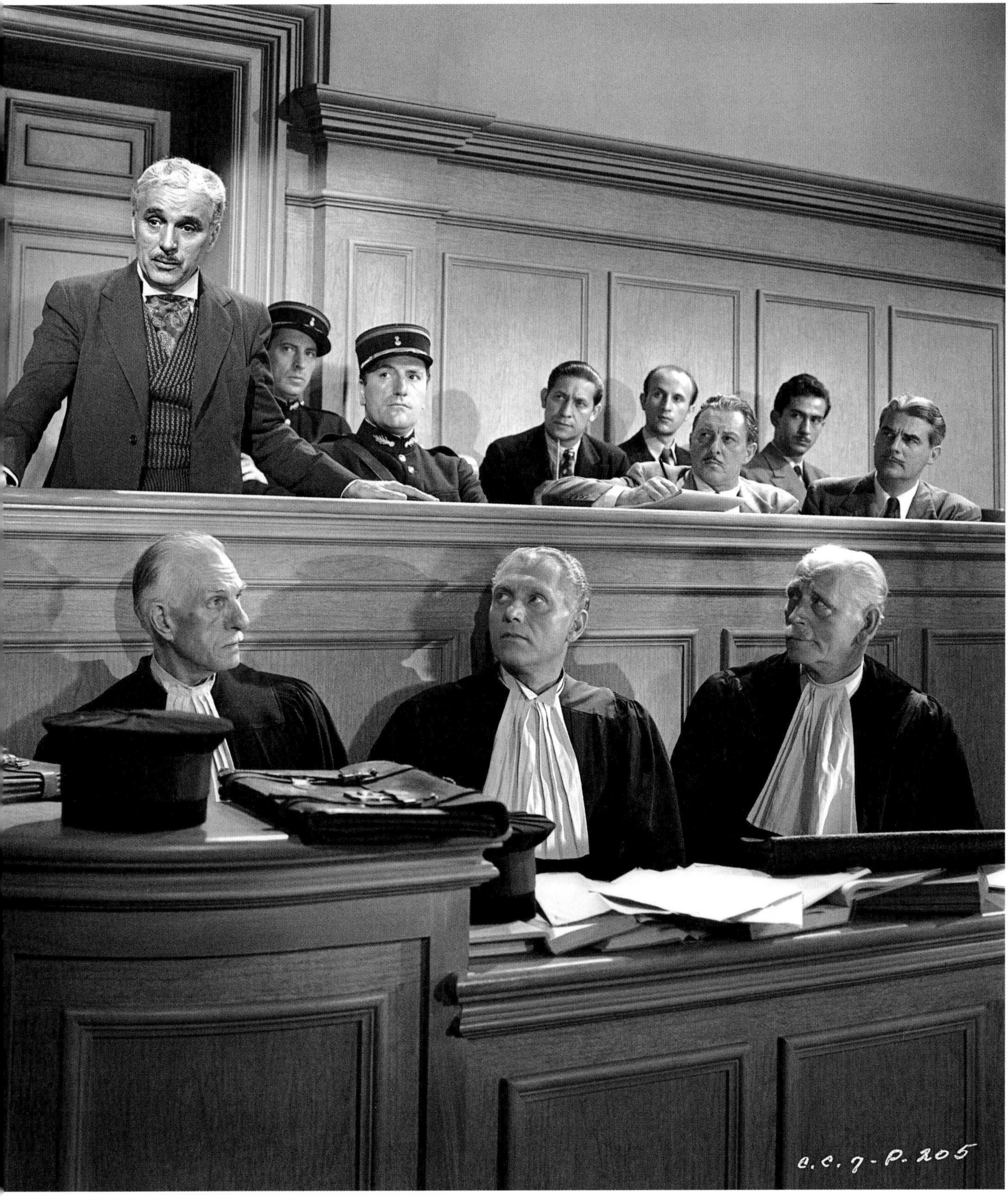
C.C.7-P.205

Maximilien Theinhardt

The sound and the Führer

An analysis of Hynkel's speech in *The Great Dictator*

Released during a time of geopolitical crisis—Europe was gradually being invaded by Adolf Hitler's armies; the United States had still not entered the war—*The Great Dictator* saw Chaplin taking a double stance. On the one hand, he presents himself as a whistle-blower who displays his idealistic humanism, particularly during the final speech of the Jewish barber who had unintentionally become "emperor of the world." On the other, *The Great Dictator*, Chaplin's first entirely talking film, could be interpreted as a metaphor for the power of speech and especially for the limits of such power. Adenoid Hynkel's speech in gibberish at the beginning of the film, a counterpart to the final speech, is a condensed illustration of those issues.

On a large stage, Hynkel, dictator of Tomainia, launches into a five-minute harangue, intercut with the interventions of an interpreter in the pay of the regime. The humor of the scene resides in the clear discrepancy between the dictator's rhetorical and gestural violence, and the interpreter's aplomb: Hynkel's words, even though incomprehensible, are obviously very much watered down by the interpreter. The interest of this scene, however, lies in the invention of a language, Tomainian, faux German sprinkled with English. Shortly before, Chaplin, who mastered no foreign language, had engaged in a similar exercise with his faux Italo-French version of "Je cherche après Titine" in *Modern Times*. The recourse to gibberish was part of the music hall tradition and of pantomime in particular, an art upon which comic actors of the silent cinema, especially Chaplin, largely relied. Meaning can be put to one side: just like silent cinema, gibberish has, in theory, the huge advantage of adapting to speakers of any language. Hynkel's speech is, however, a hybrid case.

The speech is peppered with words that are perfectly identifiable for an English speaker with a rudimentary knowledge of German. Despite all the eructations, the totalitarian discourse should be understood and even taken seriously. There are words borrowed directly from German: *strafen* (punish), *Blitzkrieg* (lightning attack) and *Juden* (Jews), which Chaplin pronounced with an English accent (dʒudən). Germanic culinary specialties also feature largely: *Wienerschnitzel* (Viennese breaded cutlet), *Sauerkraut*, "*Lagerbierten*" (deformation of *Lagerbier*, beer brewed by slow fermentation), and *Leberwurst* (liverwurst). Also noteworthy is the presence of the word "baloney," another name for "bologna sausage," the American version of mortadella: it is also a colloquial synonym for absurdity and inconsistency. Chaplin revives a tradition well anchored in propaganda speeches: the enemy is reduced to what he is thought to eat. Since World War I, the Germans were crazy about cold meats. Very ironically, when he used the word *Delikatessen*, Chaplin clearly refers to the delicatessens

Below

Hynkel making his speech at the beginning of *The Great Dictator*, 1940.

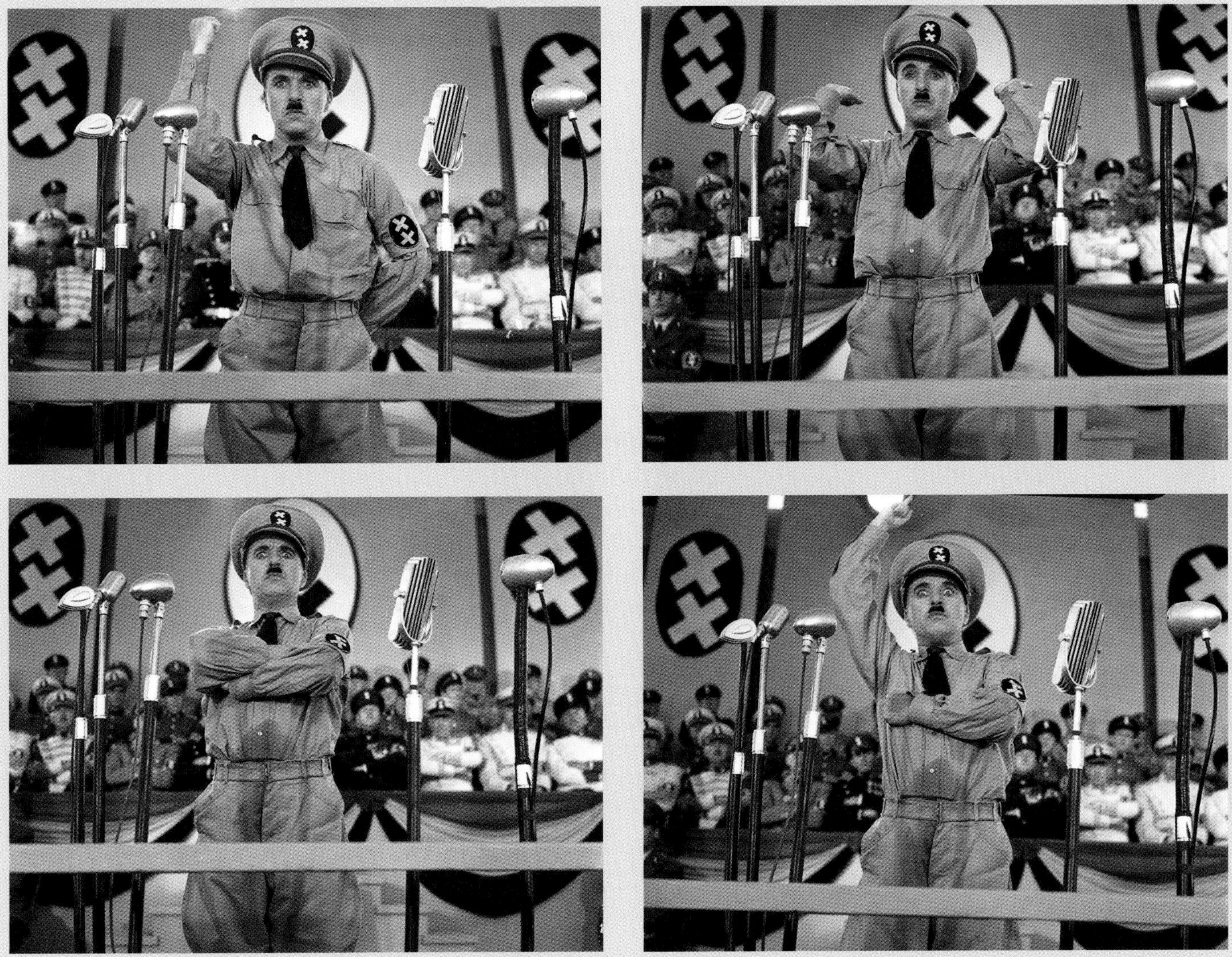

SEQUENCE"2-B" 3.

Hynkel is haranguing the crowd excitedly in jargon. He works himself up. To emphasize a point (that Tomainia, once down, is now up) he points to the ground, does the splits and pulls himself up by his pants, gesticulating skyward. Terrific cheers. The noise is faded down.

INTERPRETER: Adenoid Hynkel has just said - a few years ago Tomainia was defeated. But today Tomainia has risen and is ready to fight again.

(crowd cheers FADED UP. Hynkel drinks half glass of water, pours the rest in his pants and waves them to cool off. Then with a flick of the hand he silences the crowd and continues in jargon)

HYNKEL: (Jargon) Slutten die wiss - democracy schtoonk.

INTERPRETER: Democracy is fragrant.

HYNKEL: (jargon) Liberty schtoonk.

INTERPRETER: Liberty is odious.

HYNKEL: (jargon) Frei spielen schtoonk.

INTERPRETER: Freedom of speech is objectionable.

Left

Extract from the screenplay of *The Great Dictator*, c. 1939–40.

Right

Czech poster for *The Great Dictator*, 1947.

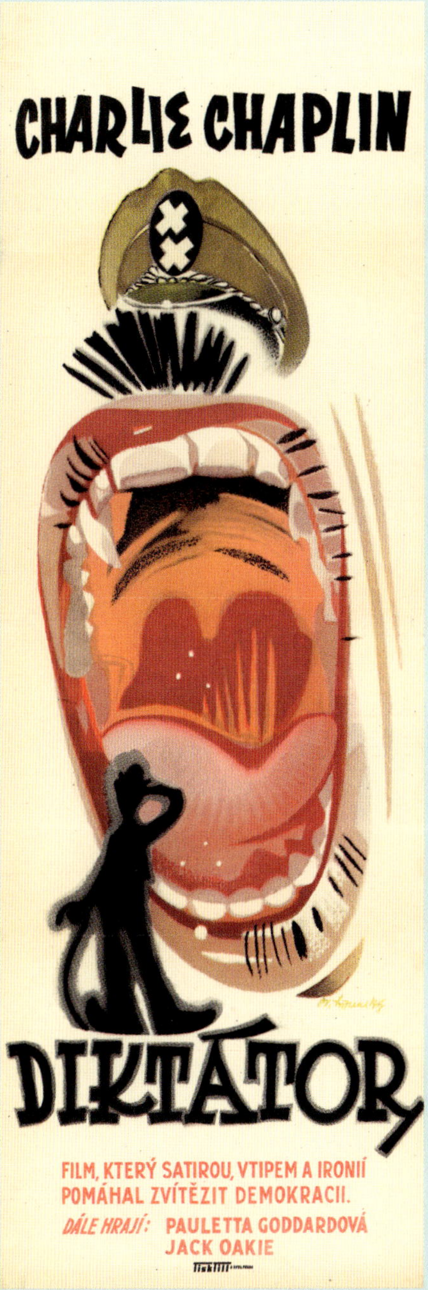

in the United States run by Jewish immigrants from Central and Eastern Europe. In the passage in which he urges Aryan women to produce more children to swell the ranks of his army, Hynkel talks of "Kinder Katzenjammer" (*Kinder*: children, *Katzenjammer*: hangover). It may be a reference to *The Katzenjammer Kids*, an American cartoon very popular at the time, which featured a family speaking in a blend of faux English and German.

Words and phrases in English, sometimes Germanized for the occasion, also interrupt the flow of faux German and mumbling ("Enough!" "Soldiers for Hynkel!" "tighten de belten!"). There are also numerous plays on words in English. Perhaps this should not be called gibberish. The Secretary of the Interior, alter ego of Joseph Goebbels, is named Garbitsch, a Germanization of the word *garbage*. Field Marshal Hermann Goering becomes Herring and more precisely, a "Bismarck Herring," a marinated herring. In his speech, Hynkel pays vibrant and fragrant tribute to his two acolytes: "Herring shouldn't smelten fine from Garbitsch und Garbitsch shouldn't smelten fine from Herring."

In Hynkel's speech, Chaplin combines pantomime with verbal humor. Only an audience from an English-speaking cultural universe, particularly North American, is actually capable of appreciating all the linguistic and comic registers of the dictator's harangue. Apart from the diatribe on the stench of democracy ("Democratzy schtunk"), which is systematically found in the different versions of the script for *The Great Dictator*, the Tomainian speech seems to have been mainly improvised during filming. The other parts of the speech were not put down on paper: only the word "jargon" appears on the documents describing them. This was, however, not the case with the gestures and the facial expressions, for which there were very precise stage directions. When the film was released in 1940, Paulette Goddard said: "[Charlie] thinks in rhyme and tempo . . . To the people who are to play a scene, he will describe it as though they were dancers . . . Doing a scene with him is so exactly like working to music that you can't help falling into it."[1] Even in a parody of a Nazi rally speech, musical and above all choreographic composition was never very far away.

1 Quoted in Jim Lochner, *The Music of Charlie Chaplin* (Jefferson, NC: McFarland & Company, 2018), 144.

Maximilien Theinhardt

Transcript of Adenoid Hynkel's speech

The Great Dictator **(1940)**

Warning: Adenoid Hynkel's speech in German-sounding gibberish was largely improvised during filming. The only reference document is the transcript made after shooting for the film's dialogue continuity. The present transcript was also made after the fact and is thus inevitably subjective. The fake interpreter's interventions are not included.

Adenoid Hynkel (AH): Ay der straf mitz hültensekt. Der Wienerschnitzel mit der Lagerbierten. Und der Sauerkraut! Ay der flutensack der flayrten. Ein Tomainia with sein strupf. Ein der flidensekta knültz. Ay if fleiner straf mit der ach—uch—ich—ach—uch—[*chesty cough*] Baloney. Baloney war sein schtritz mit sein elten zeckta üün. Ein der straf mit seiner clutch. Ay! Der strutz mit tsikatenta. In seiner trutch mitzketten. Meiner natita wie der strafen, die strafen, sie strafen.

The crowd: Heil!

AH: Democratzy schtunk. Liberty schtunk. Free spraken schtunk. Tomainia mit der grotze army in der Welt. Der grotze navy in der Welt. Mit seiner der grotze ALLES und einer du sacrifice. Aaay, alles, neine strutten tighten de belten!

Field Marshal Herring: Heil Hynkel! Ischt won der firsten.

AH: Ah, Herring. Pupschen Herring. Bismarck Herring. Bist ein hültensackta blayrten. Aaah from der hearten siegt der ailda hutz: ein Herring. Und Garbitsch. Herr Garbitsch wuntselts untz. Herring und Herr Garbitsch. Aaah. Herring shouldn't smelten fine from Garbitsch and Garbitsch shouldn't smelten fine from Herring. Herring 'n' Garbitsch. Vasült. Und der stretz. Hey der flütensack der klötensilla weinerhütten uuuh. Ein der spritz mit seiner gruttensackta flayrten. Ein zekt strittensekt. Ein zekt strittensuckt. Ein sichs strittensackt. Und der ein . . . [*chesty cough*] Enough! Djiwelsch stolz mit sein eltensekt. Aaah. Und die Aryan. Und die Aryan maiden. Ah, die Aryan maiden. Aaah der Delikatessen mit der schön. Mit der flacksen, mit der stresses. Ah, und der Holstein mit der muss. Eeeeh der muss. For der Kinder Katzenjammer. Der Katzenjammer mit der hudensackta, hiepen, heipen, hücken, weiter, dotten, guten sekt. Hey! Soldiers for Hynkel!

The crowd: Heil!

AH: Wiesayn der Aryan. Und now, der Juden [*grunt*]. Der Juden. Und der streff das Sauerkraut mit der Juden. Und der Leberwurst mit der Juden. Ein der flützensekt either, mit der Juden. Heey, der flutensack der klayrten. Hum der strengerische mit der huldensekt der flayrten und der blaytzensack der elken. Besieg! Besag! Der Juden. Ooooh, der Juden.

The crowd: Heil!

AH: Und now, schtrupff mit sein hüldensack der flayrt. Der flayrten with der hüldensack der erten. Und striff mit seiner todschtrutz. Eeeein der fluten. Der held trutz einer, nach Europe. Blitzkrieg wratsch tratz mitzikatenten. Ein feinholz schtraf mit seine und den French, ein weinholsein schtraft mit seiner Hinland, und weinholsein schtraft mit seiner Russe, weit schtrass der meine, eeeey. Eeeeey der flüzen mieder, heeey der stref. Oooh da schtinkt einer schtonken, der schtonken mit der Führer, ein schtonken mit der hull. Ein siedul der grotzes mit seine Tomainia!

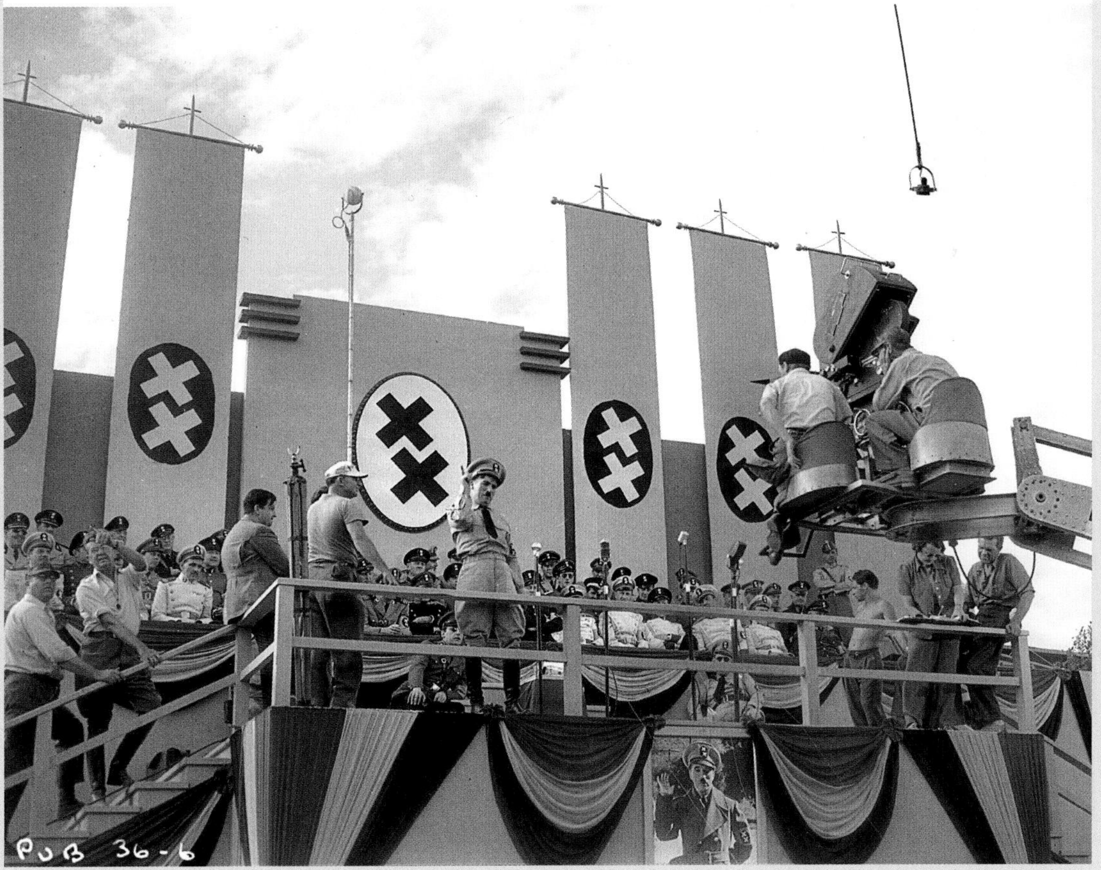

Right

Shooting Hynkel's speech scene, 1940.

Kate Guyonvarch

Chaplin's final speech from *The Great Dictator*

A long-lasting phenomenon

Although the story goes that the little tramp character was invented more or less by chance, Chaplin went on to develop him into a carefully studied character. From the tip of his shoes to the top of his bowler hat, each detail was of vital importance to the whole, and his qualities are not outdated, since hunger, poverty, homelessness and struggling to survive remain at the forefront of 21st-century news. "My character is man. I have not given him a name—he is man," explained Chaplin in 1936.

The Chaplin family, represented by the Chaplin office, is not therefore simply protecting and licensing a name and image, but the lifetime's work that these represent. Over the years, the totemic tramp figure has come to represent far more than the ragged, mischievous, resilient character from the films—now he is the epitome of Chaplin's own humanism and modernism. The worldwide mood is one of seriousness, and Chaplin remains ever in demand. His films are screened in concert halls with symphony orchestras, but also in refugee camps. Photographs and clips from *Modern Times* are regularly requested to illustrate the working conditions of today.

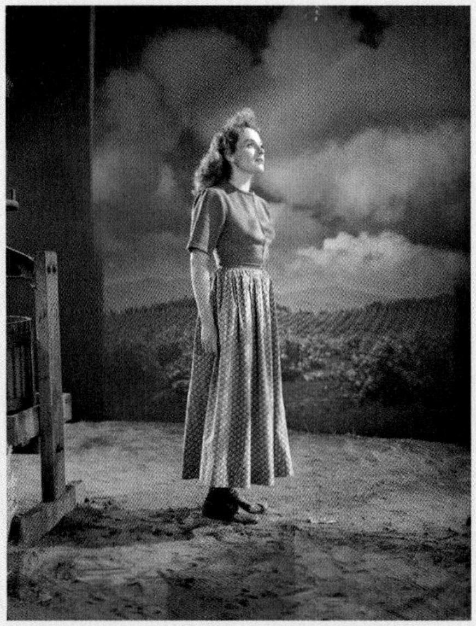

In 2003 the Chaplin office was contacted by the English band Slovo, asking to use *The Great Dictator* speech in a piece for their new album. A few months later Spanish DJ Javier Rayes Regueiro wanted to mix the speech for a dance track. Surprised, the Chaplin family agreed to this new idea, and since then there have been hundreds of requests from musicians the world over. The rights have been licensed to jazz, punk, reggae, heavy metal, rock, disco, electro bands, and more—from unknown musicians with family-and-friends-only followers to Stephen Marley, from Coldplay's use of the speech on their *Head Full of Dreams* tour in 2016, to U2's April 2019 EP vinyl release featuring Chaplin's speech mixed with "Love Is All We Have Left" from 2017's *Songs of Experience*, segueing into the famous "New Year's Day."

Paolo Nutini's "Iron Sky," incorporating the speech, was perhaps the most widely heard piece so far, later used as the soundtrack for an advertisement for Amnesty International. A ballet created in March 2019 for the Slovak National Ballet by Daniel de Andrade and Carl Davis features the speech in its entirety in one beautifully choreographed scene, where dancers and dictators move in half-darkness below Chaplin's impassioned face on screen. Alessandro Rak's animated feature film *The Walking Liberty* will contain a scene in which the characters watch the speech on a cinema screen. Composer Daniel Nelson is putting the words of the speech to new music to be premiered by the Swedish Radio Symphony Orchestra and Radio choir in autumn 2020 and performed by the Gävle and Helsingborg symphony orchestras during their 2020–2021 concert season.

Charlie the tramp always retained his jaunty walk in the face of adversity, and Chaplin the man his belief in supporting, and fighting for, humanity's "pursuit of happiness." In the late 1950s, when young Michael Chaplin misbehaved at school in Switzerland, his teacher made him copy out the text of the final speech from *The Great Dictator*, telling him to think hard about his father's words. Charlie Chaplin was very amused to hear that, but also surprised, saying he felt the speech was probably out of date. Current, renewed, unflagging interest in the speech proves him quite wrong.

Left

Hannah (Paulette Goddard) listens to the barber's message of hope, *The Great Dictator*, 1940.

Below

The barber's speech at the end of *The Great Dictator*, 1940.

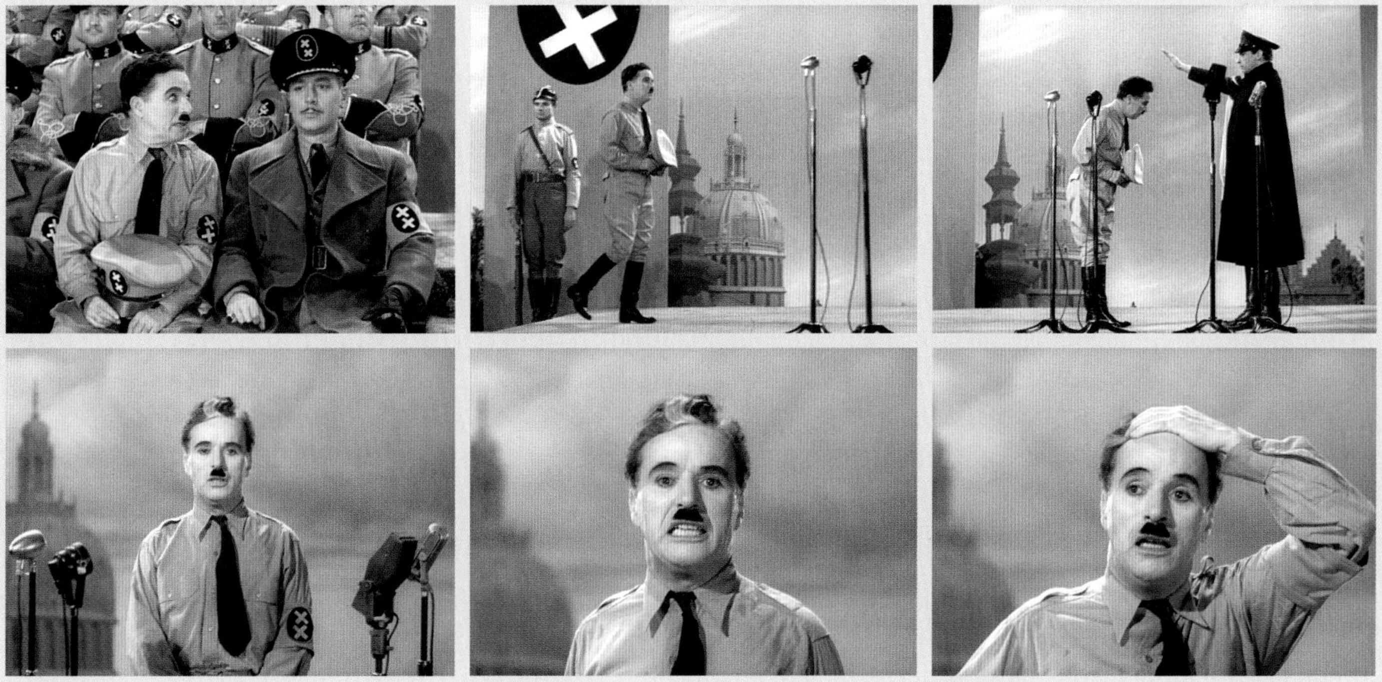

Speech from *The Great Dictator* by Charles Chaplin

The Great Dictator (1940)

I'm sorry, but I don't want to be an emperor. That's not my business. I don't want to rule or conquer anyone. I should like to help everyone if possible—Jew, Gentile, black man, white.

We all want to help one another. Human beings are like that. We want to live by each other's happiness—not by each other's misery. We don't want to hate and despise one another. In this world there is room for everyone. And the good earth is rich and can provide for everyone. The way of life can be free and beautiful, but we have lost the way. Greed has poisoned men's souls, has barricaded the world with hate, has goose-stepped us into misery and bloodshed. We have developed speed, but we have shut ourselves in. Machinery that gives abundance has left us in want. Our knowledge has made us cynical. Our cleverness, hard and unkind. We think too much and feel too little. More than machinery we need humanity. More than cleverness we need kindness and gentleness. Without these qualities, life will be violent and all will be lost . . .

The aeroplane and the radio have brought us closer together. The very nature of these inventions cries out for the goodness in men—cries out for universal brotherhood—for the unity of us all. Even now my voice is reaching millions throughout the world—millions of despairing men, women, and little children—victims of a system that makes men torture and imprison innocent people. To those who can hear me, I say—do not despair. The misery that is now upon us is but the passing of greed—the bitterness of men who fear the way of human progress. The hate of men will pass, and dictators die, and the power they took from the people will return to the people. And so long as men die, liberty will never perish . . .

Soldiers! Don't give yourselves to brutes—men who despise you—enslave you—who regiment your lives—tell you what to do, what to think and what to feel! Who drill you, diet you, treat you like cattle, use you as cannon fodder. Don't give yourselves to these unnatural men—machine men with machine minds and machine hearts! You are not machines! You are not cattle! You are men! You have the love of humanity in your hearts! You don't hate! Only the unloved hate—the unloved and the unnatural!

Soldiers! Don't fight for slavery! Fight for liberty! In the 17th Chapter of St Luke it is written: "the Kingdom of God is within man"—not one man nor a group of men, but in all men! In you! You, the people have the power—the power to create machines. The power to create happiness! You, the people, have the power to make this life free and beautiful, to make this life a wonderful adventure. Then—in the name of democracy—let us use that power—let us all unite. Let us fight for a new world—a decent world that will give men a chance to work—that will give youth a future and old age a security. By the promise of these things, brutes have risen to power. But they lie! They do not fulfill that promise. They never will! Dictators free themselves but they enslave the people! Now let us fight to fulfill that promise! Let us fight to free the world—to do away with national barriers—to do away with greed, with hate and intolerance. Let us fight for a world of reason, a world where science and progress will lead to all men's happiness. Soldiers! In the name of democracy, let us all unite!

Hannah, can you hear me? Wherever you are, look up Hannah!

The clouds are lifting, the sun is breaking through.

We are coming out of the darkness into the light.

We are coming into a new world, a kindlier world, where men will rise above their hate, their greed and brutality. Look up Hannah. The soul of man has been given wings and at last he is beginning to fly. He is flying into the rainbow, into the light of hope, into the future. The glorious future that belongs to you, to me, and to all of us!

Look up Hannah, look up!

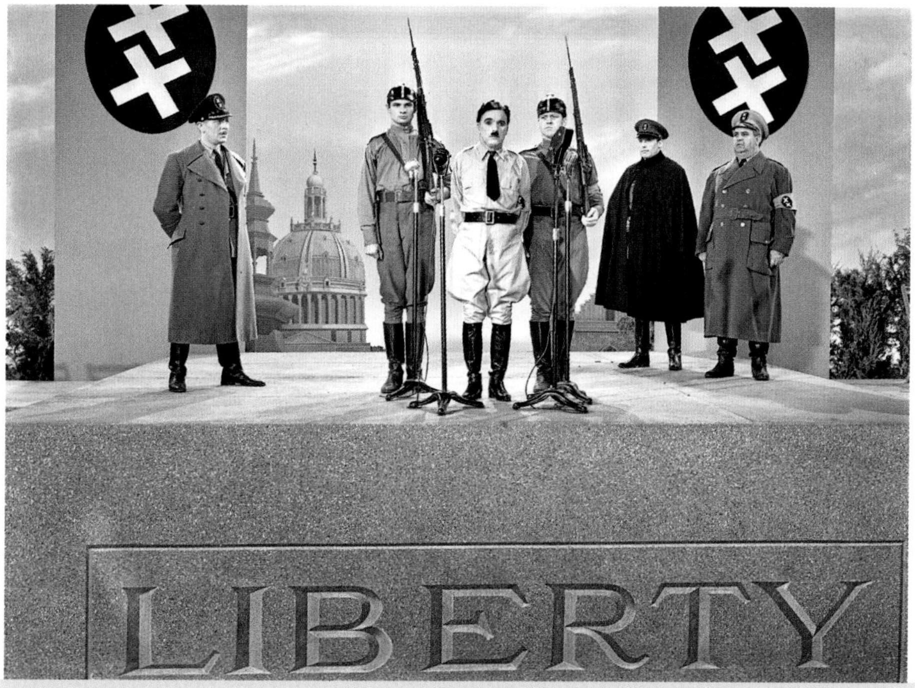

Right

Rehearsal for the final scene of *The Great Dictator*, 1940.

Chronology

Apart from a few events taken from David Robinson's biography of Chaplin, this chronology is largely based on Jim Lochner's book *The Music of Charlie Chaplin.*

1889
April 16 Birth of Charles Chaplin

1890–1891
Publication of Charles Chaplin Senior's songs "Eh, Boys?," "Every-Day Life," and "As the Church Bells Chime"

1895
The Lumière Brothers patent the association of a camera and a projector

1896
Edison presents his Vitascope projector

1898–1900
Chaplin works for the Eight Lancashire Lads

1901
May 9 Charles Chaplin Sr. dies, age 38

1906
July Sydney Chaplin joins "Fred Karno's Army"

1908
February 21 Chaplin signs his first contract with Fred Karno

1909
There are more than 9,000 movie theaters in the United States

1910
Eugène Lauste patents a "new and better method to record and simultaneously reproduce action and sound"
October 3 Start of the Karno tour of the USA which lasts twenty one months

1912
Chaplin returns to the USA for a second Karno tour

1913
September 25 Chaplin signs a contract with the Keystone Film Company at $150 per week for one year starting from December 16

1914
February 2 *Making a Living,* Chaplin's first film, released
Autumn Sydney leaves the Fred Karno Company

1915
January Chaplin starts to work for Essanay Studios for $1,250 per week and for fourteen films
November 20 *A Night in the Show* released

1916
Charlie and Sydney Chaplin, Herbert Clark and Tom Harrington create the Charlie Chaplin Music Publishing Company
February 20 Chaplin conducts John Philip Sousa's band at the New York Hippodrome
February 26 Chaplin signs with Mutual Film Corporation for $10,000 per week plus a $150,000 signing bonus
March 27 Lone Star studio opened
April 10 Essanay's expanded version of *A Burlesque on Carmen* released
July 10 *The Vagabond* released: first appearance of Chaplin onscreen with his left-handed violin
December Vaslav Nijinsky visits studio

1917
June 17 Chaplin signs with First National Exhibitor's Circuit for an unprecedented $1 million plus $75,000 signing bonus

1918
January Chaplin moves into new studio on La Brea Avenue

1919
February 5 Chaplin signs contracts of incorporation for United Artists with D.W. Griffith, Douglas Fairbanks and Mary Pickford
June 15 *Sunnyside* released

1921
February 6 *The Kid* begins theatrical release at the Strand Theatre, New York; score compiled and conducted by Strand music director Carl Edouarde

1923
September 26 *A Woman of Paris* premieres at the Criterion Theatre, Los Angeles; score compiled by Louis F. Gottschalk, conducted by Adolf Tandler

1924
February 8 Chaplin begins shooting *The Gold Rush*

1925
June 26 *The Gold Rush* premieres at Grauman's Egyptian Theatre, Los Angeles; score compiled by Carli D. Elinor, conducted by Gino Severi

1926
Warner Bros. Pictures, Incorporated starts using the Vitaphone
January 11 Chaplin begins shooting *The Circus*
June 16 Raquel Meller visits set of *The Circus*

1927
October 6 Premiere of Alan Crosland's *The Jazz Singer* with Al Jolson (considered as first talking film)
December Chaplin works on musical score for *The Circus* with Arthur Kay

1928
Paramount is the first studio to announce it will only produce talking films
January 6 *The Circus* premieres at the Strand Theatre, New York; score compiled by Arthur Kay; conducted by Alois Reiser
August 28 Hannah Chaplin (Chaplin's mother) dies in California, age 63
December 27th Chaplin begins shooting *City Lights*

1929
October 24 Wall Street Crash —beginning of the Great Depression
November 8 Chaplin begins work on musical score for *City Lights*

1930
Hays' Production Code adopted by film industry
November 14 Arthur Johnston begins work on *City Lights*
December 29 First orchestra rehearsal for *City Lights*
December 31 *City Lights* recording sessions begin

1931
Continuous musical accompaniment is abandoned; temporary decline of film musicals
January 6 *City Lights* recording sessions end
January 30 *City Lights* premiere in Los Angeles

1933
March 25 First mention of work on *Modern Times*

1935
August 30 Shooting on *Modern Times* completed
November 18–December 17 Recording sessions for *Modern Times*
December 4 Chaplin has disagreement with conductor Alfred Newman on the *Modern Times* soundstage; Edward Powell takes over the few remaining conducting duties
December 22 Sound for *Modern Times* completed

1936

February 5 *Modern Times* opens at Rivoli, New York

1938

October Chaplin begins work on *The Great Dictator*

1939

January 9–February 10 Soundproofing of studio stages

September 9 Chaplin begins shooting *The Great Dictator*

1940

June 22 Chaplin begins working on the score for *The Great Dictator*

July 3 Meredith Willson begins working with Chaplin on the score for *The Great Dictator*

August 15–23 Recording sessions for *The Great Dictator*; conducted by Meredith Willson

October 15 World premiere of *The Great Dictator* in New York

1941

June 9 Chaplin begins work on reissue of *The Gold Rush* with soundtrack

August 23 Max Terr begins working with Chaplin on score for *The Gold Rush* reissue

October 27–November 3 Recording sessions for *The Gold Rush*; conducted by Max Terr

1942

May 19 *The Gold Rush* “with music and words” released

1946

May 21 First exterior shots for *Monsieur Verdoux*

November 18 Rudy Schräger begins working with Chaplin on the score for *Monsieur Verdoux*

1947

January 9–17 Recording sessions for *Monsieur Verdoux*; conducted by Rudy Schräger

April 11 World premiere of *Monsieur Verdoux* in New York

1950

October Chaplin begins working on music for *Limelight*

December 15 Ray Rasch begins working with Chaplin on the score for *Limelight*

November 19 Chaplin begins main shooting of *Limelight*

1952

January 25 Main shooting of *Limelight* completed

June 10–17 Recording sessions for *Limelight*; conducted by Keith Williams

September 17 Chaplin family sails from New York, re-entry permit rescinded two days later

October 16 Premiere of *Limelight* in London

1953

January 5 The Chaplins move into Manoir de Ban, Corsier-sur-Vevey, Switzerland

May 23 Franck Chacksfield’s popular recording of “Terry’s Theme” from *Limelight* enters the Billboard charts at no. 19, eventually reaching no. 6

1954

July 27 “Smile” released by Nat King Cole

1956

May–June Chaplin shoots *A King in New York*

August–October Editing, recording, dubbing of *A King in New York* in Paris

December 18 Boris Sarbek begins working with Chaplin on the score for *A King in New York*

1957

January 25–29 Recording sessions for *A King in New York*; conducted by Leighton Lucas

June 22 *Mandolin Serenade* short filmed at Studio de la Mutualité in Paris

September 12 London premiere of *A King in New York*

1958

November Chaplin works on the score for *The Chaplin Revue* with Eric James

1959

January 12–14 Recording sessions for *A Dog’s Life*; conducted by Eric Spear

February 18–25 Recording sessions for *Shoulder Arms* and *The Pilgrim*; conducted by Eric Spear

September 25 *The Chaplin Revue* released

1964

September Publication of *My Autobiography*

1966

January 25–May 11 Chaplin shoots *A Countess from Hong Kong*

September 19–23 Recording sessions (in mono) for *A Countess from Hong Kong*; conducted by Lambert Williamson

September 27–28 Recording sessions (in stereo) for *A Countess from Hong Kong* soundtrack album; conducted by Lambert Williamson

1967

January 5 *A Countess from Hong Kong* released

February 16 Petula Clark’s recording of “This Is My Song” reaches no. 1 in the United Kingdom

October 30 Eric James begins working with Chaplin on the score for *The Circus*

1968

April 18–22 Recording sessions for *The Circus*; conducted by Lambert Williamson

1971

October 25–29 Recording sessions for *The Kid* and *The Idle Class*; conducted by Eric Rogers; on the 29th, a camera crew filmed Chaplin conducting the orchestra for a documentary

1972

April 10 Chaplin receives Honorary Oscar

August–September Eric James works for four weeks on the score for *Pay Day*

November 22–24 Recording sessions for *Pay Day*; conducted by Eric Rogers

1973

March 27 Chaplin, Raymond Rasch and Larry Russell win Best Dramatic Score Academy Award for *Limelight*

May 7 Eric James begins working on the score for *A Day’s Pleasure*

August 28–30 Recording sessions for *A Day’s Pleasure*; conducted by Eric Rogers

1974

February 17–27 Eric James works on the score for *Sunnyside*

April 30–May 2 Recording sessions for *Sunnyside*; conducted by Eric Rogers

1975

March 4 Chaplin is knighted by HM Queen Elizabeth II

1976

February 17–23 Recording sessions for *A Woman of Paris*; conducted by Eric Rogers

1977

December 25 Chaplin dies at Manoir de Ban, Corsier-sur-Vevey

Bibliography

A

Abel, Richard; Altmann, Rick. *The Sounds of Early Cinema*. Bloomington, Indiana University Press, 2001.
Albera, François. "Deux scénarios inédits de Fernand Léger," *1895. Mille huit cent quatre-vingt-quinze. Revue de l'association française de recherche sur l'histoire du cinéma*, no. 81 (March 1, 2017), p. 122–31. *journals.openedition.org*.
Altman, Rick. *Silent film sound*. New York, Columbia University Press, 2004.
Anthony, Barry; Chaplin, Michael. *Chaplin's Music Hall: The Chaplins and Their Circle in the Limelight*. London, I.B. Tauris, 2012.

B

Blouin, Patrice; Delage, Christian; Stourdzé, Sam. *Chaplin et les images*. Paris, NBC Éditions, 2005.
Bordat, Francis. *Chaplin cinéaste*. Paris, Éditions du Cerf, 1998.
Brownlow, Kevin. *The Search for Charlie Chaplin*. Bologna, Cineteca del Comune di Bologna, 2005.
Brownlow, Kevin; Gill, David. *Unknown Chaplin*. Photoplay Productions, 1983.

C

Cenciarelli, Cecilia; Fiaccarini, Anna; Zegna, Michela. *The Great Dictator*. Bologna, Le Mani, 2002.
Cendrars, Blaise. "Un pneu de Fernand Léger," *L'Homme foudroyé*. Paris, Denoël, 2002, p. 273.
Chaplin, Charles, *My Father, Charlie Chaplin*. New York, Random House, 1960.
Chaplin, Charlie. *My Autobiography*. London, The Bodley Head, 1964.
—. *My Life in Pictures*. London, The Bodley Head, 1974.
—. *My Trip Abroad*. New York, Harper and Brothers, 1922.
Chion, Michel. *La musique au cinéma*. Paris, Fayard, 1995.
—. *La Voix au cinéma*. Paris, Cahiers du cinéma, 1982.
—. *Les Lumières de la ville, Charles Chaplin*. Paris, Nathan, 1989.
—. *Un art sonore, le cinéma: histoire, esthétique, poétique*. Paris, Cahiers du Cinéma, 2003.
Coulondre, Ariane. *Fernand Léger, le beau est partout*. Metz, Éditions du Centre Pompidou, 2017.

D

Davies, Ann; Powrie, Phil. *Carmen on Screen: An Annotated Filmography and Bibliography*. Woodbridge, Tamesis Books, 2006.
Davis, Carl. "Charlie Chaplin's Film Music," *The Guardian*, January 1, 2011. *www.theguardian.com*, http://www.theguardian.com/culture/2011/jan/01/carl-davis-charlie-chaplin-soundtracks.
Delage, Christian; Cenciarelli, Cecilia. *Modern Times–Tempi moderni*. Bologna, Le Mani-Microart's Edizioni, 2014.
Delage, Christian. *Chaplin, la grande histoire*. Paris, Jean-Michel Place, 2002.
Derouet, Christian. *Fernand Léger*. Paris, Éditions du Centre Pompidou, 1997.
—. *Fernand Léger, une correspondance poste restante, lettres à Simone, 1931–1941*. Cahiers du Musée national d'art moderne, "hors-série/archives," 1997.
—. "Léger et le cinéma," *Peinture – Cinéma – Peinture*. Marseille, Hazan, 1989, p. 121–42.
Descargues, Pierre. *Fernand Léger*. Paris, Éditions Cercle d'art, 1955.
Duncan, Paul. *The Charlie Chaplin Archives*. Köln, Taschen, 2015.

E

Eyman, Scott. *The Speed of Sound: Hollywood and the Talkie Revolution 1926–1930*. Reprint. New York, Simon & Schuster, 2015.

F

Faure, Élie. *Fonction du cinéma: de la cinéplastique à son destin social*. Paris, Gonthier, 1964.
Fawell, John. *The Essence of Chaplin: The Style, the Rhythm and the Grace of a Master*. Jefferson, McFarland & Company, 2014.
Fiaccarini, Anna; Cenciarelli, Cecilia; Zegna, Michela. *The Great Dictator = Il grande dittatore: di Charlie Chaplin*. Bologna, Cineteca Bologna, Fondazione Cassa di Risparmio di Bologna, BIM, 2002.
Fitzsimmons, Linda; Street, Sarah. *Moving Performance: British Stage and Screen, 1890s–1920s*. Trowbridge, Flicks Books, 1999.
Flom, Eric L. *Chaplin in the Sound Era: An Analysis of the Seven Talkies*. Jefferson, McFarland & Company, 1997.
França, José Augusto. *Charles Chaplin: O "self-made-myth."* Translated by V. de Villeneuve de Mons. Lisbon, Inquerito, 1954.

G

Gehring, Wes D.; Lane, Conrad. *Chaplin's War Trilogy: an Evolving Lens in Three Dark Comedies, 1918–1947*. Jefferson, McFarland & Company, 2014.
Génin, Bernard; Loiseau, Jean-Claude *Charlot Chaplin: Du rire aux larmes*. Paris, Télérama, 2002.
Goll, Yvan. *Die Chapliniade*. Rudolf Kaemmerer, Dresden, 1920.
—. "La Chapliniade ou Charlot poète," *La Vie des Lettres*, no. 5 (July 1921).
—. *Le Nouvel Orphée: La Chaplinade, Mathusale, Paris brûle, Le Nouvel Orphée*. Paris, Éditions de la Sirène, 1923.

H

Howe, Lawrence; Caron, James Edward; Click, Benjamin Click. *Refocusing Chaplin: A Screen Icon through Critical Lenses*. Lanham, Scarecrow Press, 2013.
Huff, Théodore. *Charlie Chaplin*. New York, Schuman, 1951.

J

Jacobs, Lea. *Film Rhythm after Sound*. Oakland, University of California Press, 2014.

K

Kamin, Dan. *The Comedy of Charlie Chaplin: Artistry in Motion*. Lanham, Scarecrow Press, 2008.
Kornhaber, Donna. "Substituting Speech for Style: Technique and Discourse in Monsieur Verdoux, Limelight, and A King in New York," *Quarterly Review of Film and Video* 31, no. 5 (July 4, 2014), p. 415–34.

L

Lang, Edith; West, George. *Musical Accompaniment of Moving Pictures*. New York, Arno Press, 1970.
Lapeyssonnie, Mariange. *Charlot prend la parole aux mots*. Lyon, Aléas, 2008.
Léger, Fernand. *Fonctions de la peinture*. Paris, Gallimard, 1997.
—. "La Joconde amoureuse de Charlot," *14 rue du Dragon*, no. 1. March 1933.
—. "Réponse à l'enquête de René Clair sur le cinéma," *Le Théâtre et Comœdia illustré*. March 1923.
—. "Sur Charlie Chaplin" in *Les Chroniques du jour*, 7th year, no. 7–8 (December 31, 1926), p. 243–44.

Lochner, Jim. *The Music of Charlie Chaplin*. Jefferson, McFarland & Company, 2018.

M

Mannoni, Laurent. *De Méliès à la 3D: la machine cinéma*. Paris, La Cinémathèque française, Lienart, 2016.
Mari, Jean-Claude. *Quand le film se fait musique: une nouvelle ère sonore au cinéma*. Paris, L'Harmattan, 2007.
Marks, Martin Miller. *Music and the Silent Film: Contexts and Case Studies, 1895–1924*. Oxford, Oxford University Press, 1997.
Martin, Marcel; Chaplin, Charlie. *Charles Chaplin: présentation par Marcel Martin. Choix de propos de Charles Chaplin, scénarios, témoignages...* Updated edition. Paris, Seghers, 1971.
Maurois, André. *Les Douze Grandes Dates du Cinéma*. Festival international du film, Cannes, 1949.

N

Narboni, Jean. *Pourquoi les coiffeurs?: notes actuelles sur "Le Dictateur."* Paris, Capricci, 2010.
Nysenholc, Adolphe. *Charles Chaplin: l'âge d'or du comique*. Paris, 2002.
Nysenholc, Adolphe; Bordat, Francis. *Charlie Chaplin: le rêve: essai: contrepoint entre le créateur et sa créature*. Brussels, M.E.O., 2018.
Nysenholc, Adolphe; Noguez, Dominique. *Charles Chaplin ou La légende des images*. Paris, Méridiens Klincksieck, 1987.

P

Perry, Israel; Capitaine, Jean-Louis. *Charlie Chaplin Movie Posters*. Bilingual edition. New York, Queen Art Pub Inc., 2005.
Pitkin, Walter B.; Marston, William S. *The Art of Sound Pictures*. New York, D. Appleton and Company, 1930. *Internet Archive*, http://archive.org/details/artofsoundpictur00walt.
Portes, Jacques. *De la scène à l'écran: naissance de la culture de masse aux États-Unis*. Paris, Belin, 1997.

R

Rapee, Erno. *Motion Picture Moods: for Pianists and Organists*. New York, Arno Press, 1974.
Reeves, May; Goll, Claire. *Charlie Chaplin intime. Souvenirs recueillis par Claire Goll*. - 3rd ed. Paris, Gallimard-NRF, 1935.
Robinson, David. *Chaplin, His Life and Art*. London, Grafton, 1992.
—. *Chaplin: the Mirror of Opinion*. London, Secker and Warburg, 1984.
—. *Charlie Chaplin: Footlights with the World of Limelight*. Bologna, Cineteca di Bologna, 2015.
—. "The World of Silent Cinema," *Sight & Sound* 24, no. 2 (February 2014), p. 59–59.
Robinson, David; Marti, Jean-Christophe; Sandberg, Marc. *Musique et cinéma muet*, exhibition at the Musée d'Orsay, September 19, 1995–January 7, 1996. Paris, Réunion des musées nationaux, 1995.

S

Sandrin, Carole; Stourdzé, Sam; Mitchell, Glenn. *Charlie Chaplin: l'album Keystone: l'invention de Charlot*. Lausanne, Musée de l'Élysée, 2014.
Schwob, René; Chagall, Marc. *Une mélodie silencieuse*. Paris, B. Grasset, 1929.
Stenzl, Jürg. *Musik für über 1500 Stummfilme: das Inventar der Filmmusik im Pariser Gaumont-Palace (1911–1928) von Paul Fosse*. Vienna, LIT, 2017.
Stourdzé, Sam. *Chaplin*. Paris, MK2, Bayard, 2007.
—. *Charlie Chaplin: images d'un mythe*. Morges, IDPURE, 2011.
—. *Charlie Chaplin: un album photo*. Göttingen, Steidl, 2002.

T

Teichner, Noah; Dreux, Emmanuel. *Les comiques "du muet" face à l'arrivée du parlant: le cinéma burlesque en transition*. Thesis, Paris, Université Paris VIII, 2014.
Troufleau, Carole; Stourdzé, Sam; Terrier-Hermann, Véronique. *L'année Chaplin*. Paris, Beaux-arts SAS, 2005.
Tsivian, Yuri. "Charlie Chaplin and His Shadows: On Laws of Fortuity in Art," *Critical Inquiry* 40, no. 3 (March 1, 2014), p. 71–84.

V

Vance, Jeffrey. *Chaplin: Genius of the Cinema*. New York, Harry N. Abrams, 2003.
Vance, Jeffrey; James, Eric. *Making Music with Charlie Chaplin*. Lanham, Scarecrow Press, 2000.

W

Weis, Elisabeth; Belton, John. *Film sound: theory and practice*. New York, Columbia University Press, 1985.
Wild, Jennifer. "What Léger Saw," *Léger: Modern Art and the Metropolis*. Philadelphia Museum of Art. 2013, p. 145–51.

Filmography

Brownlow, Kevin; Gill, David, *Unknown Chaplin*, three part documentary, 156 min, 1982, rereleased by Lobster Films, 2 DVDs, 2014.

Author biographies

Francis Bordat

Professor emeritus of American civilization at the Université Paris-Nanterre, Francis Bordat has published several books and articles on the economic and sociocultural history of Hollywood, as well as on genres (musical, crime film, Western) and great directors (Ford, Lubitsch, Berkeley). A specialist in burlesque cinema and Charlie Chaplin, he is the author of *Chaplin cinéaste* (Éditions du Cerf, 1998). Former editor of the "Rivages-cinéma" series, he is co-founder and member of the Groupe de Recherche sur le Cinéma Classique Hollywoodien (CICLAHO).

Timothy Brock

Active conductor and composer specializing in concert works of the early twentieth century and live performances of silent film, his leading work in this field includes the film-score restorations of Dmitri Shostakovich, Pietro Mascagni, Erik Satie and Camille Saint-Saëns. In 1999, Brock began work for the Chaplin estate and has restored 13 scores which he conducts throughout the world, including *Modern Times*, *City Lights*, and *The Gold Rush*. He has also written over twelve new scores for silent film, from *Pandora's Box* in 1986 to *7th Heaven*, commissioned by the Orchestre Philharmonique de Radio France in 2018. He is a regular guest of the world's major orchestras including the New York Philharmonic, the BBC Symphony Orchestra and the Orchestra dell'Accademia Nazionale di Santa Cecilia.

Cecilia Cenciarelli

Director of research and international projects at the Cineteca di Bologna, which she joined in 2000, Cecilia Cenciarelli is also on the committee of directors of the Cinema Ritrovato festival. For the Chaplin Project, she coordinates the digitization, cataloging, and research of Charlie Chaplin's document and photographic archives, as well as the restoration of his films, and numerous international events, exhibitions, and publications. Since 2007 she has headed Martin Scorsese's World Cinema Project, which, in partnership with the Cineteca di Bologna, aims to safeguard, preserve, and restore the neglected cinematographic heritage of the entire world. Over the past ten years, the World Cinema Project has restored thirty-five films, including works from Brazil, Turkey, Senegal, the Philippines, Armenia, Morocco, and India.

Charles Spencer Chaplin, Jr.

Born in 1925 to Chaplin and second wife Lita Grey, he and younger brother Sydney were mostly raised by their mother and grandmother, but as teenagers they visited their father frequently and adored "stepmother" Paulette Goddard. Charles served in the US Army in Europe during World War II. He married (and later divorced) Susan Magness and they had one daughter, Susan Maree. He later married Marta Brown, which marriage also ended in divorce. He acted in several films, including in his father's *Limelight* (1952), but never managed to break into movies or theater, remaining on the periphery of Hollywood. In 1960 he wrote a biography of his father entitled *My Father, Charlie Chaplin*. He died aged forty-two.

Ariane Coulondre

Curator of the modern collections of the Musée National d'Art Moderne at the Centre Pompidou, Ariane Coulondre has curated several exhibitions, including *Fernand Léger, le Beau est partout* (Centre Pompidou Metz, 2017, BOZAR Bruxelles, 2018) and *Le cubisme* (Centre Pompidou, 2018, with Brigitte Léal and Christian Briend). She contributed to *Le Dictionnaire du cubisme* (Éditions Bouquins, 2018). Her work focuses on the avant-gardes in France and on modern sculpture. She was formerly curator at the Musée National Fernand Léger (Biot, Alpes-Maritimes).

Carl Davis

Composer of some of the world's best-known scores for fiction and documentary TV, such as *The World at War* (1973), *Hollywood* (1979), BBC's *Pride & Prejudice* (1995), and *Cranford* (2007–2009), Davis's film soundtracks include *French Lieutenant's Woman* (1981), *The Naked Civil Servant* (1975), Ken Russell's *The Rainbow* (1989), *The Great Gatsby* (2000), and *Brexicuted* (2018). Recent additions to his many ballet compositions are *Nijinksy: God of the Dance* and *Chaplin: The Tramp* (2018). Concert works include *Paul McCartney's Liverpool Oratorio*. In 1980, Carl created a score for Abel Gance's 1927 film *Napoleon*, reviving silent film performances with live orchestra. He has since scored over fifty silent films from Charlie Chaplin, Harold Lloyd, and Buster Keaton to D.W. Griffith and King Vidor.

Kate Guyonvarch

Starting as a bilingual secretary for the Chaplin organization in Paris over thirty-five years ago completely by chance, she has been there ever since and is now managing director of Roy Export S.A.S., the company that owns the films Chaplin made from the time he set up his own studios. Under direction from the Chaplin family she also manages the use of the Chaplin name and image for merchandising purposes for the company Bubbles Incorporated S.A., and oversees the access, conservation, and exploitation of the paper and photograph archives and archival film footage from the ex-Chaplin Studios in Los Angeles and the Chaplin family home in Switzerland.

Dan Kamin

Trainer of Robert Downey, Jr. for his Oscar-nominated performance in *Chaplin* and creator of Johnny Depp's comedy moves for *Benny and Joon*, Dan also played the wooden Indian that came to life in the cult horror film *Creepshow 2*. Author of *The Comedy of Charlie Chaplin: Artistry in Motion*, he is a well-known comedian and mime in his own right, performing worldwide in theaters and with symphony orchestras.

Jim Lochner

Jim Lochner is an arts journalist based in New York City. His music and lyrics have appeared in shows for TADA! Youth Theater, and he has written extensively on film music for *Film Score Monthly* and *FSM Online*, and for the record labels FSM, Varèse Sarabande, Intrada, La-La Land Records, Quartet

Records, and Disques Cinémusique. *The Music of Charlie Chaplin* is his first book.

Adolphe Nysenholc

Honorary professor at the Université Libre de Bruxelles, Adolphe Nysenholc is the author of several essays on Charles Chaplin: *L'Âge d'or du comique* (1979, new edition 2002), *La Légende des images* (1987), *Charlie Chaplin: le rêve* (2018), and on André Delvaux and magical realism (2006). Organizer of the first international Chaplin conference at the Université de Paris 1 Panthéon-Sorbonne under the patronage of Oona Chaplin (1989, proceedings published in Berlin), he is also a novelist with *Bubelè l'enfant à l'ombre* (2013) and a playwright with *Mère de guerre* and *La Passion du diable*, winner of the Prix Littéraire du Parlement de la Communauté Française.

David Robinson

British critic and historian specializing in Popular Entertainment Arts, especially cinema and music hall. As director for almost two decades of the Pordenone Silent Film Festival (Le Giornate del Cinema Muto), he has been directly involved in the provision of music for silent film accompaniment and he established the Pordenone Master classes in Film Accompaniment. Inevitably Chaplin has been central to his studies, and his fundamental book *Chaplin His Life and Art* (1985) was followed by other books on Chaplin, as well as on film history and comedy. He is also a former film critic of *The Times* (London) and former director of the Edinburgh International Film Festival. A forthcoming book is a commentary on Chaplin's last, uncompleted film, *The Freak*.

Jürg Stenzl

Musicologist of Swiss origin, Jürg Stenzl studied in Bern and Paris. First assistant then professor at the Université de Fribourg in Switzerland, he has been a professor in Austria since 1992 (Vienna, Graz) and a guest professor in Berlin, Cremona, and Harvard. He has also been teaching at the Universität Salzburg for fifteen years. His publications focus on the Middle Ages and the twentieth century, particularly the oeuvre of Luigi Nono and the history of musical performances. Lately, he has concentrated on the relationship between music and film in books on Jean-Luc Godard, Dimitri Kirsanoff, and the music used to accompany Charlie Chaplin's silent films.

Sam Stourdzé

Director of the photography festival at the Rencontres d'Arles since October 2014, former resident of the Villa Médicis, Sam Stourdzé was previously director of the Musée de l'Élysée in Lausanne, Switzerland. He has published several books and curated many exhibitions, including *Fellini, the Great Parade* and *Chaplin in Pictures*. The latter exhibition travelled the world from 2005 onwards and was presented at the Jeu de Paume in Paris, the Kunsthal in Rotterdam, the Art Museum in Helsinki and the Instituto Tomie Ohtake in São Paulo, Brazil, amongst many others.

Maximilien Theinhardt

Art historian specializing in twentieth-century art. His research focuses on parody and caricature, as well as on the porosity of the divides between avant-garde art and popular culture, notably through the illustrated humorous press and the cinema. He has helped organize several exhibitions (*Charlie Hebdo, journal (ir)responsable*, DOX, Prague, 2015; *Le Cubisme*, Centre Pompidou, Paris, 2018).

Mathilde Thibault-Starzyk

A graduate in art history and museology from the École du Louvre, Mathilde Thibault-Starzyk specialized in the registration and documentation of works. Her areas of research are the history of fashion and dress and the performing arts. She has worked on several exhibitions at the Philharmonie de Paris, notably *Barbara* as production assistant. While working as an independent registrar, she was in charge of research for the exhibition *The Sound of Charlie Chaplin*.

Right

The girl and the Tramp set off into the distance, final scene of *Modern Times*, c. 1936.

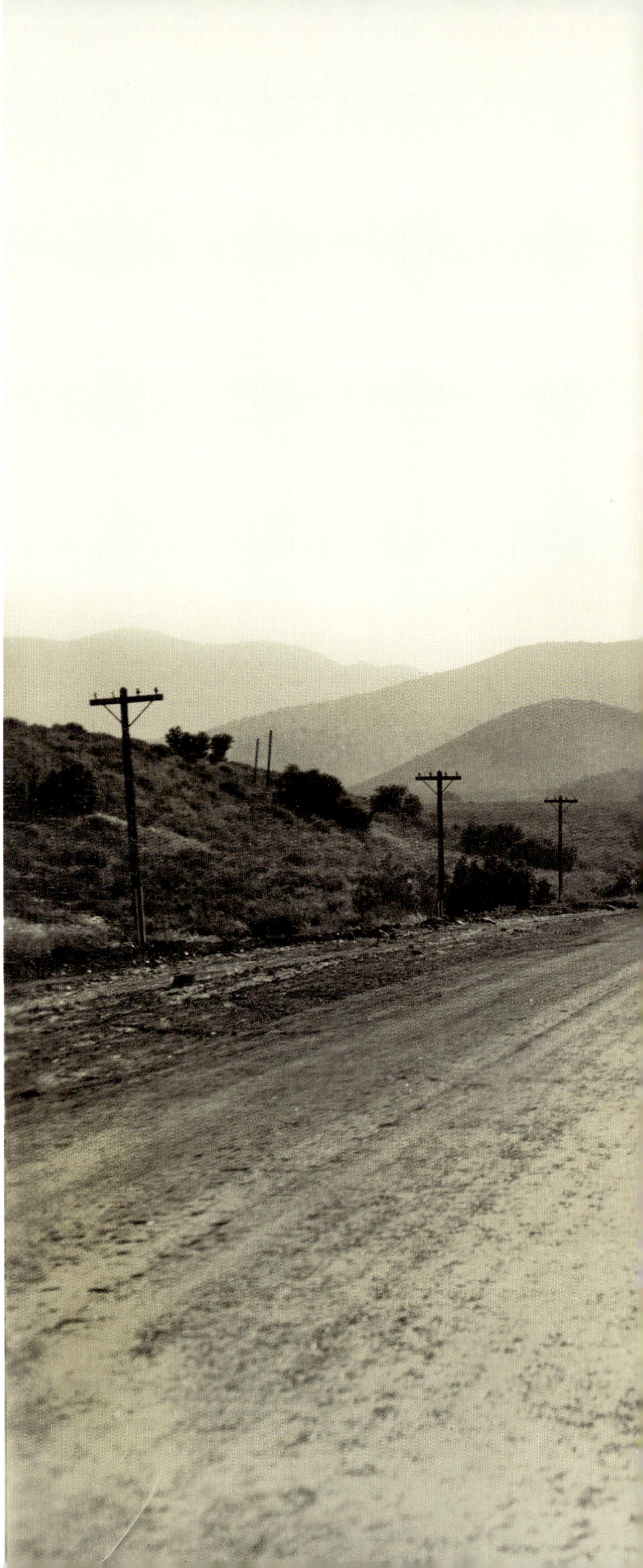

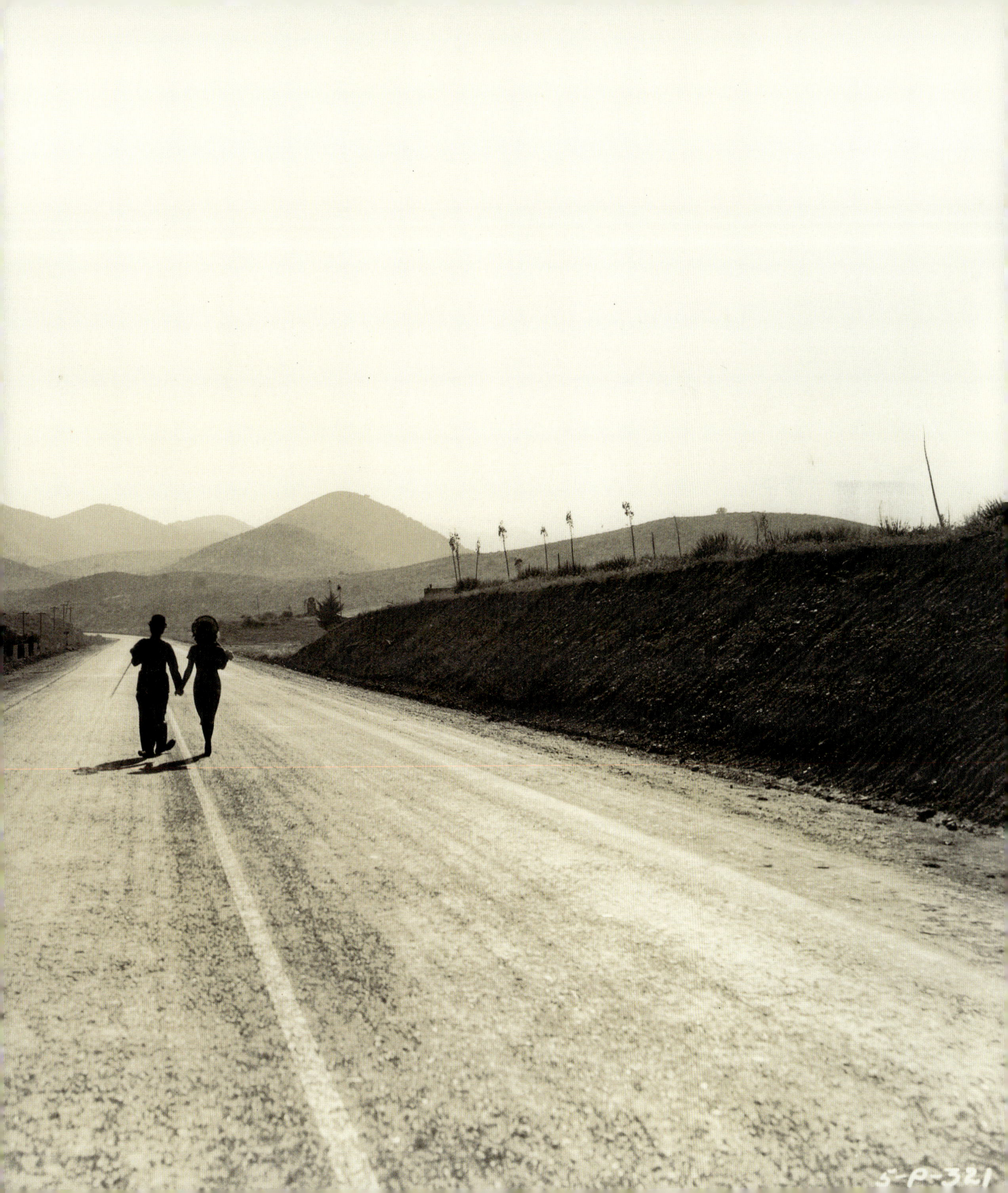
5-P-321

Photographic credits and copyrights

All images from Chaplin films made from 1918 onwards, copyright © Roy Export S.A.S.

Images and documents from the Chaplin archives, unless otherwise indicated, copyright © Roy Export Company Ltd. All rights reserved
p. 25: © Kessler Photo, Empress Theatre, Los Angeles
p. 26: Courtesy Jane Koszuta collection, www.TheRoyalZanettos.com
p. 71: © James Abbe
p. 103: © Apeda

Digitization of the Chaplin archives by Cineteca di Bologna. Digitization of certain photographs from the Chaplin archives by Musée de l'Élysée. Original documents from the Chaplin archives deposited at Archives de Montreux, PP75, Fonds Charles Chaplin. Original negatives and photographs from the Chaplin archives deposited at Musée de l'Élysée.

Other sources:
pp. 29, 42: Cinémathèque Française collection © Auguste Leymarie, all rights reserved
pp. 40, 77: © Lobster Films collection
p. 45: Cinémathèque Française collection © Henry Roberty, all rights reserved
p. 48: Cinémathèque Française collection © Paul Fosse, all rights reserved
pp. 52–53: Gaumont collection
pp. 58, 59, 152: Jeffrey Vance collection
p. 77: © Mutual 1916/Restored Version Lobster films 2013
pp. 80, 147, 148, 180, 201: all rights reserved
p. 81: Cinémathèque Française collection © Raoul Artez, all rights reserved
p. 83: The Metropolitan Museum of Art, Dist. RMN-Grand Palais / MMA image
p. 85: Cinémathèque Suisse collection, all rights reserved
p. 87: Centre Pompidou, MNAM-CCI, Dist. RMN-Grand Palais / Jacques Faujour © Adagp, Paris, 2019
pp. 88, 91, 92: © Adagp, Paris, 2019
p. 89: © Thérèse Bonney
p. 116: © Léo Kouper
pp. 118–19: Excerpts from Charles Chaplin, Jr., *My Father, Charlie Chaplin* (London: Longmans Green, 1961) © Longmans Green
p. 127: © Universal
p. 149: © Bernard Hermann

Distributed in 2020 by Abrams, an imprint of ABRAMS

ISBN: 978-1-4197-4577-5

Photoengraving: IGS-CP
Printed and bound in August 2019 by DZS Grafik D.o.o., Slovenia

ABRAMS The Art of Books
195 Broadway, New York, NY 10007
abramsbooks.com